Praise for *Quit*

"This brilliant and entertaining book documents a major flaw in human actions and decisions: the bias against quitting. I learned a lot from its compelling tales of failures and sound recommendations. You will too."

—Daniel Kahneman, Nobel Prize winner in economics and
#1 *New York Times* bestselling author of *Thinking, Fast and Slow*

"Every business school has a course in starting new businesses, but few have a course in shutting them down at the right time. This book fills that gap with brilliant new insights and fantastic stories. Quit what you are doing right now and start reading this book."

—Richard Thaler, Nobel Prize winner in
economics and bestselling coauthor of *Nudge*

"Engrossing, important, and grounded in science, *Quit* is a gem that will allow you to navigate the world more effectively."

—Katy Milkman, bestselling author of *How to Change*

"*Quit* is the rare book that is both a page-turner and a legitimately important contribution. If you've never thought of quitting as a competitive advantage before, prepare to be enlightened."

—David Epstein, bestselling author of *Range*

"There aren't many times you will say, "this book changed my life." This is one of them."   —Seth Godin, bestselling author of *The Practice*

"Only a poker player could write this classic book on when—and more importantly how—to fold a bad hand in business, investing, relationships and life."   —Ryan Holiday, #1 *New York Times*
bestselling author of *Stillness Is the Key*

"There's no wisdom that matters more in life than knowing when to persist and when to pull the plug. Annie Duke offers a wealth of knowledge to help you figure out whether it's time to let go."

—Adam Grant, #1 *New York Times* bestselling author of *Think Again* and host of the TED podcast *WorkLife*

"A game-changing book of strategy from a world-class thinker on risk and decision-making." —Shane Parrish, host of *The Knowledge Project* podcast

"The opposite of a great virtue is also a virtue. And *Quit* is the perfect dialectical complement to *Grit*. Weave these two virtues into your character and live a much more fulfilling life."

—Philip Tetlock, bestselling author of *Superforecasting*

"Quitting is not just an art; it's also a science—and there is no one so uniquely suited to teach us both as Annie Duke."

—Brian Christian, coauthor of *Algorithms to Live By*

"Not since Kenny Rogers has an expert storyteller so clearly demonstrated the importance of knowing when to hold 'em and when to fold 'em, nor presented a clearer strategy to determine when, instead of merely walking away, it's time to run."

—David McRaney, author of *How Minds Change*

"You won't want to quit reading this book, both because it is such a rewarding read and also because its lessons are so important, useful, and memorable." —Don A. Moore, author of *Perfectly Confident*

Quit

THE POWER OF KNOWING WHEN TO WALK AWAY

ANNIE DUKE

Ebury Edge, an imprint of Ebury Publishing,
20 Vauxhall Bridge Road,
London SW1V 2SA

Ebury Edge is part of the Penguin Random House group of companies
whose addresses can be found at global.penguinrandomhouse.com

Penguin
Random House
UK

First published in the United States by Portfolio in 2022
First published in the United Kingdom by Ebury Edge in 2022

This edition published by arrangement with Portfolio, an imprint of
Penguin Publishing Group, division of Penguin Random House LLC

Grateful acknowledgment is made for permission to reprint 'The Gambler'
Words and music by Don Schlitz. Copyright © 1977 Sony Music Publishing (US) LLC.
Copyright renewed. All rights administered by Sony Music Publishing (US) LLC,
424 Church Street, Suite 1200, Nashville, TN 37219. International copyright secured.
All rights reserved. Reprinted by permission of Hal Leonard LLC.

Book design by Tanya Maiboroda

www.penguin.co.uk

A CIP catalogue record for this book is available from the British Library

ISBN 9781529146158

Printed and bound in India by Thomson Press India Ltd.

The authorised representative in the EEA is Penguin Random House Ireland,
Morrison Chambers, 32 Nassau Street, Dublin D02 YH68

Penguin Random House is committed to a sustainable future
for our business, our readers and our planet. This book is made from
Forest Stewardship Council® certified paper.

*To my children, my *

CONTENTS

SECTION I
The Case for Quitting

INTERLUDE I

SECTION II
In the Losses

INTERLUDE II
GOLD OR NOTHING

SECTION III
Identity and Other Impediments

INTERLUDE III
THE ANTS GO MARCHING . . . MOSTLY 199

SECTION IV
Opportunity Cost

The Gaffed Scale

I N OCTOBER 1974, BOXER MUHAMMAD ALI PULLED OFF ONE of the greatest upsets in the history of sports when he knocked out George Foreman in the famous "Rumble in the Jungle." With that victory, Ali regained the heavyweight boxing championship, a title he had first earned when he dethroned Sonny Liston a decade earlier in 1964.

Ali faced unbelievable odds and adversity on the way to this momentous triumph. In 1967, he was stripped of his heavyweight title after refusing to serve in the Vietnam War, depriving him of the opportunity to fight for three and a half years during what should have been the prime of his career. After that layoff, he had to fight his way back into contention for another four years to get the title shot against George Foreman. By this time, Ali was nearly thirty-three and had fought as a professional forty-six times.

Foreman was heavily favored: younger, bigger, stronger, undefeated, and considered indestructible. Ali had split a pair of fights that went the distance against both Joe Frazier and Ken Norton. Neither Frazier nor Norton lasted two rounds against Foreman.

When Ali bested Foreman, he cemented his status as the Greatest of All Time.

Muhammad Ali became a symbol of grit. Against all odds, among a sea of naysayers, he had refused to give up and triumphed. Is there any greater testament to the power of persistence and perseverance when it comes to pursuing your dreams?

But the story doesn't end there.

That same grittiness led Ali to fight for seven more years. From 1975 to December 1981, Ali persisted despite repeated, unambiguous signals that he should quit. In 1977, after friends and reporters noticed signs of his physical and mental deterioration, Teddy Brenner, the matchmaker at Madison Square Garden (which had hosted eight Ali fights) begged him to retire.

Ali waffled.

Brenner followed with the announcement that Madison Square Garden would never host another of his fights. "I don't want him to come over to me some day and say, 'What's your name?' The trick in boxing is to get out at the right time, and the fifteenth round last night [against Earnie Shavers] was the right time for Ali."

A week later, Ali's fight doctor, Ferdie Pacheco, also tried to get him to retire after receiving a post-fight lab report about the condition of Ali's kidneys. After getting no response, Pacheco was the one who quit.

In 1978, Ali lost his title to Leon Spinks, who had boxed as a professional only seven times. In 1980, he barely and only under suspicious circumstances obtained medical clearance in Nevada to fight Larry Holmes, the current champion. Ali suffered such a physical beating in that loss that Holmes cried after the match.

Sylvester Stallone, who was in the audience that night, described the last round as "like watching an autopsy on a man who's still alive." Yet, Ali still wouldn't give up. Giving up wasn't how he had knocked out George Foreman. Giving up wasn't how he became the Greatest.

By 1981, Muhammad Ali couldn't get licensed to fight in America, usually a formality, with race-to-the-bottom standards between state commissions to get any marketable fight. If the world was ever screaming, "Time to hang up your gloves!," that was it. But he went ahead and fought in the Bahamas anyway.

He lost again, in an embarrassing spectacle even by boxing standards. The promotion was such a mess that they couldn't find a key to the venue. They provided only two sets of gloves for the entire undercard so there were additional lengthy delays to unlace the fighters' gloves so they could be reused. They had to borrow a cowbell to signal the start and end of each round.

Muhammad Ali obviously paid a heavy price for continuing to fight until he was nearly forty. He had already shown signs of neurological damage toward the end of his career. All those punches he absorbed after vanquishing Foreman unquestionably contributed to the 1984 diagnosis of Parkinson's disease, and his physical and mental decline thereafter.

Persistence is not always the best decision, certainly not absent context. And context changes.

The same *grit* that helped Ali become such a great champion—admired and revered almost without equal—became his undoing when it drove him to ignore signs that were obvious to anyone on the outside looking in that he should quit.

That's the funny thing about grit. While grit can get you to stick to hard things that are worthwhile, grit can also get you to stick to hard things that are no longer worthwhile.

The trick is in figuring out the difference.

Grit vs. Quit

We view grit and quit as opposing forces. After all, you either persevere or you abandon course. You can't do both at the same time, and in the battle between the two, quitting has clearly lost.

While grit is a virtue, quitting is a vice.

The advice of legendarily successful people is often boiled down to the same message: Stick to things and you will succeed. As Thomas Edison said, "Our greatest weakness lies in giving up. The most certain way to succeed is always to try just one more time." Soccer legend Abby Wambach echoed this sentiment over a century later when she said, "You must not only have competitiveness but ability, regardless of the circumstance you face, to never quit."

Similar inspirational advice is attributed to other great sports champions and coaches, such as Babe Ruth, Vince Lombardi, Bear Bryant, Jack Nicklaus, Mike Ditka, Walter Payton, Joe Montana, and Billie Jean King. You can also find almost identical quotes from other legendary business successes through the ages, from Conrad Hilton to Ted Turner to Richard Branson.

All these famous people, and countless others, have united behind variations of the expression "Quitters never win, and winners never quit."

It is rare to find any popular quote in favor of quitting except one attributed to W. C. Fields: "If at first you don't succeed, try, try again. Then quit. There's no use being a damn fool about it."

Fields was hardly a role model, creating a public persona out of characters who loved drinking, hated children and dogs, and eked out an existence on the fringes of society. That's not much of a counterbalance . . . and Fields didn't actually say it!

By definition, anybody who has succeeded at something has stuck with it. That's a statement of fact, always true in hindsight. But that doesn't mean that the inverse is true, that if you stick to something, you will succeed at it.

Prospectively, it's neither true nor good advice. In fact, sometimes it's downright destructive.

If you are a bad singer, it doesn't matter how long you stick with it. You're not going to be Adele. If you are fifty years old and set your sights on becoming an Olympic gymnast, no amount of grit or effort will make it possible for you to succeed. Thinking otherwise is as absurd as reading one of those articles about the habits of billionaires, finding out that they wake up before 4 a.m., and figuring that if you get up before 4 a.m. you will become a billionaire.

We ought not confuse hindsight with foresight, which is what these aphorisms do.

People stick to things all the time that they don't succeed at, sometimes based on the belief that if they stick with it long enough, that will lead to success. Sometimes they stick with it because winners never quit. Either way, a lot of people are banging their heads against the wall, unhappy because they think there is something wrong with *them* rather than something wrong with the advice.

Success does not lie in sticking to things. It lies in picking the *right thing* to stick to and quitting the rest.

When the world tells you to quit, it is, of course, possible you might see something the world doesn't see, causing you to rightly persist even when others would abandon the cause. But when the world is screaming at the top of its lungs to quit and you refuse to listen, grit can become folly.

Too often, we refuse to listen.

This may be, in part, because quitting has a nearly universal negative connotation. If someone calls you a quitter, would you ever consider it a compliment? The answer is obvious.

Quitting means failing, capitulating, losing. Quitting shows a lack of character. Quitters are losers (except, of course, when it involves giving up something obviously bad like smoking, alcohol, drugs, or an abusive relationship).

The English language itself favors grit, describing those who persevere with positive terms like *can-do*, *unwavering*, *steadfast*, *resolute*, *daring*, *audacious*, *undaunting*, *gutsy*, and *hardy*. Or as having *backbone*, *pluck*, *mettle*, *tenacity*, or *stick-to-itiveness*.

As readily as positive words to describe perseverance come to mind, so do the negative terms for those who quit, all of which encompass the idea that quitters are failures who don't deserve our admiration. They are *backtrackers*, *chickens*, *defeatists*, *deserters*, *dropouts*, *shirkers*, *wimps*, and *wusses*. They *give up* and *abandon* things, *waver* and *vacillate*.

We consider them *aimless*, *capricious*, *craven*, *erratic*, *fickle*, *weak-willed*, *undependable*, *unreliable*, and even *untrustworthy*. Or we call them the politically toxic *flip-floppers*.

It's not as if there aren't any negative words for grit (like *rigid* or *obstinate*), or positive words for quitting (like *agile* or *flexible*). But if you tried filling a two-by-two table with positive and negative terms for both concepts, you would soon see the imbalances.

On the perseverance side, the imbalance would be toward positive ways to talk about grittiness over negative ones. That would be mirrored by an imbalance in favor of negative ways to talk about quitters. Unlike grittiness, there just aren't that many positive words for quittiness, as evidenced by the absence of *quittiness* itself from the dictionary.

One of the biggest clues to the way that the language favors grit over quitting is that one of the synonyms for grittiness is *heroism*. Others include *bravery*, *courage*, and *fearlessness*.

When we think of perseverance, particularly in the face of danger, we picture the hero, who gets to the edge of death, faces down the abyss, and perseveres when other people would give up.

Meanwhile, people who quit are cowards.

In a world where perseverance is almost universally seen as the road to honor and success, grit is the star. Quitting, meanwhile, is either the villain (an obstacle to overcome) or, more often, a bit player (credited only as "Henchman #3" or "Cowardly Soldier").

Wrapped in Euphemism

In February 2019, Lindsey Vonn, one of the world's most famous athletes, announced on Instagram that she was retiring from ski racing: "My body is broken beyond repair and it isn't letting me have the final season I dreamed of. My body is screaming at me to STOP and it's time for me to listen."

After detailing her most recent series of injuries, surgery, and rehabilitation (much of which she had not previously disclosed), she added the following message: "I always say, 'Never give up!' So to all the kids out there, to my fans who have sent me messages of encouragement to keep going . . . I need to tell you that I'm not giving up! I'm just starting a new chapter."

In the first part of Vonn's statement, she very clearly, in all caps, says she is stopping competitive skiing. (Translation: She's quitting.) But then, in the second part of the statement, she gives a full-throated denial of the very quitting that she just announced, instead wrapping it in the euphemism "starting a new chapter."

If anybody has earned the right to proudly quit without their mettle or stick-to-itiveness questioned, it's Lindsey Vonn. Stories of her comebacks from serious crashes are almost as impressive as her unrivaled record of success. After being airlifted to a hospital from a horrible crash at the 2006 Olympics, she tried to sneak out before being cleared by doctors and competed two days later.

In 2013, after suffering a torn ACL and MCL and another fracture, having surgery, and working through a grueling rehabilitation, she reinjured both reconstructed ligaments and went through the same process *again*. She missed the Sochi Olympics and most of 2014 yet returned to win another twenty-three World Cup races between late 2014 and early 2018.

If Lindsey Vonn finds it so hard to just say that she's quitting, imagine what it's like for us mere mortals to do so. The idea of quitting is such a bitter pill to swallow that we have to take it with a spoonful of sugar. Or, in this case, a spoonful of euphemism, the most famous of which is "pivot."

If you search any major bookselling website, you will see that titles with *pivot* in them are awfully popular. Many books are simply titled *Pivot* (plus one titled *Pivot!*). There is also *The Big Pivot*, *The Great Pivot*, *Pivot with Purpose*, *Pivot to Win*, and *Pivot for Success*, among countless others.

I'm certainly not knocking these books. But whether you say "pivot" or "moving on to the next chapter" or "strategic redeployment," all of these things are, by definition, quitting. After all, stripped of its negative connotation, quitting is merely the choice to stop something that you have started.

We ought to stop thinking that we need to wrap the idea of quitting in bubble wrap and serve it soft. After all, there are lots of circumstances in which quitting is the right choice, particularly when the world tells you that you ought to, and your kidneys are failing, or you're facing another set of career-ending injuries. Or you're in a miserable marriage, or a dead-end job, or a major you hate.

Why is the word given the Voldemort treatment (The-Word-Which-Must-Not-Be Named)?

Back in the days when people bought their meat at a local butcher's shop, every comic had a gag about getting cheated by the butcher's scale. One of Borscht Belt comedian Milton Berle's famous bits went like this: "I'm beginning to question my butcher's accuracy. The other day a fly landed on his scale. It weighed four-and-a-half pounds."

What Berle was talking about was a common Borscht Belt meme of the butcher "gaffing" the scale, usually by sneaking his thumb on it, to cheat customers. A carnival's wheel of fortune could be gaffed with some mechanism that got it to stop at a certain point in its spin, guaranteeing the house would not have to pay out. Shady backroom roulette wheels could be similarly gaffed. The dice in an impromptu craps game could be gaffed.

When it comes to quitting, the scale is similarly gaffed. What Muhammad Ali, Lindsey Vonn, the aphorisms, the language, and the euphemisms are telling us is that there is a cognitive and behavioral thumb tilting the scale's balance toward persevering when it comes to weighing grit versus quit.

Science Says

Given the way the scale is gaffed toward grit, and the way we admire people who persist as heroes, it shouldn't surprise us that books about the power of perseverance, like Angela Duckworth's *Grit* and Malcolm Gladwell's *Outliers* (with its famous ten-thousand-hours trope), are so popular.

The implication of the massive, enthusiastic audience for such books is that the human condition is one of persevering too little.

But anybody who reads *Grit* as suggesting that perseverance, absent context, is always a virtue, is misinterpreting Angela Duckworth's work. She would never say, "Just stick with things and you'll succeed." She has herself written about the importance of trying lots of things (which requires that you quit lots of other things) to find the thing that you want to stick with. Duckworth, whose book makes the case for the importance of persistence, would certainly agree that knowing when to quit is a skill worth developing.

While grit might have won the battle of the popular mind, the case for quitting earlier and more often is also well established.

There is a rich universe of science studying the human tendency to persevere *too long*, particularly in the face of bad news. The science spans disciplines from economics to game theory to behavioral psychology and covers topics from sunk cost to status quo bias to loss aversion to escalation of commitment, and much more.

Some of the deepest work on the topic of the tendency to over-persist, particularly the circumstances under which we do that, has been done by Daniel Kahneman and Richard Thaler. Kahneman won the Nobel Prize in Economic Sciences in 2002, and Thaler won the same prize in 2017. When two Nobel laureates opine on the same topic, we ought to pay attention.

And what the science is telling us is that every day, in ways big and small, we act like Muhammad Ali, sticking to things too long in the face of signals that we ought to quit.

The aim of this book is to create a better understanding of those forces that work against good choices about what and when to quit and the circumstances in which we are reluctant to walk away, and to help all of us view quitting more positively so we can improve our decision-making. I've organized this material into four sections, with three interludes.

Section I will make the case for quitting as a decision skill worth developing. Chapter 1 covers why quitting is our best tool for making decisions under uncertainty, because it allows us to change course after new information is revealed. I'll also examine how the very uncertainty that makes the option to quit so valuable can make it hard to quit at all. Chapter 2 explores why, when you quit on time, it usually feels like you quit too early. Quitting is ultimately a forecasting problem, meaning that when to quit is a problem of whether the future looks dire, not whether the present is dire. And a rosy present is a hard thing to walk away from. Chapter 3 will dive into the science of quitting, showcasing the evidence that we all tend to poorly calibrate our grit/quit decisions: In particular, when the world gives us bad news we tend to persevere too long, but when we get good news, we tend to quit too soon.

In Section II, I cover specifically how your decision to quit is affected by whether you are winning or losing ("in the losses"). Chapter 4 introduces the concept of escalation of commitment, where we respond to bad news by *increasing* our commitment to a losing course of action. Chapter 5 describes why sunk costs make it so hard to walk away. I'll dive deep into the fear of waste and how the money, time, effort, or other resources we have invested in a course of action negatively impact decisions about whether to move forward. Chapter 6 offers up strategies to improve decisions about when to quit, including the importance of tackling the hardest part of a project first, as well as ways to develop benchmarks, criteria, and signals, called kill criteria, that will help ensure you quit sooner when persisting is no longer in your best interest.

In Section III, I'll get deeper into the cognitive biases that interfere with quitting. Chapter 7 explores how ownership, both of things and ideas, makes it difficult to change course, as well as the powerful pull of the status quo. I'll cover the dual effects of how the fear of uncertainty and the fear of losing associated with changing course prevent us from charting a new path. Chapter 8 looks at how our identity—and our desire for a consistent identity—becomes an impediment to quitting, and can cause us to escalate commitment to disastrous choices. Chapter 9 offers an additional strategy for mitigating the cognitive biases that make walking away so hard: a quitting coach, or someone who can see our situation from the outside and help us to change course when the time is right.

In Section IV, I examine the problem of opportunity cost. Whenever we commit to a course of action, by default we are committing to not pursuing other things. How do we know when it's time to quit one choice in favor of another, better one? Chapter 10 highlights the lessons we learn when we're forced to quit, and how to apply those lessons preemptively. Chapter 11 looks at the downside of goals, arguing that although goals are a motivating force, they can also motivate you to stick to things that are no longer worthwhile. The pass-fail nature of goals is at odds with an unfixed and flexible world, and the desire to meet a goal can keep us from seeing other paths and opportunities available to us. I'll also argue for why every goal needs caveats, as well as progress markers along the way.

I hope that as a result of reading this book, you will learn to recognize why quitting should be celebrated and how it can become a skill you can develop and use to enrich your life, encouraging you to value optionality, execute better on the things you stick with, and continue exploring so you can flexibly change with (or in advance of) a changing world.

To be clear, there are lots of hard things that are absolutely worth sticking to, and resilience and grit are going to help you do that. Success is not achieved by quitting things just because they are hard. But success is also not achieved by sticking to hard things that are not worthwhile.

The trick is in figuring out when to persevere and when to walk away. This book will help you develop the tools to do that.

So let's get to it. It's time to rehabilitate quitting.

The Case for Quitting

CHAPTER 1

The Opposite of a Great Virtue
Is Also a Great Virtue

T HERE IS NO PLACE IN THE WORLD WHERE YOU WOULD expect more stories of grit—per vertical foot, at least—than the upper reaches of Mount Everest. Such an unforgiving environment requires perseverance just to survive, much less reach the summit. You've probably heard many such stories, certainly the most famous ones.

And so, Everest also happens to be an appropriate place to begin a book about the virtues of quitting.

This Everest story is about three climbers you are likely unfamiliar with, Dr. Stuart Hutchison, Dr. John Taske, and Lou Kasischke. They were part of a commercial, guided expedition of Mount Everest, operated by Adventure Consultants, one of the most successful, highly regarded companies guiding climbers to the summit in the 1990s. Its expedition that year consisted of three guides, eight climbing Sherpas, and eight clients.

It takes several weeks of intermediate climbs to acclimatize and move equipment up the mountain before, weather permitting, the expedition members at Camp 4 can attempt to reach the summit. Hutchison, Taske, and Kasischke had become friendly and climbed together that year on the numerous treks between Base Camp (17,600 feet) and Camp 4 (26,000 feet).

Companies like Adventure Consultants had made it possible for relatively inexperienced climbers to reach the summit of the world's tallest mountain. All you needed was $70,000 to cover the costs, enough free time to spend several months in Nepal, and to be in good physical condition. This last requirement is, of course, no guarantee of success or safety. The air above 25,000 feet is too thin to sustain human life for an extended period. In addition, the average temperature during climbing season is minus 15 degrees Fahrenheit (minus 26 degrees Celsius).

Anybody who reaches the summit (or gets anywhere high on the mountain) must be capable of persevering in conditions most people could not handle.

Back at Base Camp, the expedition leader had impressed on the clients the importance of having strictly observed turnaround times for each day's climb up the mountain as they ascended from the foot of Everest to each intermediate camp and, ultimately, to the summit.

While at Base Camp, the expedition leader set the turnaround time on summit day at 1 p.m.

A turnaround time is, simply put, the time at which climbers are to stop their ascent, even if they haven't yet reached their destination, and return to camp. Turnaround times are meant to protect climbers from putting themselves in danger on the descent, which requires more skill than ascending the mountain.

Climbers on the descent can suffer from a combination of fatigue, oxygen deprivation (hypoxia), frostbite, changing weather, becoming lost or disoriented, falling into a crevasse, and darkness if they persist too long in their summit attempt. The darkness and fatigue multiply the likelihood of making a mistake and slipping on the narrow South-east Ridge, where a misstep can cause you to fall 8,000 feet to your death into Tibet, or 12,000 feet to your death into Nepal.

In fact, eight times more people die on Everest on the way down than on the way up

No client makes the sacrifices needed to get to the top of Everest with the intent of stopping short of the summit. And the pull of the summit goes beyond the amateur climbers. Assistant expedition guides prove their ability by summiting Everest, or doing it multiple times. Expedition leaders, competing with each other for business, market their successes in getting their clients to the top of the mountain. Sherpas aren't immune to the pull either. Their marketability and local standing are enhanced by summiting.

Turnaround times are there to prevent people from making poor decisions to keep going when they're in the shadow of the summit, building into a climbing plan three crucial concepts. The first is that persistence is not always a virtue. Whether it is prudent to continue up the mountain depends both on the climbing conditions and the condition of the climbers. When those conditions warrant quitting, it is a good decision to heed those signals.

The second is that making a plan for when to quit should be done long before you are facing the quitting decision. It recognizes, as Daniel Kahneman has pointed out, that the worst time to make a decision is when you're "in it." On Everest, when the summit is within reach and you have sacrificed so much to be there, you are truly in it. That is when you will be the least fit to make a decision about whether to continue on or to quit. That is why turnaround times are set long before you are ever faced with that choice.

Third, and perhaps most important, the turnaround time is a reminder that the real goal in climbing Everest is not to reach the summit. It is, understandably, the focus of enormous attention, but the ultimate goal, in the broadest, most realistic sense, is to return safely to the base of the mountain.

The Invisible Men at the Top of the World

Hutchison, Taske, and Kasischke were part of one of three expeditions trying to reach the summit on the same day and the top of the mountain was crowded. More crowded than it was supposed to be.

The evening before, the expedition leader with the least experience announced that his group would not attempt to summit the next day. Yet, around midnight (which is when summit day begins), there they were, part of what was now an unusually large group of thirty-four, setting out from Camp 4 at the same time.

Hutchison, Taske, and Kasischke had gotten stuck at the back of the pack, behind some climbers from that group. Those climbers were slow and difficult to pass because they were clumped together, which was a problem since you have to go much of the way along a single fixed rope (experienced climbers know to spread out to allow faster climbers to pass). Also stuck with them was Adventure Consultant's expedition leader, whom Hutchison asked at one point how long it would be until they reached the summit.

The reply was about three hours. At that point, the expedition leader started climbing faster, trying to get past the clump of incompetent climbers in front of them.

Hutchison held Taske and Kasischke back for a talk. Looking at their watches, it was nearly 11:30 a.m. They'd been climbing for almost twelve hours. All three climbers remembered that their expedition leader said back at Base Camp that 1 p.m. would be the turnaround time on summit day.

Hutchison announced his opinion: Their summit attempt was done. It would be well past 1 p.m. when they reached the summit, even accounting for wiggle room. They all understood that the turnaround time was meant to protect them from the dangers during the descent. Because of the harshness of the environment at 26,000 feet and above, a likely enough outcome of most of those dangers was, obviously, death.

Taske agreed to turn back, but Kasischke was reluctant to quit. He needed to summit Everest to complete the last of "Seven Summits," climbing the highest mountain on every continent. Achieving the Seven Summits requires a significant expenditure of time and money. Several of the peaks are in remote, difficult-to-reach areas. (If you think it's hard to get to Everest, try planning a trip to the Vinson Massif, the highest point in Antarctica.) Quitting would mean giving up on that goal for at least a year.

Hutchison and Taske managed to persuade Kasischke and, at 11:30 a.m., they gave up on their summit attempt. They turned around and made it—safely, uneventfully—back to Camp 4 and, later, off the mountain.

It's probably obvious to you why this isn't a famous story. It's pretty uneventful, after all. The heroes of our story got within three hours of the summit of Mount Everest, followed the rules, and abandoned their summit attempt. They never faced the brink of death. Instead, they turned around and lived.

It feels anticlimactic. Not the stuff movies are made of.

But the funny thing is that if you've read books about Everest or seen any of the movies, I'd be willing to bet that you have already heard the story of Hutchison, Taske, and Kasischke.

It's just that you don't remember them.

Our three climbers were part of the 1996 climbing season, chronicled in Jon Krakauer's famous book *Into Thin Air*, as well as the popular 1998 documentary *Everest* and the 2015 feature film also titled *Everest*. Their expedition leader was Rob Hall, one of the world's most accomplished alpinists. Hall, along with four others who reached the summit that day, died on various parts of their descent back to Camp 4.

Hall was, in fact, the guide with them at the back of the pack who told them they were three hours from the top and then attempted to sprint past the slow climbers ahead of them.

This despite Hall being the one who impressed upon them the importance of the 1 p.m. turnaround time back when they were gathered with the other clients at Base Camp. He also set and enforced turnaround times on numerous interim climbs up the mountain. He had even, the previous year, turned around with a client named Doug Hansen only 300 feet from the summit.

Hall's prudence and expertise in establishing and enforcing that turnaround time in 1995 undoubtedly saved Hansen's life. One of the other guides that year said that Hansen "was fine during the ascent, but as soon as he started down, he lost it mentally and physically; he turned into a zombie, like he'd used everything up."

Rob Hall repeatedly called Hansen during the intervening year, discounting his fee and successfully encouraging him to try again in 1996.

Hall reached the summit that next year around 2 p.m. with a small group of climbers. The others—*now* recognizing that it was getting late—quickly began descending, but Hall waited for Hansen, whom he believed was close behind.

Hansen didn't arrive on the summit until 4 p.m., by which time he was so exhausted that he was unable to climb down the near-vertical Hillary Step. Hall couldn't get Hansen down and wouldn't abandon him.

They both died.

We'll explore later in this book many of the forces that likely interfered with Hall's judgment. But for now, what his failure shows is that while turnaround times increase the chances that you'll make a rational decision about quitting, they don't guarantee it.

Amid the chaos of what happened on the mountain that day, almost no one remembers Hutchison, Taske, and Kasischke, three climbers who followed the rules and turned around. It's not just that they are uncelebrated. It's that they made no impression whatsoever.

They are invisible.

Why do so few remember these three climbers who wisely turned around? It's not because Krakauer failed to tell their tale in his book. He even noted that, "faced with a tough decision, they were among the few who made the right choice that day."

We tend to think only about one side of the human response to adversity: *the ones who go for it*. The people who continued up the mountain become the heroes of the story, tragic or otherwise. They're the ones who catch our attention, the ones who persevered, despite not having adhered to the turnaround time.

The story of the climbers who turned around on summit day was out there for the telling, but apparently not for the remembering.

There is no doubt that quitting is an important decision-making skill. Getting the decision right is sometimes a matter of life or death. That was the case on Everest. But even in this life-or-death situation, we don't seem to remember the quitters at all.

The problem with this is, of course, that we learn to get better at things from experience, either our own experience or by watching others. And our ability to learn from experience can only be as good as our memory of those experiences.

This is no less true for decisions about quitting.

How can we learn if we don't even see the quitters? Worse yet, how are we supposed to learn if, when we do see them, we view them negatively, as people not worthy of our admiration, as cowards or poltroons?

Admittedly, "poltroon" is an obscure word now, but it's a synonym for quitter that used to be quite popular, sufficiently nasty that if you called someone a poltroon, they were within their rights to challenge you to a duel. When Charles Dickinson called Andrew Jackson a coward and a poltroon in a local newspaper in 1806, Jackson challenged Dickinson to a duel, killed him, and it didn't stop Jackson from becoming president in 1829.

If calling someone a quitter is grounds to shoot them, how can we expect people to appreciate how important it is to become skilled at walking away?

Quitting Is a Decision-Making Tool

Despite the way grit and quit have been pitted against each other, they are actually two sides of the exact same decision. Anytime that you are deciding whether to quit, you are obviously simultaneously deciding whether to stick, and vice versa.

In other words, you can't decide one thing without deciding the other.

Our intrepid climbers offer a good way to think about the grit-quit decision: Grit is what gets you up the mountain, but quit is what tells you when to come down. In fact, it is the option to turn around that allows you to make the decision to climb the mountain in the first place.

Just imagine if any decision you made was last and final. Whatever you decide, you would have to stick with it for the rest of your life. Think of how certain you would have to be before you could ever make a choice to start anything. Imagine if you had to marry the first person you ever went on a date with.

Having no option to change course or change your mind would be disastrous in a landscape that itself is changing, where mountains can become molehills, and molehills can become mountains. If the mountain you've been scaling turns out to be a glacier that's starting to melt beneath you, you want to climb down it before you're washed away.

That's why, if I had to skill somebody up to get them to be a better decision-maker, quitting is the primary skill I would choose, because the option to quit is what allows you to react to that changing landscape.

Any decision is, of course, made under some degree of uncertainty, stemming from two different sources, most of our decisions being subject to both.

First, the world is stochastic. That's just a fancy way of saying that luck makes it difficult to predict exactly how things will turn out, at least not in the short run. We operate not with certainties but with probabilities, and we don't have a crystal ball that tells us which among all the possible futures will be the one that actually occurs. Even if you know for sure that a choice will work out for you, say, 80% of the time, that means, by definition, that the world is going to hand you a bad outcome 20% of the time. The problem for us as decision-makers is that we don't know when, in particular, we are going to experience the outcomes that make up that 20%.

Second, when we make most decisions, we don't have all the facts. Because we're not omniscient, we have to make decisions with only partial information, certainly far less than we'd need to have to make a perfect choice.

That being said, after you've set out on a particular course of action, *new information will reveal itself to you*. And that information is critical feedback.

Sometimes, that new information will be new facts. Sometimes, it might be different ways to think about or model a problem or a set of data or the facts you already have. Sometimes, it will be a discovery about your own preferences. And, of course, some of that new information will be about which future you happen to observe, a good one or a bad one.

When you take all these aspects of uncertainty together, it makes decision-making hard. The good news is that quitting helps make this easier.

Everyone has had the thought go through their head "If I had known then what I know now, I would have made a different choice." Quitting is the tool that allows you to make that different decision when you learn that new information. It gives you the ability to react to the way the world has changed, your state of knowledge has changed, or how you have changed.

This is why it's so important to skill up on quitting, because having the option to quit is what will keep you from being paralyzed by uncertainty or being stuck forever in every decision you make.

Silicon Valley is famous for mantras like "move fast and break things" and implementing them through strategies like "minimum viable product" (MVP). These types of agile strategies can only work if you have the option to quit. You can't put out an MVP unless you have the ability to pull it back. The whole point is to get information quickly, so you can quit the stuff that isn't working and stick with the things that are worthwhile or develop new things that might work even better.

Quitting is what allows companies to maximize speed, experimentation, and effectiveness in highly uncertain environments. If you are moving fast, by definition, you are going to have greater uncertainty. You are taking less time to gather and analyze information before acting. An MVP is meant to allow you to quit or change things before you put too much time or effort into a course of action, all while speeding up the information-gathering process so crucial to good decision-making.

Richard Pryor, when he was arguably the world's best stand-up comedian from the mid-1970s to the early 1980s, was known for his dedication to this kind of strategy for developing new material. Pryor, if a little less familiar to the current generation, is still considered among the most important comedians ever, in the scope of his success, in using comedy to break down boundaries, and in his influence on comedians ever since. Twenty years after his last stand-up work,

Comedy Central ranked him as number one of all time. In 2017, more than a decade after Pryor's death, *Rolling Stone* also ranked him number one. Practically every legendary comedian since has called him the best, including Jerry Seinfeld, Dave Chappelle, Eddie Murphy, David Letterman, Jim Carrey, Chris Rock, and the late Robin Williams.

At the height of Pryor's celebrity, not just as a comedian but as a movie star and a cultural icon, he would book a series of gigs to work on new material at the Comedy Store on the Sunset Strip. The Comedy Store was a small club but so influential that it was considered impossible to appear on *The Tonight Show* without proving yourself there first. Time on the stage there was a coveted commodity.

Pryor was so big that he could get stage time whenever he wanted. In fact, once his name appeared on the marquee, expectations soared. News quickly spread throughout LA and in the entertainment business. The line for the few tickets would stretch around the block. When he arrived onstage, the atmosphere was like the start of a heavyweight championship fight.

And Pryor would bomb.

On the first night, he would show up with nothing prepared beyond "a couple of ideas," "one or two jokes at the most." The audience would beg him to pull out trademark characters from his latest album and scream out punch lines. Once it was clear he wouldn't give the audience what they wanted (or anything new that was actually funny), the yelling subsided. He would stumble through at least a half hour of terrible material in awkward, embarrassing silence.

The next night, he'd drop everything that didn't work—which was nearly the whole set—and expand on whatever got a titter. At the end of thirty days, he had forty minutes of incredible material, the material he created for nine consecutive Grammy-nominated comedy albums, five of which won him the award.

This is the comedian's version of MVP, going to small clubs and telling jokes before they've ironed out the details, or sometimes just improvising on a topic and seeing where it goes. Jerry Seinfeld does this, as does Chris Rock and most other successful stand-ups. They get feedback from the audience and they quit the stuff that isn't working and develop the stuff that is.

This isn't just for Silicon Valley folks and iconic comedians. Trying something and having the ability to quit is vital to how we all live our lives.

A simple example we all use is dating, which is a version of MVP. You need to know much less about a person you're going to go on a date with than a person you're going to marry because you can easily choose never to see your date again. In addition, all those dates help you reveal and refine your preferences and make your decisions about long-term relationships much better.

Having the option to quit allows you to walk away when you find out that the thing that you're doing is broken. If you're near the top of Everest and the weather changes, you want to turn around. If your fight doctor lets you know that your kidneys are damaged, you can retire from the sport.

The same is true for your major, or your job, or the direction of your career, or a relationship, or piano lessons, or even something as small as a movie you're watching.

The Siren Song of Certainty

While it is true that quitting is one of your most important tools for making good decisions under uncertainty, it is also true that uncertainty is an impediment to making good decisions about quitting. That's because quitting is, itself, a decision made under uncertainty. Just as you can't be 100% sure how a decision is going to turn out when you enter into a course of action, you also can't be 100% sure how it will turn out when you are considering exiting it.

If you think about Hutchison, Taske, and Kasischke, when they first decided to climb Everest, they didn't know how it would work out. They didn't know how things would turn out when they were at Base Camp, or how summit day would go when they left Camp 4 at midnight. The same, of course, was the case when they were deciding at 11:30 a.m. whether or not to continue with the other climbers up the mountain or turn around.

When you make the decision to get married, you can't be certain of how that decision will work out. When you make the decision to get divorced, you also can't know how that decision will work out. That's true whether you are deciding about choosing a major or changing it, or starting a job or quitting it, or starting a project or abandoning it.

When you are weighing whether to quit something or stick with it, you can't know for sure whether you can succeed at what you're doing because that's probabilistic. But there is a crucial difference between the two choices.

Only one choice—the choice to persevere—lets you eventually find out the answer.

The desire for certainty is the siren song calling us to persevere, because perseverance is the only path to knowing for sure how things will turn out if you stay the course. If you choose to quit, you will always be left to wonder, "What if?" Just as the Sirens of mythology lured sailors toward their song, we are lured to persevering because we want to *know*. It's the only way to avoid those "what ifs."

The problem, of course, is that sometimes, the siren song lures you toward a rocky shoal that breaks your ship apart. Or it leads you to your death at the top of Everest.

In fact, the only time you can be sure you should quit is when it's no longer a decision, when you're at the edge of the abyss or you've already stumbled into it. Then you have no choice but to abandon course.

I challenge you to put yourself in the position of climbers near the top of the mountain. Imagine having spent all that time and effort and money. Imagine the sacrifices that you and your family have made for you to get to the top of Everest. You are within a few hundred feet—just a few hours—from the summit.

Could you turn around without knowing for sure whether you could have made it, after everything you put yourself through and all you've asked of others? How much of a burden would it be having to live with "What if I hadn't quit?" for the rest of your life?

Most people in that situation could not do it. Hutchison, Taske, and Kasischke did, but a much larger number—those who died that day and many others who barely escaped death—were unable to resist the call to persevere.

The Super Bowl Is a Corporate Graveyard

Just as you have to exercise skill in choosing which hills to climb, you also need skill in choosing when to climb down.

As the world changes, we should be quitting stuff that isn't working or is no longer what people want or what we want. We should be surveying the landscape, both to understand when that may happen as well as to find something better we can turn our attention to.

It turns out that just because you're on a big mountain, you aren't necessarily on particularly solid ground, even if you're near the top. When Tom Brady won his seventh Super Bowl in 2021, it was another reminder not just of his excellence but also of the astonishing length of his career. In fact, scanning a list of the advertisers from Brady's first Super Bowl back in 2002, nineteen years earlier, you can see that Brady also outlasted many once successful and very prominent companies. The list is now a virtual corporate graveyard: AOL, Blockbuster, Circuit City, CompUSA, Gateway, RadioShack, and Sears.

In case you are wondering why it's so important to be good at quitting to adeptly navigate a changing world, all you have to do is look at that list. If you could afford $2 million for thirty seconds of airtime in 2002 (it is over $5 million now), along with the production and agency costs of making an ad you think will stand out, you were a big, successful company. And presumably, you were working hard at trying to stay a big company, and hopefully get even bigger.

All those companies were smart enough to build something very successful. They had the money and the resources to survey the landscape really well. Yet in each case, the world changed on them, and they failed to quit on time, persisting into oblivion.

Take the example of Blockbuster. New competitors, including Netflix, sprung up. New and disruptive technology (streaming) was developed. Blockbuster, when presented with the opportunity to acquire Netflix, refused. Then, it persisted in its business of renting physical copies of entertainment content to people coming in person to their store locations.

We all know what happened to Blockbuster, and what happened to Netflix.

Looking at Blockbuster and the rest of that list, you realize that the scale must be gaffed against quitting not just for individuals but for businesses as well. This should not be surprising because businesses are a collection of individuals.

The road to sustained profitability for a business is not only about sticking to a strategy or business model (even one that has been profitable in the past). It is also about surveying and reacting to the changing landscape. Similarly, for each of us on an individual level, the road to happiness is not in sticking blindly to the thing that we're doing, as so many aphorisms cajole us to do. We need to see what's going on around us so we can do whatever will maximize our happiness and our time and our well-being.

And that usually means doing more quitting.

"Know When to Hold 'Em, Know When to Fold 'Em": But Mostly, Fold 'Em

As Kenny Rogers sang in *The Gambler*, "You gotta know when to hold 'em, know when to fold 'em, know when to walk away, and know when to run."

Notice that three of those four things are about quitting. When it comes to the importance of cutting your losses at poker, Kenny Rogers got it.

A poker table, it turns out, is a very good place to learn about the upside of quitting. Optimal quitting might be the most important skill separating great players from amateurs. In fact, without the option to abandon a hand, poker would be much more like baccarat, a game of no skill because there are no new decisions you get to make once the cards are dealt.

Top poker players are better at quitting than amateurs in a variety of ways. The most obvious is that they know when to fold 'em.

Deciding which hands are worth playing and which hands are not is the first and most consequential choice a player makes. And pros are just better at that choice, playing a mere 15% to 25% of the two-card starting combinations they are dealt in Texas Hold'em. Compare that to an amateur, who will stick with their starting cards over half the time.

In the battle of whether to hold 'em or fold 'em, amateurs usually hold 'em. Professionals usually fold 'em. This may be, in part, because in the choice between holding 'em and folding 'em, only holding 'em lets you know for sure that you never miss out on raking in a pot that you might have won if you had just stayed in the hand till the last card.

There's an old saying in poker that goes "Any two cards can win," meaning that if you stick with your hand, there is always some possibility, no matter how slim, that even a terrible hand can triumph.

Unfortunately, it doesn't go on to say, ". . . but not enough of the time for it to be profitable."

I remember many, many nights at a poker table when a player sitting next to me would nudge me after a hand to let me know that the cards they folded would have won the pot. It would occasionally get ridiculous, like when they had folded a seven-deuce at the beginning of the hand (the mathematically worst two-card starting combination you can be dealt, so it's a no-brainer to fold) and the five community cards would end up including seven-deuce-deuce. They would invariably lean over and groan, "I folded seven-deuce. I would have made a full house!"

I'd tell them, "There's a way to avoid that."

"How?"

"Just play every hand all the way to the last card."

That advice might have been absurd, but I was making the point that a necessary part of succeeding in poker is to fold some hands that might have won. To be good at the game you just have to learn to live with that. Playing every hand you are dealt is an easy and fast way to go broke since you would be playing too many hands that aren't profitable in the long run. That would also make poker more like baccarat, taking out a key element of skill, the option to fold.

Even playing 50% of your hands comes at a great price. But what you get in return for that cost is peace of mind. When you hold 'em instead of fold 'em, you experience a lot less of the pain of knowing that you could be throwing away a winner. You won't have to deal with the version of "What if?" on steroids: watching players throwing chips into a gigantic pot and seeing someone else rake it in, knowing that could have been you if you just hadn't folded your hand.

For most players, that peace of mind is a potent force, another siren song. It's one of the main reasons why amateurs play so many hands.

If folding is difficult for amateurs at the beginning of the hand, it's even more difficult once a player has committed money to the pot. It is hard to overcome the urge to protect the money you have already bet, regardless of the likelihood that the next bet is a favorable choice.

Because of the uncertainty during the hand—not being able to see the other players' cards and not knowing the cards that are yet to come—you can't be sure how that particular hand will turn out. That pushes most players toward continuing rather than cutting their losses because if they stay in the hand, they still preserve some hope of winning it. In contrast, if you fold 'em, that's the way to *guarantee* that you lose a pot and any chance of getting back the money you just bet.

If you generally land on the side of playing your starting hand, and you keep sticking with your hand to the end, you will be more likely to avoid the regret of folding a hand that would have won.

You will also quickly go broke. The best poker players avoid that trap.

In addition, great players know when to walk away. When experts are in a game, they are more likely than other players to recognize when the game conditions aren't favorable or when they're not playing well. And, given that they recognize those things, they are more likely to quit the game because of it.

Quitting a game is a decision fraught with uncertainty because it is never clear exactly why you are losing. While you could be playing poorly, you could also be playing really well but still losing in the game because of an unlucky run of cards. In other words, if you want to blame your losses on luck and keep playing, you can always find a way to do that. Quitting a game is the same as admitting that you might not be good enough compared with the other players, that you might not have an edge in the game that you're playing in. That's a blow to the ego few are willing to take.

Just like folding a hand is the only way to guarantee losing that hand, quitting a game when you're losing is the only way to guarantee that you won't get those chips back in that game. That all makes quitting when you are losing difficult.

Are expert poker pros perfect at these decisions? No. In fact, sometimes they are far from perfect. But they are better at making quitting decisions than their opponents, which is all you need in order to win.

When you think about it, almost all our decisions involve the same kinds of uncertainty. Should we quit the job? Should we change the strategy? Should we abandon the project? Should we turn around on the mountain? Should we shut down the business?

These are hard problems. We're not omniscient. We don't have crystal balls or time machines. All we have is our best assessment of an uncertain and changing landscape and the hope that we have honed our quitting skills enough to walk away when conditions turn against us.

This is the fundamental truth about grit and quit: The opposite of a great virtue is also a great virtue.

Chapter 1 Summary

- We tend to celebrate people who respond to adversity by soldiering on. The quitters, in comparison, are invisible.
- If we don't notice the decision-making of the quitters, it's hard to learn from them.
- Quitting a course of action is sometimes the best way to win in the long run, whether you're cutting your losses at the poker table or getting to climb another day.
- Quit and grit are two sides of the exact same decision.
- Decision-making in the real world requires action without complete information. Quitting is the tool that allows us to react to new information that is revealed *after* we make a decision.
- Sticking with a course of action is the only way to find out for sure how it will turn out. Quitting requires being okay with not knowing what might have been.
- Having the option to quit helps you to explore more, learn more, and ultimately find the right things to stick with.

CHAPTER 2

Quitting On Time Usually Feels Like Quitting Too Early

F ROM STEWART BUTTERFIELD'S FIRST EXPOSURE TO THE internet as a college freshman in 1992, he was drawn to its potential to facilitate human interaction, especially beyond the limits of geographic boundaries.

A decade later, in 2002, he cofounded a company to build a massive multiplayer online role-playing game. The concept was called *Game Neverending*, where players accumulated objects by working cooperatively to create an entire world. Thousands of players loved the prototype, but the company found the funding environment unfriendly in the immediate wake of the dot-com crash. As Butterfield told me, "Not very many people were interested in investing in anything to do with the internet, but especially not something frivolous like a game."

In 2004, unable to secure capital, the venture ran out of money.

In a final desperation move, they salvaged one feature of the game, an inventory of objects the players accumulated, represented by a shoebox of photos. This became Flickr, one of the first photo-sharing websites. Within a year, Butterfield and his cofounders sold it to Yahoo for $25 million.

Stewart Butterfield left Yahoo in 2008 and returned to the idea of creating an open-ended, cooperative, world-building online game. He rounded up some of the folks from his Flickr days and cofounded another gaming company, Tiny Speck, whose first product was an even more ambitious game, *Glitch*.

Computing power had advanced one hundredfold. His whole team of engineers and designers were more experienced and capable. Flickr afforded him a track record, plus the funding environment was much more favorable. This all gave him greater access to venture capital. The company raised $17.5 million from venture investors including Andreessen Horowitz and Accel.

They launched the game publicly on September 27, 2011. *Glitch* looked amazing and had a vividly imagined story line, described by fans and reviewers as "Monty Python meets Dr. Seuss."

By November 2012, the game had a devoted following of about five thousand diehard users, who were playing at least twenty hours a week. The problem was that these players, who paid a monthly subscription fee, represented less than 5% of more than a hundred thousand users who signed up to try out the game for free.

Over 95% of new users played *Glitch* for less than seven minutes and never returned.

Butterfield, his cofounders, and his investors recognized the problem. They had to attract as many as ninety-five to one hundred new users to end up with just one paying player. They decided to get more aggressive with customer acquisition. Their strategy had been low-key, doing PR and relying on word of mouth. Now they stepped up marketing, taking out paid ads and involving affiliate networks to get more people to try out the game.

They executed the new marketing plan and it was working. Over the weekend of November 10–11, the last weekend of the push, they got ten thousand new accounts. Daily active users, over the previous fifteen weeks, had been growing by more than 7% per week. The number of super hard-core players, playing at least five days a week, had been growing by over 6% per week.

Yet, on the Sunday night after that stellar weekend, Stewart Butterfield found himself stressed and unable to sleep. In the middle of the night, he had a revelation, which he acted on the next day, Monday, November 12.

He sent an email to his investors that started with, "I woke up this morning with the dead certainty that Glitch was over."

This took the other founders and the investors completely by surprise. By all appearances, things were going fine. In fact, they were more than fine. *Glitch* just experienced its greatest growth ever. They were still well capitalized, with $6 million in the bank. Yet Butterfield was telling them he was quitting *Glitch* and offering to return the remaining capital to his investors.

In the midst of all the company's good news, what was bothering Butterfield so much he couldn't sleep? What was motivating him to shut down the company?

The answer is that Stewart Butterfield was able to peek into the future, allowing him to see things others couldn't see (or didn't want to see). When he looked at the range of possible outcomes for *Glitch*, the probability was just too high that the game would end up being a money pit.

They had just experienced their highest growth in new accounts, but he saw a future where they would have to sustain week-over-week growth of 7% for thirty-one weeks just to break even. And that was assuming the new users they acquired were going to convert to paying customers at the same historical rate, a pretty big assumption since it stood to reason that the more eyeballs they got, the lower the quality those eyeballs would be. Even the most recent ten thousand new users had cost more to acquire and were of lower quality than earlier marketing efforts had produced.

Worse, over time, paid ads would increasingly reach the hundreds of thousands who had already tried and quit *Glitch*. As the ads saturated the core gaming audience, their potential for new users would depend on people with little background or interest in online gaming. That would lower *Glitch*'s already low conversion rates. The game could continue its growth only by churning through massive numbers of new accounts.

All these growth metrics, despite the increasing challenges, would have to hold up as Tiny Speck burned through its capital on marketing for eight months, just to get to breakeven. For the game to succeed financially, Tiny Speck would eventually need hundreds of thousands of paying users, which would mean tens of millions of people trying out the game. To get there, it would have to endlessly throw money at acquiring new users, who would be of lower and lower quality, to capture more eyeballs to find those diehards that would support the game.

The math just didn't work.

Stewart Butterfield had every reason to deny or ignore what he had seen in his peek into the future. *Glitch* was a great game. It creatively expressed the vision of the founders. It was beloved by a community of *Glitch* gamers. There was growth in new users.

You would expect that every instinct from the founder of such a venture would be to continue. Butterfield had devoted four years to *Glitch*. Most importantly, he had staked his reputation on the project. As he explained to Reid Hoffman in a *Masters of Scale* podcast in 2017, "You have to convince investors, and you have to convince the press, and you have to convince potential employees, and you have to convince customers. And I had done a lot of convincing of people to come work on this project, to leave whatever they were working on before, quit their job, get poorly paid in exchange for equity. . . ."

Despite all this, he knew quitting was the right decision. He told his investors, "I think I knew this six weeks ago and I mistook denial for prudence (in the sense of making sure that we didn't give up too early). But there are just too many things in the 'against' column."

To everybody else, it felt like he was quitting too soon. But to Stewart Butterfield, peeking into the future, he recognized that maybe he hadn't quit soon enough.

After he explained his reasoning to the others, it is unclear whether or not he persuaded them to see what he saw. But it didn't much matter. If he was no longer on board, there was no point in continuing.

Most people in that position would not do what Butterfield did. Despite everything that makes sticking the easier choice—his years of commitment to the project, the encouraging recent results, his cofounders and investors wanting to continue, the pain he felt at having to follow through on this decision and what that meant for his employees—he was able to quit.

This may seem like an unhappy ending. Butterfield was so passionate about his concept of a collaborative multiplayer game that he devoted a decade to trying to make it happen. Now he had fallen short for a second time.

But quitting effectively, when the context warrants it, ought to be the definition of a happy ending. It is just hard for us to see it that way because we process quitting as failure.

Stewart Butterfield saw that he had a losing hand and he decided to fold before he had burned through Tiny Speck's remaining capital. He stopped the company from throwing $6 million at a bad investment, freeing that money up to invest in other things that would be more likely to win. He also spared Tiny Speck's employees from being trapped in a failing business, working for little money and the promise of equity, by promptly acting when he determined that equity wouldn't be worth *their* effort.

These things were good for Butterfield, good for his investors and cofounders, and good for his employees. Shouldn't we view that as a happy ending on its own?

This raises another valuable lesson about quitting. When you quit, you live to fight another day, sometimes literally. Hutchison, Taske, and Kasischke, by turning around, lived to continue with the rest of their lives. When poker players fold a hand, they are cutting their losses so they have chips to invest in another, better hand. If they walk away from the table when they're not playing well, they don't go broke and leave themselves without a bankroll to play in another game where they have a better chance to win.

When Stewart Butterfield walked away from *Glitch*, he freed himself up to develop another product. Which he promptly did, exploring the potential of turning the *Glitch* development team's internal communications system into a standalone productivity tool. The tool basically combined the best parts of email, instant messaging, and texting, allowing team members to communicate in real time and share documents and other materials.

Everybody at the company loved it. Everybody who knew about it loved it. Within two days of quitting *Glitch*, the team was moving on with this new thing, including the investors who decided to roll their capital into this new product.

During the time they used it at Tiny Speck, it didn't even have a name. On November 14, Butterfield came up with a code name for the tool, based on the acronym for "Searchable Log of All Conversation and Knowledge."

Slack. It stuck.

In August 2013, Slack announced its product launch. In June 2019, Slack went public. On its first day as a public company, its market capitalization was $19.5 billion. In December 2020, Salesforce agreed to buy Slack for cash, stock, and assumption of debt in a deal valued at $27.7 billion.

There's a temptation to think, "Now *that's* what makes it a happy ending, because Slack is what came out of that decision to quit." But make no mistake, even if Butterfield had never pursued Slack and just returned the capital to his investors, that would be a happy ending on its own. The fact that he turned Tiny Speck's internal communications tool into a unicorn just makes it even happier.

Quit While You Still Have a Choice

The story of *Glitch* highlights one of the fundamental problems of quitting.

Quitting on time will usually feel like quitting too early.

If you quit on time, it's not going to seem like anything particularly dire is happening at that particular moment. That's because quitting is a problem of being able to glimpse at the range of ways the future might play out and see that the likelihood that things will turn out poorly is too high to make it worth your while to continue.

At the moment that quitting becomes the objectively best choice, in practice things generally won't look particularly grim, even though the present does contain clues that can help you figure out how the future might unfold. The problem is, perhaps because of our aversion to quitting, we tend to rationalize away the clues contained in the present that would allow us to see how bad things really are.

Stewart Butterfield did see how bad things were, despite all appearances. He looked at what was happening to the quality of new users and how many of them stuck around to figure out what the future had in store for *Glitch*.

Most of us, in Butterfield's place, would focus on a rosy version of the present, or at least one that is not so bad that it would warrant quitting. After all, you've created a great online game that has attracted a community of five thousand die-hard customers. It looks amazing. Your investors are encouraged. Your cofounders are happy. You just had your best month ever and acquired a lot of new customers.

You have $6 million in the bank. You just have to work on the problem of how to get more people to stick. Everyone else is encouraged and expects to continue.

Or you're near the top of Everest, only three hours or so from the summit. You have plenty of oxygen. You're just moving a little slow, but the climbing conditions look pretty good, good enough that most people are continuing upward.

The ideal time for Muhammad Ali to walk away might have been after he regained his title from George Foreman. Obviously, that would have required superhuman time-traveling skills, maybe omniscience. But it was after he had just achieved his life's ambition, and certainly before he suffered renal and neurological damage.

Teddy Brenner and Ferdie Pacheco didn't need omniscience to see, after the Earnie Shavers fight in September 1977, the high likelihood and severity of negative outcomes if Ali persisted beyond his midthirties in this dangerous profession.

That was still four years before he actually quit.

It shouldn't be surprising that making good decisions about quitting requires mental time travel since the worst time to make a decision is when you're in it. That's when you are in the present, facing down the decision whether or not to cut your losses, unable to see past what is happening right now.

When we do think about the future, we are often considering our hopes, our goals, our ambitions. That optimism means that, too often, we allow a disastrous future to hurtle toward us, noticing it only as it's arriving on our doorstep.

There is a well-known heuristic in management consulting that the right time to fire someone is the first time it crosses your mind. This heuristic is meant to get businesses to the decision sooner, because most managers are reluctant to terminate personnel, hanging on to them too long.

Dismissing an employee who isn't working out is, of course, a form of quitting (from the employer's perspective). Companies have to face down this situation all the time. To manage their workforce, they have to decide whether to let underperforming personnel go.

Hiring is a much more uncertain decision than most people want to believe. You have a job candidate's CV, their references, and a few interviews. That's the equivalent of entering a long-term relationship based on a couple of dates and having two mutual friends. The hiring success rate of managers has long been estimated at just 50%, which completely squares with the uncertainty involved. How much can you know about whether a new hire will work out before they've actually done the job for a while?

What mitigates the risk associated with such an uncertain decision is that employers have the option to let employees go, just as employees have the option to quit. Of course, that means you need to be good at exercising that option. But the decision to fire someone is itself a decision made under uncertainty, which, as we've already explored in several circumstances, contributes to our tendency to persist too long.

That's why the heuristic about when to fire someone is well known but not often put into practice.

The mistake of keeping people too long after you recognize it's not working out carries with it a heavy price tag. Geoff Smart, a management consultant and expert on the topic of hiring talented teams, has found from studies done with his company's clients that, in hard costs and lost productivity, an average hiring mistake costs fifteen times that person's salary. Of course, once the hiring mistake has been made, hanging on to that employee too long contributes to that cost.

This is true of all our delays in changing course. If we don't cut our losses when it's warranted, those losses will continue to accumulate.

This exposes a common misconception about quitting. We are reluctant to walk away when we should because we have the feeling that doing so will slow our progress or stop it altogether.

But it is the reverse that is actually true.

If you stick to a path that is no longer worth pursuing, whether it's a relationship that isn't going well, or a stock that you're invested in that's losing money, or an employee that you've hired who isn't performing, that is when you lose ground.

By not quitting, you are missing out on the opportunity to switch to something that will create more progress toward your goals. Anytime you stay mired in a losing endeavor, that is when you are slowing your progress. Anytime you stick to something when there are better opportunities out there, that is when you are slowing your progress.

Contrary to popular belief, quitting will get you to where you want to go faster.

Thinking in Expected Value

To get the stick-or-quit decision right, you need to make an educated guess at the probability that things will go your way and the probability that things will go against you, in order to figure out if the good stuff will occur enough of the time to warrant continuing on your path.

Essentially, you need to think in *expected value*, which is what Stewart Butterfield was doing.

Expected value (or EV) helps you answer two questions. First, it tells you whether any option you are considering is going to be, on balance, positive or negative for you in the long run. Second, it allows you to compare different options to figure out which is the better choice, the better choice being simply the one that carries the highest expected value.

To determine the expected value for any course of action, you start with identifying the range of reasonable possible outcomes. Some of those outcomes will be good and some will be bad, to varying degrees, and each of those outcomes will have some probability of occurring. If you multiply the probability of each outcome occurring by how good or bad it might be and add all that together, that gets you the expected value.

As a simple example, imagine that you are flipping a fair coin, meaning the coin has a 50% chance of landing heads and a 50% chance of landing tails. Let's say for this example that if the coin lands heads, you will win $100, and if it lands tails, you will lose $50. If you multiply the $100 you will win by 50% (how often the coin lands heads), you get $50, which will be your expected long-run gains. Multiplying the $50 loss when the coin lands tails by 50% gets you negative $25, your expected losses in the long run. Subtracting $25 from $50 gets you a net gain of $25. So this coin flip proposition carries a *positive expected value* of $25.

Notice that even though the probability of the coin landing tails is the same as the probability of the coin landing heads (both will happen 50% of the time), your expected value is positive because your profit is greater when you win than your loss is when the flip goes against you.

You can also get a positive expected value even if what you can win is much less than what you can lose, as long as your chances of winning are great enough to make up for the losses. For example, if you can win $50 when the coin lands heads or lose $100 when the coin lands tails, but you will win the flip 90% of the time and lose just 10% of the time, your expected value is $35.

That's a bet you should take.

Likewise, there are situations where your expected value can be positive despite having only a small chance of winning. Imagine flipping a coin that lands tails 99% of the time and heads 1% of the time. When the coin lands tails, you will lose $100, but when the coin lands heads, you will win $100,000. Even though you will win money only one out of one hundred times, the win is big enough to make the bet positive expected value, to the tune of $901!

(Of course, that's a much riskier bet than the other two bets. Managing risk is the subject of many other books, but not this one.)

When thinking in expected value, the first step is to ask, "Does the course of action I'm considering (either a new course of action or continuing what you're currently doing) have a positive expected value?"

The second step is to compare that expected value with the expected value of other options you might be considering. Because time, attention, and money are limited resources, and we only have a limited number of things that we can do in our life, when we're thinking about whether we should stick to something, we need to ask, "If I were to switch and do something else, would that have a higher expected value than the thing I'm currently doing?"

If you figure out that another path carries a higher expected value, then walking away from the path you're currently on and switching to the new one will get you to where you're going faster.

No matter whether you are thinking about flipping coins or buying stocks where wins and losses are measured in money, or you are thinking about who to marry or where to live, where wins and losses are measured in happiness and quality of life, expected value is a helpful concept for determining whether the path you are on is worth sticking to.

Stewart Butterfield used expected value to decide whether to continue developing *Glitch*. As a cofounder of a start-up, he was dealing with an endeavor that had a low probability of success but a huge potential payoff.

The vast majority of start-ups, obviously, don't become Slack or Netflix or Twitter or Facebook. Most start-ups fail. Even so, the probability of success can still be just high enough to make pursuing that big idea worthwhile.

This reveals what was bothering Stewart Butterfield. On his trip to the future during his sleepless night on November 11, 2012, he saw that Tiny Speck didn't have a high enough probability of becoming a unicorn to make it worth persevering.

There was some future world in which he could turn *Glitch* into a unicorn, but the likelihood was too remote to justify going for that billion-dollar-plus exit. He could see the writing on the wall, but when you are a good quitter, often you're the only one able to read it. At the time when he told his cofounders and investors on November 12, he understood that quitting had a better expected value than continuing.

In essence, Stewart Butterfield was thinking like a poker player. Winning poker players aren't thinking about trying to win a single hand, come what may. They know that while any two cards can win, only some hands can win enough of the time to make them worth pursuing. Poker players are making decisions based on whether playing or folding will have the greater expected value. In other words, if they played the hand out over and over again, which choice (staying or folding) would be the more profitable decision in the long run?

Obviously, we're not omniscient and most of us aren't going to be as good at doing this mental time travel as Stewart Butterfield, but every single one of us is capable of getting some peek into the future and that's going to help you be better at your quitting decisions.

Quitting Decisions Are Expected-Value Decisions

In the summer of 2021, I received an email from a reader who wanted help working through a decision about whether to quit her job.

Dr. Sarah Olstyn Martinez felt she had reached a crossroads in her professional life. She had been an emergency room physician for sixteen years, having fallen in love with emergency medicine from the first moment in 2005 when she rotated through a hospital ER during her one-year internship after medical school.

Mount Sinai Hospital, where Olstyn Martinez did her internship, was a leading trauma center in Chicago. Its neighborhood, North Lawndale, is considered one of the most dangerous in the city. According to a 2019 study on trends in firearm violence based on emergency room data, "it is accurate to say that Mount Sinai sees a large percentage of the total firearm violence that occurs in Chicago."

It was great training and she loved the experience of working in a leading trauma center. The internship worked out so well that she did her four-year residency in emergency medicine.

In 2009, she moved to Austin, Texas, and became an ER doctor at the hospital where she worked for the next twelve years. This, too, was a job she loved.

People have the idea that an ER doctor is running around pumping people's chests, constantly doing crazy life-and-death stuff. Of course, there is some of that, but, as Olstyn Martinez describes it, the essence of the job is more about the daily challenge of dealing with the wear of seeing humanity at its loneliest and most heartbreaking.

For example, on one shift in 2021, her first patient was a ninety-year-old woman brought in from a nursing home. She was so ill that she wasn't verbal and Dr. Olstyn Martinez couldn't get ahold of any family to help her figure out what was wrong.

In the next room, a woman in her sixties complained that someone was trying to poison her because every hit off her crack pipe gave her palpitations.

She vehemently denied the possibility that the crack was the problem, since she had been smoking it for twenty years.

It was both emotionally challenging and engrossing work. But inside the ER community, handling the hard aspects of the job is what makes ER doctors special. As Olstyn Martinez put it, "One of the underlying themes of emergency medicine is, if you're not full-on suffering and in the trenches and digging yourself out of patients, you're [a wimp]."

At the start, the benefits of her career clearly outweighed the costs. The satisfactions included saving lives, serving the community, being a highly skilled and effective problem solver, and being part of the community of ER doctors handling the exposure to so many raw, trying situations.

An additional benefit of working in the ER was that it provided Olstyn Martinez with a needed work-life separation.

She had scheduled shifts and when they ended, she could attend to the rest of her life. Whether it was going to the gym or taking her dog to the vet, she had space away from her job. This became especially important with the births of her two daughters in 2014 and 2017.

But then, her circumstances changed.

In addition to her ER shifts, Dr. Olstyn Martinez became the hospital's director of emergency and trauma services in 2015 and, in 2020, senior director of patient care quality for twelve emergency departments in the hospital's healthcare system. Over the course of those years, as her administrative responsibilities expanded, the negatives started to grow.

While Dr. Olstyn Martinez clearly excelled at the additional position as director, as evidenced by the further expansion of her responsibilities in 2020, the mounting administrative tasks allowed her to work only six shifts as a doctor in the ER per month. That meant limited time doing the part of her profession she had originally fallen in love with.

Because of her expanded workload, especially during a period of growing financial constraints in medical practice and administration and (of course) the pandemic, the stress of the job increased and took its toll. The boundary between her career and the rest of her life evaporated. This was no longer a job that she could leave behind at the end of an ER shift. She couldn't turn her brain off. She received a non-stop stream of texts and emails, all representing fires she had to put out. There was no downtime.

Increasingly, she felt she was not fully present in her personal life. That hurt her the most with her two young daughters. At eight o'clock one night, she became aware that her seven-year-old had been trying to get her attention, repeating, "Mom. Mom? Mom! MOM!!" When she finally looked up, her daughter said, "You aren't listening to me because you're looking at your phone. You're always on your phone."

And she was right.

Olstyn Martinez was used to handling a challenging load, but she knew it was negatively impacting her and her family. She was bringing it all home. She could feel it physically. She had trouble sleeping. Her hair actually started falling out.

The equation of the things she loved about her work and its costs started to flip for her.

She thought about quitting for over a year, but never acted on it. Then in 2021, a friend offered to recommend her for a job at an insurance company. Olstyn Martinez waltzed through the interview process, and it soon became clear she was going to have to make a decision, and fast.

But she found herself unable to figure out whether or not to take the new position and quit her old one.

That's when I heard from Sarah. I wrote back and we soon got on a call.

After listening to her story, I asked her a simple question: "Imagine it's a year from now and you stayed in the job that you're currently at—what's the probability you're going to be unhappy at the end of that year?"

She said, "I know I'm going to be unhappy, one hundred percent."

I followed up by asking, "If it's a year from now and you switched to this new job you're considering, what's the probability you're going to be unhappy?" She said, "Well, I'm not sure."

"Is it one hundred percent?"

She said, "Definitely not."

At that moment, she realized, "Oh, wait a minute. I'm always going to be unhappy if I stay. If I switch, sometimes I'll be unhappy, but sometimes I won't. Sometimes, I'm going to find real fulfillment in the job that I'm switching to, and that has to be better."

All that I had done was to reframe her quitting decision as an expected-value problem. She was considering two options: staying in her job or quitting to take the new position at the insurance company. Which one carried the greater chance of increasing her happiness and making her feel better about her relationship with her children?

She realized taking the new job had the higher expected value.

Dr. Olstyn Martinez's story reminds us that expected value is not just about money. It can be measured in health, well-being, happiness, time, self-fulfillment, satisfaction in relationships, or anything else that affects you.

Time Travelers from the Past

I often talk about thinking in expected value as a kind of mental time travel, propelling yourself into the future to glimpse the range of possible outcomes and take some reasonable guess at how likely each of them is.

This time travel, as a means to becoming a better quitter, works in both directions. Sometimes, like Stewart Butterfield or Sarah Olstyn Martinez, you are looking into the future by using the clues that the present moment offers you. But other times, you can get the benefit of listening to a message *from the past*.

Hundreds of people had climbed high on Everest before summit day in 1996. Those past climbers had figured out the appropriate turnaround times, whether they were Rob Hall in 1995, Tenzing Norgay and Sir Edmund Hillary in 1953, or any of the climbers in between. At 11:30 a.m., as Hutchison, Taske, and Kasischke were making a difficult quitting decision, those people from the past tapped them on the shoulder and let them know, "Now is the time to turn around."

Retired four-star admiral William McRaven, one of the world's most respected figures on military strategy, U.S. foreign policy, and counterterrorism operations, whose participation in ten thousand Navy SEAL missions during his thirty-seven-year career included organizing and overseeing the successful raid on Osama bin Laden, echoed the importance of this aspect of time travel in successfully navigating decisions about whether to persist or abandon course while on a military mission.

Admiral McRaven is a longtime student (as well as teacher, speaker, and author) of military history. When we spoke, he pointed to a wall of bookshelves behind him stuffed with books and said, "Probably three quarters of the books behind me are history books about battles that went well and battles that went wrong."

He talked about how those history books help him access time travelers from the past. As he explained, "Is it Clausewitz coming forward to tell me something? Is it Napoleon coming forward to tell me something? Is it Norman Schwarzkopf coming forward to tell me something?"

Admiral McRaven's own experience on all those missions also allows past versions of himself to transmit important messages forward in time. "When you see another target later in your career, you say, 'You know what? I did something really similar to that twenty years ago.' People looking at it that are new say, 'There's no way you can do that.' I tell them, 'Oh yeah, we can. I've done it.'"

When you are making a decision about whether to quit, you need to listen to those people from the past who are giving you important advice. Sometimes, the person sending you a message is someone who has traveled a similar path before you. And sometimes, the person traveling from the past is an earlier version of yourself.

Flipping Coins

In 2013, economist Steven Levitt, coauthor of the wildly popular book *Freakonomics*, put up a website inviting people who visited to flip a virtual coin to help them make a close decision about whether to quit or stick.

Participants would register what they were struggling with, among a variety of types of decisions. Many of these were big life decisions, like "Should I quit my job or stay?" or "Should I leave my relationship or continue on?" or "Should I stay in college or drop out?" In other words, these were the normal types of choices you can imagine people would have trouble making.

The site would assign one side of the decision, like stay in your job, to heads, and the other side of the decision, like quit your job, to tails. When users clicked on the image of the coin, they were shown the randomized outcome of the virtual coin flip.

You might be skeptical that people would go to a website to flip a coin to help them make a life-changing quitting decision. But twenty thousand people over the course of a year actually did this.

Obviously, these people must have felt that the choice of whether to quit or to persevere was so close, so 50-50, that flipping a coin to help them decide seemed like a reasonable option. It stands to reason that if these decisions were, in reality, as close as the coin flippers felt they were, they would be equally likely to be happier if the coin landed heads or if it landed tails, whether they ended up sticking or quitting.

That is, after all, the definition of a close call.

But this isn't what Levitt found. When he followed up with the coin flippers two and six months later, he discovered that for the big life decisions, people who quit were happier on average than people who stuck, whether they quit on their own or after the coin flipped in favor of quitting.

While the decisions may have felt close to the people making them, they were not actually close at all. As judged by the participants' happiness, quitting was the clear winner.

Because people were much happier when they quit what they considered a close decision, that shows that people are generally quitting too late. That's exactly what was happening with Sarah Olstyn Martinez. She thought it was a close call, but once I put it in terms of expected value, she realized it wasn't close at all.

Underscoring that point, Levitt concluded, "The results of this paper suggest that people may be excessively cautious when facing life-changing choices."

The corollary of this is also true. When people quit on time, it will usually feel like they are quitting too early, because it will be long before they experience the choice as a close call.

This is consistent with the idea that the scale is gaffed against quitting. It turns out that our psychology puts a thumb on the scale such that by the time we think the options of quitting and sticking are 50-50, it's not even in the vicinity.

This book will go deep into the cognitive and motivational forces that gaff the scale in favor of persisting, as well as practical strategies for recalibrating the scale. For now, you can consider this simple heuristic as a rule of thumb: *If you feel like you've got a close call between quitting and persevering, it's likely that quitting is the better choice.*

Jumping the Shark

In 1985 or 1987 (accounts differ), a pair of University of Michigan students, Jon Hein and Sean Connolly, were talking about signals that their once favorite television shows had started an irreversible decline. That discussion spawned the famous phrase "jumping the shark."

The definitive instance they identified was from the classic, beloved TV series *Happy Days*, which first aired in January 1974. At the show's peak, it had over thirty million viewers. Hein and Connolly decided *Happy Days* jumped the shark in episode 91 (season 5, in September 1977), when, famously, Fonzie, a character who was the leather-jacketed embodiment of cool, literally jumped over a shark.

Just to set up such a story, the show had to get Fonzie from Milwaukee to California. They arranged this by having some Hollywood talent scouts pass through town. Their limo breaks down and they "discover" Fonzie and invite him out to Hollywood to audition. The rest of the show's cast makes the trip with him.

It culminates with Fonzie, out in Hollywood, on water skis, jumping over a shark, Evel Knievel style. If this doesn't seem ridiculous enough, he does it while wearing his trademark leather jacket and a pair of swim trunks.

Thanks to that origin, jumping the shark has become the ultimate pop culture burn, widely used to identify when something good turns bad. It's now applied to washed-up TV shows, movie franchises, actors, and even athletes, politicians, and social media influencers.

In hindsight, we can see the moment when somebody should have quit. When your favorite quarterback hangs on a few years too long, it's easy to spot the exact point when they started the decline from their peak. It's easy to look back at a relationship and realize when things began to go irreparably downhill. It's easy to look back and see the moment when it was clear that Blockbuster was going to lose to Netflix.

We have an expectation that people ought to have seen in foresight what we can so easily see in hindsight. And when they don't, we can't believe how obtuse they are. That's the point of jumping the shark. It's mocking someone who doesn't quit on time, no matter that it's much harder to see the shark in foresight, to pull a Stewart Butterfield and see it in advance.

But the sad thing is that as much as we make fun of people who quit too late, when someone does manage to quit on time, we mock them for quitting too early.

That's the quitting bind.

The Quitting Bind

In the 1990s, Dave Chappelle became a popular stand-up comedian and actor. On the strength of his growing following and a successful HBO special, Comedy Central debuted *Chappelle's Show* in 2003. It became an instant hit, called "a singular juggernaut in the annals of American television comedy." After the first season, Comedy Central's new parent, Viacom, gave him a $55-million deal for two more seasons. The deal also gave him the freedom to do outside projects and a share of DVD sales, which reached record levels.

His passion was performing stand-up for a live audience, so he continued touring. It became clear that he was unhappy with how stardom and celebrity interfered with his passion. At a sold-out show in Sacramento in June 2004, he walked offstage after audience members continually shouted the catchphrase from his most popular sketch. When he returned to the stage, he lectured the audience and admitted, "The show is ruining my life."

In May 2005, Chappelle left production of season 3 of *Chappelle's Show*. He walked away from his huge contract (and negotiations for an even greater fortune). The entertainment world threw a collective fit at Chappelle's decision, because people couldn't understand why somebody who was at the top of their game, whose show was a juggernaut and who was being offered such a lucrative deal, would leave.

Quitting in that situation seemed so confounding that a narrative caught on that squared this widespread bafflement: Something must be wrong with Chappelle. The show was falling apart. He disappeared. He had a drug problem. He checked himself into a mental health facility.

None of this was true.

Dave Chappelle quit because he was able to travel to the future where he could see two things. First, he was unhappy in that future. Chappelle knew that continuing with the show would affect the quality of his life in an increasingly negative way.

Second, he could see the shark. He sensed that he was close to crossing the line between his audience laughing *with* him and laughing *at* him. The show was going to go downhill, and his growing unhappiness would contribute to that.

As Chappelle put it in an interview two weeks later, "I want to make sure I'm dancing and not shuffling." Near the end of the ninety-minute interview, he asked, "Is that enough to prove I'm not smoking crack or hanging out in a mental institution?"

This same kind of disappointment bubbled up when Phoebe Waller-Bridge announced in 2019 that she was ending *Fleabag*. In its two seasons (six episodes in 2016 and six in 2019), the show earned massive worldwide acclaim. After the second season, the show won six Emmy Awards, including Outstanding Comedy Series, Outstanding Lead Actress in a Comedy Series, Outstanding Directing for a Comedy Series, and Outstanding Writing for a Comedy Series. Despite Waller-Bridge's explanation that ending the series was consistent with the arc of the title character, fans, feeling abandoned, have been begging incessantly for a season 3.

Over the history of TV, a handful of other shows have quit on top, including *I Love Lucy* and *Seinfeld*. Typically, the public sentiment was that those shows should have kept going. Generally, whether it's

Lucille Ball and Desi Arnaz, Jerry Seinfeld, Phoebe Waller-Bridge, or Dave Chappelle, people feel the creators are quitting too soon if they *haven't* yet jumped the shark.

Dave Chappelle relocated with his family to the small Ohio town where he grew up. He returned to performing, slowly and occasionally, but on his own terms. In 2013, he began touring again. In 2016, he agreed to a deal with Netflix, paying him $20 million per stand-up special. He hosted *Saturday Night Live* the week after the 2016 presidential election, for which he won an Emmy in 2017. He was awarded the Mark Twain Prize for American Humor in 2019.

You can see many similarities between Dave Chappelle and Stewart Butterfield. Both quit at times when their endeavors were going well, because they both had the foresight to see that the future didn't look good no matter how good the present looked to an untrained eye.

Quitting freed Chappelle, as it did Butterfield, to explore other opportunities that would bring him greater happiness and creative satisfaction.

There were even common elements in how their quitting would be perceived (or how they thought it would be perceived). Chappelle, of course, had to deal with the whole world thinking that he must be on drugs or having a mental breakdown. Butterfield didn't experience anything like that, but he was concerned that people would perceive the decision as capricious, preemptively letting his investors know, "Just make sure this part is clear: I'm not doing this because I'm restless or bored."

This behavior, expertly exercising the option to quit, baffles us. In trying to make sense of the world, we will impute all sorts of things. The quitters are cowards, or crazy, or flighty. This is the human tendency when we don't understand things. We try to make sense of them.

Often, our sense-making is unkind to the quitter.

Chapter 2 Summary

- Quitting on time usually feels like quitting too early.
- The hardest time to make a quitting decision is when you're in it.
- Our intuition is that quitting will slow down our progress. The reverse is actually true. If you walk away from something that is no longer worthwhile, that frees you up to switch to something that is more likely to help you achieve your goals—and you'll get there faster.
- When the time is objectively right to quit, nothing particularly dire will be happening right at that moment. Getting the timing right means looking into the future and seeing that the chances things will go your way are too slim.
- Thinking in expected value helps you figure out if the path you are on is worth sticking to. EV is not just about money. It can be measured in health, well-being, happiness, time, self-fulfillment, satisfaction in relationships, or anything else that affects you.
- If you feel like the choice between persevering and walking away is a close call, it's likely that quitting is the better choice.
- In hindsight, we can see when someone has waited too long to quit, and we tend to be harsh in our judgment of those people. But when someone quits before it seems obvious to others, we mock them for quitting too early. That's the quitting bind.

CHAPTER 3

Should I Stay, or Should I Go?

I N THE CENTURY OR SO BETWEEN HENRY FORD'S DEVELOP-
ment of mass production for automobiles and the development of
ridesharing apps, taxicab drivers were the forebears of "the gig
economy." The majority of cab drivers have always been independent
contractors. They don't make an hourly wage. Unless they own their
own medallion, they are renting the cab, paying a fixed fee per twelve
hours.

Because they are not employees, they don't have to drive the entire
twelve hours and, indeed, they frequently don't. They get to choose—
and have to choose—during that twelve-hour shift when they're
driving and when they are not.

That makes the behavior of cab drivers a nice place to study quitting behavior.

When a cab driver sets out on their workday, there is a lot of uncertainty about all the things that can favorably or unfavorably affect
their earning conditions. There are some patterns to how many fares
there are, but as they drive around, they will learn more information

about those conditions. They should always be looking at the prospective earning conditions and deciding, based on what they see, "Should I stay, or should I go?"

Old-school economists, under the rational actor theory, would predict that drivers will maximize the number of hours they're driving when there are lots of fares and they're earning the most money. Likewise, they will minimize the number of hours that they're driving when there's no one to pick up.

This is similar to the goal of top poker players in terms of when they keep playing in a game and when they quit. They want to maximize the number of hours that they're playing well and earning the most money, and minimize the number of hours that they're playing poorly or the game conditions aren't good.

As we've found with so many things that old-school economists predicted about what rational actors would do, things don't work out as predicted when you look at the actual behavior of human beings. The field of behavioral economics is predicated on the idea that there are circumstances in which we are systematically irrational. The behavior of cab drivers (and most poker players) definitely fits in that category.

Behavioral scientist Colin Camerer, a professor at Caltech and a pioneer in neuroeconomics, studied cab driver behavior with a stellar group of collaborators, including George Loewenstein, Linda Babcock, and Richard Thaler. They collected trip sheets of nearly two thousand New York City cab drivers.

They found that cab drivers don't make particularly good decisions about when to keep driving. And the mistakes the drivers made were two-sided, both in quitting too soon in good market conditions and persisting too long in bad ones.

Instead of maximizing their driving time when fares were plentiful and minimizing their unproductive time, they were likely to quit early when there was a lot of demand for their services. When there were few fares, they'd work the full twelve hours, wearing themselves out driving around for little benefit.

Camerer and his colleagues queried drivers (as well as fleet managers) to understand the heuristic they used to decide when to keep driving and when to quit. They discovered that the drivers set a daily goal for how much they wanted to earn and used that to determine when to stop working, ignoring the more useful information about earning conditions they discovered during their daily shift.

Drivers would quit early when they could easily pick up more rides, not because they thought the next hour on the road wouldn't earn them much but simply because they had reached their income goal for the day. For the same reason, they would work long into unproductive shifts because they didn't want to leave the road before they had hit their target.

It seems very clear that the cab drivers were not thinking in expected value.

If they hit their daily goal early, it meant, by definition, that driving conditions were very good. That means the heuristic they were using was causing them to quit at a time when the amount they expected to earn in the next hour was at the top of the spectrum. Likewise, when they had worked many hours and were still far from their goal, they would keep driving when, by definition, the amount they expected to earn was low.

How much did this inverted quitting behavior cost the drivers? It turns out a lot.

Camerer calculated that the drivers would make 15% more income if they worked the exact same number of hours but allocated those hours based on demand. In fact, if drivers just chose a heuristic that was random, like working the same number of hours each day regardless of conditions, they would make 8% more than they were with the strategy they were using.

If the drivers were better at figuring out when to quit and when to stick, they would get to where they want to go—making the most money out of their cab—faster, 8% to 15% faster. Clearly, there is a huge cost to bad calibration between sticking and quitting. The cab drivers made decisions that hurt them in both directions, quitting too soon *and* sticking too long.

Up to this point, we have been focused on how quitting on time usually feels like quitting too early. That's what Steven Levitt's work tells us. But the cab drivers show us that there are specific circumstances under which we do actually quit too early, when we aren't gritty enough. That is, after all, why there is a wildly popular book called *Grit* that grew out of Angela Duckworth's influential and substantial work on the topic.

That we make both types of errors, sometimes sticking too long and sometimes giving up too early, shouldn't be that surprising because whether to stick or quit aren't separate decisions. They are one and the same. Whenever you choose to stick, you are, by definition, not quitting. The reverse is true when you choose to quit.

It stands to reason that if we are bad at one side of the equation, we will also be bad at the other.

The cab drivers quit too early when the going was good and kept driving too long when the going was bad. If we can understand the circumstances under which we commit these errors, it will help us get to the bottom of why we are so bad at quitting and how we might get better at it.

Paper Gains and Paper Losses

The behavior of 1990s New York cab drivers is consistent with a classic study, published in 1979, by Daniel Kahneman and Amos Tversky, which found a related miscalibration between sticking and quitting.

Kahneman and Tversky, starting in the 1970s, identified behavioral factors explaining when and why we frequently depart from perfectly rational decisions. Their 1979 paper described what has become a cornerstone of behavioral economics, prospect theory.

Prospect theory is a model of how people make decisions, accounting for systematic preferences and biases involving risk, uncertainty, gains, and losses. One of the key findings of prospect theory is *loss aversion*, recognizing that the emotional impact of a loss is greater than the corresponding impact of an equivalent gain. In fact, losing feels about two times as bad to us as winning feels good to us.

When we're choosing among new options, loss aversion causes us to favor the ones that have the lowest absolute loss associated with them, even if those options come at a lower expected value. In other words, our aversion to taking a loss causes us to make decisions a rational actor would not.

Imagine being given the following two propositions that offer you the choice between a sure thing and a gamble. In each case, which option would you choose?

A. I owe you $100. I offer you the choice of taking the $100 or flipping a coin. If it lands heads, I'll give you $200. If it lands tails, I'll give you zero. Do you take the flip?
B. You owe me $100. I offer you the choice of paying me the $100 or flipping a coin. If it lands heads, you'll wipe the loss off the books. If it lands tails, you'll owe me $200. Do you take the flip?

If you're like most people, and like Kahneman and Tversky's participants (and the participants in all the studies replicating this aspect of prospect theory), you'll choose to quit when you're ahead, taking the sure $100 gain in the first scenario. That probably makes sense to you. After all, why would you want to risk giving up the $100 you already have in your pocket on the flip of a coin?

But when you're behind, like in the second scenario, you'll choose to take the gamble and flip the coin. That probably also makes sense to you. If you are already down $100, why not jump at the chance to get that $100 back?

Of course, for both propositions, you are breaking even in the long run no matter which option you choose. If you are up $100 when offered the coin flip, you can walk away with a sure win of $100 if you turn the coin flip down or you can gamble. If you take the flip, half the time you'll walk away with $200 and half the time you'll end up with nothing, for an identical win of $100 in the long run.

If you are down $100, the two options again offer identical long-run results. You can either take the sure loss of $100 if you don't flip the coin or you can take the gamble. If you flip the coin, you will erase the $100 loss half of the time and lose $200 the other half of the time, for an expected loss of $100 in the long run.

What the gamble *does* offer you, if not a difference in how much you might expect to win or lose in the long run, is the chance to change the outcome. The gamble offers the chooser the opportunity to inject luck into the equation, turning a sure thing into a more uncertain short-run outcome.

That difference exposes an asymmetry in when we want to walk away and when we want to gamble. When we are *in the gains*, we don't want to recruit luck into the equation, luck that might wipe out what we have already won. We want to quit while we're ahead.

But when we are *in the losses*, we'll take the gamble, recruiting luck into the equation in the hopes that we can wipe out what we have already lost. All of a sudden, uncertainty doesn't bother us. When we're losing, we *want* luck to be involved.

When we are coming to a decision fresh, having not yet incurred any losses or gains, loss aversion creates a preference for options associated with a lower chance of incurring a loss. It makes us risk averse and stops us from getting started, from choosing options where we might lose.

But when we have already accrued losses on paper, we become risk seekers. Daniel Kahneman subsequently characterized this as *sure-loss aversion*.

Sure-loss aversion makes us not want to stop something we have already started. That is because the only way to make sure we turn those paper losses into realized losses is to quit and refuse the gamble. Taking the option to flip the coin opens up the possibility of avoiding having to do that.

When we have a gain on paper, we are averse to taking on any risk that might cause us to lose that which we have already won. Now we want to ensure that we can turn that paper gain into a realized gain so we refuse the gamble.

Kahneman and Tversky wanted to find out if these tendencies were strong enough that people would be willing to pay for the opportunity to lock up a sure gain, as well as to pay for the opportunity to avoid a sure loss.

Imagine we changed our two propositions as follows:

A. I owe you $100. I offer you the choice of taking the $100 or flipping a coin. If it lands heads, I'll give you $220. If it lands tails, I'll give you zero.
B. You owe me $100. I offer you the choice of paying me the $100 or flipping a coin. If it lands heads, you'll wipe the loss off the books. If it lands tails, you'll owe me $220.

Notice that now neither of these is a break-even proposition.

When you are up $100, flipping the coin gets you $220 half the time and gets you $0 the other half. That means that risking the $100 you have already won by flipping the coin will net you $110 in the long run. So this new proposition is now a choice between that $110 long-run profit if you gamble and taking the sure win of $100 if you quit and walk away. If you refuse the coin flip now, you are also refusing that $10 in extra profit.

Kahneman and Tversky found that, indeed, people are willing to give up this extra profit to lock in the sure win. They will *pay* to avoid their win evaporating with the flip of a coin, and the regret that comes along with it.

In our example, they would be passing up a return on investment of 10%, ten times better than any savings account you could park that money in. Yet most people quit rather than take advantage.

On the other hand, when you have that $100 loss on paper and you are offered a proposition where half the time you're going to wipe that loss off the books but half the time you are going to have to pay $220, that now carries a *negative* expected value of $10. It is now a choice between taking a sure loss of $100 or taking the gamble that will lose you $110 in the long run. That means that if you choose to flip the coin, you are losing $10 more than you would if you just quit and took the sure loss.

Kahneman and Tversky found that people will, indeed, pay for the chance to recruit luck into the equation, which is the only way that they can turn the sure loss around.

A rational actor would take the coin flip in the first case and refuse it in the second. But as with so much else, people do not behave rationally when it comes to sure losses and sure gains. The choice about when to stay and when to go gets inverted.

Given these findings, let's amend our quitting aphorism to say: Quitting on time usually feels like quitting too early, and the *usually* part is *specifically when you're in the losses.*

Quit While You're Ahead?

It's not surprising, given that quitting has such a terrible reputation, that there is no shortage of well-known advice discouraging people from quitting.

But there is one aphorism that actually encourages people to quit:

Quit while you're ahead. Just as so many of those inspirational quotes lauding unlimited persistence are bad advice, this single piece of pro-quitting wisdom, despite surviving for more than four hundred years, is no better.

Quit while you're ahead amplifies the exact irrationality that Kahneman and Tversky found.

Occasionally, quitting while you're ahead is, of course, reasonable advice, specifically when you have managed to win at something that is a losing long-run proposition. Like baccarat or craps. Imagine that you were playing baccarat and you were up a few hundred bucks. That would be lucky because for every dollar you bet in the game, you are losing 2.5 cents. Over the long run, if you keep playing, your gains will evaporate because, as they say, the house always wins.

That's a good time to quit while you're ahead. When the next hand you play will be a losing proposition.

But when people quit while they're ahead it's generally not because they've come to their senses that they have gotten lucky, having overcome losing odds. They quit when they're ahead simply because of the fact that they are ahead, no matter whether the situation they are in is one that is favorable or unfavorable in the long run. If they happen to quit a losing proposition it is probably accidental. They just don't want to risk losing what they have already accrued, even if they have to pay a cost to quit.

That is, after all, the point of what Kahneman and Tversky found.

The real advice we should give people is more complicated than you can fit in a four-word slogan: Quit while you're ahead . . . when the game you are playing or the path you are on is a losing proposition. If you are in a situation that carries with it a negative expected value, by all means quit. But keep going when you have a positive expected value.

But that makes for an unwieldy aphorism. Try fitting that on a coffee cup.

Take the Money and Run

Retail traders—nonprofessionals who are actively trading online— also show the same tendency to quit when they're ahead and stick when they're behind. Alex Imas, now a professor at the University of Chicago's Booth School of Business, along with several colleagues in 2020, replicated this well-known finding of Kahneman and Tversky in a non-laboratory setting.

Traders on the platform, at the time they opened a position, set orders to close out the position when it reached a certain price above or below the contract price. These are known as take-profit (or take-gain) orders and stop-loss orders. (While poker players don't gener-ally establish take-gains, they do often set stop-losses, quitting games after they've lost a certain amount of money.)

Notice that adhering to a stop-loss order forces the traders to turn a loss on paper into a realized loss, while a take-gain order does the opposite, causing the trader to keep gains on paper at risk if the trade goes against them. This is like committing in advance to refuse the coin flip when you are down $100 and taking the coin flip when you are up $100.

The researchers wanted to find out if the traders stuck to their take-gain and stop-loss orders or if they looked more like Kahneman and Tversky's participants, preferring to keep gambling when they were losing and quit when they were winning.

As Alex Imas explained to me, "Almost nobody hits their take-profit order. They exit manually before that." In other words, traders will quit earlier than the take-profit order would tell them to, in order to lock up a sure win, regardless of whether continuing to hold that position would be a winning decision. When they have a win on pa-per, they don't have any interest in recruiting luck into the equation any further, risking losing gains that they could put in their pocket.

(I hope it's becoming very clear how bad the advice "quit while you're ahead" really is, because it's encouraging our natural tendency to be irrational in these situations already.)

On the other hand, when traders are losing, they cancel their stop-loss orders, preferring to gamble that the position will recover and they won't have to turn their loss on paper into one that's realized, a decision that carries with it the risk of accumulating bigger and bigger negative returns.

Our goal, obviously, should be to persist when we have a positive expected value, regardless of whether we have already won or lost to a prior course of action. Because these decisions are made under uncertainty, we rarely know for sure whether sticking or quitting is the best choice. In the same way that it's easier for the cab drivers to see if they've met a daily goal, it's easier for any of us to see whether we're ahead or behind so we use that signal to determine whether or not to persevere.

The result is that we'll quit when we're ahead, even if we're giving up good opportunities to win more. If we're behind, we don't want to quit, even if persisting—to try to get to the other side of zero—is more likely to make things worse.

I saw this routinely in poker. When most players were offered the slightest pretense to quit a game when they were ahead, they couldn't get their chips off the table and over to the cashier fast enough. But it's also true that when they were in the losses, they were superglued to the seat. Many times, I saw otherwise skilled poker players lose money in a game and refuse to quit when they were drunk, tired, angry, or just not capable of playing well.

This quit-while-you're-ahead strategy costs poker players real money, causing them to minimize the hours when they're playing well, because that's correlated with winning, and maximize the hours they're playing poorly, because that's correlated with losing.

Make no mistake, this is costing you money too. Whether it's in the stock market or some other investment, this behavioral tendency is affecting your bottom line.

How Smart Is the Smart Money?

Obviously, the traders blowing through their stop-loss orders were not experts. But if they were, would that tendency evaporate? If you've got enough experience and expertise in something, do you become better at these quitting decisions?

That would be consistent with what happens in poker. Expert players make better decisions about when to fold a hand and when to walk away from a game. And it turns out that experience also helps cab drivers become better quitters.

In a 2015 paper, Henry Farber, an economist at Princeton, looked at data on cab driver behavior spanning 2009 to 2013. He found that veteran drivers, while not perfect, did make better decisions about when to keep driving and when to quit than newer drivers.

If experience makes poker players and cab drivers better calibrated, maybe expert investors are better at decisions about when and what to sell than retail investors.

Klakow Akepanidtaworn, along with a group of colleagues including Alex Imas, asked this exact question and the answer is . . . *sort of*.

The researchers' analysis did show that expert investors overcome the mistakes commonly made by retail traders. These portfolio managers did not follow the simple heuristic of quit while you're ahead and stick while you're behind. But the analysis also showed an asymmetry in the quality of their buying and selling decisions.

The researchers looked at data from sophisticated market participants, over seven hundred institutional portfolio managers, with average assets under management valued at nearly $600 million. Not surprisingly, they found that expert investors' decisions about what to buy performed much better than a benchmark that just indexed the market. The average stock purchased by these portfolio managers outperformed the benchmark by more than 120 basis points, annualized (or 1.2 percentage points).

These investors spend most of their time finding great strategies and theses to invest in, and they profit from their research and expertise. You can see just how much their decisions about when to enter into a position are outperforming the benchmark in the chart below that tracks their excess returns over time.

But what about their quitting decisions? How are their decisions about which stocks to sell performing?

To understand how good these expert investors were at sell-side choices, Akepanidtaworn, Imas, and their colleagues benchmarked the investors' actual selling decisions against a hypothetical strategy

Return Buy–Return Hold

Akepanidtaworn, Klakow, Rick Di Mascio, Alex Imas, and Lawrence Schmidt, "Selling Fast and Buying Slow: Heuristics and Trading Performance of Institutional Investors," *SSRN Electronic Journal* (2019), doi.org/10.2139/ssrn.3301277.

where they just randomly picked which stock to sell from among the holdings that they had in their portfolio at the time of the sale.

In other words, when they exited a position, how did their quitting decisions compare with just throwing darts at their portfolio and selling whatever equity the dart landed on?

Pretty poorly, it turns out.

The advantage these experts have in buying equities isn't mirrored when they sell them. While they're earning 120 basis points in excess returns on their buy-side decisions, they're *losing* 70 to 80 basis points, annualized, on their sell-side decisions. That means they would be better off if they just chose randomly from their portfolio to decide what to sell.

You can see this in the chart below, which shows how much they are losing over time, as compared to throwing darts.

Akepanidtaworn et al., "Selling Fast and Buying Slow."

For these expert investors, much of the significant excess returns that they generate by their decisions about what stocks to add to their portfolios is lost in their selling decisions due to opportunity cost. You can think of it this way: If they had picked what to sell randomly they would have had more money to invest in better opportunities.

Whether it's investors of any stripe, cab drivers, Kahneman and Tversky's participants, poker players, or people climbing Everest, we can see that this lack of skill in quitting comes at a great cost.

The authors dug into the data to try to understand what strategy these expert investors were using to decide what to sell. They found that when the investors sold, it was mostly to generate funds for their next positions. That dictated the timing. Then, as for which stock they sold to free up those funds, the researchers discovered that the investors were using a heuristic that had little to do with expected value. Rather, they tended to sell stocks only if they were either extreme winners or extreme losers in the portfolio.

In other words, when buying, these expert investors were trying to find positions that would be a good bet going forward. When selling, it appears that they were not doing as much, if any, of that work, either in the timing of taking off positions or the future prospects of those positions.

The best quitting strategy would be to examine all your holdings, not just the ones at the tails of your portfolio, and decide which were going to generate the least value going forward and sell those. That would maximize the value of the portfolio as a whole. This is, after all, their buying strategy, and they execute it with skill and success, by using amazing data-driven strategies to generate excess returns.

That raises the question of why, in such a data-rich environment, they aren't noticing the problem with their decisions about when to quit or using the data to model a solution to the issue.

Getting Feedback on the Things You Don't Do

When it comes to quitting, we have a feedback problem. When we're doing something, we are naturally tracking it. We know how it's turning out, because it's the path that we are on. If we're climbing Everest, or running a company, or in a relationship, or in a job, we're tracking those things because we're *in* them. That's the timeline we're on.

But when we exit those things, there is a twofold problem in getting feedback.

First, for most things we quit, there is no obvious data available for how it would have gone if we had stuck to it. It's merely a hypothetical or a counterfactual. What if I hadn't shut down that business? What if I had stayed at that job? What if I had changed majors or changed colleges?

Instead of data, all we have are those "What ifs?"

This makes it hard to compare whether the choice we made to quit was better than a choice to stay the course would have been. We don't have anything to directly compare it with, except as it might exist in our imagination.

Second, when we quit things, we usually follow the idiom *out of sight, out of mind*. We don't naturally track things that we're no longer in. This is likely what is causing the problem with the portfolio managers. When they enter into a position, they're tracking that every day, because it's part of the portfolio. But once they exit, they're not tracking it in the same way, because the position is now off their books. It's no longer part of their P&L statement, not as far as they can see in any obvious way.

The tragedy of all of this is that these investors are in the rare situation where the data actually exists to know the quality of their decisions. They can get answers to questions like: Did I sell at the right time? Did I sell too early? Did I sell too late? Should I have chosen something else out of my portfolio to sell that would have performed better against the benchmark?

When these researchers looked into this, they found the investors were continuing to lose to these quitting decisions simply because they weren't doing the analysis to find out.

Traders sometimes create shadow books of the things they were thinking about buying but didn't, to track how those decisions might have gone. A solution I've recommended to clients working in financial markets is to use the same strategy to solve the feedback problem on sell-side decisions. Create a book that tracks those sell-side decisions and see how they're doing compared to a benchmark of how they would have done if they randomly sold something different in the portfolio at the same time.

There are many situations where there is nothing to track that might tell us how things would have gone if we had just stayed the course. But the problem for the portfolio managers has an obvious solution. They need to track their selling decisions as rigorously as they're tracking their decisions to buy.

Chapter 3 Summary

- A key finding of prospect theory is *loss aversion*, the phenomenon whereby the emotional impact of a loss is greater than the corresponding impact of an equivalent gain.
- Loss aversion creates a preference for options associated with a lower chance of incurring a loss. It makes us risk averse.
- When we are in the gains, we have a tendency to quit too early in order to avoid the risk of giving those gains back. In other words, we like to quit while we're ahead.
- When we are in the losses, we become risk seekers. We want to keep going, hoping we can avoid ever having to realize the loss. Daniel Kahneman has characterized this as *sure-loss aversion*. In other words, we like to stick when we're behind.
- Quitting on time usually feels like quitting too early, and the *usually* part is *specifically when you're in the losses.*
- Retail investors show this pattern of quitting when they're ahead and sticking when they're behind.
- Even expert investors don't get their quitting decisions just right. They outperform on their buying decisions but underperform on their selling decisions.
- We naturally track and get feedback on the things we are doing. But once we quit something, we also quit keeping track of that course of action. This creates a problem with getting high-quality feedback, which in turn makes it hard to hone our quitting skills.

Quitting When the World Is Watching

El Capitan is the world's most famous—and most impressive—rock. Located within Yosemite National Park, "El Cap" is massively wide, with more than seventy recognized climbing routes. From the base to the summit, it's 3,000 vertical feet.

The first ascent, in 1958, involved a team that spent forty-six days over sixteen months drilling bolts into the granite, pulling themselves up on ropes.

Fifty-eight years later, in 2016, elite rock climber Alex Honnold decided to take climbing the rock formation to an insane, barely imaginable level. On an extremely difficult route called Freerider, he was going to climb "free solo." All by himself. All in one day. From base to summit without installing or even using bolts or footholds beyond what nature made available. And without using ropes to assist his climb or, more important, to stop or limit what could happen if he fell.

Honnold confided in a few folks—almost all elite climbers themselves—that he was considering free soloing via Freerider. He agreed to let his friend Jimmy Chin film his process for what Chin imagined would be an amazing documentary, not only because Honnold was one of the few climbers who would consider something so dangerous but because no one had ever tried a free solo ascent of El Capitan.

Nearly all climbers use ropes for safety when rock climbing. The human body can rarely survive a fall greater than eighty feet. For rock formations hundreds or even thousands of feet in vertical height, falling means dying.

Even the world's most skilled climbers (who consider themselves "free" climbers) acknowledge and accommodate the inevitability of gravity. Free climbers remain attached to ropes for safety but don't use those ropes to assist their climb, in the same way trapeze artists or wire walkers would use a net (or ropes) to catch them only if they fall. Free climbing is considered a test of climbing skill that has the benefit of forgiveness if you slip more than eighty feet above the ground.

Free solo climbing is the same test of skill, but you die the first time you make a mistake because there are no ropes to stop your fall from a fatal height. This is why there are so few free solo climbers, and most of the famous free solo climbers are no longer with us.

Such a feat is the ultimate pass-fail test. Tommy Caldwell, another elite, hard-core climber and friend who helped Honnold practice, said, "Imagine an Olympic gold-medal level athletic achievement, that if you don't get the gold medal, you're going to die. That's pretty much what free soloing El Cap is like. You have to do it perfectly."

Filming Honnold was also a difficult, expensive, and delicate process. Chin recruited a camera crew of experienced rock climbers. Like Chin and Caldwell, most of them were friends with Honnold. They had to figure out placing, setting up, and operating ten cameras at different spots on the route. They also had to do it invisibly, making sure to not interfere or assist with the climb.

Honnold spent several months in 2016 practicing—with ropes—the intricacies of all thirty sections (known as "pitches") of the Freerider route. His training on the route was frequently documented by the film crew, including the time he slipped while practicing on Pitch 6, Freeblast Slab (480 feet up). He was attached to a rope, so his fall was "just" thirty feet, still far enough that he sprained his ankle and tore a ligament.

Three weeks after his injury, only partially recovered, he resumed practice and soon decided to attempt his free solo climb, before the coming winter weather closed his window for 2016.

The documentary crew filmed it all.

On the morning of his attempt, he woke up at 3:30 and began climbing in the dark. The camera crew had to simultaneously stay out of sight and get to their positions. When he reached Pitch 6, a camera picked him up from a distance, with his headlamp as the only illumination.

Hanging off the mountain at Pitch 6, Honnold felt he couldn't trust his feet.

This was a perfect setup for making a bad decision about whether to continue the climb. He had invested months preparing. Money had been spent. Several other climbers had devoted time to helping him prepare, some hanging off the rock to film him. Many of them were his close friends, including Jimmy Chin, who was filming Honnold's attempt.

Chin had a bunch of footage, but putting that together into a documentary without a big summit attempt would be like trying to sell a *Rocky* movie that ends with the training montage. There was no documentary if all Honnold did was climb 480 feet to Pitch 6 and turn around.

Worse, this was the end of the season. "Wait until next year" could mean the same thing as "never" when you're depending on the behavior of a free solo rock climber still wanting to do this the following year—or even being alive to try.

Despite all the forces working against Honnold giving up at that moment, he purposely fouled his attempt by pulling on a nearby protection bolt. From a microphone placed in his chalk bag, he said, "This sucks. I don't want to be here. I'm over it."

He climbed down. The whole crew climbed down. The group dispersed and Honnold returned to his van (which was also where he had been living) and drove 350 miles home to Las Vegas.

Alex Honnold came back the next June, the crew reassembled, and he successfully summited, free solo. *The New York Times* called it "one of the great athletic feats of any kind, ever." Jimmy Chin and codirector Elizabeth Chai Vasarhelyi released the documentary, *Free Solo*, in 2018.

It won the Oscar for Best Documentary Feature.

Practically everyone who watches *Free Solo* is amazed by the difficulty of what Honnold was attempting, the danger, and the skill involved (not to mention the process of documenting it all). Obviously, as a physical feat, Alex Honnold's free solo ascent in June 2017 was, indeed, amazing, seemingly without equal.

But much less obvious was the *mental feat* of quitting and turning back on Pitch 6. Once he made the decision to go for it and start climbing that morning in 2016, every force—except, obviously, gravity—was pushing him to persist. He had invested months in training. His friends, in addition to investing their time and money in the effort, were literally risking their lives to film the attempt. An entire film project was at stake.

Understanding what made Honnold's decision-making so exceptional will help us gain insight into the forces that push all of us to persist too long, and the strategies that might help us become more Honnold-like in our decisions about when to stick and when to quit.

In the Losses

CHAPTER 4

Escalating Commitment

TOWARD THE END OF THE 1930s, HAROLD STAW'S PARENTS were among the millions of Americans who moved their families from the East Coast to Southern California, the latest frontier for chasing the American Dream. Shirley Posner's family had made a similar move to Los Angeles, where she met Harold. They fell in love, married in 1940, and had two kids of their own while Harold worked in a defense plant in Los Angeles during World War II.

After the war, Harold and Shirley settled in San Bernardino, along the eastern end of an area known as the Inland Empire, sixty miles from Los Angeles. The war years had been good for LA, a center for defense production. As that prosperity spread, much of the Inland Empire transitioned from farms and citrus groves to residential areas.

Harold's stepfather and mother operated a grocery store, and Harold and Shirley followed suit, purchasing a neighborhood store. They turned a small profit but after several years Harold could see the writing on the wall. Large supermarket chains were taking over and it would eventually be impossible for a mom-and-pop operation to compete.

Harold needed to find a more promising business.

By 1952, he noticed a unique opportunity in Fontana, ten miles to the west of San Bernardino, along the route of a new freeway that was supposed to one day reach all the way to Los Angeles. Fontana was a booming factory town. Kaiser Steel had opened a huge factory during World War II and it became even busier once the United States entered the Korean War.

Harold thought all those workers—mostly new arrivals to the area who were now earning a good wage—represented a market he could sell appliances to. Because the factory's workers all belonged to the steelworkers union, his store would sell exclusively to members of the union, like a PX on a military base.

At the start, he had little beyond his idea. With the small amount of money the Staws got from selling the grocery store, Harold could only afford to lease a tiny property that had previously housed chickens. But with the help of Shirley and their two young children, he enthusiastically swept the space clear of chicken feathers and opened the Union Store.

He didn't have money for much inventory—the entire operation was, literally, bare bones—but he used the limitations of the space and his budget to offer discounted prices. Customers could look at several floor models. If they saw a refrigerator or a stove they liked, he ordered it for them from the manufacturer.

Harold's idea turned out to be a visionary first step in building a successful retail chain. The converted chicken coop did so well that Harold expanded to a larger property in Upland, another twelve miles west on the freeway as construction continued. The Upland store had more space, more inventory, and now featured housewares in addition to appliances. Harold expanded his customer base by opening the store to members of other unions (and then dropped the membership requirement altogether).

The fifties were a period of unbridled growth for Harold Staw and, it seemed, everything around him. The population of the Inland Empire grew nearly 80% during the decade. The Greater Los Angeles area (a sprawl eventually covering 34,000 square miles), increasingly linked by the rapidly expanding California highway system, became one of the fastest-growing and largest metropolitan areas in the world. Seemingly endless waves of people flocked to the opportunities and lifestyle promised by Southern California. Those people found good jobs, earned growing incomes, started and built families, became homeowners, and eventually moved into bigger homes.

They needed appliances. They needed housewares. They needed a lot of consumer goods, and Harold Staw was just the man to sell to them.

Harold opened an even bigger store, now renamed ABC, in Montclair (just another three miles west on the freeway). He negotiated a fifty-year lease on the property. Its profitability far exceeded anything he could have imagined when he was in Fontana or could have achieved in Upland.

In quick succession, he began buying out competitors, expanding, and, in one case, merging with another owner of a pair of stores. The ABC Store in Covina—halfway to LA from San Bernardino on the still-expanding freeway—was cavernous, over 100,000 square feet. It was the largest retail outlet in California, if not in the entire country. Harold made these into true one-stop shopping centers. In addition to offering everything from clothing to housewares to large appliances, he leased space to specialty service providers like insurance agencies and optometrists.

By the beginning of the sixties, ABC Stores was a major retail chain in Southern California. In 1961, Harold Staw expanded with his biggest deal yet, a merger with Texas-based discount retailer Sage Stores. Sage came from roots familiar to Harold. Whereas he started by specializing in selling to union members, Sage began by selling to government workers. (Sage was an acronym for "state and government employees.")

Staw became the largest shareholder and CEO of the combined company, named Sage International. A public stock offering in 1962 initially valued the company at $10 million, with the Staw family owning more than 30%.

Harold Staw's rise, in common with most success stories, came from a combination of skill and luck. Remarkably, he bootstrapped himself from practically nothing to a position of significant wealth (and potentially even greater wealth to come). His main starting assets were brains, grit, and nerve, and he used them to capitalize on favorable developments that he foresaw but were themselves outside his control: the demographic shifts of the baby boom generation and the growth of consumer culture.

Those favorable trends continued in Southern California into the sixties (and beyond), but the opportunities for discount retailing became so lucrative that they eventually attracted competitors Harold Staw couldn't outfox, outfight, or buy out.

The year of the merger with Sage was also the year the first Kmart opened.

Kmart itself later got shoved out of the way by Walmart and Target (which both opened their first stores in Arkansas and Minnesota, respectively, in 1962 as well), but in the sixties, it was time for Kmart to do the shoving. This was especially true in California. S.S. Kresge, a national chain of already successful five-and-dimes, built its first Kmart north of Los Angeles in San Fernando in January 1962. By the end of the year, there were already eighteen Kmarts around the country.

Kmarts sprang up within a short distance of Harold's stores, sometimes right across the street or down the block. The chain had the muscle to undercut his prices. Because it used the same strategy of locating and operating its expanding empire at the expense of other local retailers, the independent discounters in California started falling by the wayside.

Toward the end of the sixties, ABC (still the name of the California locations) had ceased to be profitable.

In Texas, Sage remained successful, continued to open new stores, and thrived. Kmart had not yet expanded significantly into Texas. Even Walmart, founded in adjacent Arkansas, didn't come to Texas until 1975. This was good for the parent company because Sage's growth offset the increasing losses at ABC.

But it was problematic for Harold Staw. He was the CEO of Sage International and its largest shareholder, but the Texas store operators (who owned a significant block of shares through the merger) became increasingly upset that they were subsidizing Harold's losses in California. They wanted to get rid of the ABC stores; sell them off while they still had some value. That meant getting rid of the part of the company Harold had built.

The choice seemed clear enough.

Harold was running a company with good assets (in Texas retailing) and bad assets (in California retailing). He had no good answer to Kmart's competitive threat. In addition, his Texas shareholders were threatening to revolt, recognizing that Sage International (in which he was and would remain the largest shareholder) would be much more profitable without those California assets.

Yet, Harold wouldn't sell or close them. Those ABC locations were his babies. He created them. He nurtured and grew them. They were the embodiment of so much work and so many smart, well-timed decisions.

By the beginning of the seventies, the resentment of the Texas shareholders erupted into a proxy fight and an expensive, messy lawsuit.

The unkindest cut came when one of his closest friends, who was also his longtime lawyer, switched over to the Texas side, filing their lawsuit.

Even in the face of this turmoil at Sage International, he refused to part with ABC. Instead, he negotiated a settlement in which he gave up any interest in Sage International's profitable assets and became the sole owner of its unprofitable ones. The Texas shareholders took back their Sage stores, Harold's partners in the earlier merger took back their two California stores, and Harold was left with the rest of the California stores.

To keep competing with Kmart, Harold started taking the wealth he and Shirley had accumulated over two decades and invested it in a futile attempt to save his business.

Within a few years, a piece of good luck fell in his path, in the form of an offer by Fred Meyer Inc. to buy him out. Fred Meyer was a successful regional discounter founded in Oregon and looking for a foothold in California. At the time, it had over forty stores in four states and had been a public company since 1960.

He turned the offer down.

Harold Staw eventually lost all of his retail operations, along with all his family's accumulated wealth. The only thing that kept him and Shirley from becoming completely destitute was that fifty-year lease on the Montclair property. After ABC Stores was long gone, he was able to earn a bit of income by leasing it to other storefronts.

Ironically, many of those tenants succumbed to the same refusal to adapt to the changing business landscape that was Harold's undoing. CompUSA, for instance, made the list of 2002 Super Bowl advertisers that later went out of business as well as the list of Harold's tenants.

From the outside looking in at what happened to Harold Staw, it's easy to see that he was ignoring some pretty clear signals that he was now in a losing game: his inability to compete with Kmart, the flight of the other independents in the face of the new environment, the attitude of his former merger partners, his close friend and attorney taking sides against him.

If he didn't have an opportunity to jettison ABC and profit from a position in Sage, he certainly had the chance afterward to get out on the favorable terms offered by Fred Meyer. Yet he nevertheless *chose* to keep investing in the doomed effort, eventually pouring in almost everything he had accumulated.

The mystery of it all is *why*: What blinded such a nimble, flexible decision-maker to the clear signals right in front of him? How could some of the same behavior that helped him thrive (through grit, determination, and stick-to-itiveness) end up causing his failure (through inflexibility, intractability, and maybe even some hubris)?

It seems that if we can get to the bottom of this mystery for Harold Staw, then we can do it for a lot of other people, including ourselves.

Knee-Deep in the Big Muddy

The very first sentence of one of the earliest and most influential academic papers identifying our tendency to persist in losing endeavors, even in the face of strong signals that we ought to quit, states very simply why such behavior is so confounding:

"Intuitively, one would expect individuals to reverse decisions or to change behaviors which result in negative consequences."

The author of that seminal 1976 paper, "Knee-Deep in the Big Muddy: A Study of Escalating Commitment to a Chosen Course of Action," is Harold and Shirley's son, Barry Staw.

At the same time his father was stubbornly fighting his losing battle with Kmart and some of his own shareholders, Barry Staw was studying to become one of a generation of social scientists developing fresh approaches to figuring out why we get stuck in losing endeavors, persisting too long in the face of bad news, and the strategies that work best for getting better at walking away.

Staw came of age during the Vietnam War and viewed the U.S. involvement in that conflict as a paradigmatic example of how easy it is to get stuck in things once we've started them. He saw the U.S. involvement in the Vietnam War as a living, breathing, high-stakes, slow-motion train wreck of an example of our inability to quit.

The desire to unlock the mystery of why became the driving force behind his work. The title of his landmark 1976 paper, "Knee-Deep in the Big Muddy," was even a reference to Pete Seeger's 1967 anti-war song, "Waist Deep in the Big Muddy."

By the end of the war, it was widely believed that the war was unwinnable, yet even decision-makers aware of this could not extricate the United States, instead responding with what Staw later called an *escalation of commitment* to the losing course of action, responding to the growing awareness that there was no real path to victory for the United States by *increasing* the nation's commitment to the war.

Staw pointed to the revelation from the Pentagon Papers, a secret Department of Defense history of that war published over government objection by *The New York Times* and *The Washington Post*, that Undersecretary of State George Ball warned LBJ in 1965 of the inevitable entrapment in the conflict, "Once we suffer large casualties, we will have started a well-nigh irreversible process. Our involvement will be so great that we cannot—without national humiliation—stop short of achieving our complete objectives. Of the two possibilities I think humiliation would be more likely than the achievement of our objectives—even after we have paid terrible costs."

Johnson, of course, did not follow the warning, and that's exactly what happened. The Vietnam War cost the United States nearly $200 billion (which, adjusted for inflation, is about $1 trillion). It killed 58,000 American soldiers and injured another 300,000. It ended

Lyndon Johnson's political career, costing him a chance at a second term. The war created a generational distrust in government and authority in general.

This problem with escalation of commitment to unwinnable wars is a familiar refrain. Once the United States got into Afghanistan, it took twenty years to get out, despite three different presidents promising to do so. After two decades of involvement and a cost of $2 trillion, the Taliban regained control only days from the time American troops withdrew, revealing the fact that this was a war the United States was never really winning.

Staw's central insight about escalation of commitment is that the phenomenon is not confined to matters like the Vietnam War, a complex geopolitical conflict with national pride wrapped up in it. His laboratory and field experiments show that whether it is on the level of an individual, an organization, or a governmental entity, when we're getting bad news, when we are getting strong signals that we're losing—signals that others plainly see—we don't merely refuse to quit. We will double and triple down, making additional decisions to commit more time and money (and other resources) toward the losing cause, and we will *strengthen* our belief that we are on the right path.

Barry Staw might have only realized it later, but his body of work on escalation of commitment helps us understand how the grit that helped Harold Staw build a business empire could be his undoing, how his father could ignore such clear signals that he should get out of the California business until he was eventually left with nothing but a lease on the Montclair property.

Waiting until It Hurts

We know that when the stakes are high, it can be hard to walk away. But some of the more fascinating discoveries in the field are about just how *low* the stakes can be when we escalate our commitment. One study, published a year before "Big Muddy," was about the simple act of waiting.

Psychologists Jeffrey Rubin and Joel Brockner conducted an amusing experiment to answer two questions: How long will people wait for something that never arrives, and what price will they pay to continue waiting? It turns out people will wait a surprisingly long amount of time, and they will pay an amount that clearly exceeds the value of what they were waiting for.

The researchers offered students a payment of up to $8 ($45 in today's dollars) for successfully completing a crossword puzzle in a speed test. To get the full amount, they had to complete the puzzle in less than three minutes, with the amount they would earn declining for each additional minute beyond those three minutes, eventually all the way to $0. They could quit at any time, even if they didn't solve any of the clues in the puzzle, and earn $2.40 for participating, but only if they quit before the elapsing time started eating into that payment.

Because several of the words were very difficult, they could request a crossword puzzle dictionary (this being in the days before everyone had internet access), but there was only one available and they were told that several other participants were also working on the puzzle in other rooms. That meant they would have to stop working while they waited for the dictionary to become available, but the clock would continue to run.

Unbeknownst to the participants in the study, there was no dictionary so the wait would be indefinite.

Just over half the participants waited for the nonexistent dictionary *beyond* the time when the prize for completing the puzzle declined to less than $2.40. In the words of the authors, they waited "beyond this 'point of no return,' having been entrapped in a conflict from which there was no longer a satisfactory escape."

Escalation of commitment is costly. If the participants had walked away sooner, they would have made more. It may feel like quitting slows us down, but Rubin and Brockner show that it is persistence that is often the culprit.

The work on escalation of commitment over the last forty-five years—in different laboratory experiments, field experiments, and explanations of commonly observed behavior—has shown that this type of entrapment in losing causes occurs across a variety of settings and circumstances.

There are all sorts of ways we get stuck in our decisions. Presented with the opportunity and the relevant information, we will over-persist, rejecting the chance to quit and backing up our original decision by spending even more resources to try to save the endeavor.

This is true whether it involves spending more time waiting in line or waging an unwinnable war, or staying in bad relationships and bad jobs too long, or pouring money into a car that's worth less than the repairs are costing us. It's why a house can become a money pit. It's why we won't leave a terrible movie because we have already started watching it. It's why businesses continue to develop and support products that are clearly failing, or pursue strategies long after conditions have changed.

George Ball was right. That kind of behavior is the rule.

Persevering in the face of tall odds, as Ali or Rob Hall did, is not exceptional. Quitting a losing course of action before certain failure is. People like Stuart Hutchison, Stewart Butterfield, and Alex Honnold are the exceptions.

Chapter 4 Summary

- When we are in the losses, we are not only more likely to stick to a losing course of action, but also to double down. This tendency is called *escalation of commitment*.

- Escalation of commitment is robust and universal, occurring in individuals, organizations, and governmental entities. All of us tend to get stuck in courses of action once started, especially in the face of bad news.

- Escalation of commitment doesn't just occur in high-stakes situations. It also happens when the stakes are low, demonstrating the pervasiveness of the error.

CHAPTER 5

Sunk Cost and the Fear of Waste

I N 2008, CALIFORNIA VOTERS APPROVED THE ISSUANCE OF $9 billion in bonds for building a high-speed rail system connecting Los Angeles and San Francisco. The system, capable of traveling up to 220 miles per hour, would also connect Californians all along the route in potentially transformative ways.

The economic engines of the state are the coastal centers in the north (the Bay Area and Silicon Valley) and the south (Los Angeles and San Diego). The greater speed and mobility would allow the rest of the state in between to participate in the prosperity concentrated at the north and south coasts. It would also relieve the overdeveloped real estate markets in those northern and southern metropolitan areas by allowing people a reasonable commute from greater distances.

When the bond issue passed, it was estimated that the route would be completed in 2020, at a cost of $33 billion, and that the rail system would be generating yearly operating revenue of $1.3 billion by 2020, with an operating surplus of $370 million, making the system self-supporting and increasingly profitable thereafter. The bonds that were issued covered only about a quarter of the expected cost to complete the project, but the rest would be made up in federal funds, additional state funds, and public-private partnerships.

These projections and plans all came from the California High-Speed Rail Authority (or, as it refers to itself, "the Authority"). The Authority has been responsible from the beginning for planning, designing, building, and operating the system. They are the decision-maker, along with oversight from the governor and the state legislature.

The Authority creates a new business plan and updates projections every two years. As the costs and completion dates have continued to climb in these updates, it has also become increasingly clear that the plans and projections—neither the original ones nor the later revisions—have not had any connection with reality.

In a stunning example of how far off the mark the Authority's forecasts have been, remember that estimate of $1.3 billion in operating revenue for 2020? The Authority fell short of that number.

How far short? $1.3 billion short. No part of the line is operational.

Given the accuracy of the Authority's past projections, there is no basis for believing that the revised estimates of 2029 (for initial service) or 2033 (for completion) are reasonably achievable. This shouldn't be too surprising since they approved building the first segment in 2010 (twenty-five miles between Madera and Fresno), but they didn't break ground *for another five years*.

A good signal that the end of construction will be late: when the *beginning* of construction is delayed by half a decade.

Why is this all taking so long? It turns out there are two titanic engineering obstacles to connecting the central, interior part of the planned route with the key metropolitan areas at either end of the state. First, they have to figure out a way to build track over or blast through the Tehachapi Mountains, which is necessary to connect Bakersfield with Los Angeles to its south. That issue pales in comparison to a second bottleneck, a portion of the Diablo Range known as the Pacheco Pass that stands between the Central Valley and the Bay Area to its north.

It's not as if the Authority had no way to know about the existence of these barriers in 2010. The Tehachapi Mountains and the Pacheco Pass have been around for at least five million years, certainly at the time the Authority put together the route, along with the plan to blast through the mountains and build long tunnels underneath.

In 2018, the Authority admitted the tunnels under the Pacheco Pass present "the highest uncertainty in terms of cost and schedule." They know there will be enormous expenses and difficulties blasting through mountains, contending with technical geological obstacles, and crossing an active seismic fault. But what they don't know is whether, how, when, or at what cost they can do this.

In 2020, the Authority admitted the enormity of the engineering challenge. The project's tunneling corridors (including the Pacheco Pass and the Tehachapi Mountains) "make up nearly 80 percent of the total estimated cost" of completion.

You might assume that, after finally recognizing that addressing the two bottlenecks will be uncertain and, possibly, both intractable and prohibitively expensive, the Authority would figure out the details of solving those challenges before doing any additional building. After all, if you can't figure out how to connect LA to San Francisco at a cost in the realm of what taxpayers are willing to bear, what's the point of building any other track?

Yet, in 2019, instead of seizing what seemed like, from the perspective of an outsider looking in, the perfect moment to shut the whole thing down, Governor Gavin Newsom approved a plan to complete a section of track connecting Bakersfield to Merced in the north, completely unconnected with the two engineering bottlenecks. Merced is 110 miles from San Francisco, on the wrong side of the Pacheco Pass.

And Bakersfield is 100 miles from LA, on the wrong side of the Te-hachapi Mountains.

Once they complete that track, the plan is to turn their attention to construction connecting San Francisco and Silicon Valley, two areas already pretty well connected by roadways. Even worse than the redundancy of building that section of the route, both areas sit to the north of the Pacheco Pass.

So, in a move that defies common sense, the plan is to keep building without addressing the issues that will eventually be responsible for at least 80% of the cost of the bullet train. Because it is cheaper and easier, they are going to build a very fast train that won't actually go *from* anywhere or *to* anywhere, at least not anywhere people reasonably expected from the promise at the outset of the project in 2008.

This approach makes about the same amount of sense as executing a plan to put condos on the moon by building the condos on Earth first and waiting until they are built to figure out the whole "How do we get them on the moon?" part.

Consequently, the current projections of initiating service in 2029 or completing the line in 2033 seem wildly optimistic and, essentially, meaningless. That also applies to any value placed on the projections of the cost of the bullet train itself. As of June 2021, the Authority had spent more than $8.5 billion in planning and building high-speed rail infrastructure. And the estimated cost to complete the system has already exploded from $33 billion to as much as $105 billion.

Those estimates don't even fully include blasting through mountains and building tunnels in the north and the south, because the Authority has only in the last few years identified the enormity of this problem but not figured out the details, specifically the detail of what such a massive undertaking will cost.

Given where the project stands now, it's a good bet that if the decision-makers had known then what they know now about how much the bullet train would cost and how long it would take, it wouldn't have been approved in the first place.

But having started the project, the Authority seems unwilling to quit and cut their losses.

The Sunk Cost Effect

When it comes to out-of-control public works projects like the bullet train, if you are at all familiar with the behavioral economics space, the first thing that probably comes to your mind is "That sounds like a sunk cost problem."

Richard Thaler, in 1980, was the first to point to the sunk cost effect as a general phenomenon, describing it as a systematic cognitive error in which people take into account money, time, effort, or any other resources they have previously sunk into an endeavor when making decisions about whether to continue and spend more.

A perfectly rational decision-maker would consider only the future costs and benefits in deciding whether to continue with a course of action. In other words, if continuing on has a positive expected value, a rational actor would persevere. If it has a negative expected value, they would quit.

Forty years of experiments and fieldwork across a variety of domains show that people behave as Thaler hypothesized regarding sunk costs. In decisions about whether to move forward, they *do* take into account what they've already spent. They do this because they irrationally think that the only way to recover or justify the costs is if they continue on.

Put simply, the sunk cost effect causes people to stick in situations that they ought to be quitting.

To illustrate, imagine this simple thought experiment: A band you love is coming to town for an outdoor concert. On the day of the show, it is freezing cold, rain is pouring down, and that is expected to continue all night. A friend tells you they have an extra ticket and they are happy to treat you to the concert. You thank them but decline, because, as much as you love the band, you have no interest in standing in the crowd, soaking wet for hours, risking hypothermia.

Now imagine that you had bought a ticket when they originally went on sale for $95. It's the day of the show and it is freezing cold, rain is pouring down, and that is expected to continue all night. Do you go to the concert?

If you're like most people, your gut tells you there is a difference between these two scenarios. In the second case, people are much more likely to choose to go, because they don't want to waste the ticket that they have already bought.

This exposes the sunk cost error. In the first case, you are coming to the decision of whether to go to the concert fresh. You haven't already purchased the ticket or had any plans to go. You are weighing the future costs and benefits only, the discomfort of being outdoors for hours in unpleasant weather conditions against the pleasure of seeing the band you love perform live.

If you decided that the costs of going outweigh the benefits when offered a free ticket, then that means the costs of going also outweigh the benefits when you have already purchased a ticket.

The fact that you spent money on the ticket should matter very little, in fact not at all, because those costs are already sunk, the money is already spent. But so often we think, "If I don't go, I'll have wasted the money that I blew on the ticket."

And the effect is stronger the more the ticket costs. Imagine if, instead of $95, you had spent $150 or $250 or $500. As the price tag grows, so does the effect of sunk costs.

Another simple way to understand the sunk cost effect is to think about investing in the stock market. In deciding whether to purchase an individual stock, all that matters is whether it has positive expected value going forward. Do you believe you're going to make money on the purchase? That's how you do it when it's a fresh decision, but when you already own the stock and the price has declined since you bought it, you are more likely to hold on to it, trying to win back what you've already lost in the position.

That's why retail traders blow through their stop-losses.

But this is irrational. If you wouldn't buy a stock today, you ought not hold it today, because a decision to hold is the same as a decision to buy.

The sunk cost problem is echoed in Kahneman and Tversky's work exploring people's willingness to accept gambles depending on whether they are winning or losing going into the proposition being offered. That echo isn't surprising, because their 1979 work, which became part of the foundation of prospect theory, comprised one of the sets of results that Thaler was trying to make sense of in his 1980 paper.

As you'll recall, Kahneman and Tversky started participants off with a loss, and then they offered them the choice between walking away or paying for the opportunity to take a gamble that might erase the loss from their books.

Of course, we know people tend to prefer the second option, to take the gamble rather than cut their losses, because they're taking into account the money that they already owe. We know that because there's no doubt that if you offered someone (who has neither won nor lost any money yet) a 50-50 coin flip where they could win $100 or lose $120, no sane person would take that gamble. But that's just what the participants who had a loss on the books in Kahneman and Tversky's study were willing to do.

There's a simple elegance to Kahneman and Tversky's proposition. You can see the decision error, free of complicating factors like how the participants got into the losing position or whether they realized their expected value was negative. In these experiments and those that followed, the math is made clear and transparent to the participants.

This is not an error of calculation. This is an error of cognition.

In a simple hypothetical like the concert, you can also see the error pretty clearly. It likely makes sense that a choice of how much you want to see the band versus how much you don't want to spend hours in the cold and freezing rain shouldn't depend on whether or how much you paid for the ticket.

But this cognitive illusion is very strong. Just because you know it's an error in theory doesn't mean that you won't fall for it when you are facing down these kinds of decisions.

You can think about it like a visual illusion. You can look at an illusion where two squares are sitting on backgrounds of different colors, and one square looks brown and the other looks orange. But when you remove the backgrounds, you see the squares are, in reality, the exact same color. The effect of the contrast with the backgrounds causes you to see the squares as different hues.

But no matter how many times I show you that the squares are the same color or explain to you what's happening in your visual cortex to cause the illusion, when you look at them again with the backgrounds returned, you still see one square as brown and one as orange. You cannot unsee it.

It is similarly difficult to "unsee" sunk costs when making decisions about quitting.

When "Public Works" Is an Oxymoron

The sunk cost error's fingerprints are all over the California bullet train. If most anyone were asked to start the project today as a new endeavor—knowing about the exploding costs, currently as much as $105 billion but likely to increase significantly, and how hard it will be to blast through those two mountain ranges—it seems obvious that the answer would be a hard no.

In addition to the direct costs of the project, there is the issue of opportunity costs. Every dollar that California sinks into the project is a dollar that could otherwise be allocated to something that would create more value and a greater public good for the taxpayers whose money is funding the endeavor.

But imagine how gutsy a politician would have to be to abandon the project, knowing they're going to have to defend themselves against charges of having "wasted" more than $8 billion on a train that was never completed. The pressure to keep going to "recover" those costs is enormous.

When it comes to these types of public works projects, sunk cost is a familiar refrain.

Decades earlier, between the mid-1970s and 1984, the Tennessee-Tombigbee Waterway* lived out the same fate as the bullet train, becoming one of the most expensive public works projects ever undertaken by the federal government. Jimmy Carter tried unsuccessfully to shut it down as a waste of money. *The New York Times* noted that "congressmen from other regions called it a $2 billion boondoggle, the worst kind of pork barrel politics."

Ironically, bloated past costs became the justification for *not* abandoning the project.

The completion of the waterway hinged on a group of senators (from the states where the money was being spent) who successfully argued that "to stop the project after a great deal had already been spent would represent a waste of taxpayers' money." As Alabama senator Jeremiah Denton said, "To terminate a project in which $1.1

---

*Psychologists Hal Arkes and Catherine Blumer documented this case in a landmark 1985 paper about the sunk cost effect.

billion has been invested represents an unconscionable mishandling of taxpayers' dollars."

Senator Denton wasn't intending it, but I'm not sure that there has ever been a clearer explanation of the sunk cost fallacy.

New York's Shoreham Nuclear Power Plant, the subject of a field study by Jerry Ross and Barry Staw, was another, much more expensive public works project that similarly suffered from escalating commitment. The plant's initial estimated cost back in 1966 was $75 million for completion in 1973. Just getting the approval from the Atomic Energy Commission to *start* construction exceeded both the initial cost of the entire plant and blew past the original completion date.

In 1979, the people responsible for the project claimed the plant was 80% done. In 1983, it was still not completed and a spokesman for the plant's owner clearly admitted the sunk cost problem, pointing out that if the decision were a fresh one, they would not continue: "If we had known that we were talking about a $3 billion plant and all the other travail that has gone along the way—the licensing, the political problems—I think we might have chosen not to."

And yet, continue they did! It wasn't for *another* six years and spending $2.5 billion *more* that the still unfinished plant was discontinued.

It's easy to look at these fiascos, roll your eyes, and think, "Typical government waste." But the sunk cost effect makes us all, in ways big and small, build a track from nowhere to nowhere, refusing to quit because we don't want to lose what we've already spent.

It could be someone staying in their money pit of a house. Our track to nowhere could be refusing to quit our college major even though it's making us unhappy, because we already took so many classes and put so much time into it. Or we don't leave a career we spent years training for, because that would mean our training was for nothing. Or we keep watching a bad movie because of the time we've already spent watching it.

Because we put time or effort or money into anything we have started, the sunk cost fallacy affects all of our decisions about whether to stop.

Katamari

There was a popular video game that came out in 2004 named *Katamari Damacy*. It was a silly game, strangely addictive, with a grandiose but simple plot. You control the actions of a tiny prince, whose father, the King of All Cosmos, gives him a katamari (Japanese for "clump"), a sticky ball you roll around different locations, picking up trash and debris off the floor, the ball growing bigger and bigger as it accumulates more stuff.

Why are you on this mission? The king had gotten drunk and accidentally destroyed a bunch of stars and constellations. You have to grow the ball until it's big enough to become a star to replace the ones the king destroyed. It's a goofy plot, but no goofier than whatever is supposed to be motivating you to eat dots and fruit in *Pac-Man* or fit together block formations in *Tetris*.

The katamari can't roll over anything bigger than itself. If it does, the impact knocks some things off, making your ball even smaller. At the beginning, your katamari is only big enough to pick up things like ants, thumbtacks, and buttons. Running into a mouse can be a catastrophe.

But as you successfully pick up debris, the ball gets bigger. Then you're terrorizing the mouse. You're rolling over batteries, plates of food, radios, shoes, pets. Cows, bears, sumo wrestlers, cars, monsters, buildings, islands, mountains.

As one reviewer put it after listing some of the mundane little items, "25 minutes later the bloody thing is ripping rainbows out of the ground."

Like the katamari, rolling around collecting debris, which makes it grow in mass and collect more and even bigger debris, there is a self-reinforcing aspect to the sunk cost fallacy that we really need to watch out for.

When we embark on an endeavor, we also accumulate debris—the time, money, and effort we have spent. As we accumulate costs, the mass grows, escalating our commitment and making it more and more difficult to quit. *That* decision to persevere then makes us accumulate more costs, which then makes us even more likely to continue the next time we consider quitting. And that keeps adding weight to the scale in favor of persevering.

The whole thing snowballs.

You can see this with the students waiting for a crossword puzzle dictionary that never comes. Once they start waiting, the time they've already spent causes them to wait longer, which increases the time they've put into waiting, which causes them to wait even longer still. All the while their compensation is evaporating.

We've all had that happen, even for something as simple as standing in a grocery line.

When we're approaching the fresh decision of which grocery line to choose, we act like an Einstein. We're not just looking at the length of the different lines, but we're taking into account an initial read of the speed and experience among the cashiers. We're factoring in the location of customers who don't have their payment ready, or seem distracted by their children, or are fumbling with coupons, or have items stored beneath their cart.

But once we're in the line and we invest time waiting, we don't apply the same rigor to the decision about whether to switch to a new line. When we see the cashier in the next line race through three customers as the cashier in our line makes small talk while cashing out just one, do we cringe or roll our eyes? Definitely. Do we change lines? Hardly ever.

And the longer we wait—the more time we sink into the line we have chosen—the more unwilling we are to switch lines. That's how we get entrapped.

A relationship that's not working out turns into a game of *Katamari*. Your friend complains about being in a bad relationship. If you ask, "Why don't you just break up?" they'll frequently say, "Because I've put so much time into trying to make this relationship work." Sometimes, they'll even say, "I put my heart and soul into it." The more time they put in, the less likely they are to break it off, which leads to them investing more time to get it to work. That makes them even less likely to break up. And so on.

No wonder that once you have this talk with a friend, you end up having it over and over again. Their dysfunctional relationship keeps rolling up mass—living arrangements, friends, pets, consumer purchases, property—until they're ripping rainbows out of the ground.

We saw something similar happening with Sarah Olstyn Martinez, before she was able to see her quitting decision for the expected-value problem that it actually was. As she put more time into her career, it became harder to quit. She had already put fifteen years in before she started thinking about changing careers. By the time she contacted me, another year had elapsed, creating even more friction against quitting.

This is one of the reasons that retail traders hold on to losing positions. Imagine you're in that situation: Once you're losing in a position, you cancel your stop-loss order because you want to recover your losses. That often causes you to accumulate even more losses, making you even less likely to give up on the position.

I could see the escalating commitment happening in front of my own eyes at the poker table. Players would lose, and they would start to bet more to try to recover the losses that they had previously accumulated, which then would make them bet even more still. That decision would generate more losses, which made them bet more still, and sometimes even move up in stakes.

They would become entrapped.

And that is why Stewart Butterfield and Alex Honnold are so exceptional.

Both were able to cut their losses despite the tremendous resources they had already poured into achieving their goal. Butterfield had devoted four years and spent more than $10 million of his investors' money when he quit working on *Glitch*. Honnold had been training for months to summit El Capitan, yet even with a friend's film crew hanging off the mountain documenting his preparation and the completion of the film hinging on his attempt, he was still able to quit short of the summit in 2016.

How Big Does the Katamari Grow?

In Barry Staw's classic 1976 experiment, "Knee-Deep in the Big Muddy: A Study of Escalating Commitment to a Chosen Course of Action," he set out to ask how much prior commitment to a course of action influences future decisions about whether to stick or quit.

He discovered that the answer is *a lot*.

Staw recruited groups of business school students who were tasked with individually deciding how a corporation should allocate certain R&D funds between two of its divisions. To help with the choice, the students were given ten years of historical financial performance about the company and the two divisions under consideration.

The participants each had to make an all-or-nothing decision about which department should receive the $10 million in R&D funds, meaning they only had two options: allocate the entire $10 million to one division and give no funds to the other or vice versa.

Given the data provided to the students, there were reasonable arguments for allocating the funds to either of the two divisions. While one division was more profitable, the other was growing more quickly.

Indeed, the participants, who were all coming into this decision fresh, split about 50-50 on which division they chose.

What Staw wanted to find out was whether this initial decision about which division got the funds would affect future allocation decisions, particularly once the participants learned their first choice turned out poorly. In other words, Staw was exploring whether people who carry a loss into a new allocation decision would be more likely to persist, continuing to direct funds to the same division they had previously sunk resources into.

To answer that question, he gave all the students a simulation of the next five years of financial results for the company. Regardless of which option they directed the funds to, the additional data showed that the division they chose suffered from half a decade of stagnant sales and deepening losses, significantly underperforming the division they passed over.

After being shown this performance data, the participants were then given a new budget of $20 million, which they could now allocate *proportionally* across the two divisions. Staw hypothesized that students receiving negative feedback on their first decision would *increase* their commitment to their original cause, favoring that same division in the second allocation.

Indeed, that is what he found. The participants allocated, on average, over $13 million of the $20 million to the division that they originally directed the R&D funds to, and just under $7 million to the one they did not initially choose.

To really hit the point home, he also had a separate group of participants come to the $20 million allocation fresh, as a new decision. They were shown the same financial results and informed of a $10 million R&D allocation five years earlier (by a since-departed financial officer) to the division that subsequently underperformed. In this case, they were not the ones who initially made the decision to sink the R&D funds into one division or the other.

When these fresh participants allocated the $20 million proportionally across the two divisions, they gave an average of just $9 million to the division that received the prior funds, much less than the $13 million allocation by the participants carrying with them the sunk cost debris of having personally incurred the prior losses.

Putting it into sharp focus, the participants responsible for the first, money-losing decision *directed nearly 50% more* of the $20 million to that same division, compared with others with the identical information and corporate history but no personal responsibility for prior policy.

Staw's work reveals just how much past history with a decision can influence you to escalate commitment when someone fresh to the decision might quit. He also recognized in "Big Muddy" that those decisions to persist have a self-reinforcing quality: "Due to a need to justify prior behavior, a decision maker may increase his commitment in the face of negative consequences, and this higher level of commitment may, in turn, lead to further negative consequences."

Staw's findings also begin to peel back the curtain on what was going on with his father. Given that Harold Staw's California stores had been losing for a long time and things were getting worse and worse, it is something of a head-scratcher that he turned down the buyout offer from Fred Meyer Inc.

But his son's work gives us a glimpse into the why of it all. Harold Staw's accumulating losses, as he continued bailing out his failing California stores, escalated his commitment to the point where he turned down opportunities to exit short of near-total ruin.

Mental Accounting

There's a saying among top poker players that poker is one long game.

It's a reminder that the particular hand they're playing is not the last hand they'll ever play or that any particular day that they're play-ing is not the last day they'll ever play. A poker player will play thou-sands upon thousands of hands over their lifetime, so in the grand scheme of things whether or not they lose one single hand of poker matters very little. What matters is that they're maximizing their ex-pected value over all those days and all those hands. That's what they mean by one long game.

This mantra is meant to help expert players overcome the sunk cost fallacy, expressed in poker as wanting to protect the money you've already invested in a single hand by not folding, or not wanting to quit a game when you're in the losses. Of course, what applies to poker applies to life as well.

We all need this kind of reminder because of a quirk in our men-tal accounting.

When we start something, whether it's putting money into the pot in a hand of poker, or starting a relationship or a job, or buying a stock, we open up a mental account. When we exit that thing, whether it's folding a hand, or leaving a relationship or job, or selling the stock, we close that mental account.

It turns out that we just don't like to close mental accounts in the losses.

If we're losing in a hand of poker, we don't want to fold because that means we have to realize the loss of the money we put in the pot. If we're losing in a poker game, we don't want to quit because it means that we have to leave with less money than we started with. If we're in a relationship or a job, we don't want to walk away because we'll feel like we will have wasted or lost all the time and effort that we put in.

Of course, that's irrational. What really matters is maximizing your expected value across *all* the things you start, across all of your mental accounts. If you're investing in a number of stocks, some are going to win and some are going to lose. What matters is whether you're winning across your whole portfolio not whether any one investment is up or down.

But that's not how we naturally think. We don't think about the whole portfolio of stocks we own. Each is associated with its own mental account that we don't want to close out unless we are in the gains.

What's true for one stock or one hand of poker is just as true for an individual decision or a project, or climbing a mountain, or opening a discount store in a converted chicken coop. When we start any of these things, we open a mental account. When things start going poorly, we don't want to quit because we don't like to close accounts in the losses.

This is why poker players remind themselves that poker is one long game. We would all do well to remember that life is one long game as well.

The Hardest Cost to Bear

The greater the sunk costs, the harder it becomes to quit. And the greatest cost is, of course, the loss of human life. That makes decisions about whether or when to exit a war heartbreakingly difficult.

Retired four-star general Tony Thomas, commander of U.S. Special Operations Command (USSOCOM), served in Afghanistan on missions between 2001 and 2013 (except for a year when he served in the Iraq War). He attended many military funerals and gave an American flag to many gold star families. He described to me those humbling experiences and how those tragic losses amplify the types of sunk cost problems we all face, making it particularly difficult for a country to extricate itself from a war once it has started to incur those losses.

On one occasion, a gold star mother, having just lost her son, gripped his hand and said, "Stay on this and finish it." The general's knees almost buckled. At that moment, he wanted to run through a wall for her.

The unspoken message, never expressed at these funerals but which he felt was on the minds of all those grieving parents, was, "Tell me my child didn't die in vain."

It's understandable why a gold star parent would say, "Keep going so my child didn't die in vain," and it's impossible not to be moved by such an emotional request. We all feel some of that weight, whether we are involved in deciding policy going forward or just members of the public for whom those soldiers and their loved ones made that sacrifice. You can't be a person with feelings without being sensitive to that.

But the reality is that when it comes to decisions about whether to continue or withdraw, what matters is whether the next life is worth putting at risk, as much as we instinctively want to take into account the lives already lost. If we continue, are our chances of getting the outcome we want worth risking additional lives and imposing those losses on other families?

The Difference between Knowing and Doing

There are lots of intuitions people have about cognitive biases, including the sunk cost fallacy. One of the most common is that if you are educated on the topic and know about it, that will stop you from committing the error.

I know it seems we've already spent a lot of time on stories about scaling mountains. But to demonstrate the difference between knowing and doing, please indulge me while I tell one more.

This one is about an experienced outdoorsman and mountain

climber named Jeffrey R., who had set a goal for himself of climbing the one hundred highest peaks in New England. In the climbing community, this is considered a significant achievement. Several of the peaks do not have official trails and can be reached only along snowmobile tracks, old logging roads, or herd paths. Some of those involve "bushwhacking," where a climber has to force their way through forested or overgrown areas.

Jeffrey R. had climbed ninety-nine of the peaks and was climbing the last one, Fort Mountain, in Maine. When the weather turned bad and a fog came in, his climbing partner decided to turn around. Jeffrey R. disagreed and continued climbing alone.

His body was found several days later. He apparently fell to his death.

Why am I telling you this story, so similar to some of the others? One person turns around. The other continues to go on, with tragic consequences.

The Jeffrey R. in this story is Jeffrey Rubin, the same Jeffrey Rubin who, with Joel Brockner, studied the behavior of people waiting for a crossword puzzle dictionary that never came, and followed it up with an impressive and influential body of work on escalation of commitment right up to his death in 1995. If anybody understood the problem of being entrapped in a course of action, unable to cut your losses even in the face of clear signals that you ought to be quitting, it would have been him.

Yet he became entrapped that day.

This should be a warning to all of us. Don't think that, just because you've read up to this point in the book or understand the sunk cost fallacy, this knowledge alone is going to help you overcome it. If Rubin was unable to quit, that should open our eyes to how hard it is for the rest of us.

Knowing is not the same as doing.

You Can't Jedi Mind Trick
Being Fresh to a Decision

A lot of people who know about the sunk cost fallacy tell me they've come up with a solution. Essentially, regardless of the history they have with the decision, they ask themselves, "If I were approaching this decision fresh, would I want to enter into this course of action?"

As an example, imagine you own a stock that's trading for less than the amount you bought it for. In other words, you're in the losses. You would ask yourself, "If I were looking at this as a new opportunity, would I be a buyer or a seller?" If you would make a fresh decision to buy the stock, you would continue to hold it (because holding means you continue to own the stock, meaning it is the same as buying). If you wouldn't buy the stock, then you would sell it.

Does this Jedi mind trick actually work?

We can, once again, look to Barry Staw for the answer.

In one of the follow-ups to the "Big Muddy" experiment, Itamar Simonson and Staw asked participants to make a corporate decision about allocating marketing funds to two products, a nonalcoholic beer and a lite beer. The first decision was, again, an all-or-nothing choice of which product should receive an additional $3 million in marketing support. After making their choice and receiving a simulation of three years of results based on that choice, the participants made a second decision as to how to split another $10 million marketing budget between the two products.

The investigators tested several possible ways of mitigating escalation of commitment to the product that received the initial $3 million in marketing funds. One of those ways was the Jedi mind trick, where they asked some of the participants to approach the decision fresh, specifically instructing them to do an analysis listing the pros and cons of allocating funds to each product *going forward*.

Despite the instruction to look forward rather than backward when making this new decision, the participants made a similar allocation ($5.1 million) to the product they earmarked the original funds to as compared to those who made the same prior, losing decision but were not given instruction to just look forward. In contrast, participants who actually came to the second allocation fresh gave just $3.7 million to the product that lost money after receiving the earlier addition of marketing funds.

The instruction to treat it as a new decision did practically nothing to reduce escalation of commitment.

Just knowing about the sunk cost effect doesn't help. The Jedi mind trick doesn't help. That's a lot of bad news about sunk cost.

It's about time we get to the good news.

Chapter 5 Summary

- The sunk cost effect is a cognitive illusion where people take into account resources they have previously sunk into an endeavor when making decisions about whether to continue and spend more.
- The sunk cost effect causes people to stick in situations that they ought to be quitting.
- When deciding whether to stick or quit, we are worried that if we walk away, we will have wasted the resources we have spent in the trying.
- You might be experiencing the sunk cost fallacy if you hear yourself thinking "If I don't make this work I will have wasted years of my life!" or "We can't fire her now, she's been here for decades!"
- Sunk costs snowball, like a katamari. The resources you have already spent make it less likely you will quit, which makes it more likely you will accumulate additional sunk costs, which makes it again less likely you will quit, and so on. The growing debris of your prior commitment makes it increasingly harder to walk away.
- We don't like to close mental accounts in the losses.
- Knowing about the sunk cost effect doesn't keep you from falling prey to it.
- You can't trick yourself into not taking sunk costs into account by trying to view the situation as a new choice. Asking whether or not you would continue if the decision were a fresh one doesn't mitigate the sunk cost effect the way you might intuitively think it would.

CHAPTER 6

Monkeys and Pedestals

WHEN ERIC TELLER WAS IN HIGH SCHOOL, HIS FRIENDS thought his hairstyle looked like AstroTurf, so they started calling him Astro. He leaned into the nickname, adopting it from there forward, even painting Astro, the cartoon dog from *The Jetsons*, on the side of his car in college.

Astro Teller earned his PhD in artificial intelligence at Carnegie Mellon University in 1998. While in grad school, he cocreated an interactive gallery installation fusing portrait art and computer science. He also wrote the first of two novels he has published.

Between that time and 2010, he cofounded and grew five companies. One was a hedge fund that chose investments through techniques from machine learning. Another became a successful company in wearable body monitors. He was also a professor at Stanford.

In 2010, with Larry Page, Sergey Brin, and Sebastian Thrun, he developed the in-house innovation hub at Google. Page and Brin were two of Google's cofounders. Thrun, then a VP, was formerly a professor at Carnegie Mellon and Stanford. He has been an innovator in robotics, headed the company's autonomous car project, and subsequently founded Udacity, an online education provider.

They originally called the venture "X" as a placeholder because they considered the name a relatively unimportant detail to be determined later. X remains the company name, which is convenient because Google later changed *its* name to Alphabet.

Teller became the CEO of X, though his actual job title is "Captain of Moonshots." His only requirement for accepting the position, granted by Google's founders, was that he had complete autonomy over the company. Even though X is a subsidiary of Alphabet, he has always insisted on cultural separation.

X has become a famous incubator and developer of ideas in the nontraditional tradition of Bell Labs, Xerox PARC, and Thomas Edison's laboratories. X's mission is to build and launch technologies to "improve the lives of millions, even billions of people."

They're specifically in the business of identifying and accelerating world-changing ideas. That means they reject plenty of good ideas because the change those ideas create would be too incremental for their mission. One of X's slogans is "10x impact on the world's most intractable problems, not just 10% improvement."

Teller might be the perfect person to be running an innovation lab with such lofty goals. Deep, revolutionary thinking didn't just show up on his doorstep. His paternal grandfather was Edward Teller, the legendary physicist who was one of the inventors of the hydrogen bomb. His maternal grandfather was Gerard Debreu, a Nobel Prize–winning economist and mathematician. His father was a philosopher of quantum mechanics, and his mother was a clothing designer and teacher of gifted children.

Innovation, literally and figuratively, is in his blood.

X is an innovation hub but it's not about any innovation at any cost or on any time horizon. X has a very specific charter: to take their best ideas from concept to commercial viability in a five-to-ten-year time horizon. It's not enough that the idea is a world-changing solution, or even that the proposed solution is possible. They also have to know that the economics will work, so that it will become self-supporting and profitable.

The reasoning behind the five-to-ten year time horizon is that if the solution could be developed in fewer years, somebody else is probably already working on it. If it is going to take longer than a decade, the technology might be outdated by the time it gets to market.

Once a project reaches the point where it is polishing its product or scaling operations, it "graduates" from X. X's most famous graduate was one of its first projects, a self-driving car. In 2017, it became Waymo, an Alphabet company. As of early 2021, Waymo had a valuation of $30 billion. Other projects reaching commercialization include Google Brain (one of the largest-ever neural networks for machine learning), Verily Life Sciences (a collection of medical technologies, like a smart contact lens that monitors glucose levels), and Wing delivery drones.

Many of the projects that didn't make it were amazing, innovative ideas aimed at global problems. Project Loon was developing technology to create a grid of giant, high-flying balloons to provide internet access to a billion people in the world's last unconnected communities. Project Foghorn aimed to convert seawater to fuel as a clean, abundant alternative to oil.

X takes a lot of big swings, knowing that most will be whiffs. Teller looks at each project as buying an option on the future. Like most options, you have to keep paying to hold it, in increasing amounts.

As he told me, "We're going to buy a thousand options over the next couple of years. We need only four a decade to get to Sundar [Pichai, CEO of Alphabet]." Teller sees his job as being smart about building a portfolio of value as cheaply as possible.

Even when your owner is Alphabet, you have limited resources of time, money, and attention. What that means is Teller has to identify the projects that aren't going to pan out as quickly as possible. To pursue radical ideas, he has to be a radical loss-cutter. Every dollar they save by getting to no quickly is a dollar they can spend on something that *could* change the world.

To help X-ers become better quitters, Astro Teller has come up with a unique mental model that has been woven into the fabric of X: monkeys and pedestals.

Imagine that you're trying to train a monkey to juggle flaming torches while standing on a pedestal in a public park. If you can achieve such an impressive spectacle, you've got a moneymaking act on your hands.

Teller recognizes that there are two pieces to becoming successful at this endeavor: training the monkey and building the pedestal. One piece of the puzzle presents a possibly intractable obstacle in the way of success. And the other is building the pedestal. People have been building pedestals since ancient Greece and probably before. Over two-plus millennia, pedestals have been thoroughly figured out. You can buy one at a furniture store or a hardware store, or turn a milk crate upside down.

The bottleneck, the hard thing, is training a monkey to juggle flaming torches.

The point of this mental model is to remind you that there is no point building the pedestal if you can't train the monkey.

In other words, you ought to tackle the hardest part of the problem first.

"Monkeys and pedestals" has become part of the language of the organization. When X-ers give project presentations, you'll see #MONKEYFIRST and icons of monkeys. That's their way of identifying the hard thing they have to do for the project to be worth pursuing.

The lesson here is, when you're starting your business, the first thing you tackle shouldn't be designing the perfect business card or investing in the most beautiful logo or coming up with the coolest name.

After all, that's how X got its name in the first place.

Getting the Monkey Off Your Back

Project Foghorn, X's initiative to develop technology to convert seawater into fuel, offers an example of how the monkeys-and-pedestals mental model works. The first monkey would be proof of concept, but they already had that from the scientists they were partnering with whose recent work attracted their attention to the innovation. The second monkey was commercial viability. They would have to produce the fuel at a cost that was significantly lower than the current price per gallon for gasoline to get broad adoption in the market.

At the time they started, $8 per gallon of gasoline equivalent would be competitive in the most expensive markets, like Scandinavia. The first hurdle was the prohibitive cost of building pipes in the ocean. They thought they found a solution by partnering with existing desalination infrastructure. But they quickly realized that the worldwide capacity of those existing plants would barely make a dent in their production needs. Plummeting costs of traditional fuels at the time didn't help matters.

They realized they couldn't tackle the monkey. Because it was too unlikely they would become price competitive in the next three years, they shut down Foghorn.

Sometimes, applying monkeys and pedestals means you shut down something after two years, or five years, or, as was the case with Loon (the project to connect remote areas with internet access), nine years. It doesn't really matter whether it's two or five or nine years, as long as you're shutting it down sooner than you otherwise would have.

If you are able to cut your losses earlier, that's a huge win. An added bonus is that it frees you up so you can turn your limited attention and resources to more fruitful endeavors that have a higher expected value, reducing opportunity costs.

"If we find the Achilles' heel," Teller told me, "thank God we found the Achilles' heel after $2 million instead of after $20 million."

Astro Teller clearly understands that quitting gets you where you want to go faster.

The sooner you figure out that you should walk away, the sooner you can switch to something better. And the sooner that happens, the more resources you're saving, which you can then devote to more fruitful endeavors.

One of the beautiful things about the monkeys-and-pedestals mental model is that sometimes it helps you quit before you start.

Years ago, X looked into developing what's now known as a hyperloop, an experimental high-speed rail system. The concept was fine. Building the physical infrastructure wouldn't be very hard from an engineering standpoint.

The monkeys for the hyperloop to be viable were things like whether you could safely load and unload passengers or cargo, and whether you could get the system up to speed and get it to brake without incident. A couple hundred yards of track wouldn't tell you anything about whether you could conquer those challenges. In fact, Teller and the team at X figured out that you would have to build practically the whole thing before you knew whether it worked. You would have to build a bunch of pedestals before you could find out if the monkeys were intractable.

They quickly decided not to pursue it.

One of Teller's valuable insights is that pedestal-building creates the illusion of progress rather than actual progress itself.

When you are doing something that you already know you can accomplish, you're not learning anything important about whether the endeavor is worth pursuing. You already know you can build the pedestal. The problem is whether you can train the monkey.

On top of that, Teller realizes that when you're building pedestals, you are also accumulating sunk costs that make it hard to quit even as you find out that you may not be able to train the monkey to juggle those torches. By focusing on the monkey first, you naturally reduce the debris you accumulate solving for something that's, in reality, already solved.

We can see this illusion of progress that pedestal-building creates with the California bullet train. We've built countless miles of train tracks over flat land everywhere. They essentially figured that out over 150 years ago, making railroad companies among the most profitable in the world in the last quarter of the nineteenth century. This is infrastructure that we already know we can build.

That means that any track you build on the interior of the line is going to be a pedestal. And yet the first piece of track they approved in 2010 was on flat land between Madera and Fresno.

Astro Teller also understands a subtler but no less important point, that we have a tendency, when we butt up against a monkey that is proving difficult to solve, to turn our attention to building pedestals rather than giving up.

We prefer that illusion of progress to having to quit and admit defeat.

Here again, this is on full display with the California bullet train. Having butted up against the big monkeys of the Pacheco Pass and the Tehachapi Mountains, the Authority turned to building two more pedestals, the track connecting Bakersfield to Merced and, if they finish that, the track connecting San Francisco to Silicon Valley approved by Governor Newsom in 2019.

Had the decision-makers in California approached the project's problems as X does, using monkeys and pedestals, they may have shut down that project as quickly as X shut down the hyperloop. Instead, their katamari keeps growing, making the bullet train harder and harder to abandon.

Butting up against a monkey that you can't solve and turning to pedestal-building is a disaster on two fronts. Not only are you continuing to pour resources into something after the world is giving you signals that you won't succeed, but those are resources you could be devoting to something better. For every dollar the Authority continues to sink into the bullet train, that's a dollar not available for other big ideas with a greater likelihood of benefiting the taxpayers of California.

Monkeys and pedestals boils down to some very good advice:

Figure out the hard thing first.
Try to solve that as quickly as possible.
Beware of false progress.

Kill Criteria

We already know that we're not particularly good at responding rationally in the moment to signals that tell us that we ought to quit. In fact, we tend to react to bad news by *increasing* our commitment rather than cutting our losses. Just knowing about the problem doesn't help, nor does the Jedi mind trick of saying, "What if I imagine coming to this decision fresh?"

But there is something that can help.

If we can identify in advance what the signals are that we should pay attention to and make a plan for how we will react to them, we can increase the chances that we'll cut our losses when we ought to.

Essentially, when you enter into an endeavor, you want to imagine what you could find out that would tell you it's no longer worth pursuing. Ask yourself, "What are the signs that, if I see them in the future, will cause me to exit the road I'm on? What could I learn about the state of the world or the state of myself that would change my commitment to this decision?"

That list offers you a set of *kill criteria*, literally criteria for killing a project or changing your mind or cutting your losses. It's one of the best tools for helping you figure out when to quit closer to on time.

Kill criteria could consist of information you learn that tells you the monkey isn't trainable or that you're not sufficiently likely to reach your goal, or signs that luck has gone against you.

We can imagine potential kill criteria for many of the examples we've explored. For Harold Staw, it could be that if the profitability of your stores drops below a certain threshold, you might look to sell. Or your kill criteria could be in the form of a loss limit where, if you had to personally contribute additional money to keep the stores going (or contribute beyond a certain amount), you would sell or close the business. Or, in the extreme case, it could be that trusted advisers are telling you to abandon course, like if your best friend and lawyer switches sides in a lawsuit.

In the case of *Glitch*, a kill criterion might be if you haven't reached a certain number of sticky customers by a particular date, you'll quit.

Given the California bullet train, you can imagine a lot of applicable kill criteria, like quitting if your original projected budget has more than tripled.

One of the clearest examples of a kill criterion is the turnaround time on Everest. If you haven't made it to the summit by 1 p.m., you cannot safely descend to Camp 4 before dark, so you must abandon the climb.

Back in 1992, Itamar Simonson and Barry Staw explored the effect of this type of advance planning as part of the same study in which participants made an original allocation to one of two beer products, got bad news, and then got the chance to make a second allocation.

The researchers wanted to find out if advance planning would help participants make allocations that look more similar to those of participants who came to the decision fresh.

As you'll recall, participants making the second ($10 million) allocation as a fresh decision gave $3.7 million to the product that received the earlier funds, compared with just over $5 million by participants who made that earlier, losing choice. We already know that asking the participants to do a fresh analysis of the pros and cons looking forward didn't change behavior.

But another strategy that did work was having one group set benchmarks in the form of minimum targets for sales and profits in advance of the first decision. Those participants, after getting the data about the poor performance, allocated just $3.9 million to the same product they chose earlier. Their allocation now looked the same as those of participants who were actually fresh to the decision. And it was a big reduction compared with others who made both allocations but hadn't set benchmarks.

This is in line with lots of subsequent work that's been done on all sorts of precommitment contracts. Whether it comes to following through with diet plans or work plans or study plans, these types of precommitment contracts get people to act more rationally.

Essentially, kill criteria create a precommitment contract to quit.

Funnel Vision

You can likely imagine lots of applications of kill criteria in your personal life. When you start dating someone, think ahead. What could be happening that would make you think that it was time to end the relationship? Or, in the case of a single date, what would make you want to end the date? You could do that with going to a particular college, picking a major, starting a career, or taking a job.

An obvious and high-value application of kill criteria has to do with funnel management for a business's sales function. A big problem for sellers is managing all the opportunities at the top of the funnel: Which do you pursue? And, once you've started pursuing a lead, when do you give up on it?

It's in a company's interest to make sure its sellers are spending their time pursuing the highest-value opportunities, based on a combination of the probability of closing and the potential size of the contract.

Of course, a lot of these challenges aren't unique to sales. Once you start to pursue a sales lead, you're putting time and effort into it. That time and effort makes it hard for you to abandon the lead, making it harder and harder for you, as you dump more resources into it, to give up and cut your losses.

In addition to costing yourself the investment of resources on losing or lower value leads, there are also opportunity costs. You have limited resources. Every minute you spend on something with a low expected value is a minute you don't have for other opportunities of greater value.

These problems are even bigger when you have sellers who, by temperament, don't like to let go of a possible sale until the bitter end. Sellers are gritty by nature. That attitude, similar to poker players who won't want to fold a hand as long as there is any chance of winning it, gives you the peace of mind that you never have to give up on anything and wonder "What if?" But, also like poker players, that's a bad use of resources, and a prescription for eventually going broke.

Setting out kill criteria can be very valuable to making decisions within the sales function more rational and efficient.

As an example, I worked with one of my clients, mParticle, to help them develop and implement kill criteria in their sales process. mParticle is a SaaS (software as a service) company that offers a customer data platform (CDP) that helps teams unify their customer data and connect it to various marketing and analytics APIs (application programming interfaces).

When I started working with them, their sellers were having difficulty letting go of low-value leads, partly because the culture reinforced the notion that walking away from an opportunity would make the company lose ground.

A sales professional's time is a valuable and limited resource. Any time spent on a low-value lead is time they can't spend on higher-value leads, or developing new opportunities. That means that if they don't quickly identify and quit the likely dead ends, that is what will, in reality, slow progress.

Creating a set of kill criteria would help the team to cut their losses faster when the signs were clear.

To develop such criteria, we started by working with the sales team to generate a list of signals that would tell them that an opportunity wasn't worth pursuing. To do that, we sent out the following prompt to the sellers and the sales leadership:

Imagine you were pursuing a lead that came through an RFP (request for proposal) or RFI (request for information). It's six months from now, and you have lost the deal. Looking back, you realize there were early signals that the deal was not going to close. What were they?

In general, this idea of casting yourself into the future, imagining a failure, and then looking back to try to figure out why is called a *premortem*. Using a premortem is a great tool to help develop high-quality kill criteria.

This particular prompt targeted the early signals of failure that the sellers (and all of us) tend to overlook, rationalize, or ignore. In other words, we were looking for the kinds of indicators of things not going well that intuitively we should pay attention to, but don't.

We asked members of the team to respond to the prompt outside of a group setting, independently and asynchronously, so we could get the broadest range of answers, uninfluenced by the opinions of others. We also had them answer this as a hypothetical, not pegged to a particular opportunity they were currently pursuing or had lost. We did it this way because we know that when people are facing down the decision to quit or analyzing an opportunity they have just lost, that's when their perspective is going to be the most biased.

There were several signals repeatedly mentioned in the responses, including: the prospective customer never had an executive attend any of the meetings, the request was clearly written with a competitor in mind, or the prospect went straight to pricing before seeking any other information.

We then turned these signals into a set of kill criteria. Some signals on the list were strong enough that if you saw one of them, you would stop pursuing the lead with no further action. As an example, if the prospect immediately went to price, that was considered a strong enough sign that the lead was a dead end, as it signaled that the potential customer was just using the seller as a stalking horse to beat a competitor down on price.

But other signals required further action. For each of those, we identified the information that the seller needed to discover, as quickly as possible, from the potential customer. Depending on what they found out, the seller would either continue to pursue the deal or quit.

For example, if there was no executive in the room during the first few meetings (a less certain kill criterion), the seller was instructed to offer up executive alignment at the next meeting. The seller would explain to the potential customer that, in their experience, deals go more smoothly when there are executives from both sides in the room, and offer to make sure to have an executive from their side at the next meeting if the potential customer would do the same. If the lead refused the offer, the seller would kill the deal.

Creating this set of kill criteria helped the sales team manage their funnel more efficiently, ensuring the sellers were spending more of their time on the highest-potential opportunities and killing the low-potential ones as quickly as possible. These kill criteria also gave mParticle's sellers another way to win. Company evaluations of sellers, obviously, still involve how much revenue they generate, but now they also include how well sellers follow kill criteria in managing their leads.

For naturally gritty people who live to close the deal, giving them that extra way to win is crucial to getting them to quit when the time is right.

We tend to associate the idea of funnel management with sellers or investors. But every one of us has a funnel we are managing: the interests we can pursue, the classes we can take, the projects we can do at work, the jobs we can apply for, the people we can date.

We all have to make these choices about which opportunities to pursue and which to skip or quit. As we're making those choices, we want to spend as little time as possible on the things that aren't worthwhile and as much time as possible on the things that are.

You can set kill criteria before you accept a position at a company, or before you decide on your major or what college you're going to, or the house that you want to buy, or the place that you want to live. When you're shelling out money for a concert ticket, you can think about what the weather conditions would have to be for you to eat the cost and stay home.

Kill criteria work well for investing in the market. Setting a stop-loss or a take-gain are examples of kill criteria, but you could also set criteria more broadly, asking yourself in advance what the signals in the market might be that would cause you to change your investment strategy.

The good news about kill criteria is that you haven't missed your chance to set them once you have already started an endeavor. At any point, no matter whether it comes to someone you are dating or a house you already own or an investment you are in or a college you are attending, you can think about some time frame in the future, imagine you are unhappy with your situation, and identify the benchmarks you will have missed or the signals you will be seeing that will tell you that you ought to walk away. You may not have set a stop-loss or take-gain when you bought a stock but you can set one now.

After all, the present is always in advance of something.

States and Dates

The best quitting criteria combine two things: a state and a date. A state is just what it sounds like, an objective, measurable condition you or your project is in, a benchmark that you have hit or missed. A date is the when.

Kill criteria, generally, include both states and dates, in the form of "If I am (or am not) in a particular state at a particular date or at a particular time, then I have to quit." Or "If I haven't done X by Y (time), I'll quit." Or "If I haven't achieved X by the time I've spent Y (amount in money, effort, time, or other resources), I should quit."

For mParticle, one of the kill criteria was a lack of a decision-maker in the room, triggering an offer of executive alignment for the next meeting. Translated into states and dates, "If I can't get an executive in the room (the state) by the next meeting (the date), then I'll kill the deal."

You don't have to look any further than X's charter for an example of the interaction of states and dates. X's projects must have the potential to be 10x world-changing (a state), capable of becoming commercially viable (a state), within five to ten years (a date).

Admiral McRaven offered a unique, high-stakes application of this concept of states and dates when describing the planning for Operation Neptune Spear, the raid on Osama bin Laden. The operation was broken down into 162 phases. Each phase told you what state you would have to achieve to continue, and what state you might be in that would cause you to quit during that phase. Because this was all planned out in advance, it left McRaven, as he told me, with only about five command decisions he might have to make on the fly once the mission had commenced and they were already in it.

He gave two examples of the criteria that would cause them to kill the mission. If at any point they fell an hour behind schedule, they would abort. Or, if they discovered that, at any time up to 50% of the way to bin Laden's compound, they had been detected and compromised by the Pakistani government, they would turn around. If they were compromised beyond the 50% mark, that would be a command decision McRaven would have to make on the fly.

The raid, of course, was a success and McRaven never had to exercise the kill criteria. But that's not true of all missions. A famous example is "Operation Eagle Claw," the 1980 attempt during the Carter administration to rescue American hostages being held by Iran. One of the kill criteria set for the operation was that if the aircraft inventory fell below six operational helicopters (owing to mechanical troubles, accidents, or other causes), they would abort the mission. They sent eight helicopters to the first staging area, but only five arrived operational, triggering that kill criterion, so they aborted. Had they not set such conditions in advance, one can easily imagine how difficult it would be in the moment, with the stakes so high, to make the decision to abandon the attempt.

The importance of thinking about states and dates in setting kill criteria in advance has been developed and tested in situations with the highest possible stakes, affecting large numbers of people and gigantic, world-changing decisions. But the concepts are broadly applicable to your personal decisions, where you are trying to spend your resources on things that matter and avoid pedestal-building when you ought to be quitting.

Kevin Zollman, a professor at Carnegie Mellon University and a game theory philosopher, offered up an excellent example of states and dates as it applies to seeking academic jobs. There are relatively few tenure-track positions for those who have earned PhDs in the humanities. That limited supply is pretty well known, and not likely to change by much.

There are two big problems a newly minted PhD faces in their quest for a tenure-track position that make setting out kill criteria in advance of their search crucial. The first is that, within the humanities, leaving academics is considered a one-way decision. If you choose to quit academia, it's incredibly hard to go back. Knowing that the decision is last and final will make it harder for people to quit, even when the signals are pretty strong that they should.

The second issue is that there are lots of pedestals that you can build within the humanities in the form of endless adjunct professor and postdoctoral positions you can secure. These jobs aren't tenure-track positions but they offer the illusion of progress, that you are advancing in your career.

It's easy to move from one pedestal to another, from a postdoc to an adjunct and so forth, thinking that your big break is right around the corner. Of course, with every pedestal, you're accumulating sunk costs, putting more time and effort into the endeavor, making it harder and harder to walk away.

To avoid becoming entrapped, set benchmarks, in the form of states and dates, in advance. Find out the average time it takes a newly minted PhD to secure a tenure-track position and circle that date on the calendar as a quitting deadline. If, for example, that's four years from the time you get your PhD, then if you haven't secured a tenure-track position (the state) within four years (the date), you ought to quit.

If your goal is to be an Olympic sprinter, figure out how fast the best runners in the world were running the 100-meter dash at fifteen years old, or eighteen years old, or as college sprinters. You can mark those milestones along the way and if you are hitting them, keep going (as long as the pursuit still brings you happiness), and if you miss them, quit and pursue a new goal.

This way, you can spend more of your time on the things that are worth pursuing.

You can apply states and dates to relationships. If your goal is marriage (or an equivalent long-term commitment), then if your relationship partner hasn't proposed (or accepted your proposal or otherwise demonstrated a long-term commitment) by a certain date, you should move on and find someone who is as excited about committing to you as you are to them.

You can do the same for career advancement. If you're working at an entry-level position that has some prospect for advancement, figure out as early as you can the interim milestones for those who succeed, whether it's raises, or initial promotions, or additional responsibilities, or whatever is specific in that company or practice. Get information about when others who've succeeded got those signals on the way up and include those states and dates in your kill criteria.

Better, Not Perfect

When I was playing poker, I applied a bunch of kill criteria that helped me be a better quitter (of hands and of games). One example was a stop-loss. If I lost a certain amount, I would quit. This was especially important at the start of my career, because novice players are particularly poor at judging whether they're losing due to their poor play or because of bad luck. (Take-gains don't make sense in poker, so I didn't employ that tool.)

After turning pro, I still maintained a stop-loss. Elite poker players are still going to be worse at making quitting decisions when they're in it, especially if they're in it *and losing*. So, even after I gained experience and got a better understanding of the quality of my play and the short-term swings of luck, I still set loss limits.

I also realized that I played better in sessions of six to eight hours or less, so I committed to quitting after I played that long. Because I was more aware of the importance of game conditions, I also committed to quit if the quality of the players in the game drastically changed in an unfavorable way as some players cashed out and new ones took their seats.

Those kill criteria helped me to become better at quitting games. But was I perfect? Not even close.

Did I always walk away when I reached my loss limit? No. When I had access to funds at the casino, there were times that I grabbed some more money and kept playing.

Did I always stop after playing six to eight hours? Definitely not. There were times when I played for more than twenty-four hours at a stretch. Likewise, there were absolutely times when I convinced myself that I was still in a good game, even though the players who made the game so good had left and been replaced by much tougher ones.

I was far from flawless, but I did better than I would have without those kill criteria. In the one long game of my poker career, I'm confident my bottom line benefited because I was able—some of the time—to reduce the mental and financial resources I spent in negative expected-value situations.

The important thing is to be better, not perfect. After all, we're only human and we're operating under conditions of uncertainty. It's hard to time quitting decisions perfectly.

Astro Teller knows that they don't always quit at the exact right moment at X. He's fine with that because they do better overall since they are always trying. "This is exactly why X produces such outsized returns. Not because we're perfect at what we aspire to, but because we're so relentlessly aspiring to it that we're modestly successful and that turns out to be enormous."

Taken together, the monkeys-and-pedestals mental model and kill criteria help us overcome our aversion to closing accounts in the losses. First, they both get you to no faster, which naturally limits the losses that you have to absorb when you quit. And the less you are down, the easier it is to walk away.

Second, when you set out clear kill criteria in advance and make a precommitment to walk away when you see those signals, you are just more likely to follow through, even when you are losing. Anytime you can make a decision about cutting your losses in advance, you'll do better at closing those mental accounts.

Chapter 6 Summary

- Monkeys and pedestals is a mental model that helps you quit sooner.
- Pedestals are the part of the problem you know you can already solve, like designing the perfect business card or logo. The hardest thing is training the monkey.
- When faced with a complex, ambitious goal, (a) identify the hard thing first; (b) try to solve for that as quickly as possible; and (c) beware of false progress.
- Building pedestals creates the illusion that you are making progress toward your goal, but doing the easy stuff is a waste of time if the hard stuff is actually impossible.
- Tackling the monkey first gets you to no faster, limiting the time, effort, and money you sink into a project, making it easier to walk away.
- When we butt up against a hard problem we can't solve, we have a tendency to turn to pedestal-building rather than choosing to quit.
- Advance planning and precommitment contracts increase the chances you will quit sooner.
- When you enter into a course of action, create a set of kill criteria. This is a list of signals you might see in the future that would tell you it's time to quit.
- Kill criteria will help inoculate you against bad decision-making when you're "in it" by limiting the number of decisions you'll have to make once you're already in the gains or in the losses.
- In organizations, kill criteria allow people a different way to get rewarded beyond dogged and blind pursuit of a project until the bitter end.
- A common, simple way to develop kill criteria is with "states and dates:" "If by (date), I have/haven't (reached a particular state), I'll quit."

Gold or Nothing

When seven-year-old Alexandra "Sasha" Cohen first became interested in figure skating in 1992, American women had medaled in every Winter Olympics going back to 1968. By the time she started competing in high-level junior competitions, women's figure skating was the most watched Winter Olympic event. American skaters like Kristi Yamaguchi, Nancy Kerrigan, Tara Lipinski, and Michelle Kwan were household names.

A huge U.S. audience watched qualifying events and non-Olympic championships, looking for the next superstar. Four years younger than Kwan and two years younger than Lipinski (who retired after the 2002 Olympics), Cohen was one of thousands of athletic young girls in highly competitive, demanding local programs, laser-focused on filling that role.

Sasha Cohen went on to become one of the best figure skaters of her time. From the late nineties through her silver-medal performance at the 2006 Winter Olympic Games in Turin, Italy (at age twenty-one), she was a top performer in elite junior, national, and international competitions.

Cohen rose to prominence at just fifteen, finishing second at the 2000 U.S. Figure Skating Championships to Michelle Kwan who, by that time, had already won two World Championships and an Olympic silver medal. Kwan was unmatched in the U.S. Championships, winning in 1996 and then in eight straight years, from 1998 to 2005.

Cohen was right behind her. Excluding 2001, when she had to withdraw due to a stress fracture in her back, between 2000 and 2006, this was her performance line at the U.S. Championships: silver, silver, bronze, silver, silver, and gold. Only Michelle Kwan (and reigning Olympic champion Sarah Hughes in 2003) finished ahead of Sasha Cohen.

As a seventeen-year-old, she finished fourth in the 2002 Olympics in

Salt Lake City and earned gold medals in six Grand Prix competitions in 2002–2003 (including the Grand Prix of Figure Skating Final in 2003). She won six other international events between 2001 and 2005, and medaled at the World Championships in 2004 (silver), 2005 (silver), and 2006 (bronze).

During Cohen's time in figure skating, her focus and persistence was what we expect of the world's top athletic performers. She started skating at seven and was competing regularly by eleven, when she began home-schooling to maximize her time practicing, training, and competing. The intensity of her commitment led to numerous injuries and related set-backs. She continued to suffer from the back problems that took her out of the 2001 U.S. Championships, limiting her competitive schedule in 2004 and 2005.

But 2006 looked like it was going to be Sasha Cohen's year. Michelle Kwan, now twenty-five, had been training for an Olympic bid but withdrew from three late 2005 competitions due to a hip injury. She also withdrew immediately before the start of the U.S. Championships in January, ending her eight-year winning streak.

Cohen earned gold, finally becoming U.S. champion.

Kwan petitioned for a medical waiver to compete in the Olympic Games, received it, but then had to withdraw when she suffered an injury during her first practice in Turin. This signaled the end of Michelle Kwan's com-petitive skating career. Cohen was now the heir apparent to America's skating dynasty, which included medals in ten consecutive Olympics, five of them gold, including in three of the previous four Olympics.

Cohen held the lead after the short program and the gold medal was hers to lose. But less than thirty seconds into her long program in the fi-nals, she fell. As a testament to how great she was, despite the fall and the instant realization that she would not win, she performed so flawlessly that she still earned silver, adding to her long list of accomplishments.

Maybe, if she hadn't suffered that fall, she would have retired from competition, having won the gold. She already had a bad back and recently suffered through a hip injury. By the next Olympic Games, she would be twenty-five, the same age as Michelle Kwan in her 2006 Olympic attempt, which ended with her inability to compete due to three separate injuries.

Instead, in April 2006, just two months after the Olympics, she announced she would return and try for a spot on the 2010 team. She took a break from competition but not from figure skating. She spent 2006–2009 in a similarly demanding skating environment.

A reward for a successful career in American figure skating is the chance to perform in professional exhibitions and touring in *Champions on Ice* and *Stars on Ice*, and Cohen reaped that reward, headlining from 2007 to 2009.

Sasha Cohen was unhappy with touring. It was lucrative work but, as she described it, "it wasn't the life that I wanted to live. I didn't want to be hanging out in the bowels of an arena and doing the same thing over and over, like *Groundhog Day*."

That leaves one to wonder, if she was so miserable, why didn't she quit?

Cohen has wondered this herself, coming to no clear answer. She just couldn't bring herself to retire, which she considered "too permanent and too final. It would end an identity. . . . I think I had to get to the point that I was so unhappy that I wasn't functional."

She felt obligated to try to make the Olympic team one more time. Skating was her identity, and persevering was her identity. To do otherwise, "it would be weak, or I'd be giving up because it was hard if I didn't make the effort."

In May 2009, she began training to return to competition. After withdrawing from two Grand Prix events due to tendinitis in her right calf (another in the inevitable accumulation of physical setbacks from fifteen years of commitment to such demanding work), she competed in the 2010 U.S. Championships. She needed a top-two finish to qualify for the Vancouver Olympics, but finished fourth.

She was finally done with figure skating, though it was more through circumstances than choice. The competitive window for female figure skaters closes at twenty-five. She aged out, which she "didn't interpret as quitting. It just seemed like I'm free."

Although her skating career is in her distant past, her legacy remains. Because of her 2006 silver medal, which extended the streak of U.S. success in women's figure skating to eleven consecutive Olympics, she remains, as of 2022, the last American woman to earn an Olympic singles figure skating medal.

After she was forced to quit skating, she created a happy life for herself. At twenty-six, she started college, fifteen years after her last time in a classroom. She earned her degree from Columbia University in 2016, the same year she was inducted into the U.S. Figure Skating Hall of Fame. She became an investment manager at Morgan Stanley, married, and is mother to two children, born in January 2020 and August 2021.

There is a lot to be learned about quitting from Sasha Cohen's story. There is the obvious accumulation of sunk costs from all the time, money, and effort devoted to her career, both by herself and her family. There was loss aversion and an inability (until she was forced) to visualize her life on the other side.

But as we will explore in section III, there are broader lessons from her experience having to do with identity. Sasha Cohen had much in common with many others in this book, including the climbers trying to reach the summit of Everest, like the late Doug Hansen: so much already devoted to the endeavor, the emphasis on an all-or-nothing goal, and a feeling that coming close was a failure that had to be addressed by trying again.

In large part, we are what we do, and our identity is closely connected with whatever we're focused on, including our careers, relationships, projects, and hobbies. When we quit any of those things, we have to deal with the prospect of quitting part of our identity. And that is painful.

Identity and Other Impediments

CHAPTER 7

You Own What You've Bought
and What You've Thought:
Endowment and Status Quo Bias

N 2006, ANDREW WILKINSON FOUNDED METALAB, A COM-
pany that designs and builds mobile apps for tech companies. It
was instantly profitable and grew quickly. Its client list includes
Apple, Google, Disney, Walmart, and famously successful start-ups
like Slack.

Over the years, he used some of those profits to start more than
twenty companies. In addition, one of those, Tiny, founded in 2014,
has invested in and bought dozens of internet businesses. Because of
Wilkinson's reputation for doing fast deals, being a hands-off buyer,
and holding for the long term, he's been called "Warren Buffett for
startups."

Wilkinson's entrepreneurial spirit was apparent from an early age.
While attending high school in the early 2000s, he started a tech news
website called MacTeens.com, along with some friends. He worked
hard at the project, even snagging an interview with Steve Jobs. The
site was so successful that, between managing staff, negotiating ad

deals, and creating content, it became a full-time job. The project took so much time that he barely graduated.

After briefly studying journalism in college, he dropped out and started MetaLab. In 2009, finding that he wanted a way for his team to share to-do lists, he decided to build his own to-do list tool. The idea became a software product called Flow, which he funded and pursued until 2021.

The market for SaaS tools, like Google Docs and Slack (which hired MetaLab in 2013 to design its interface), has exploded since then, but at the time he conceived of this idea, the market was nascent. He was early to the space, correctly foreseeing the potential market size for this type of product. MetaLab had become successful enough that he had the resources to bootstrap Flow, to fund the company on his own rather than seek outside investors such as venture capital firms.

After nine months of work with two developers from MetaLab, Wilkinson succeeded in producing a beta version of the to-do list tool. He described his immediate pride in the product: "It was actually really cool. From day one, it was a huge hit."

The beta version of Flow quickly got to $20,000 in monthly recurring revenues and was soon growing by 10% a month. The product was hot. All the big venture capital firms reached out to him.

Among the community of people who incubate new ventures (and the larger community of people who follow what those people are up to), there has long been a spirited debate about the pros and cons of venture funding versus bootstrapping. Wilkinson was among those very publicly siding with bootstrapping as the better option, both for himself and as a general strategy. This obviously contributed to his refusal of all the offers of venture money coming his way.

Flow was a spartan operation but, not surprisingly for a new company in this space, it was still significantly outspending its promising initial sales. Wilkinson willingly wrote the checks to cover the growing expenses. He had capital, a product he was in love with, and a frequently expressed desire to avoid the dilution that comes with taking on outside investors.

Although Flow's initial success confirmed that there was demand for a SaaS tool that helped teams manage and share to-do lists, he recognized that the potential demand meant others would try to enter the space.

Shortly after starting Flow, Wilkinson began hearing about another product named Asana. He had reason to be concerned about Asana. It was cofounded and run by Dustin Moskovitz. Moskovitz was a cofounder of Facebook, a billionaire, and someone who had enormous credibility and name recognition with potential investors, employees, and prospective users.

When Asana went live in late 2011, Wilkinson breathed a sigh of relief. "It was ugly! It was designed by engineers. Complicated and hard to use. Not a threat in the slightest."

By comparing Flow with this debut version of Asana, he felt validated. "With a team a quarter of the size, and a fraction of the money, we had built what I felt was a superior product."

After Asana debuted, Dustin Moskovitz reached out to Andrew Wilkinson and they met for coffee in San Francisco, where Asana had its office. At the meeting, Moskovitz was very open about how much cash they had and the talent they were bringing into the company.

Wilkinson came away from the meeting believing the message was that Asana had superior resources and Flow wouldn't be able to keep up. Much later, Moskovitz publicly made it clear that his memory of the meeting was quite different. He thought he was exploring the possibility of Asana and Flow teaming up, maybe through an acquisition, to better take on the bigger, established competitors in the space.

It is hard to know why they interpreted what happened at the meeting differently. But the way Wilkinson heard it was certainly consistent with his beliefs about bootstrapping and venture funding. It also reinforced his viewpoint that Flow was the scrappy underdog and Asana, rather than being another struggling new venture, was one of "them" in an us-versus-them war of bootstrappers versus VC-backed founders.

Within a few months after the release of Asana's paid product (in April 2012), it had completed three rounds of funding, the last of which saw the company raise $28 million at a $280 million valuation.

Wilkinson could have considered that a negative for Flow. After all, its main competitor was thriving, was flush with funds, and was clearly a hot property in the venture market. Instead, he treated this as good news for Flow's prospects. If experienced venture investors thought Asana was worth $280 million, then his company with its superior product must be worth much more.

At this point, Flow was outspending its monthly revenues by a factor of two or three, with greater spending necessary if keeping up with Asana was a priority. When his concerned CFO brought this up, Wilkinson told him they needed to hold on. Based on his reasoning that Flow had to be worth more than Asana, it was clearly worthwhile to continue investing his personal funds in the product.

This self-mounted crusade against Asana quickly became a war of attrition. To make Flow available across multiple platforms (as Asana did), upgrade it with features customers wanted, and market at even a fraction of Asana's level, Flow's cash burn rate quickly doubled.

Wilkinson maintained his belief that continuing to pour money into Flow was justified because of the quality of Flow's product. "We started burning money on ads and hiring sales people just to keep a toe hold, but mostly we focused on making the product better than theirs. Our one remaining advantage."

As they continued to add features to the product, more bugs

started to appear (a well-known issue in software development). Despite the regular cash infusions, the engineering and design team was understaffed and overworked. They found themselves unable to keep up with the endless stream of bug reports from customers. Month-over-month growth slowed from 20% to 5%.

In September 2015, Asana launched a new version, which didn't remotely resemble the product Wilkinson had viewed so negatively in its original form. It now had all the features Flow had and all those he wished Flow had. It worked on more platforms and, in contrast to Flow, was not plagued by bugs.

By this time, Flow's burn rate was $150,000 per month. Wilkinson's total investment was more than $5 million, with no end in sight. The world was telling him that in this case, a scrappy, bootstrapped company trying to fight a well-funded, venture-backed company was a losing battle. Yet, he still didn't shut it down, continuing on for seven more years, until he had eventually put $11 million into the company. During this period, he saw revenue growth slow and then stop, while Asana (along with other competitors in the space) kept making their product better.

In the midst of all this, he fielded an offer to acquire Flow for $6 million. He refused, because he had $11 million into it and he didn't want to have to realize the sure loss of $5 million. Classic sunk cost fallacy.

Finally, after twelve years and, as Wilkinson put it, "$10MM+ lit on fire," he saw what had long been clear to everyone else. Asana was better by every measure: marketing, product, features, support, integrations. Flow downsized to a shadow of its former self, breaking even (with little growth) on less than a third of its former annual recurring revenue.

More significantly, Andrew Wilkinson let go of his aspirations for Flow. As of 2021, it was still technically operating but he had realized that he would never make his investment back and Flow would never own a large chunk of the productivity-tool market.

Wilkinson's story demonstrates how ownership can interfere with our ability to walk away, especially when the thing we own, we created.

An Oenophile among Economists

When we own something, we value it more highly than an identical item that we do not own. Richard Thaler was the first to name this cognitive illusion, calling it the *endowment effect*. In fact, he introduced the endowment effect in that same 1980 paper where he coined the term "sunk cost." He described the endowment effect as "the fact that people often demand more to give up an object than they would be willing to pay to acquire it."

Thaler offered the example of a distinguished economist friend who bought a case of good wine in the late fifties for $5 a bottle. A few years later, the wine had greatly appreciated in value. His wine merchant offered to buy the wine for $100 a bottle. Despite having never paid more than $35 for a bottle of wine, he declined to sell any bottles for $100. Yet, he also declined to buy any additional bottles at that price. This is very odd behavior. His refusal to sell communicated that anybody buying his bottles would be paying less than what the bottles were worth. Yet having determined it was too much of a bargain to sell any of the wine, he refused to take advantage of that bargain himself and buy an identical bottle at the same price.

The bull market for bottles of Bordeaux continued. In 1991, eleven years later, Thaler, along with Daniel Kahneman and fellow economist Jack Knetsch, updated the situation of their friend and his wine. The wine was now selling at auction for $200 a bottle. Their friend would occasionally drink some of the Bordeaux, but he was still neither "willing to sell the wine at the auction price nor buy an additional bottle at that price."

The story gave them all a good laugh, but they found it puzzling from an economic standpoint. Because he had the opportunity to sell the bottles at a profit, the sunk cost effect didn't explain this behavior. Instead, Thaler hypothesized that it had something to do with the wines being in his possession, the fact of ownership. That ownership caused him to value his bottles more highly than bottles not in his possession.

If an economist can fall for this illusion, even after his friends have been poking fun at him in academic journals for years, imagine how bad this is for the rest of us.

Over the past forty years, researchers in well over a hundred subsequent studies have replicated and expanded on Thaler's initial work. The early demonstrations of the endowment effect in the lab were quite simple.

In one of Jack Knetsch's early experiments, students signed up for the task of completing a questionnaire. Before filling it out, one group of participants received their payment in the form of a coffee mug. A second group received payment in the form of a big chocolate bar.

(A third group was offered a choice between the two as a fresh decision with no prior ownership of either. This group split pretty evenly, favoring the mug 56%–44%.)

Knetsch wanted to know whether ownership of the mug or the chocolate bar among the first two groups would change how the participants valued those items. To do that, after completing the questionnaire, he gave the participants in those groups a chance to switch their payment for the other item. In other words, the students with the mug could trade for the chocolate bar, and the students with the chocolate bar could trade for the mug.

If there was no effect of ownership, you would expect that the first two groups, after trading when they preferred the other item, would end up with the same proportion of mugs and chocolate bars as those who came to the decision fresh. About half the participants in each group would trade, perhaps slightly more in the group that started with the chocolate bar and slightly fewer in the group starting with the mug.

But that's not what Knetsch found. It turned out that endowment to an item, even for such a brief period of time, had quite a strong effect on how much value they attached to the items. Of those given the mug, 89% declined to trade it for the chocolate bar. Among those given the chocolate, 90% favored the chocolate and only 10% traded it for the mug.

Knetsch, along with several other collaborators (including Thaler and Kahneman) ran additional experiments to uncover the disparity that the endowment effect creates in buying and selling prices. These studies were an attempt to replicate the behavior of their economist friend, who simultaneously thought $200 was too much to pay for a bottle of wine but the same amount was too little to sell it for.

One of the experiments involved paying some participants with cash and some with a coffee mug. Those receiving the mug answered the questionnaire and then were asked, "What is the minimum amount you would accept in cash for your mug?" When those receiving cash finished the questionnaire, they were shown a mug and asked, "What's the maximum you would pay for it?"

For something as simple as a coffee mug with a school logo on it, the disparity in buying and selling prices was amazingly large. If you got the mug, your minimum selling price was at least *double* the maximum price someone getting the cash would pay to buy it. The ratio has held up in decades of later experiments using visors, sweatshirts, boxes of pens, and seemingly just about anything an experimenter could scrounge from the university bookstore.

The results of these experiments are also consistent with our common experiences.

You have a car and you're thinking about selling it. When you look up the Kelley Blue Book value, you think, "No way. My car is worth more than that." Or "It's worth at least that much. Clearly, it's at the top end, if not more." But then, when you're out shopping for a car and you see an identical car where they are asking for the top end of Kelley Blue Book, your reaction is "These people are ridiculous. Highway robbery. There's a ding in the fender."

The endowment effect has obvious applications to quitting behavior. Selling something you own is the equivalent of quitting; you are quitting your ownership. Not selling something you own is a form of persistence. When you are deciding whether to sell your wine, or your car, or your house, you are choosing whether or not to persist in owning those things.

Also, If You've Known It, You Own It

The original basis for the endowment effect was loss aversion. Simply put, if we weigh losses greater than gains of similar amounts, then we are more worried about losing something we already own than we are eager to acquire the identical thing we don't own.

Decades of research since have established that we can become endowed to things for additional reasons other than loss aversion. In the process, a broader understanding of what we think we own has been developed.

The original work on the endowment effect was about the physical ownership of objects and the additional value we impute to those objects once they are in our possession. But as Carey Morewedge and Colleen Giblin pointed out in a 2015 review of the literature, we can become endowed to much more than physical objects. As the research on the endowment effect has expanded, it has become increasingly clear that we can also become endowed to our beliefs, our ideas, and our decisions.

As we carry around beliefs and ideas, they become our possessions. We own what we've bought *and* what we've thought.

When we commit to a course of action, it means that, in some sense, we now own that decision. The value we attach to things, whether they are bottles of wine or our commitment to an endeavor, is likely going to be greater than those same things when they belong to others, and greater than others think those things of ours are worth.

The endowment effect is particularly strong if the thing you own you also built. This is known as the IKEA effect, for obvious reasons. Most furniture you buy from IKEA, you have to put together yourself. We'll value that nightstand that we built much more than an identical one that was preassembled.

The IKEA effect is one of the reasons we have to be super careful about pedestal building. If you build something you are already certain is buildable, like starting the California bullet train with the route between Madera and Fresno, or building between Bakersfield and Merced or between San Francisco and Silicon Valley, you are creating a twofold problem. Without finding out useful information about whether you can complete the line, you put in time, effort, and money, which creates a sunk cost issue. In addition, you've become endowed to the thing you have built, which makes it even harder to abandon course.

If you are going to gaff the scale against quitting by adding endowment into the mix, at least make the thing you've become endowed to something that represents real progress at solving a hard problem.

The Endowment Effect

The endowment effect helps unlock the mystery of why Harold Staw *twice* would not sell his stores. In his battle with the Texas shareholders, in which his good friend and lawyer defected to the other side, he was endowed to the California stores in a way that those on the other side of the suit were not. He was unwilling to sell the California stores, stores he had created and built, to protect the value of the Texas stores, stores he had not created and built.

When Fred Meyer Inc. came along and offered to buy him out, he again thought the price was too low, despite the fact that his stores were drowning in losses. At every step of the way, he viewed the business that he built from a chicken coop into an empire as worth more than those looking at the value from the outside. They saw the faltering business for what it had become in a way he could not.

The endowment effect also offers insight into why Andrew Wilkinson put so much of his personal wealth into Flow. Wilkinson's story is a particularly good illustration of the layers of cognitive debris at work in our over-persistence.

Wilkinson was endowed to Flow in multiple ways. To start and most simply, Wilkinson was the actual owner of Flow. Plus, it was his idea. He thought of it. He created it.

He immediately fell in love with his product and that feeling intensified when he compared it to Asana, a similar type of product that he immediately described as "ugly," "complicated," and "hard to use." Flow was a beautiful, functional coffee mug, while Asana was a candy bar he wouldn't touch. It's hard to say whether his belief in the value of Flow was reasonable at the beginning, but it certainly wasn't reasonable during the last several years of his commitment to the losing venture.

The endowment effect was clearly causing Wilkinson to overvalue his product, but you can also see how this mixed with the sunk cost effect to create a very destructive cognitive brew. When he was at the point where he had already decided to scale back his commitment to Flow, he nevertheless turned down an offer to sell it for $6 million, because that wouldn't allow him to recoup all of his $11 million in losses.

The endowment effect adds more mass to the katamari, beyond what is already added by the sunk cost effect. As you start on a course of action and as you make subsequent decisions to continue on that course of action, not only are you accumulating more sunk costs, but you're becoming more endowed to your ideas, to the belief that you're on the right course. As you build things, whether they're train tracks, or bookshelves, or relationships, or essays that you've written for classes, the endowment effect gaffs the scale even more, further escalating our commitment to failing causes.

Pro Sports Teams and Their Escalating Commitment to High Draft Picks

After two decades of exploration of escalation of commitment in the lab, Barry Staw set out to validate his findings in the field. One of the first places he looked was in professional sports decisions about roster management. In a 1995 study, Staw and Ha Hoang explored whether there was an effect of a player's draft order on their subsequent playing time and career length in the NBA, independent of their skill level.

When an NBA team uses a high draft pick to acquire a player, this is a real-world, high-stakes decision where sunk cost and endowment are potential issues. Spending a high draft pick to acquire a player burns a valuable, limited resource and comes with a higher salary paid to that player. Endowment also comes into play because teams are making a very public decision, a decision that they own. Because the teams with the worst records receive the highest picks, their first-round pick very clearly links the team's future with that player.

Would sunk cost and endowment influence future decisions to play and retain those highly drafted players more than other equally productive players?

You might be surprised, given the strong incentives of NBA teams to field their best players, that the answer is yes.

The NBA and other professional sports leagues offer a unique environment in which to study quitting behavior. Decision-makers in pro sports get a lot of continuous, quick, clear feedback on player productivity. Pro basketball is a data-rich environment, with many objective measures of player performance for scoring (points, field goal percentage, free throw percentage), toughness (rebounds and blocks), and quickness (assists and steals). The coach and team management are highly motivated to use the best players in the right situations and, obviously, to win.

In contrast, in the rest of the world we make most of our decisions without that level of information for calculating the expected value of different options with any precision. When we're deciding which of two applicants to hire for a job (or which of two jobs to take), we don't have nearly as much information as NBA executives have when they're deciding which of two players to start or keep on the roster for another season.

Our educated guesses are a lot less educated.

That means that when coaches and executives make errors in player decisions, they can't just chalk it up to not knowing the data. This is similar in transparency to the options offered to the participants in Kahneman and Tversky's original studies on prospect theory. When the participants turned down a positive expected-value bet or accepted a negative expected-value bet, it wasn't because they didn't know whether the bets were favorable or unfavorable. Despite the clarity of the choice, you could see that people were willing to take bad bets when they were in the losses and refuse good bets when they had a gain on paper they could turn into a sure win by quitting.

In the NBA, much more so than in Kahneman and Tversky's studies, personnel decisions are high stakes and you would expect a tremendous amount of motivation to get them right. But just as with the gambles participants accepted and refused, the choices NBA executives make are not always rational.

Staw and Hoang wanted to know whether, when comparing two players of equal skill, the player chosen higher in the draft would get more playing time, have a longer career, and be less likely to be traded. To find out, they analyzed the draft order of the 1980–1986 NBA drafts, nine measures of player performance, minutes of playing time for five seasons, career length, and whether a player was traded.

It turned out that draft order did have an independent effect on future playing time and roster decisions. "Results showed that teams granted more playing time to their most highly drafted players and retained them longer, even after controlling for players' on-court performance, injuries, trade status, and position played."

During the first five years of the players' careers, draft order was a significant predictor of playing time. After teams had one year of playing data, first-round picks played 552 minutes more in their second NBA season than did second-round picks of equal skill. Each additional downward spot in a player's draft order decreased their playing time by 23 minutes (i.e., the second pick in the first round played 23 minutes more over the season than the third pick in the first round).

Once a team picked a player in the first round, that player stayed in the league an average of 3.3 years longer than second-round picks with similar on-court performance. Each incremental decrease in draft order increased the likelihood of the player being cut by 3%. They also found second-round draft picks were 72% more likely to be traded than first-round players, with the likelihood increasing by 3% with each incremental decrease in their draft order.

If we can see this escalation of commitment even in a data-rich, high-stakes environment where you can actively measure the quality of the player, it shouldn't be surprising that employers hang on to their employees too long. Or that students demand much more than their coffee mug is worth to trade it. Or that an economics professor won't sell his bottles of wine at a price he also won't buy one for.

In 1999, Colin Camerer and Roberto Weber attempted to replicate Staw's results with updated data (from players chosen in the 1986–1991 NBA drafts) and additional variables and methods that could rule out other explanations. Their results closely matched Staw's. Because of the additional variables, they found the escalation-of-commitment effects were not as strong, but still significant enough to declare they "constitute the most conclusive available field evidence of irrational escalation."

To be fair, both Staw's and Camerer's analyses of the NBA took place before the *Moneyball* era in sports, where decision-making became much more driven by analytics. One could argue that data wasn't used or appreciated in the same way it is today. You could then ask, Does the effect of sunk cost and endowment in professional sports still hold up today?

Quinn Keefer, an economics professor at California State University San Marcos, has conducted several field studies since the mid-2010s on the effects of draft order and player compensation on playing time in the NFL and the NBA. These studies involved decisions in the post-*Moneyball* era. He also used advanced analytics measuring player performance. Although the effect sizes were diminished, they were still significant, replicating the original findings from the 1980s and 1990s.

To anybody who thinks they can be objective about quitting decisions, the results of the field studies in major professional sports should be super alarming. You've got smart people, a data-rich environment, a tight feedback loop, and a lot of motivation. For most of the quitting decisions we make, we have much less information and we have longer, noisier feedback loops.

The Status Quo Is Hard to Quit

The endowment and sunk cost effects live together in a way that amplifies escalation of commitment. Status quo bias adds to the mix of cognitive forces gaffing the scale.

Simply put, the status quo is the path you're already on or the way you've always done things. The bias is that we have a preference to stick with those decisions, methods, and paths that we've already set upon, and a resistance to veering from them into something new or different.

That's true whether it's thinking about a career switch, like Sarah Olstyn Martinez or Sasha Cohen, or breaking off a relationship and dating someone new, or changing majors or colleges. For NBA teams, once a player is on the team, they become part of the status quo. If you bench or trade or cut them, you're veering from that status quo.

In a seminal 1988 paper, Harvard economist Richard Zeckhauser and Boston University economist William Samuelson introduced the term "status quo bias." They presented both lab experiments and field studies demonstrating that individuals overwhelmingly stick with the status quo option, even when that option is associated with a lower expected value. The bias is widely acknowledged, robust, and has been established as applying to decisions by individuals and organizations.

The status quo represents a mental account that we already have open, which has sunk costs associated with it, the time, money, or effort that has already been put into the way we've been doing things. Closing that account by switching to a new option can make us feel like we are wasting those resources we have already spent.

We also become endowed to the status quo, taking ownership of the decisions that have kept us in that groove and anything we have created along the way.

Another of the factors that cause us to hew to the status quo is an asymmetry in the way we experience loss aversion. We are much more bothered by the downside potential of changing course than we are by the downside potential of staying on the path we're already on.

We can see this at work in Dr. Olstyn Martinez's dilemma. She clearly recruited loss aversion into her thinking about changing careers. "What if I go and do the new thing and get a bad outcome?" That's part of what was creating the friction that was stopping her from taking the new role.

Meanwhile, she wasn't nearly as averse to the prospect of the same bad outcome—unhappiness—from staying in her current job, even though she had already acknowledged that unhappiness was a 100% certainty if she didn't quit.

She was thinking about the potential losses associated with each path in an asymmetric way.

John Maynard Keynes, one of the most influential economists of the twentieth century, summed up this phenomenon well when he said, "Worldly wisdom teaches that it is better for reputation to fail conventionally than to succeed unconventionally." Succeeding unconventionally carries with it the risk of experiencing failure as a result of veering from the status quo.

A higher chance of failing is more tolerated on paths that don't rock the boat. After all, what's the go-to defense in a postmortem after we make a decision that doesn't work out? "I followed procedure," or "I stuck with the status quo," or "I made the consensus choice."

Failing conventionally doesn't feel as bad, nor is it treated as such by the people who are judging you.

Wrapped within all these forces interfering with quitting decisions is that we do not think of sticking with the status quo as an active decision in the same way that we view switching as one. We are much more concerned with errors of commission than errors of omission (failures to act). We're more wary of "causing" a bad outcome by acting than "letting it happen" through inaction.

This phenomenon is known as omission-commission bias.

Switching to something, like a new job or a new major or a new relationship or a new business strategy, is perceived as a new decision, and an active one. In contrast, we don't really view the choice to stick with the status quo as a decision at all.

You've probably heard people (including yourself), when thinking about taking a new path, say, "I don't want to make a decision right now." You likely accepted that as a reasonable thing to say. But once you step back and think about it, you realize that deciding not to change is itself a decision. At any moment, when you're pursuing a goal, you are choosing to either stay on the path you're on or change course. Sticking with the path is as much of a decision as choosing to quit.

In fact, the decision about *whether* to stay or go is by definition the same choice.

One of the steps to becoming a better quitter is to not accept "I'm not ready to make a decision right now" as a sentence that makes sense. At every moment of your life, you have a choice about whether to stay or whether to go. When you choose to stay, you are also choosing to not go. When you choose to quit, you are also choosing to not continue. It's crucial to start realizing that those are the same, active decisions.

When Sasha Cohen realized traveling from arena to arena skating in ice shows was not the life she wanted, not quitting was as much of a choice as her decision to retire after her last Olympic Games. The same was true for Sarah Olstyn Martinez during her last few years sticking to her job as an ER doctor and director and her eventual decision to quit. Harold Staw and Andrew Wilkinson were making a choice when they continued to subsidize the losses in their businesses.

Had Hutchison, Taske, and Kasischke decided to continue to the summit when they found themselves three hours short of it at 11:30 a.m., that would have been as much of a choice as the decision to turn around. Had Stewart Butterfield chosen to continue pursuing *Glitch*, that would have been as much of a choice as his decision to shut it down.

But omission-commission bias causes us not to view these decisions as equivalent. That's why we accept that explanation of "I'm not ready to make a decision yet" from others and why we accept it from ourselves. Of course, what that really means is "I'm not ready to veer from the status quo."

The next time that you find yourself saying, "I'm just not ready to decide yet," what you should actually say is "For now I think that the status quo is still the best choice." Maybe you need more information to know whether to switch. But what shouldn't stop you from quitting (or getting that information) is that it's too scary to switch because loss aversion is too intense.

Better the Devil You Know

Adding to the ruckus, we prefer what we know to what we don't know, to what is ambiguous and undefined. Whatever you're already doing, whether it's working out or not, you have a lot more certainty about than something that you've never experienced before.

Thus, the aphorism "Better the devil you know than the devil you don't know."

You can see this clearly with Olstyn Martinez. When I asked her whether she was happy in her current position, she easily answered. It was already a known quantity, and she knew she was unhappy. But when I asked whether she would be happy in the new job, she said she didn't know, an expression of uncertainty about what might lie ahead if she switched, because she had never experienced being in that position. That uncertainty contributed to her fear of quitting.

By asking her if she would be happier in the new job more than 0% of the time, that helped her see that there was some certainty in changing jobs. Specifically, she had a better chance of getting to where she wanted to go faster if she switched.

In that moment, she realized the devil that she didn't know was the better choice.

The Price of Sticking

In addition to how this bias against quitting affects our personal lives, all the forces that encourage status quo choices cause organizations to pay a massive price. Professional sports happen to provide many examples of poor quitting behavior in the form of persistence with strategies that are demonstrably failing.

One of the most visible examples is how remarkably slow NBA teams have been to take advantage of the benefit of three-point shots. Many people have documented this, including Michael Mauboussin and Dan Callahan in a September 2021 paper about overcoming barriers to change in sports and business.*

The NBA adopted the three-point shot in 1980. By 1990, the shooting percentages for long-range shots made them a higher expected-value choice than a two-pointer. This despite players of the era rarely practicing three-pointers. Mauboussin and Callahan quoted Larry Bird, who said that other than before the All-Star Game's annual three-point competition, "I can't even remember practicing the shot."

---

*As Mauboussin and Callahan noted in their paper, many of the strategies that teams have been slow to adopt were covered in a March 2020 talk Richard Thaler gave at the MIT Sloan Sports Analytics Conference. Thaler's talk included NBA three-point shots and two-for-one opportunities, bunts and stolen bases in MLB, and NFL fourth-down decisions and draft picks.

Bird won the first three of those competitions in 1986, 1987, and 1988, before missing almost the entire 1988–1989 season due to injury. He was already an all-time great, the best three-point shooter of his generation, one of the best pure shooters ever, and legendary in his dedication to practice. Imagine how much *greater* he could have been had he maximized the value of that shot.

One of the early mistakes teams made was in thinking about the math wrong. Teams were comparing the value of three-point shots versus (all) two-point shots, rather than the value of three-point shots versus two-point shots that are taken just inside the three-point line. The disparity in expected value really grows when you look at the choice that players actually have to make, which is between a perimeter two-pointer or a slightly longer three-point attempt. The answer to that comparison is clear and was clear within a decade of the league's adoption of the rule: Getting three points instead of two (a 50% increase) is worth far more than the few percentage points of difference in accuracy between the two shots.

The math was figured out by the early nineties. But, stunningly, it wasn't until the 2014–2015 season that three-point attempts on a league-wide basis started exceeding two-point attempts.

Here are some of the other well-known and documented failing strategies that pro sports teams were slow to quit: always punting on fourth down in the NFL (instead of going for it); always attempting extra-point kicks after touchdowns (rather than two-point conversions); MLB teams positioning infielders in the traditional spots (rather than shifting); MLB teams bunting and stealing bases as an offensive strategy; NHL teams' reluctance to pull their goalie earlier or when facing smaller deficits.

There are huge rewards in professional sports for innovating (or just following successful innovators). The innovators and rapid adopters have excelled, like the Oakland A's and the Tampa Bay Rays in baseball and the Houston Rockets in basketball, producing consistently winning teams with historically low payrolls. In football, the New England Patriots have built a two-decade dynasty without the benefit of those coveted top draft choices.

The cost of status quo bias is actually much greater in business than in sports. In sports, if you don't innovate or adapt, you may lose games or fans, but your franchise still exists. A sports team will have a chance to catch on and catch up. In the business world, you often aren't afforded that chance because by the time you catch on, you may already have been pushed out. When you look at the graveyard of advertisers from the 2002 Super Bowl, you can see this frequent cause of death. Whether it was Blockbuster or RadioShack, that's part of what happened.

In business as well as in personal decisions, we've seen how all these cognitive effects—loss aversion, sure-loss aversion, the sunk cost effect, endowment, status quo bias, and omission-commission bias—create a heady brew that makes it hard for us to quit on time.

It turns out there is one more ingredient in that cauldron: identity, which we turn our attention to next.

Chapter 7 Summary

- The endowment effect is a cognitive bias where we value something we own more than we would if we didn't own it.
- We can be endowed to objects but also to our own ideas and beliefs.
- Endowment is an obstacle to quitting because when we irrationally value things we own, we miscalculate their expected value. We might think the company we started or the project we devised or the belief we have is worth more than it actually is.
- We prefer to stick with the status quo.
- We are more tolerant of bad outcomes that come from sticking with what we are already doing than bad outcomes that come from switching to something new. This phenomenon is part of omission-commission bias.
- When you say, "I'm just not ready to decide yet," what you are really saying is, "For now, I am choosing the status quo."
- Even in highly data-rich environments like professional sports, sunk cost, endowment, and status quo bias distort decision-making.

The Hardest Thing to Quit Is Who You Are: Identity and Dissonance

THE RISE AND FALL OF SEARS, ROEBUCK AND CO. IS WELL known, from the publication of the first Sears mail-order catalog in 1896 to its bankruptcy in 2018. For the first thirty years of Sears's existence, it sold merchandise only through mail-order catalogs. The birth of the Sears catalog took advantage of developing trends that helped the new company revolutionize retailing.

Two thirds of Americans lived in rural areas, with practically no access to mass-produced goods. The expansion of railroads, along with an 1896 U.S. Postal Service program called Rural Free Delivery, massively expanded mail service. Thanks to the initial *Book of Bargains* (532 pages), people living in small towns and on isolated farms suddenly had the opportunity to buy bicycles, buggies, clothes, furniture, farm equipment, sewing machines, patent medicines, and, it seemed, everything else in the world.

Sears quickly became a phenomenally successful seller of consumer mail-order merchandise. When founder Richard Sears retired in 1908, his fortune was estimated at $25 million.

To help Sears fuel its massive growth, Goldman Sachs underwrote the company's $40-million initial public offering in 1906. Sears was the first American retailing company to go public. Its growth was considered so impressive that its IPO was one of the first to publicize its price-to-earnings ratio. When Goldman Sachs celebrated its 150th anniversary in 2019, it cited the Sears IPO as a historical highlight, also noting its astounding size: "In 2018 dollars, the offering would translate to US$26.2 billion."

Sears continued to grow rapidly over the next decade and a half, until the 1920s presented a number of challenges to its business model: the mobility created by the automobile, greater competition, an agricultural depression, and a demographic shift into cities.

Sears responded by pivoting within its consumer business from catalog sales to retail stores.

By 1929, Sears operated more than three hundred department stores. Sears even thrived during the Depression, nearly doubling its number of retail locations. After World War II, the company continued to grow and expand. Between 1941 and 1954, annual sales tripled to $3 billion. During the next two decades, annual sales tripled again, to $10 billion, as Sears became a staple and anchor tenant in hundreds of shopping malls throughout suburban America.

By the beginning of the 1970s, Sears was the face of American consumer culture. Its annual revenue was approximately 1% of the U.S. GNP. Two out of three Americans were shopping at Sears within any three-month period.

In 1969, Sears announced plans to construct a new headquarters, which would be the world's tallest building. In 1973, it completed the 110-story Sears Tower.

Sears had barely moved into its namesake skyscraper when it confronted challenges to its retail operations more serious than anything it had faced in the previous half century. As was the case in the twenties, demographic changes and improved competition had a lot to do with it.

Sears, which had cultivated and nurtured its image with American consumers since the 1890s, found itself trapped in that image. On the one hand, the spread of low-price retailers (especially Walmart, Kmart, and Target) ate into Sears's image as the thriftiest place to shop. Sears was too top-heavy to compete on price with the new chains and was fighting a losing battle for that business as the chains grew. On the other hand, more affluent consumers became attracted to the upscale image of department stores like Saks Fifth Avenue, Nordstrom, Macy's, and Neiman Marcus.

Ironically, it was the company's expansion into suburban shopping malls that introduced many shoppers to those competitors. In addition, Sears's breadth of offerings had turned from an advantage to a disadvantage. Not only did the malls open the door to competing department stores, but they also offered specialty retailers (such as the Gap and the Limited) a chance to reach a huge consumer market.

Sears found itself in a second losing battle for customers.

Year-to-year merchandising income fell 13% from 1978 to 1979 and fell again by 43% from 1979 to 1980. Between 1978 and 1980, the retail division's return on investment dropped from more than 15% *higher* than the industry median to 31% *lower*. Its return on investment was nearly 40% below Walmart's.

Sears tried addressing its well-known retailing problems in numerous ways, none of which arrested its continued decline. Sears was no longer the most successful retailer and, by the early nineties, had ceased to be the biggest. In February 1991, Walmart and Kmart both passed Sears as the number-one and -two retailers.

The final chapters of Sears's decline are especially well known: outdated, decrepit, or shuttered retail locations; repeated promises to fix or update the stores; the disastrous 2005 merger with Kmart (referred to by at least one publication as "a double suicide"); the evaporation of investment capital; and the long-expected bankruptcy in 2018.

That's the familiar story of the life and death of a once great retailer. But the story that's less well known is the story of Sears, the financial services company. *That* Sears thrived even as the retail company was faltering.

This story starts in 1899, just three years after the first Sears catalog, when they opened a banking department. In 1911, they followed by selling to customers on credit.

In 1931, as car ownership was increasing among their customer base, Sears saw a market opportunity to sell auto insurance to their patrons. They founded Allstate, whose insurance products were initially offered through their catalog and, three years later, at locations inside Sears retail stores. Allstate became a thriving member of the Sears family.

By the 1950s, Allstate expanded its sales locations beyond Sears stores and became a diversified seller of insurance, including auto, personal liability, life, health, commercial, and property.

The seventies were a period of significant growth for the financial services operations. The Sears in-store credit card was more popular than Visa or Mastercard. Nearly 60% of American households had one. Allstate had established itself as one of the nation's largest casualty insurers.

By the late seventies, as Sears tried to address its faltering retail business, it also started aggressively expanding its footprint in the financial services industry.

In October 1981, Sears announced two major acquisitions. First, it bought Coldwell Banker, the nation's largest real estate brokerage firm, for $175 million. Second, it bought Dean Witter, one of the largest securities brokerage firms, for $600 million. In 1985, Sears followed up these acquisitions by creating a new general-use credit card to compete with Visa and Mastercard, the Discover card.

By the beginning of the nineties, Allstate, Dean Witter, Discover, and Coldwell Banker were successful, growing, profitable subsidiaries of Sears. Those assets had a combined market value at that time of more than $16.6 billion. They were, and (excepting Dean Witter) still are, household names that you likely didn't know Sears once owned.

This leads one to wonder, given that Sears owned such enviable brands, how could they possibly have gone bankrupt?

It turns out quitting is the culprit. Or, more specifically, quitting the wrong things.

As the retail stores became a drag on overall financial performance, the institutional investors who owned most of the company's stock pressured management to do something.

Management's response? In September 1992, Sears announced that it was breaking up its financial services empire. It was going to sell those assets and use the money so Sears could "get back to its retailing roots."

Over the next two and a half years, Sears divested itself of all those profitable assets. It sold 20% of Allstate in an IPO raising over $2 billion. It also distributed the remainder of Allstate's value to shareholders in a stock dividend valued at $9 billion. It divested itself of Dean Witter Discover in the same two-part process, raising $900 million in an IPO and distributing the remaining stock (valued at approximately $4.5 billion) as a dividend. Finally, it sold Coldwell Banker outright for $230 million.

Sears, of course, never approached getting out from under its retail problems and went bankrupt. The successful financial services businesses it created, wisely acquired, and skillfully operated went on to thrive.

Allstate's October 2021 stock market valuation was nearly $40 billion. It is the largest publicly held insurer of personal lines, insuring about sixteen million households.

Less than five years after Sears spun off Dean Witter Discover, Morgan Stanley bought the company for $10 billion in stock, representing 40% of the combined entity's value. By October 2021, Morgan

Stanley's stock market valuation was over $180 billion. That valuation does not include the value of Discover, which became a separate public company in 2007 (as Discover Financial Services). Discover's stock market valuation in October 2021 was almost $40 billion.

Coldwell Banker merged with some other real estate companies and went public as Realogy Holdings in 2012. Realogy was involved in 1.4 million home transactions in 2020 and had a stock market valuation in October 2021 in excess of $2 billion.

As a retailer, from the midseventies on, Sears found itself in a losing fight. By the beginning of the nineties, the gap between Sears and competitors on all sides had only grown. As of this same period, Sears was also operating an increasingly successful financial services business.

When Sears had to make the choice of which assets to sell and which to keep, from the perspective of someone on the outside looking in, the choice should have been easy. Whether that outsider was a rational financial professional or one of the corporate raiders Sears feared were circling, the answer would have been to run with the financial services assets and run *from* the losing retail game.

Yet, Sears did the opposite. It escalated its commitment to the retail stores and sacrificed everything else it owned to finance the fight.

Why did this happen?

Part of the problem is the fact that you likely only know (or remember) Sears as a retail company. "Sears" and "retail" are synonymous.

Retail was their identity.

If they had held on to the financial services assets and shuttered or sold the retail company, they would have, in some sense, ceased to be Sears, at least the Sears that everyone knew them as. That's the choice that they faced.

When it comes to quitting, the most painful thing to quit is who you are.

The Cult of Identity

In 1954, Leon Festinger, one of the most famous psychologists of the twentieth century, came across a newspaper story about a doomsday cult.

An interesting feature of a doomsday cult is that the cult predicts an exact date when the doom is going to come, in this case, December 21, 1954. That's the reason why the story caught Festinger's eye, because he wanted to know what would happen to the members of the cult when that date arrived and the world did not end, when they learned clearly and unambiguously that the beliefs that caused them to join the cult and all that comes along with that were incorrect. Would they quit or would they stick with it?

Festinger, along with colleagues Henry Riecken and Stanley Schachter, were among the first psychologists asking these questions, publishing the classic field study about their findings, *When Prophecy Fails*, in 1956.

The story that the researchers read was about a suburban housewife, Marian Keech, who had been receiving messages from space aliens of superior intelligence from a planet named Clarion. According to those messages, a cataclysmic flood would submerge much of the western hemisphere on December 21.

The psychologists contacted Keech and learned she was one of the leaders of the Seekers, whose members believed the world would end on that date and that aliens would be sending a spaceship at midnight on the day of the flood to rescue the true believers.

The followers of this cult made a series of life-altering commitments. They quit their jobs, stopped attending school, and ended friendships and family relationships with skeptics and non-followers. They sold or gave away their possessions.

The psychologists infiltrated the small group of cult members to observe how people in this real-life situation would behave once their beliefs had been disconfirmed. Festinger's team spent as much time as they could with Keech and her followers in the run-up to December 21.

By early evening on December 20, fifteen people had gathered at Marian Keech's house to wait for the spaceship and the end of the world. As midnight approached, everyone sat in the living room, their coats in their laps, the silence broken only by the ticking of a pair of mantel clocks.

When one of the clocks struck midnight and the aliens did not come, there was a moment of confusion, until one of the believers pointed out that the other clock had not yet chimed midnight, so the first clock must have been fast.

A few minutes later, the other clock struck twelve and, still, no aliens arrived. Two of the Seekers were sufficiently convinced by the absence of a midnight ride to Clarion that they didn't wait around for a flood. They went home and did not return, which is the behavior you would expect from a rational person whose beliefs (no matter how wacky) had just been so manifestly disproved.

This left eight true believers and Festinger's observers.

The well-known finding reported in *When Prophecy Fails* was that the other eight members were not willing to quit their belief in the prophecy, even though it was demonstrably false. To the contrary, the members actually escalated their commitment.

Although the Seekers had previously shied away from media attention, they now actively sought it out. As Keech relayed a flurry of new messages from Clarion explaining the situation, making new predictions, and promising additional imminent appearances, the members gave frequent and lengthy interviews and issued news releases about the latest contacts with the aliens. They engaged anyone curious to learn about their group, regardless of the sincerity of their interest or potential motives.

Surprisingly, the two members of the group who had been the most skeptical in the run-up to the prophesied end of the world, Cleo Armstrong and Bob Eastman, became the most zealous after, especially Cleo. Her father, Dr. Thomas Armstrong, a physician in a small college town, had become a leader, along with Keech, of the Seekers. Her mother, Daisy, was also a believer. Bob Eastman considered Dr. Armstrong as his mentor and practically lived with the family by December.

A parade of events in the final days before doomsday left Cleo and Bob doubtful of what they had committed to. They attended and listened to recordings of two seances hosted by a psychic named Ella Lowell. The proceedings devolved into a bumbling series of confusing, inconsistent, and contradictory predictions and messages. Cleo and Bob were also disillusioned by the gullibility of the other Seekers in blindly believing the authenticity of messages supposedly delivered from Clarion that were obvious pranks from local teenagers.

Yet, "in the days following the 21st, their behavior took an astonishing turn. Though it might be most plausible to expect that they would give up their beliefs following disconfirmation, quite the reverse happened."

During the cult's PR offensive on December 22 and throughout the week, Cleo frequently took over for her father and Marian Keech to answer reporters' questions. In contrast to her prior conduct with reporters (avoiding them completely or lying to rid herself of them), she willingly became a voice for the beliefs of the cult.

Five months later, she found herself on the garage ramp of a local hotel waiting all night yet again for the aliens to arrive. Ella Lowell had contacted Dr. Armstrong and told him that his family would be picked up on that date at that location. Cleo, now a college student, failed to get permission from her dormitory for the overnight absence, perhaps because she believed it wouldn't matter once she was on her way to Clarion.

For someone who was wavering in their beliefs in December, before the aliens failed to show, this escalating commitment, to the point of spending all night waiting in a garage for a spaceship, is bizarre.

Being in a cult becomes an integral part of your identity. You are a Seeker. You believe in the prophecy. Membership becomes who you are, particularly because the beliefs you are committing to are so extreme, as are the actions you take based on those beliefs. Cutting off your family and friends. Giving up all your possessions. Exposing yourself to ridicule from the outside world.

We want our identity to be consistent over time. Because our beliefs form the fabric of that identity, we are also motivated to keep our beliefs intact. If the cult is your identity, then how can you maintain consistency if you discover information that conflicts with the beliefs that caused you to join the cult in the first place?

Now, you might scoff at the behavior of the Seekers and say, "These people have nothing to do with me because, obviously, they're nutty. *They joined a cult.* Why would you expect them to be rational?"

But what you need to understand is that we're all in a cult of our own identity.

Why did Sears choose to sell off its profitable assets to save the retail part of its business, which had been faltering for over a decade and a half? Sears was trapped in its identity as a retail company. That's how it defined itself and that's how the world saw the company as well.

If Sears had sold off its retail business, that's the moment it would have ceased to be Sears, at least the Sears that the public knew it as.

There's no doubt that Sasha Cohen's identity was "Sasha Cohen, the figure skater." By the time she was twenty-five, she had devoted eighteen years of her life to skating, persisted through terrible injuries, and was world-famous. That was how she thought of herself and that was how the public viewed her. This is part of what explains why she was willing to suffer, miserable with the grind of performing on the endless circuit of ice shows and exhibitions. Quitting would have meant, in some sense, abandoning who she was.

You don't need to be world famous for these issues of identity to have a deep effect on your ability to cut your losses. This is true for everybody. When you say, "I'm a teacher," or "I'm a coder," or "I'm a doctor," or "I'm a gamer," you're making a statement about who you are.

Adults ask children, "What do you want *to be* when you grow up?" We don't ask, "What job do you want?"

We are asking who they will be, not what they will do. This is a difference with quite a large distinction.

And children get that. "I'm going to be a firefighter," or "I'm going to be a doctor," or "I'm going to be a basketball player."

When your identity is what you do, then what you do becomes hard to abandon, because it means quitting who you are.

Cognitive Dissonance

Festinger posited that cognitive dissonance explained the Seekers' behavior after the aliens failed to show. He theorized that we experience dissonance when new information conflicts with our prior beliefs. When that happens, it makes us uncomfortable, and we want to make that discomfort go away. So we rationalize away the new information so we can defend our prior beliefs.

Elliot Aronson, one of Festinger's early students and himself a pioneer in social psychology, explained that in resolving such conflicts, "we frequently get ourselves into a tangled muddle of self-justification, denial, and distortion."

We have the intuition that when the world tells us our beliefs need updating, when new information conflicts with a belief we have, we will resolve that conflict by changing our belief. But all too often, like the cult members, we rationalize away the new information so we can defend our prior belief and stick to it.

That way, we don't have to admit that we made a mistake or that something we believed wasn't true.

"I *didn't* abandon my family and give away all my worldly goods for no good reason."

Here's a simple example. You put a political sign in your yard for a particular candidate because you support them. Their policies align with your values. You volunteer at their campaign office. You canvass for them. You put campaign bumper stickers on your car. Then, information comes out that the candidate was involved in a horrible scandal. The scandal is sufficiently bad that if you had heard this at the beginning of the election cycle, before you had made your choice, you would not have supported them in the first place.

But you've already publicly asserted your support of the candidate. Your neighbors know you support them. So does anybody who has visited your house or driven by and seen the sign on your front lawn.

What do you do now? Dissonance theory predicts that you won't yank all those signs out of your yard or peel the sticker off your car. Instead, you'll continue your support, even escalating your commitment, by rationalizing away the new information. The other party is trying to smear your candidate. The establishment is trying to bring them down. One of the things that you love about them is that they thumb their nose at the establishment.

It's not just new information that can create a conflict with your past beliefs. Sometimes your own actions can cause dissonance.

Imagine that you believe yourself to be a truthful person and one day you're late to work because you're hung over and you slept through your alarm. When your boss asks you why you didn't get in on time, you say that traffic was really bad.

That action of lying conflicts with your belief about yourself as a truthful person. That creates dissonance. So do you suddenly start thinking of yourself as someone who lies? No. You rationalize away the untruth that you told your boss.

"It didn't hurt anybody. I don't do this on the regular. This was an exception to the rule."

Whether it is your own actions or new and disconfirming information, when it comes to a battle between the facts and changing your beliefs, the facts too often lose out.

Like the other forces we've explored, cognitive dissonance adds debris to the katamari, making it harder to quit. Every time you rationalize away new information in order to cling to a belief, that belief becomes more tightly woven into the fabric of your identity. The act of rejecting the facts becomes circular. Now the next time you discover conflicting information or your actions don't align with your beliefs, you're going to be even more motivated to stick to those beliefs.

This explains why some of the Seekers could have rejected such clear signals that Marian Keech did *not* have a direct line to superintelligent beings from another planet. Forced to square the failure of the aliens to show or the flood to arrive with their decision to cut off their families and friends and get rid of their worldly goods, they rationalized away the absence of the doom.

Their devotion may have staved off the end of the world. This was all a test and the Seekers passed it. There was no spaceship because the aliens were *already* on Earth, about to reveal themselves.

That's how they resolved the conflict, just as we all do.

The Mirror and the Window

When it comes to identity, we all want to maintain a positive self-narrative. We want to think well of ourselves. We want to believe that we're consistent and rational, that we don't make mistakes, that the things we believe about the world are true.

When we look in the mirror, we want to see someone we can think well of.

We also want others looking in on us to view us the same way. We worry that if others see inconsistency between our present and past decisions or actions, they will judge us as being wrong, irrational, capricious, and prone to mistakes.

The desire to maintain a positive self-image contributes to the problem with quitting. When you quit, you're closing a mental account, and we know that we don't like to close those accounts in the losses.

If you abandon a belief, that is the moment you admit you were mistaken. If you set out on a course of action and change your mind, that's when you go from "failing" to "having failed." And if you have failed, doesn't that mean you made a mistake to start in the first place?

Of course, the answer is no. But that's not how it feels to us.

If you're in a cult and you quit, why did you join in the first place? Why did you give away all your money? Why did you cut off your family?

If you quit figure skating, what does that mean for all of that time you put into that effort? Does that mean all those decisions were wrong? Does that mean you've failed in your goal?

This desire to maintain internal consistency, as we've already seen, stops us from quitting. As does the worry that other people are going to judge us as harshly as we judge ourselves.

Barry Staw demonstrated how much harder it is to quit when we're worried about being judged by others. Recall that in "Big Muddy," participants who committed funds to one of two divisions of a company and then learned that it subsequently performed poorly escalated their financial commitment to that same division in comparison to people who came to that decision fresh. While those coming fresh to the $20-million allocation gave $9 million to the money-losing division that previously received additional funding, those who made that previous decision gave it $13 million under otherwise identical facts.

This escalation seems to be clearly influenced by a desire to maintain internal consistency. If I allocated the money to that division in the first place and then I change course, wouldn't that mean that the original choice was a mistake?

Does this escalation of commitment get worse when you add in the motivation to be viewed by others in a positive light?

In 1979, with Frederick Fox of the University of Illinois, Staw explored just that question, asking if the desire for *external* validation further increases funding to the division they favored in the earlier decision.

To answer that question, some participants were told that their position as a financial officer with the company was only on an interim basis. Their $20-million allocation might make or break whether or not they held on to that job. They were also told, after they had made the first funding decision, that the board of directors had been skeptical of the decision and reluctant to approve it.

That group of participants further increased their commitment, now allocating *$16 million* to the division they chose earlier. That's a huge adverse effect, nearly a 25% increase over those who made the previous allocation to that division and about a 75% increase over people fresh to the choice.

Why is there such an amplification of this irrational behavior when participants are told that other people will be evaluating their decision?

We are all trying to defend ourselves against *how we imagine* other people are going to judge us. We get it in our heads that if we don't stick to our original choice, that will reflect negatively on us.

The irony is that this desire to be viewed as rational causes us to become less rational in the decisions we make.

When a person knows they're going to be evaluated, it's reasonable for them to expect that their decisions will be judged against the standard of what a rational person would decide in their situation.

You might think that would move your decisions to a more accurate place, but the opposite is true. Thinking about how you will be judged if you quit makes you move further from that benchmark of rationality.

You end up quitting less and committing more.

Out on a Limb

It turns out that the popularity of your belief is inversely correlated with your determination to fight for it no matter what. As Katy Milkman, a professor at the Wharton School and author of the 2021 bestseller *How to Change*, along with John Beshears, now of the Harvard Business School, have demonstrated, when you stake out a position that is out of the mainstream, you are more likely to escalate your commitment in the face of disconfirming information.

These researchers weren't studying anything as wacky as a doomsday cult. Instead, they looked at eighteen years of corporate earnings estimates and updates of more than six thousand stock analysts.

An important part of a stock analyst's job is making and updating estimates of corporate earnings. When we think about financial analysts, we think about a profession that is very rational and very analytical. The word "analyst" is right there in the name of the job.

Milkman and Beshears wanted to find out what happened to analysts who made earnings estimates that were way out of the consensus when those estimates later turned out to be far off actual earnings.

Would the analysts stubbornly stick to their original forecast, or would they revise the projections based on the new information?

Not surprisingly to a reader of this book, there was a lot of stubbornly sticking. The analysts escalated their commitment to their extreme position, despite the information that actual results were not bearing out the forecast.

This seems like cognitive dissonance and identity at play. They made a projection that was non-consensus. They did it in a public way. When the actual earnings conflicted with their prediction, they doubled down, just like the cult members did when the aliens didn't show up.

Stock analysts don't have a financial incentive for sticking to inaccurate estimates. In fact, it's quite the opposite. The authors found that analysts don't benefit from the attention of being a contrarian or a lone wolf. Rather, the analysts were *punished* for their stubbornness when they made incorrect earnings forecasts.

If they were punished for maintaining those forecasts, why would they do it?

The need to maintain consistency is strong, and appears to be even stronger once you've veered from the status quo. When you take these extreme positions, you're increasing the distance between yourself and the pack. That distance makes your position more integral to your identity, a part of the way that you define yourself as compared with other people.

To underscore this point, Milkman and Beshears looked at how analysts reacted to updated earnings information, depending on whether their estimates were out of consensus or in the mainstream. If extreme positions become more integral to who we are, we ought to see less escalation of commitment from those with consensus positions.

That's exactly what they found.

Analysts who made consensus forecasts that later turned out to be far off actual earnings seemed perfectly willing to update those forecasts. It was only the analysts who had made extreme predictions who were so stubborn.

This was one of the problems Andrew Wilkinson had in cutting his losses on Flow. He took an out-of-consensus, very public position about the superiority of bootstrapping to venture backing. That led to him turning down the flood of venture capital offers coming in. He later admitted the importance he attached to that position and those statements. "I glorified that, and that was my identity. I really valued that." As his venture-backed competitors started to outpace him, it likely influenced his continued commitment, long after the world showed him that his investments did not have a positive expected value.

The lesson in all this is that we need to be careful about tying our identity to any single thing that we believe. And we need to be particularly cautious when a belief is outside the mainstream and public because it is so much harder to let go of those beliefs, facts be damned.

Mistaken Identity

The tragedy of all this is that the way we imagine other people view us is often wrong. That means that some of the irrational decisions we make about quitting are based on a mistaken fear of how we're going to look to other people.

Those imaginings, frankly, are often unkind and ungenerous to those around us because we assume that if we quit, even if it's obviously the right thing to do, other people are going to think that we failed. That we're capricious or weak. In these scenarios, we don't believe there's going to be any empathy or understanding of why we might have made the choice that we did.

But that harsh view of others is usually unjustified. It turns out that when we do quit, other people often don't think that way at all. Those worries we've projected onto others are just head trash we're carrying around.

That's what happened with Sarah Olstyn Martinez. "I was worried my fellow ER doctors would think I was a wimp, a sellout who couldn't hack it. I was worried about how my supervisors were going to view me." She dreaded giving her boss notice, because she assumed he would be angry or upset.

When Olstyn Martinez finally did give her notice, her boss was actually very understanding. By the end of the talk, he apologized for failing her, for not making the job less stressful so that she could have persevered. Her operations director said the same thing, which was very validating to hear.

We may quickly outgrow the made-up childhood tales of frightening ogres, dragons, and witches. The scary stories that replace them, about the judgments of others, continue to torment us as adults but are no more real.

A Ray of Hope

For all the stories of those unable to quit, whether due to identity, sunk cost, status quo bias, or any of the forces that gaff the scale, you are not doomed to succumb. We know that Stewart Butterfield, Sarah Olstyn Martinez, and Alex Honnold are just three of the examples that offer us hope.

For businesses, like Sears or Blockbuster or ABC Stores, we can see identity's hand in the death of an enterprise. But, again, not every business is destined for that fate. There are notable examples of companies that turned away from the core businesses that were synonymous with their identities, and built enduring success by doing so.

As strongly as Sears was identified in the public mind as a retailer, Philips was known as the company that sold light bulbs. That was their identity. After all, for many of us growing up, when you had to change a light bulb, the name "Philips" was right there on the carton. The bulb itself had "Philips" printed on it.

Both Sears and Philips were founded in the 1890s. In 2012, decades after Sears started its death spiral, Philips was the world's largest manufacturer of lighting products, selling in 180 countries. Since the 1960s, Philips has also been famous for its consumer electronics, having invented cassettes, CDs, VCRs, and DVDs.

Not only were they endowed to those products, having developed the technology, but again, their name was right there on them.

Despite all that potential for the company's identity to cause resistance to change, as of 2020 Philips no longer sold *any* lighting products. Its three business segments, comprising 98% of sales, are Diagnosis & Treatment, Connected Care, and Personal Health.

Philips is now a healthcare company with nearly €20 billion in annual sales.

Like Sears with financial services, Philips began developing its healthcare operations early, in connection with its better-known lighting business.

In 1914, the Philips brothers started what would now be called an innovation hub, a lab to create new products. In 1919, Philips began producing X-ray tubes. Since then, it has continued to invest heavily in research and expand into the healthcare space. By 2014, nearly a century after they started producing X-ray tubes, health technology represented 40% of their business.

Just as the vast majority of the public had no idea that Sears owned Allstate or any of its other financial services assets, the same was true for Philips and its healthcare technologies. If you asked a person on the street a decade ago, "What does Philips produce?" they would have said, "They make light bulbs and televisions."

While Sears sold off its profitable assets to escalate its commitment to its core identity, retail, Philips did the opposite, announcing in 2014 it was selling off its core lighting business to focus on its healthcare operations. In 2016, the company divested itself of 25% of Philips lighting through an IPO. It also announced it was going to sell off the remaining 75%, which it did by the end of 2019.

Unlike Sears, Philips split into two companies and stuck with the part that was lesser known but offered greater expected value going forward.

We know what the cognitive and identity-driven traps are when it comes to quitting. Somehow, these remarkable individuals and companies have managed to overcome those obstacles. We can, with an understanding of the science involved, learn from these examples and craft a model to be better at quitting ourselves.

Be picky about what you stick to.

Persevere in the things that matter, that bring you happiness, and that move you toward your goals.

Quit everything else, to free up those resources so you can pursue your goals and stop sticking to things that slow you down.

We have already explored some strategies for achieving this: identify the hard part and tackle that first to avoid false progress; think about the conditions under which you would quit well in advance of having to face that decision down; create precommitment contracts and kill criteria.

We now turn our attention to another strategy: Get outside help.

Chapter 8 Summary

- When it comes to quitting, the most painful thing to quit is who you are. Our ideas, beliefs, and actions are part of our identity.
- When new information conflicts with a belief, we experience cognitive dissonance.
- To resolve the conflict, we can either change the belief or rationalize away the new information. Too often, we choose the latter.
- Dissonance can also result from new information coming into conflict with our past actions.
- We have a desire to maintain internal consistency, where our past beliefs and actions line up with our present beliefs and actions.
- We also want others to view us as consistent. We worry that if others see inconsistency between our present and past decisions, beliefs, or actions, they will judge us as being wrong, irrational, capricious, and prone to mistakes.
- When we know or believe our decisions are being evaluated by others, our intuition is that we will be more rational, but the opposite is true. External validity *increases* escalation of commitment.
- The more extreme a position is, the more cognitive gymnastics we'll do to defend it. The facts are more likely to persuade you away from the consensus opinion than a fringe view.
- Fears about how others will view us if we quit are usually overblown.

CHAPTER 9

Find Someone Who Loves You but Doesn't Care about Hurt Feelings

RON CONWAY IS BEST KNOWN AS ONE OF THE GREATEST angel investors of all time. But he ought to be equally well known for his skill as a quitting coach.

Conway, the founder of SV Angel, an early-stage venture fund, has been investing in start-ups since the nineties and is a legend in the venture-capital community. His list of successful angel investments may be unmatched, including many of the most famous companies of the last twenty-five years, including Facebook, Google, PayPal, Dropbox, Airbnb, Pinterest, Twitter, and Snapchat.

Conway is obviously great at picking winners.

Starting a new venture requires grit. Conway is known for his ability to help founders navigate the challenging ups and downs of growing what begins as nothing more than a vision into a successful, world-changing company.

You are likely not surprised that someone of Ron Conway's stature provides enormous value by helping these founders to develop the right strategic vision, stick to it, and make it work. But you might be surprised that he is especially proud of his ability in helping founders figure out when it's the right time to quit.

He sums up his philosophy in three words: Life's too short.

What Conway recognizes is that we all have a limited time on this planet to devote to different opportunities we might pursue. Founding, running, and growing a start-up is already brutally hard work. In his experience, founders tend to be driven, gritty, and brilliant individuals. People with these qualities are in great demand at established companies, for jobs with comfortable hours and great pay. But founders have all chosen a different path, and what comes with that path is hundred-hour workweeks, unrelenting stress, and practically no pay. Famously, some founders have gotten most of their sleep—which isn't much—in their parents' garage or on the floor of their office.

Obviously, the chance to change the world and the outsized rewards that come with succeeding can make it worthwhile for them to persevere. But in Conway's thinking, life's too short to take on all that suffering once it's clear that the probability is too high that those things are out of reach.

Even for someone with Conway's nose for value, only about 10% of the start-ups he invests in will make money. That means, by definition, that 90% of these ventures will fail. Doing anything *but* encouraging someone with so much promise to move on would be cruel, a sad waste of human potential.

That's what Conway means when he says, "Life's too short."

Of course, it's almost never the case that the founders can recognize for themselves the moment when their journey is no longer worth continuing, because they're on the inside looking out. Conway, as a knowledgeable outsider with a wealth of experience, can see it before they can see it for themselves. He considers it his duty to help these founders understand the futility of persevering, so these brilliant people can move on to more worthwhile opportunities.

The first obstacle Conway faces is the most obvious one: getting founders to actually recognize that the venture is failing and that it's time for them to walk away. Conway is battling the host of cognitive and motivational forces that make it hard for these entrepreneurs to do that. They're the founders of the company. They own it. It's their idea. It's part of their identity. They put a tremendous amount of time and effort and money into it. They've sacrificed so much.

What would it mean if they quit now? Would it mean it was a mistake to start? That they wasted their time? Wouldn't they be quitting who they are?

Nevertheless, when he recognizes that things aren't going well, he'll sit down and share his point of view with the founder. Inevitably, they disagree, adamant that success is right around the corner. These entrepreneurs are usually skilled at selling their vision, and they use every bit of that skill to try to persuade him.

"This is just a rough patch." "We just need to finish the next version of the build." "It's just going to take time for the product to catch on." "I know exactly what to do to turn things around."

What does Conway do to counter these vehement arguments? Nothing.

He agrees with them that they can make it work. He doesn't try to convince the founders that they're wrong.

Instead, he asks them what success would look like over the next few months. And he asks them for *specifics*. That conversation allows him to sit down with the founder and set performance benchmarks that would signal that the company was heading in the right direction. Then, they agree when to revisit those benchmarks and, if the venture is falling short, to have a serious discussion about shutting it down.

This probably sounds a lot like Conway is using kill criteria, and that's because he is.

The founder comes away from the conversation believing they've convinced Conway they can turn it around. Conway's opinion, you've probably guessed, hasn't changed. He comes away still believing that if the founder could see what he sees, they would shut the endeavor down that day. But he knows it's generally futile to try to persuade them right then.

Having set these kill criteria, which the founder has helped generate, Conway has markedly increased the probability that, when they revisit the issue, the founder will be able to see past their own biases and come to the right decision.

The deftness of Conway's approach is that he's able to take founders who are facing down the decision, who are less rational because they're in it, and refocus their attention on some point in the future. That refocus allows the founder to be more rational about the choice.

What comes with this quitting strategy is that the founder is going to continue to put a few more months of time, money, and effort into something that Conway can clearly see is failing. But he considers those extra months spent as a huge win, because it gets the founder to shut the endeavor down much sooner than they otherwise would have.

Without this type of intervention, founders, who are gritty by nature, all too often continue to grind it out until the bitter end. Giving up a few months to save years is a trade worth making, because it frees up the founders much sooner to move on to something that has a better chance of succeeding.

Even so, after the company has missed the benchmarks, Conway often gets pushback. That's not surprising because none of these things work perfectly. These tools are just trying to get us to no faster and more often than we otherwise would.

One of the most common ways that the founders push back is by claiming that they have a duty to the investors to give it everything they have. Beyond that duty, they believe that if they don't keep going, instead returning the remaining capital, their backers will think less of them, view them as a failure, and never want to invest in anything they do in the future.

Just like the rest of us, founders are often irrational in their imaginings of what others will think or how they'll react, and Conway is right there to help them see that they've got it wrong. Because he's an investor himself, he's uniquely positioned to offer these founders a more accurate perspective of the people they're imputing these things to.

In this instance, in practically every way, investors think the *opposite* of what the founders assume.

There is no honor in spending every last bit of investor money pursuing an endeavor that's failing. Returning capital to investors is the responsible choice under those circumstances and demonstrates the ability to make the hard decision when it's the right thing to do. It shows an understanding of expected value and the ability to respond to new information and changing circumstances with flexibility rather than rigidity.

Those are all traits of someone they would *want* to invest in again.

Conway points out that, contrary to the founders' beliefs, returning capital *increases* the chances that those investors will want to work with them again. He even offers examples of when he has done this in his own investing career.

It's not just a feeling of obligation to investors that makes it hard for founders to cut their losses. They also think they owe it to their employees to keep going. If they shut the company down, those people will be out of work. They've worked closely with the founder, putting their heart and soul into it, giving up so much in their lives to help make it work. Even Stewart Butterfield, who was steadfast in the decision to shut *Glitch* down, echoed this concern.

Doesn't the founder owe it to their employees to persevere?

Conway, again, points out that life's too short, and that applies to the employees' lives as well.

Joining a start-up means working for little pay in exchange for the promise of equity. These talented individuals are willing to make that trade because they believe they are building something world-changing and, if successful, they will reap the benefits of doing so. Once it's clear that's not going to happen, continuing on is just trapping them in an endeavor that's going to fail. It's stopping them from being able to move on to something better.

Just as Conway doesn't want to see the founders trapped in something that's failing, the founders shouldn't want that for their employees.

In an ideal world, we would be as rational about our quitting decisions as someone who is fresh to the choice. But we know that we can't do that. Once you have a history with a choice, with all the accumulated debris that goes along with that, you will be subject to the forces that make it hard to walk away.

Essentially, what Ron Conway is doing is offering the fresh perspective to his founders that all of us have trouble seeing when we're in it. That perspective, and his deft use of kill criteria, are what make him a legendary quitting coach.

(Over) Optimism

Helen Keller said, "Optimism is the faith that leads to achievement."

This belief that optimism will get you to where you want to go faster is deeply embedded in popular culture, as evidenced by a host of perennial bestsellers, such as Norman Vincent Peale's *The Power of Positive Thinking*, Napoleon Hill's *Think and Grow Rich*, and *The Secret*, to name just a few. Combined, these three titles alone have sold over seventy-four million copies. And let's not forget the classic children's book *The Little Engine That Could*, with its message of "I think I can."

The mandate, soaked up by a massive audience, is unchanged. Just believe in yourself and your chances of success will increase.

Even William James, the father of modern psychology, said, "Pessimism leads to weakness, optimism to power." James believed in the power of positive visualization, which he described with an example involving, of all things, mountaineering. He asserted that if you're climbing a mountain and get stuck in a spot where you need to take a "bold dangerous leap," you should imagine that you can do it, that confidence will help you succeed. But if you waver through self-doubt, you'll leap in despair and fall into a crevasse.

Don Moore, a professor at the Haas School of Business at University of California, Berkeley, has called out the absurdity of James's example. In his 2020 book, *Perfectly Confident*, Moore makes the point that even if optimism helps you in that situation, there must be limits to *how much* it helps. Let's say that sufficiently energetic optimism could help you leap a six-foot crevasse. If it's a twenty-foot leap, there's no way you're better off with optimism than with a realistic calibration of your confidence.

And Moore literally has the scars to prove it. He humbly admits, "Believing in myself did not prevent my feet from getting burned on [a] fire walk."

Moore, along with colleagues Elizabeth Tenney of the University of Utah and Jennifer Logg of Georgetown University, has explored whether people actually believe that more optimism will lead to better performance. Their 2015 paper examines performance on a variety of tasks, ranging from math problems to *Where's Waldo?* puzzles.

The researchers led some participants to be optimistic about their likely performance. When others were asked to guess at how well those participants would do as compared with ones who were not so optimistic, Moore and his colleagues found that people do, indeed, believe in *The Little Engine That Could*. The people who think they can get up the hill or finish more math problems or find Waldo were rated as more likely to actually do it.

This unfettered belief in the power of optimism is, of course, widespread in Silicon Valley, which makes Ron Conway a contrarian in a world where being overly optimistic is not only considered a job requirement for founders but is also actively encouraged. And that ethos is reflected in founders' actual beliefs. A survey of three thousand entrepreneurs found that 81% of founders put their odds of success at 70% or better and a third of founders put their odds of success at 100%!

Given that only about one in ten of the ambitious ventures Conway invests in generates a positive return, that optimism borders on the delusional.

Of course, if optimism actually improves performance, delusional confidence might be worth it. If you are in a business where you only have a 10% chance of success, maybe being optimistic improves your chances to 40%. Even if that is far short of the 70% shot you think you have, that boost might be worth the cost of being poorly calibrated.

Moore and his colleagues tested just this idea, looking to see if the more-optimistic participants had better performance on the math problems or found Waldo more often. While they did find that more-optimistic people stuck to the tasks longer, the optimists failed to perform measurably better on these tasks than the people who were less optimistic.

In other words, they quit later, but to no benefit.

What is true for grit is true for optimism. Optimism gets you to stick to things that are worthwhile. But optimism also gets you to stick to things that are no longer worthwhile. And life's too short to do that.

The problem is that optimism causes you to overestimate both the likelihood and magnitude of success. That means that any calculation of your expected value will be wildly out of whack.

The result? Optimism unchecked by realism prevents you from quitting when you ought to walk away.

Ron Conway, of course, expects and wants confident founders. He wants them to be positive about themselves and their employees, but not to the point of sticking to something that is a dead end.

It's hard for these driven entrepreneurs to flip a switch between optimism and realism. They need the help and perspective of a good quitting coach. Even then, that quitting coach needs patience because if there is such a switch, the founders are the ones who have to flip it.

The Difference between Being Nice and Being Kind

When I asked Daniel Kahneman what he thinks the secret is to being a good quitter, he told me, "What everybody needs is the friend who really loves them but does not care much about hurt feelings in the moment."

When you are in it, facing down the decision about whether to walk away or stay the course, that is when your decision-making is the most vulnerable to the host of cognitive biases that make it hard for you to quit. Kahneman's insight is that an outside observer, like a friend or a loved one, is much more likely to have a rational view on your situation, because they are not in it with you.

The problem is that when you are the outside observer and you can see that somebody is on a losing path, you are likely to think that withholding the hard truth is the nice thing to do, because you know it will hurt them to hear it. But in sparing their feelings, in trying to be nice, you're denying them the opportunity to see what you see.

The reason you're trying to spare their feelings is *because* you love them. But you're only sparing their feelings in the short run. They are hurtling toward a future where they fail, and that will hurt them much more.

We all need someone who loves us but who also understands that it's better for our long-term happiness to speak out loud the unpleasant truth when the path we are on is one we need to abandon.

That's the point of what Daniel Kahneman said.

When you find that friend, ask them to be your quitting coach, to be that person who helps you figure out when to abandon course.

If Daniel Kahneman, whose life's work has been studying cognitive biases and decision errors, needs a quitting coach, then everybody needs one. Kahneman's happens to be fellow Nobel laureate Richard Thaler.

Most of us aren't lucky enough to have somebody of that stature play that role for us, but we should all try to find someone to be that person in our life who tells us the truth, whether it's a close friend, a mentor, a coworker, a sibling, or a parent.

They just have to be someone who has our long-term best interests at heart and is willing to tell us what we need to hear, not what we want to hear.

Of course, almost all of us have experienced the opposite, where someone spared our feelings rather than helping us see the situation for what it was. You break up with someone and, all of a sudden, your close friends tell you, "I thought you should have ditched them months ago." Or you quit your job and people in your family say, "I could tell you were miserable. It sure took you a long time to figure that out."

Of course, when they tell us those things, we all have the same reaction: "If you knew that all along, why didn't you say so earlier?"

And the answer is always the same: "I didn't want to hurt your feelings."

You can get over hearing that you should quit something. But if you spend months or years in a job or a relationship that's not contributing to your long-term happiness, that's time you can never get back.

Andrew Wilkinson experienced this himself after he had to fire the CEO of one of his businesses. Several of his friends told him they could see for a while that it was necessary. When he asked, "Then why didn't you tell me?" they said, "We didn't want to upset you."

That was aggravating to hear as Wilkinson immediately realized that if his friends had been honest about what they saw, he would have gotten to the decision earlier, saving him valuable time and resources.

That's why Ron Conway is so proud of the role that he plays for his founders, and why he considers it such a big win when he can offer that fresh perspective to get them to quit.

When it comes to business endeavors, career choices, or decisions about your personal life, we should all be striving for two things: First, you should find at least one person to be your quitting coach. Second, you should try to serve in that role for the people you love.

Some Coaches Can Pull the Plug

While a quitting coach can help by offering you a fresh perspective, uncontaminated by your growing katamari, you're ultimately still the one who has to choose to walk away, and that means you can ignore the advice of your quitting coach. Having a coach improves the chances that you're going to get to quitting sooner than you otherwise would without one. But, just like Conway's founders, a lot of times you're going to rebuff the attempt.

Of course, sometimes there are situations where the person who's the quitting coach actually has the authority to make the quitting decision. For example, managers can force people to shut down projects or sales leaders can force sellers to stop pursuing leads.

The combination of kill criteria and a quitting coach who has the power to step in to force the quitting is the most efficient and effective way to get people to cut their losses, especially if those people are particularly gritty.

Navy SEALs, by the simple fact that they made it through SEAL training, are legendary for their grittiness. We all remember the classic scenes in movies of grueling training where recruits have to prove they can endure conditions that would make most people give up. There's that famous brass bell, which the trainees can ring to end the punishment of submersion for hours in freezing water, days without sleep, and constant physical trials. The ones that become SEALs are the ones who refuse to ring the bell. They are literally selected because the Navy found it impossible to make them quit.

Admiral McRaven knows that part of his job is reining in people who, on their own, would literally die rather than give up. As he put it, "You want them to be that guy that charges the machine gun nest and saves people and wins the Medal of Honor. You need those kids, but you also need commanders that can say there's a time and place for that, and it's not on every mission."

Of course, McRaven's advantage was that, as commander, when a mission butted up against kill criteria, he was the one who was responsible for deciding to quit. He could abort on his own authority, regardless of whether the Navy SEALs wanted to continue (which was probably always).

Ron Conway would love to be in McRaven's position, a quitting coach who can take over the reins. Instead, when he sees the start-up is failing and knows it's right to shut it down, he has to let the founder keep going until they agree to quit because that's the founder's decision, not Conway's.

We've all been in that frustrating situation where we've had to watch somebody keep going when we know they should turn around. Wouldn't it be so much better if you could just take over and make the decision for them, especially since the person who's least equipped to make a rational decision about quitting is the person facing down that choice?

We've all felt that frustration, but make no mistake, we've all also been on the other end of that equation. It's *our* decision whether to quit, and *we're* the ones least equipped to make a rational choice.

If you've ever wanted to take over the reins from someone else, that must mean that sometimes you would be better off handing the reins over to a quitting coach.

Divide and Conquer

We can turn back to Barry Staw to see how powerful handing off the reins to somebody else is as a quitting strategy. In 1997, along with Sigal Barsade of Yale University and Kenneth Koput of the University of Arizona, Staw studied decisions by banks about approving and servicing business loans. When a bank issues a loan, there are people at the bank responsible for making and approving that decision. If the borrower makes timely payments and eventually pays off the loan, there are no further decisions to be made about it.

But when a business has trouble making its payments, the borrower might ask for another loan in an attempt to save their business or they might also ask to renegotiate the terms of the contract. In addition to determining whether to approve those things, the bank has to decide, because it is legally required to provide accurate financial reports to shareholders and regulators, whether to keep counting that loan as an asset or write it off and realize the loss.

For all of these decisions, you can see the potential for escalation of commitment. Given what we know so far, you might surmise that when a loan is in trouble, the people who made the original lending decision, to avoid having to recognize the initial loan as a loss, would be more likely to approve a second loan or a change in terms than someone who is fresh to the decision.

That's exactly what Staw and his colleagues found when they looked at nine years of loans at 132 California banks. When there was management turnover, new management was much quicker to acknowledge when a loan was in trouble. Having not made the initial decision to approve the loan, they were much more likely to write it off as a loss.

I suppose one lesson from Staw's data is that if you have a business that's gotten a loan and you're now in financial trouble, you should go back to the same person who originally lent you the money. You're much more likely to get it.

On a more serious note, this suggests a good strategy for businesses that want to get better at their quitting decisions: *When possible, divide and conquer.* Have the people who make the decisions to start things be different from the people who make the decisions to stop those things.

For clients of mine who are institutional investors, I have suggested that type of strategy as a way to improve their sell-side decisions. Have the committee approving what to buy be different from the committee approving what and when to sell. Of course, that's only practical when the team is large enough.

In many business situations, there are ways to divide the labor. But if you're an individual, you can't split yourself in two. You can't do the Jedi mind trick of pretending to be a separate person, coming to the decision fresh.

That's yet another reason to try to find yourself a quitting coach, because it allows you to implement something closer to this divide-and-conquer strategy.

The Importance of Giving
and Getting Permission

For your relationship with your quitting coach to work, you have to give them permission to act in that role. That includes explicitly committing to being open to hearing the hard truths that they may have to tell you. That's why Richard Thaler is an effective quitting coach for Daniel Kahneman, because Kahneman has given Thaler permission to tell him the things that he doesn't want to hear.

When you ask for advice without such an agreement, the person you're asking will tend to err on the side of being nice, nice in the sense of cheerleading and telling you what they think you want to hear. Even if you are really ready to hear the hard truth, if you don't communicate that to the person you're seeking counsel from, they will usually assume you just want reassurance. And that's all you'll get.

When you're on the other side of the equation, acting as the counselor, you also need to understand that when somebody asks for your advice, this doesn't necessarily mean that they actually want to hear your honest opinion. Not unless they've explicitly given you permission to do so.

Andrew Wilkinson told me how he learned this from experience. After having to fire that CEO and finding out that none of his friends had told him what they could clearly see from the outside looking in, he resolved to give his unvarnished opinion whenever someone came to him for advice.

They ask him for advice. He gives them brutal honesty. And nothing good comes of it. He doesn't change their mind. In fact, he finds that they'll double down and become adamant about proving him wrong. In other words, typical escalation of commitment.

When people ask for advice, don't confuse that with being given permission.

Instead, when someone comes to you, it's better to use Ron Conway's approach, which can be summarized in these four steps.

STEP 1 | Let them know that you think they should consider quitting.

STEP 2 | When they push back, retreat and agree with them that they can turn the situation around.

STEP 3 | Set very clear definitions around what success is going to look like in the near future and memorialize them down as kill criteria.

STEP 4 | Agree to revisit the conversation and, if the benchmarks for success haven't been met, you'll have a serious discussion about quitting.

Implicit in steps 3 and 4 is that the person you're counseling has now given you permission to speak freely and bluntly about abandoning course.

Of course, all the while, you should remind them that life's too short.

Permission on both sides of the equation is key to a fruitful relationship between a coach and the person seeking the coaching. Even when someone seeking that advice gives permission, it's still better when you can help them get to the decision for themselves, as opposed to telling them what to do.

When Sarah Olstyn Martinez reached out to me, she gave me permission to have an honest conversation. Even so, I didn't tell her what decision she should make. I just asked her questions that helped her by framing her choice as an expected-value problem. That allowed her to see it for herself quite quickly.

If you're in a leadership position, Astro Teller provides an outstanding example of how to be a great quitting coach. He helps the people at X be better at shutting things down by tackling monkeys, avoiding pedestals, and setting kill criteria that increase the chances that they'll get to a rational decision faster. This is all part of his creating a culture that doesn't just destigmatize quitting but celebrates it.

Quitting is hard, too hard to do entirely on our own. We as individuals are riddled by the host of biases, like the sunk cost fallacy, endowment effect, status quo bias, and loss aversion, which lead to escalation of commitment. Our identities are entwined in the things that we're doing. Our instinct is to want to protect that identity, making us stick to things even more.

If there's one thing that you've learned from this book, it's that just knowing about the problem, doing a thought experiment of taking somebody else's perspective and trying to see it from the outside, looking in on yourself, is something you cannot do. That's why Daniel Kahneman thinks he needs a quitting coach, and why we all ought to see that need.

Life is just too short to be spending our time on things that aren't worthwhile. We all need people around us who will tell us when we're on the wrong path.

Chapter 9 Summary

- Optimism makes you less likely to walk away while not actually increasing your chances of success. That means that being overly optimistic will make you stick to things longer that aren't worthwhile. Better to be well calibrated.
- Life's too short to spend your time on opportunities that are no longer worthwhile.
- When someone is on the outside looking in, they can usually see your situation more rationally than you can.
- The best quitting coach is a person who loves you enough to look out for your long-term well-being. They are willing to tell you the hard truth even if it means risking hurt feelings in the short term.
- Decisions about when to quit improve when the people who make the decisions to start things are different from the people who make the decisions to stop those things.
- Getting the most out of a quitting coach requires permission to speak the truth.

The Ants Go Marching . . . Mostly

If you've ever watched a nature show or, really, any cartoon with ants in it, the classic image that probably comes to mind is of the ants walking in a single line toward a common destination. *The ants go marching one by one, hurrah, hurrah!* That's how we imagine them. And forager ants really do march that way.

Mostly.

When you look closer, what you'll see is that while most of the ants are marching in line to and from a food source, there is always a certain percentage of the foragers that seem to be wandering around aimlessly. They aren't following the program.

They look suspiciously like freeloaders, shirking their responsibility to bring food back to the nest. Are they ants with an attitude? Are they rebels? Lazy malingerers? Ant anarchists? Anti-establishment ants?

It turns out that these ants serve a crucial purpose and that purpose has a lot to do with quitting.

To figure out what's going on, it helps to understand how ants get in that line in the first place.

When ants enter a new territory, all the foragers are wandering around, scattered across the area, the opposite of that classic marching-in-line that we expect to see. That's because there is no established food source yet and the ants are searching for one.

When an ant finds food, it brings it back to the nest. Along the way, it lays down a chemical scent called a pheromone trail, which is faint when it comes from just one ant. Any other ants that pick up that scent will follow the same trail. And if the food source is high enough in quality, they too will find food and lay down a pheromone trail of their own along the same path back to the nest.

As the chemical scent gets stronger, other ants will begin to follow along the trail. The better the food source, the greater the traffic, which in turn makes the trail stronger and stronger. That's how you end up with the classic image of ants marching in one line.

The trail is like a pheromone katamari.

The choice of how you allocate your time to finding new things or taking advantage of things you've already discovered is part of the classic explore-exploit problem.* How much time should you spend exploring the landscape for new opportunities and how much of your time should you spend exploiting things that are already positive expected value?

Exploitation in this sense doesn't mean manipulating or doing something underhanded. It just means that you're taking advantage of an opportunity that you already have.

For a company that has an established product, resources devoted to continuing to market, produce, and sell that product are spent on exploiting something they have already discovered, like Blockbuster exploiting its profitable business model of renting and selling videos in physical stores. On the other hand, resources spent on research and development of new products or strategies are being devoted to exploration, the discovery of new products or business models the company might pursue. Because companies have limited resources, you can immediately see the importance of figuring out the explore-exploit balance. If they don't get it right, exploring too little, they stop innovating, sticking with what used to work until they are out of business.

Of course, the same is true in our personal lives, with how we allocate our resources of time, money, effort, and attention between exploring new opportunities and sticking with the ones we already have.

---

*Optimal stopping is an explore-exploit problem. How long should you keep exploring alternatives before you choose one? For example, when you're looking for an apartment, what's the optimal number of places that you should look at before you stop and just pick one? Optimal stopping is not a topic of this book. That's more of a game theory problem as opposed to a cognitive problem, which this book is focusing on. But if you're interested in those types of problems, I highly recommend *Algorithms to Live By*, by Brian Christian and Tom Griffiths.

When academics think about this explore-exploit problem, they often turn to ants as an example of the appropriate balance between the two.

That brings us to the puzzle of the wandering ants. If the pheromone trail is such a reliable signal and almost all the foragers quickly pick up on it and start exploiting the food source, what's going on with these few others?

The answer is that these ants are continuing to explore the territory. This serves a vital purpose for the colony for two reasons.

First, sometimes the ants will be forced to quit the food source that they're exploiting. After all, food sources can be unstable. The ants can get bad luck. The food source can disappear. The colony is better off if they have a backup plan. These ants continuing to explore are looking for just that.

Second, even if the food source remains stable, it doesn't mean that there isn't a better food source available than the one they're currently exploiting. Just because the ants have a good thing going, it doesn't mean that there's not a better thing out there.

If all the ants go into exploitation mode and 100% of them march in lockstep along that same pheromone trail, they'll never discover that better food source, because none of them will be looking for it.

That's bad for the ants' survival, because if there is a higher-quality food source out there, the ants ought to be switching to it but they can only switch to something if they know about it.

That's why it turns out that the ant-anarchists aren't anarchists at all.

There's a lesson here, of course, for us humans. When the ants first get to a territory, they're exploring it for opportunities. Once they find an opportunity, a high-quality food source, they start to exploit that. But some percentage of them never stop exploring. That allows them to discover backup plans. Those backup plans are really good to have when the ants are forced to quit, when the ants get unlucky and the food source goes away. But just as important, sometimes when they're searching for a backup plan, they find something even better than their Plan A.

That's the way that we need to think too. When we find something that's working for us, whether it's a job, a career, a product that we're developing, a business strategy, or even a favorite restaurant that we love going to, continuing to explore what other options might be available is a good strategy in a world as uncertain as the one that we live in.

Never stop exploring.

That's the topic that we turn our attention to in the last section of this book.

Opportunity Cost

Lessons from Forced Quitting

W HEN MAYA SHANKAR WAS SIX YEARS OLD, HER MOTHER brought a small violin down from the attic of the family's Connecticut home. Maya's mother had taken the instrument, which belonged to her mother, with her from India when she emigrated to the United States. Maya's three older siblings had already deemed the instrument too uncool. But Maya was instantly taken with it.

She quickly demonstrated prodigious talent. At the age of nine, she auditioned and was accepted into the precollege program at the Juilliard School, the legendary performing arts conservatory in New York. Every Saturday, her mother drove her to and from Juilliard for an intense, ten-hour boot camp.

Maya excelled, so much so that at thirteen she scored a coveted audition with Itzhak Perlman, who is widely considered one of the greatest violinists of all time, having earned sixteen Grammy Awards, a Grammy Lifetime Achievement Award, and four Emmys.

Perlman accepted her as a private student. Maya Shankar, having achieved so much so soon, was on a path to a stellar career at the highest levels of professional music.

All that was taken away when, one day during the summer before her senior year in high school, she tore a tendon in her finger while playing a difficult section of Paganini's Caprice no. 13.

She underwent surgery to repair the tendon, but the pain persisted. Over the next year, she tried performing through the discomfort by taking anti-inflammatories. She was eventually diagnosed, in addition to the torn tendon, with juvenile rheumatoid arthritis. That diagnosis meant that not only did she have to give up playing the violin, but also she was facing a future where she would experience pain every day and eventually perhaps be unable to walk.

It was a sudden end to a promising career.

The question is, what does someone do when they're forced to quit the goal they've been working toward their entire life? The answer is, of course, that they have to start looking for a new goal to aspire to.

For all of us, there are times in our lives when the world makes us stop what we're doing. When you're in a relationship, your partner can decide to break up with you even when you would prefer to stay. People lose their jobs all the time. Your employer could be unhappy with your performance and let you go for that reason. Or it could have nothing to do with your performance and the company you work for may need to make cutbacks or may just go out of business. The same can be true when you're the one running the business. An employee might quit on you. A reliable contract might jump ship to a competitor. You might run out of capital and be forced to shut down.

Sometimes, you make the choice to quit and sometimes the world makes that choice for you.

It's obviously painful when the decision to quit is not our own. But eventually, when that happens, we all have to pick ourselves up, dust ourselves off, and look for something new to do.

And that's exactly what Maya Shankar did. After getting over the initial resentment of having her passion—her identity—literally torn away from her, she applied to college and was accepted at Yale. During the summer before her freshman year, she found one of her sister's old course books in the basement, Steven Pinker's *The Language Instinct*. The idea of studying linguistics, as she puts it, "lit up my brain."

She graduated with a degree in cognitive psychology from Yale, received a Rhodes scholarship, and earned her PhD from Oxford.

While studying at Oxford, Shankar learned that her rheumatoid arthritis had been misdiagnosed. That news was a reprieve from a future she had feared would be limited by a degenerative physical condition. And possibly, it meant a way back to the violin. She performed a few times and started looking for concerto competitions to enter, but playing violin at an elite level was no longer an option because of the scar tissue built up in her hand from past surgeries.

After getting her doctorate, she returned to the United States and completed a postdoctoral fellowship at Stanford University's Cognitive and Systems Neuroscience Laboratory. While there, she realized that she was unhappy in the daily life of a neuroscientist, because the work she was doing meant spending hours alone, stuck in a basement lab, administering and reading fMRIs.

She craved collaboration. She wanted a social aspect to her work.

Being forced to quit the violin had taught her that about herself. With the perspective that comes with the passage of time, Shankar had realized that while there were many things she loved about playing the violin, there was one thing in particular that she really disliked: the solo part of being a solo violinist.

In the basement of the Stanford lab, it dawned on her that she was working solo again, the very feature of her time as a violinist that she had figured out was not for her.

So she quit.

Shankar decided that once she completed the postdoc, she would abandon her career as an academic. She did this despite the cognitive headwinds she was facing. The same headwinds that so many people whose stories this book has told have also had to face. Indeed, those are the same obstacles that we all have to overcome.

Obstacles like sunk cost, the ten years of time and effort she'd put into pursuing her degree. Her endowment to the research programs she had created and conducted, as well as all the awards, fellowships, and degrees she had earned along the way. What came along with those degrees was a PhD after her name, which was very much a part of her identity. Dr. Maya Shankar.

I suspect that one of the reasons she was able to walk away and overcome all those things gaffing the scale was that her previous experience with forced quitting had taught her that whenever you're pursuing a goal, there are always other opportunities you're neglecting. You simply don't see them because you're not looking for them.

Having quit, she was once again in a position of having to figure out what to do next.

There was no easy or natural next move for Shankar. As she told me, "What does a postdoc in cognitive neuroscience do when you realize you don't want to be an academic or become a general management consultant? The paths were not obvious."

At a wedding, she ran into her adviser from Yale, Dr. Laurie Santos, and they arranged to meet for tea. Santos told her about incredible work in applied behavioral economics that was happening in the government, specifically using the power of defaults to encourage positive behavior. These defaults are known as nudges, made famous in the bestseller *Nudge*, by Richard Thaler and Cass Sunstein. Santos connected Shankar to Sunstein, who introduced her to President Obama's science advisor, Tom Kalil, deputy director of the Office of Science and Technology Policy.

She pitched Kalil the idea of creating a new position for her, putting together a team of behavioral science experts to advise federal agencies on policies based on behavioral insights. He liked her ideas and hired her as a senior behavioral science adviser. She initially had no budget, no mandate, and no team. But within a year, she had put together a cross-agency group of behavioral scientists, policy experts, and program makers, founding and chairing the White House's first-ever Social and Behavioral Sciences Team.

When Obama left office in January 2017, Shankar also departed, moving on to become Google's global director of behavioral science. In 2021, she also became the creator, host, and executive producer of the podcast *"A Slight Change of Plans,"* no doubt inspired by the significant, far-from-slight changes in her own plans.

Maya Shankar's career has been punctuated by abrupt changes and, whether she was forced to quit or quit voluntarily, she has more than landed on her feet.

Obviously, things don't always work out that well. A torn tendon doesn't always end up with a Rhodes scholarship. Walking away from academics doesn't always end up with a job in the White House or a senior position at Google.

But even if most of us aren't destined to achieve the things that Maya Shankar has achieved, there is still something in her story for all of us to learn. If she hadn't torn her tendon, she never would have pursued cognitive psychology, a path that eventually led to the White House and then Google, because she wouldn't have been looking for something else to do.

You won't always find something better when you're forced to quit, but sometimes you will. The problem is that most of us never discover those other opportunities because we can't see what we're not even looking for.

The lesson here is that we shouldn't wait to be forced to find a Plan B. We should always be doing some exploration, especially because sometimes Plan B can turn out to be better than the thing you're already pursuing.

In the Meantime

Up until the age of twenty-six, I was on a career path to become an academic and researcher. That path began in my first week as an undergraduate at Columbia. I was applying for work-study jobs and saw a posting for a research assistant to Dr. Barbara Landau, a cognitive scientist specializing in first language acquisition. I got the job and worked for her for four years, the whole of my time at Columbia. Barbara became a mentor and a friend and encouraged me to study with her mentors at the University of Pennsylvania, the legendary Lila Gleitman and her equally legendary husband, Henry.

I spent five years at Penn, earning a National Science Foundation fellowship and completing my doctoral coursework as well as the research for my dissertation. In the winter of my last year of graduate school, I secured a handful of prestigious job talks at places like New York University, Duke, University of Texas at Austin, and University of Oregon. I was on my way to securing a tenure-track position.

But also, during that last year, I was battling chronic stomach problems, which were causing me a lot of discomfort and making me nauseous all the time. I had seen a doctor and gotten a diagnosis of gastroparesis, a potentially dangerous disorder where your stomach doesn't empty properly. My plan was to tough it out, get through my job talks, finish my dissertation, and then turn my attention to my health.

But my body had a different plan.

A few days before my first job talk at NYU, my illness became acute, and I ended up in the hospital for a couple of weeks, unable to keep any food or liquid down. I had to delay going on the job market. I was forced to make the decision to take some time off from school to recuperate and address my health.

Because my body demanded I take a leave from graduate school, I no longer had the fellowship that provided me with a modest stipend to live on.

I really needed money.

That's when I started playing poker as something to do in the meantime. This was a decade before poker became ubiquitous on television and before internet poker was a thing. For most people, it probably never crossed their mind that poker could even be a job.

But it just so happened that my brother, Howard Lederer, had already been playing poker for ten years, earning a living in New York in high-stakes games that included some of the best players on the East Coast. He had also already achieved success on a bigger stage, having made the final table of the annual World Series of Poker Main Event in Las Vegas at the age of twenty-three, becoming, at the time, the youngest player to ever have achieved that.

While I was in graduate school, he started offering to fly me out and put me up at the Golden Nugget to hang out with him during his annual trek to the World Series. I jumped at the opportunity since I obviously couldn't afford a vacation like that on my own.

It was on those trips that I first tried my hand at some low-stakes poker. Having watched my brother play for hours when I was in college, when we both lived in New York, I understood enough about the game to have some modest success.

When I was abruptly forced to take a leave from academics, it was my brother who suggested that I play poker to make ends meet, until I could finish my dissertation and get back on the academic track.

My circumstances imposed a lot of limits on what I could do to earn a living. I didn't know how I was going to feel from day to day, so I needed flexible hours. I fully intended to become a professor sometime in the next year, so I also needed to do something that I could easily quit when that time came.

Poker fit my needs well. If there's a game going on, you can play or not play whenever you want. You can pick which days you work, what time you start, and when you want to leave the game. And if you want to quit poker for something else, you don't have to give notice or worry you're inconveniencing someone who's depending on you.

The rest of my story is pretty well known. I fell in love with the challenges of poker, even the version being played in the place I started, the smoky basement of a bar in Billings, Montana. I had been studying learning and cognition and poker was a real-life, high-stakes application of those subjects. I loved the constant test of excelling in an environment with so much uncertainty, especially figuring out how to overcome the very same biases that we've talked about in this book.

I didn't go back to Penn the next spring . . . or the spring after that.

I stuck with poker, eventually earning a World Series of Poker championship bracelet, winning the WSOP Tournament of Champions and the NBC National Heads-Up Poker Championship, and having a very fruitful and long career. What was supposed to be something "in the meantime" ended up lasting for eighteen years.

For me at age twenty-six, any career other than academics was practically unexplored territory. Even as far as poker was concerned, when I was playing on those trips to Las Vegas, it never occurred to me that it was anything beyond something that I played for fun on vacation, and maybe something that I would keep playing occasionally as a hobby throughout my life.

I enjoyed the game and made some money playing during those vacations, but thinking of poker as some kind of opportunity was so silly that I actually joked about it with Lila. When I first saw her back at school after one of those trips, I told her mischievously, "I had so much fun playing poker that I almost didn't come back."

We both had a good laugh about it.

For me to even think about poker as a serious career option, it took being forced to leave school, missing my chance to move to the next step of my academic career for at least a year, desperately being in need of an income, and having severely limited options because of the state of my health.

For both me and Maya Shankar, and anybody who's been forced to exit the path they've been so passionately pursuing, those can be moments of discovery. Sometimes, forced quitting gets you to explore new opportunities, like when Maya discovered her love of cognitive science. And sometimes, being forced to quit gets you to see options that have been right under your nose all along in a new light.

That's what happened to me with poker.

What Ants Can Teach Us about Backup Plans

The world is uncertain. Whatever you've decided to pursue—a project, a sport, a job, a relationship—may not be there tomorrow. The world might force what you're pursuing away from you. Or you might be the one who chooses to abandon it when the circumstances of what you're doing change. You could be in a job you've loved with a boss who's been a mentor to you, but that boss could leave and be replaced by someone toxic. You could be living in an apartment you love and your new upstairs neighbors take up midnight clog dancing. You could be climbing a mountain and a heavy fog could roll in.

In all these situations, the expected value of your path is not the same as when you initially chose it.

It's not always the world that changes. Sometimes, it's you that changes. Your tastes, preferences, and values evolve over time. A job you love in your twenties might not be a job you love in your thirties. Maybe when you're younger, high-pressure and eighty-hour workweeks are just what you're looking for. But in your thirties, you may value your time differently, and be less willing to sacrifice time with your family to advance your career.

No matter whether it is the world that is changing or you that is changing, sometimes you have the choice about whether to quit and sometimes the world makes that choice for you.

Realistically, we're all going to face one of those two situations for something important, and probably many times throughout our lives. In either case, exploring other opportunities and at least having a *start* on a backup plan is a cornerstone of making quitting easier.

Ants have this right.

If they find something that seems amazing, like a watermelon that rolled off a table on a back patio and broke to pieces, at least a few of them are still looking for other sources of food. After all, that watermelon can disappear after the family cleans it up or hoses down the deck. So, even while the watermelon is still there, some ants keep exploring.

We humans, unfortunately, often don't explore until we're forced to.

Maya Shankar's watermelon was the violin. Mine was cognitive psychology. Combined, we did zero intentional exploring of backup plans because it never occurred to either of us that we would be forced to quit. Neither of us started looking around for something else we might like to pursue as long as we had the equivalent of an exploitable food source. This is also true of so many of the people that we've met in this book.

While Stewart Butterfield was focused on *Glitch*, he didn't even notice the unicorn right under his nose. Slack was there the whole time, but it took quitting *Glitch* for him to see its potential. That very thing had happened to Butterfield one time before, when it took running out of capital for *Game Neverending* to realize Flickr's potential.

Sasha Cohen was forced to quit figure skating because she aged out. That freed her up from something that she was unhappy doing to go explore the other things she might pursue. Eventually, she earned a degree at Columbia, became an investment manager at Morgan Stanley, and started a family. She found a lot more happiness than she had experienced during the last few years of her career, miserable on tour, but only after she was forced to go looking for it.

The ants strike the right balance between exploiting and exploring. The strength of the pheromone trail determines the percentage of foragers that continue to explore, but no matter how strong that scent is, the number of ants exploring never drops to zero, which makes perfect sense. The planet that the ants inhabit always contains some uncertainty. Things change. Virtually nothing stays the same or lasts forever.

Of course, we're living on that same planet. And we should take that lesson for ourselves.

Ants have done extremely well for themselves. They have survived for more than one hundred million years. They've thrived in every kind of climate and territory. They've become so good at surviving, in part, because they're always exploring.

Simply put, that bit of exploration provides the colony with a backup plan, *before* they are forced to quit a food source. In addition, that makes it possible for ants to find something better.

We as humans would do well to follow the ants' example and always have some exploration going on. We ought not wait to be forced to quit to do so.

Once, when I was speaking to a group of sales professionals, at the end of the talk one of them asked me if they should be taking calls from recruiters, even though they really loved the job they were currently in.

I told them of course they should take those calls. First, their job could go away. The company (a start-up) might go out of business or have to cut back on its sales force. Having those relationships with recruiters would certainly be beneficial under those circumstances. Similarly, something could happen within the company that changed the way that the salesperson felt about their job. The product could start faltering, or they could get a new head of sales who they didn't get along with. In that case, knowing what other options were available would make it a lot easier to make a rational decision about whether they should stay in their current position or leave.

And, nothing could change. They could still have a good thing going with this job, and still love it, but if they didn't do some occasional exploring with those recruiters, they would never discover when there's a better thing out there.

This is where ants have it all over humans, because an ant would never ask me that question. They would just take the call.

Notes from the London Underground

Like ants, when a commuter moves to a new town or gets a new job in a new location, they start off exploring all sorts of different ways to get to work, to try to figure out the most efficient route. But unlike ants, once they find one they like, that quickly becomes the status quo, at which point they go the same route morning and night and stop exploring alternatives.

Unless they're forced to.

That happened in 2014 to many of the two million people making two trips per day on the London Underground network (also known as "the Tube"). The Tube includes eleven lines, 270 stations, and over 400 kilometers of track, which means there are lots of different ways to get from point A to point B.

In January 2014, Britain's largest transport union announced a forty-eight-hour strike, starting on the evening of Tuesday, February 4th. When the strike started, 171 of the 270 stations closed for those two days. That meant that a lot of commuters were forced to explore alternate routes.

So what happened when many of these commuters, just for those two days, had to find a new way to get to work? Shaun Larcom of

Cambridge, with colleagues Ferdinand Rauch of Oxford and Tim Willems of the International Monetary Fund, looked at the data to find out the answer to this forced-quitting question.

What they found was that, prior to the strike, a lot of people had been taking the long way to work. It might seem surprising that so many commuters had not found the shortest possible route, but one look at the London Underground map and you can understand why.

The map is clearly not drawn to scale. Its simplicity, orderliness, and symmetry have made it one of the world's most recognizable transit maps, but it's impossible to use as a means of comparing the distance or time from point A to point B on different lines.

When this big disruption happened, 70% of commuters had to find a new route to work for those two days. After the strike ended, about 5% stuck with the new commute they had discovered. Those people reduced their travel time, on average, by more than six minutes per journey. Given an average journey of thirty-two minutes, those who permanently switched cut their commuting time by approximately 20%, meaning they saved twelve minutes a day, a full hour a week, and four hours a month.

Those alternate routes were right under those commuters' noses the whole time. But it took being forced to quit their usual way to work for them to explore a better one.

Imagine how many more people might have made a switch if the strike had lasted longer and they had to explore for more than two days. That's a valuable lesson in why we should be exploring even if we're not forced to. Many Londoners apparently learned that lesson because, in addition to the 5% who permanently switched, the researchers found that even after the strike there was increased exploration of alternatives among commuters.

Having had the experience of being forced to quit, the commuters started behaving more like ants.

Just One Day

Mike Neighbors is a legendary women's college basketball coach. In his first eight seasons as head coach (2013 through 2021), including four years at the University of Washington and four at the University of Arkansas, his accomplishments are nearly unmatched by NCAA Division I coaches of that tenure: 176 wins (second all time) and six players drafted into the WNBA, which no other coach has achieved within that period.

Coach Neighbors attributes a lot of his success to quitting.

After more than a decade of working his way through the ranks at several schools as an assistant coach, he finally got his chance as a head coach at the University of Washington in 2013. He inherited a program in which his student athletes played or practiced six days a week, which was the status quo for college basketball teams. The NCAA mandates that Division I players get a minimum of one day off athletic activities each week, and pretty much every NCAA coach treats that minimum as a maximum.

After many years of losing, the Huskies had rebounded in the previous two seasons under coach Kevin McGuff (who brought Neighbors in as an assistant). When McGuff took the head coaching job at Ohio State, it was on Neighbors to fulfill the rising expectations.

His team immediately stumbled, losing its first two games, including a horrific loss, 91–77, in the home opener to the University of Portland, a team the Huskies beat by 20 points the year before under Coach McGuff.

They improved a little, going into the Christmas break 6–4, but Neighbors could see he needed to make some changes. Minor injuries were piling up and he realized his starters couldn't play heavy minutes in games given the intensity of practices.

During the holiday break, he had the time and space to mull over how he might turn things around, and on the cross-country flight back to Washington, he decided to make a drastic change.

He resolved to cut out one additional day of practice a week, giving his players two days off instead of one.

He decided to make this unconventional move because his team was plagued by injuries. Their bodies were wearing out, and he knew from all his years as an assistant coach that those injuries would accumulate as the season went on. He surmised that the extra day of rest would get his players more time on the court when it mattered most—during games.

To understand the boldness of this decision, you have to realize that no other Division I coach was doing this. This was at the end of 2013, long before the language of self-care became part of the zeitgeist. He knew he was taking a risk and he would take the blame if this decision didn't work. But in his words, if the Huskies, and his coaching career, were going down, they were going to go down *his* way.

After the Huskies returned from break, when most coaches were trying to squeeze every single moment of practice out of players that the NCAA rules would let them get away with, Coach Neighbors shocked the program with the announcement of his plan to give the team an extra day off.

Coach Neighbors was immediately criticized from every direction. He heard, from within the men's basketball program, "They're just giving up. They're not even trying." When he let his mentors know about this plan, they told him, "Man, you do that and you're going to get fired." His top recruit and best player, freshman Kelsey Plum, fought him on the decision: "We're not practicing hard enough. This is weird. It's not going to work."

Plum changed her opinion and her teammates fully bought in based on the changes they noticed, starting with a game the next month against number-three-ranked Stanford, who had beaten them by 35 points the year before. Now, in Neighbors's first game on national

TV, they broke Stanford's sixty-two-game Pac-12 road winning streak, with a shocking upset victory, 87–82.

It wasn't a fluke. Washington finished the season strong, earned a bid to the WNIT, and won three games before losing in the quarter-finals. In his second season, the Huskies made a return to the NCAA tournament. A year after that, they made it to the Final Four. In the senior year of that recruiting class, they were one of the best teams in the country, finishing 29–6 and making the Sweet Sixteen. Each team won more games than the team the year before.

When that class graduated, Neighbors's alma mater, the University of Arkansas, asked him to turn around its women's basketball program and he became head coach of the Razorbacks. In his first four seasons at Arkansas, the program had the best run of success in its history.

Coach Neighbors's teams didn't become less competitive or start winning less because of the extra day off. They started winning more.

And that extra day off didn't just give them more wins on the court. That extra day gave those players time and space to explore other opportunities and interests that they wouldn't have been able to explore if they had to be on the court for that extra day of practice. They used that day in ways that benefited them long after their college basketball careers.

It's amazing what you can accomplish in just one day.

Some players with aspirations of playing in the WNBA, like Kelsey Plum, spent the extra day in the gym. She went on to have one of the greatest college basketball careers of all time and was the number-one pick in the 2017 WNBA draft.

Other players used the time to do extra studying, which helped raise their GPAs, obviously good for their future career prospects. Some explored new potential careers. One player worked toward getting her real estate license. She became one of the most successful Realtors selling high-end houses in the Seattle area. Another player used the day off to secure an internship with Nike. She went on to work there after graduation and advanced rapidly in the company.

A lot of people believe (especially in sports but also in plenty of other activities) that you need single-mindedness to succeed and if you have a backup plan, that's going to make you more likely to fail. But Coach Neighbors blew up that concept. Even though a lot of his players created a backup plan for themselves during that day of exploration, his teams did even better.

Diversifying Your Opportunities

Coach Neighbors made the choice to give his players an extra day off because he was trying to reduce injuries, but what came along with that was that his players were able to use that time to diversify their interests, skills, and opportunities. This is similar to what the ants are doing. The ants, by continuing to explore, are diversifying the portfolio of food sources for the colony. That diversification helps mitigate the effects of bad luck. If a food source dries up, they have other options already available to them.

The power of diversification is, of course, well known in the investment world. Investors want a diversified portfolio for the same reason the ants do, to reduce the impact on their bottom line in case any one of their investments craters.

That's not just true for investors or ants. For any of us, having a diversified portfolio of interests, skills, and opportunities helps to protect us from uncertainty.

If there were no uncertainty and you knew, for a fact, how everything would turn out, then you wouldn't need to be diversified. Your food source would always be there for you, and it would always be the best one. One investment, the one certain to have the highest expected value, would be all you'd need in your portfolio. You'd only ever pick the best job and you'd never lose it.

But, of course, that's not the way the world actually is. And that's why you want to take the call from the recruiter. Because that exploratory conversation might protect you in case the company you work for goes out of business, or there are layoffs, or you just decide that you don't like your job anymore.

Even though unintentional, having poker in my portfolio allowed me to have something to turn to when my academic career was put on hold. Having Flickr and Slack in his portfolio afforded Stewart Butterfield a quick recovery after *Game Neverending* and *Glitch* didn't pan out.

One of the goals for all of us should be to, as much as possible, maximize the diversification of interests, skills, and opportunities in each of our portfolios.

There are all sorts of ways you can execute on that in your own life. For example, in your job, it's a good idea to explore other functions by asking to participate in any onboardings or trainings that might be available to you, as long as that doesn't have a negative effect on the work you're primarily responsible for.

Exploring those other functions benefits you in several ways. It will maximize the number of jobs that you're qualified for and it allows you to sample other careers you might not have otherwise considered. Then, if your job goes away for some reason, you will have more things that you can move on to.

Sometimes, you might discover that you like a different function better than the one you're currently doing. Having the new skills in your portfolio, developed through exploration, allows you to switch to that new function more easily.

It's the same idea for your education. Don't come to college dead set on only one major. Think about several majors that have features or future career paths that might interest you. When you're choosing courses, pick the ones that satisfy a requirement for as many majors as possible. That will help you maximize the number of options open to you and diversify the skill sets that you're developing. In choosing one major over another, consider picking the one that leaves the most career opportunities open.

In your first year of college, you should essentially strive to "date" as many majors as possible. When it comes to personal relationships, that period of exploration (dating) helps you make better decisions about who you eventually commit to. But unlike a committed relationship, in just about anything else, whether it comes to your education, your career, or hobbies, or even the route you take to work, the amount of exploration you're doing should never go to zero.

Diversification doesn't just afford you a softer landing if you're forced to quit. It also helps you to make more rational decisions about walking away from something that's no longer worth pursuing. That's because it's easier to walk away when you know what you're walking *toward*.

Having other options available takes away some of the uncertainty about what comes next that can prevent you from quitting.

Philips certainly demonstrates how it's easier to quit when you know more about what you're walking toward. The Philips brothers, more than a century ago, started an innovation lab so they could diversify their portfolio by developing new products and technologies. That lab started the company on the path to medical technology. By continuing to diversify its portfolio of products, it could quit opportunities of lesser quality, including its core lighting business, and move into the better ones it had discovered along the way.

Of course, like everything else that potentially improves quitting behavior, just because your portfolio is diversified doesn't necessarily mean that you're going to make great choices about what to quit and what to keep pursuing. After all, Sears built a lucrative and growing financial services empire that it chose to forgo in order to try to save its flailing retail business.

But having other opportunities at least gives you a chance to make better choices about what to quit and what to stick to. Continuing to explore new opportunities to increase the diversification of your portfolio helps you when you're forced to quit, when the thing you're doing is no longer worth pursuing, and when you do have a good thing going, by allowing you to see when there's a better opportunity out there.

In any case, no matter the reason that you might be quitting, you need to always remember that what you think is a backup plan will often turn into your Plan A.

The Great Resignation

In March and April of 2020, when COVID first hit the United States hard, the pandemic created a massive forced-quitting event. In just those two months, twenty million people lost their jobs, at one point at a rate of one million per day.

For the approximately twenty-eight million people in the United States employed in the retail, accommodation, and food service industries, work just stopped. There were no customers. Huge numbers of these businesses closed, temporarily or permanently. So many of the others had to lay off, furlough, or drastically cut the hours of their remaining employees. The level of uncertainty for these workers and businesses remained especially high through the end of 2020.

When people started feeling more comfortable returning to stores, hotels, and restaurants, you would assume that after all that uncertainty, those who had been laid off from those jobs would be eager to get back to work. But something surprising happened. Beginning in April 2021, there was a second wave of mass quitting, only this time it was voluntary.

The Great Resignation had begun.

In April, nearly 4 million people voluntarily quit their jobs, the highest number since the Bureau of Labor Statistics started counting in 2001. The highest rate of quitting was by workers employed in service jobs, the very same people who were forced to quit at the beginning of the pandemic. More than 1.3 million of those workers quit in April. In other words, during that month alone, about one in twenty people working in service jobs quit.

Almost the same number of employees in those industries voluntarily quit in May. A new quitting record was set in June, which was broken again in July. And again in August.

Why did so many people who had lost their jobs during the pandemic decide to quit when those jobs came back?

Based on what we've learned in this book about quitting decisions, we can take some educated guesses.

First, the people who lost their jobs at the start of the pandemic were forced to explore other options that might be available to them to earn a living, something that they wouldn't generally have done under other circumstances. That gave them a better sense of the landscape and allowed them to see opportunities they might have been neglecting.

Second, it also allowed them to reexamine their own preferences. In the same way that Maya Shankar figured out that she didn't like solo work, being forced to quit gets you to ask yourself what the features are that you like and don't like of the work you have been doing. Do you want to be physically present in a workplace or do you prefer to work remotely? Do you want something with more flexible hours? Do you love your job? Do you find it fulfilling? Is there something else that would make you happier? It might seem that people would ask themselves those questions all the time, but it often takes being forced to walk away for people to take a second look.

Third, when you're currently employed, you have a mental account open. Being forced to quit caused all those people to close those accounts. We know that when you have an account open, it's difficult to walk away. You feel like a failure, that you fell short, or that you gave up. There are so many cognitive forces working against you. But when there was this mass layoff, those people who were forced to quit got to close those mental accounts, wiping the slate clean.

When that happens to you, your katamari goes back to being a small clump. Now you're more like the ants entering a new territory, exploring the area to see what's there.

Relieved by forced quitting of all that debris, it was easier for those who lost their jobs to ask themselves, "How much do I really like what I'm doing?" It was also easier for them to rationally answer that question, especially because they were essentially forced to explore alternatives. A lot of people found out that they didn't want to keep doing the thing they were doing, and they wanted to switch to new opportunities.

Of course, you can only switch to something new if there are opportunities to switch to, and alongside the Great Resignation was the Great Reopening. When things opened back up, that came with record job creation. For those people who had wanted to switch, there were lots of opportunities to switch to.

The Great Reopening essentially created a more diversified portfolio of opportunities for people who were looking for them.

This greatly accelerated growth in new jobs occurred across many industries, but the surge in voluntary quitting and switching was more concentrated among the people who had been forced out of their jobs during the beginning of the pandemic. Like the riders of the London Underground after the lines opened back up, those who had lost their jobs continued to explore even after those jobs came back online.

They learned the lesson the ants have down pat: *Don't wait to be forced to quit to start exploring alternatives.*

Left to our own devices, we tend to focus on the thing we're doing, practically to the exclusion of anything else. It's not just that we don't explore other opportunities. We don't notice them when they're right in front of us. We become myopic. That inability to see other things that might be available, on top of all the other forces gaffing the scale against quitting, makes it hard to switch what we're doing because, after all, how can you switch to something that you don't even know exists?

That myopia is what we're going to turn our attention to next.

Chapter 10 Summary

- Being forced to quit forces you to start exploring new options and opportunities. But you should start exploring before you're forced to.
- Even after you have found a path that you want to stick to, keep doing some exploration. Things change, and whatever you are doing now may not be the best path for you to pursue in the future. Having more options gives you something to switch to when the time is right.
- Exploration helps you to diversify your portfolio of skills, interests, and opportunities.
- A diversified portfolio helps to protect you against uncertainty.
- Backup plans are good to have especially because some backup plans can turn out to be better than what we're already pursuing.

CHAPTER 11

The Myopia of Goals

THE 2019 LONDON MARATHON WAS THE BIGGEST IN THE event's history, with more than 42,000 runners completing the 26.2 miles. With so many entrants, it is not surprising the race was filled with unusual stories and achievements. Guinness World Records announced thirty-eight titles that day, including "fastest marathon with two runners handcuffed together (mixed)," "fastest marathon dressed as a Christmas tree (male)," and, weirdly, four minutes slower than the Christmas tree, "fastest marathon dressed as a tree (male)."

And then there is the story of Siobhan O'Keeffe. O'Keeffe trained four months for the event and was hoping to finish in about five hours. Her ankle started hurting four miles into the race and kept getting worse. Even so, she continued running, ignoring the signals her body was sending her.

After another four miles, her fibula bone snapped in half.

Why would someone in the type of escalating pain that O'Keeffe was feeling continue running until their leg broke?

If someone planning on running a marathon *knew* they would break their leg at mile eight, we all certainly share the intuition that they wouldn't even start the race. And if you asked someone, given that they did start the marathon, whether they would quit running *before* breaking their leg, given the level of pain that must precede such an injury, their answer would also be an emphatic yes.

O'Keeffe breaks our intuition. And the case gets even stranger.

Medics advised her to stop running—no surprise there, her fibula bone had snapped in half—but she refused. She ran the last eighteen miles in nearly unbearable pain and *finished the marathon* in 6:14:20.

You might think this is a bizarre, weird, one-off story, but it's actually not as uncommon as you'd suspect. In fact, that same day, in the same marathon, at the same distance into the race, *another* runner broke his foot and ran the remaining eighteen miles on it. Steven Quayle, eight miles in, stepped on a loose water bottle, injuring his right foot, calf, and hip. The pain kept getting worse. By mile sixteen, he had to stop at a physio tent for medical assistance, the first of four or five such stops made before finishing in 3:57:33.

Four weeks later, in the Edinburgh Marathon, Mike Lewis-Copeland fractured his fibula at mile sixteen. The pain was unlike anything he had ever experienced, but he kept limping along, dragging that leg, counting down those last ten miles, until he finished in 4:30.

In the London Marathon in 2014, Graham Colborne did the exact same thing as Steven Quayle did five years later: eight miles in, stepped on a water bottle, broke a bone in his foot, and ran the remaining eighteen miles in absolute agony.

A quick Google search turns up several other stories, just from the London Marathon. In 2012, Darren Oliver broke his leg a mile into the event, and ran twenty-five miles in severe pain to finish. In the 2021 marathon, Angie Hopson was in pain from the start. It became so excruciating that she had to stop after six miles, but only briefly. She ran the last twenty miles only to find out the next day that she had done it with a broken leg.

Many of these injuries happened to dedicated distance runners. By continuing to run in pain, they weren't just risking their health or the pain of a more serious injury. They were also jeopardizing their ability to train and run in future races, something they clearly loved and prioritized in their lives. Both Oliver and Hopson lamented how much time they would have to miss before running again. Lewis-Copeland, who had completed the London Marathon in 2019 before fracturing his fibula in Edinburgh, acknowledged that his recovery and rehabilitation was going to keep him from his plan to run in six more marathons that year.

Why do these runners disregard their pain to the point where continuing to push through means that some body part breaks? And again, after the injury, why do they continue on, putting their future ability to run another race at risk?

Because there's a finish line.

Finish lines are funny things. You either reach them or you don't. You either succeed or you fail. There is no in between. Progress along the way matters very little.

When we consider how off base our intuition is that we will walk away when circumstances make it clear that we ought to, these marathon runners help us to understand why we've got it so wrong. Once you start the race, success is only measured against crossing the finish line. And even a broken leg won't make us quit when facing the choice between falling short or continuing on in pain.

The Problem with Pass-Fail

The benefits of setting goals are well known. Goals define your North Star and give you something to strive for. They motivate you to persist when things get tough. It's been repeatedly demonstrated that goals that are both challenging and specific get you to work harder and are more effective than goals that are more amorphous and general. If you say, "I want to run sixteen miles a week" or "I'd like to raise my GPA by half a grade in the next semester," you'll make more progress toward achieving those things than if you say, "I'd like to run more" or "I want to try harder in school."

But just because there are a lot of benefits to setting goals doesn't mean that there isn't a downside to them as well. As you might already suspect, clearly defined finish lines should come with a warning: *Danger, you may experience escalation of commitment.*

Maurice Schweitzer of the Wharton School and Lisa Ordóñez, then of the University of Arizona, along with several other scholars including Max Bazerman, Adam Galinsky, and Bambi Douma, coauthored a number of papers making the case that goals have a dark side. They point to numerous negative consequences of goal setting, several of which interfere with rational quitting behavior. In particular, they note the pass-fail nature of goals, their inflexibility, and how pursuing them leads to ignoring other opportunities that might be available.

The point the authors are echoing is that, while goals do help us to be grittier, grit isn't always a virtue. As you already know, grit is good for getting you to stick to hard things that are worthwhile, but grit also gets you to stick to hard things that are *no longer* worthwhile.

In part, what makes goals effective is that they get you to focus on the finish line and motivate you to keep going. But the duality is that goals also keep you from quitting in a bad situation because they focus you on the finish line and motivate you to keep going.

Why? In part, because they are graded as pass-fail.

To understand why the pass-fail nature of goals can impede progress and increase escalation of commitment, consider this thought experiment. Which feels worse? If you never try to run a marathon, or if you make the attempt and have to stop after sixteen miles? In the first case, you never train for a marathon, never start one, and never finish one. You run zero miles. In the second case, you decide to try, you train, you start, and sixteen miles in you have to quit.

I think that we all share the intuition that the latter case would feel worse, even though that version of you trained for distance running and actually ran 16 miles of a 26.2-mile race, compared with the version of you that never got off the couch.

The reason it feels worse is that if you don't try, if you never start the race, there is no failing to reach the finish line because you never set that as a goal for yourself in the first place.

The pass-fail nature of goals impedes your progress because it stops you from starting things for fear of being unable to complete them. No doubt, the person who trained and ran sixteen miles of a marathon is better off health-wise than the person who never started. If your goal is to be healthier, the person who tried has clearly made more progress toward that goal.

But for so many of us, that fear of falling short makes us not want to start.

As Richard Thaler quipped, "If a gold medal in the Olympics is the only grade that passes, you do not want to ever take your first gymnastics class."

Once we set a goal, that's what we measure ourselves against. If we're running in a marathon, anything but 26.2 miles is a failure. This is how goals exacerbate escalation of commitment, because anything short of the finish line is unacceptable to us. It doesn't matter what's happening in the world or what's happening in our bodies. We don't want to feel like we've failed.

We'll just keep running toward the finish line until our leg snaps.

When it comes to our aversion to closing accounts in the losses, the pass-fail nature of goals makes this problem worse. As soon as you set a goal or a target, you put yourself immediately in the losses, at least in relation to your distance from the goal. As soon as you cross the starting line, you are now short of the finish line.

When an economist talks about being in the gains or losses, they're talking about whether you are currently winning or losing as compared with where you started. But as is so often the case, when it comes to goals, our cognition cares very little for what economists have to say.

Being in the losses is as much a state of mind as anything else. We don't see ourselves as being in the gains, even though we've gone farther than where we started, because we're not measuring ourselves by how far we are past the starting line. We're measuring ourselves by whether we're short of the finish line.

Because we don't want to close mental accounts in the losses, we're just going to keep running toward the finish line, even if we feel our leg is about to snap, and even after it does.

If you turn around 300 feet from the summit of Everest, you will feel like you failed. That must have been the feeling that stuck with Rob Hall and his client Doug Hansen when they turned around that close to the summit in 1995, the year before the expedition chronicled in Jon Krakauer's book. Never mind that Hansen climbed more than 28,000 feet, something few humans have ever accomplished.

Hansen expressed this feeling of failure from the previous year so poignantly when he told Krakauer, "The summit looked soooo close. Believe me, there hasn't been a day since that I haven't thought about it."

When Hall convinced Hansen to come back and try again, that started them both in the losses. They opened a new account, a second attempt to summit Everest, and anything short of reaching that summit would mean failing yet again.

Hall felt compelled to let Hansen reach the finish line this time, and so he, otherwise regarded as an extremely methodical guide and expedition leader, waited two hours at the summit for Hansen to arrive, long after the turnaround time he set for his clients. Of course, that ended in tragedy for both of them.

Progress along the way should count for something, but we discard it because goals are pass-fail, all-or-nothing, yes-or-no. There's no partial credit given.

Altogether, the pass-fail nature of goals can impede progress, cause escalation of commitment, and stop us from considering the progress we make along the way as a success.

The shame in all this is that those finish lines are often arbitrary.

If you complete 5 kilometers in the context of a 5K, you've succeeded. But if that's as far as you run in the context of a half-marathon, that's a failure. If you run 13.1 miles in the context of a half-marathon, that's a success, but in the context of a full marathon, you have failed. And successfully running 26.2 miles becomes a failure if you were attempting an ultramarathon.

To understand why Sasha Cohen endured three years of misery after the 2006 Olympics, we just need to think about the pass-fail nature of goals. Her finish line, going into the 2006 Olympics as the favorite, was to win a gold medal. She fell short, both literally and figuratively, when she stumbled in her long program and had to settle for silver.

Second best in the world counts for little when the goal is to be first. And so she continued to skate unhappily in shows, sticking around to try once more in 2010 to reach the finish line. When she finished two places short of making the 2010 Olympic team and finally aged out, that forced her to close that mental account. She felt free, relieved of the burden that the pass-fail nature of goals imposes.

Goals work, but sometimes they work to the point where they make us ignore clear signs that the goal is not worth continuing to pursue. When a goal is all-or-nothing, your choices are essentially not to start or stick to the goal no matter what.

This is part of what creates the paradox of quitting. The beauty of having the option to quit is that it makes it easier for us to make decisions under uncertainty. Whenever we make a decision, whether it's starting a race, or starting up a mountain, or starting a business, or starting a relationship, we're making that decision with incomplete information in a world that's stochastic. We're under the influence of luck. The world can change. We can change.

For almost anything that we choose to believe or choose to do, we'll have the option to change our mind or walk away at some point in the future. When we face that decision, we'll generally have much better information than at the time we made the original choice to start.

But that option to quit is only helpful if we actually use it. The problem is that we don't, and here we see why. Once we start, we put ourselves in the losses. We're short of our goal, the progress along the way counting for almost nothing.

That makes us keep heading toward the finish line, broken leg be damned.

Fixed Objects in a Changing World

Exacerbating the pass-fail problem is that once we establish a goal, we rarely revisit it. Goals tend to be set-it-and-forget-it. The finish line doesn't move.

If there were no uncertainty and the world didn't change, that wouldn't be a problem, because whatever North Star you were striving for would not only be the exact right North Star for you but also would remain as such. Of course, the world is uncertain and the world does change. That means that our goals ought to change in response. But the goals we set are remarkably unresponsive to new information.

Whenever we set a goal, we're making trade-offs. There are all sorts of different things that we value—money, time with our family, time for hobbies, time for friends, our health, the feeling of helping other people, so on and so forth. There is no goal we can set that can allow us to maximize every single thing that we value.

By their nature, goals will privilege certain things we value over others. Essentially, we're asking ourselves, "What do I want to achieve, and what am I willing to give up to get it?" Presumably, the benefits of pursuing the goal will outweigh the costs.

A goal is the expression of that balancing act. In other words, we're trying to maximize our expected value and the goals that we set for ourselves are supposed to help us do that.

As an example, if you set a goal to complete a marathon, there are things you expect to get and things you expect to give up. The sense of accomplishing something hard could be important to you. Or the goal reflects the importance you place on fitness. Or it could be how great it feels to you to be outside running. Or it could be lots of other things. What you want and its relative importance are specific to you.

The same is true for what you're willing to sacrifice in terms of other things you might value. Training for a marathon will naturally mean sacrificing time with your family or your friends, or pursuing other hobbies you might enjoy. Most of us value our physical comfort and you clearly have to give up some degree of that. Routine discomfort and injuries are part of distance running and training. You're likely factoring in that you're going to have to spend a certain amount of time outside when it's cold or raining, and sometimes get out there in those conditions early in the morning, instead of sleeping in.

In setting goals for your career, you also do this kind of cost-benefit analysis. If your goal is to get on the management track of a Fortune 500 company, you're prioritizing certain things you value (such as advancing in your career or wealth) in favor of other things you're willing to give up (such as having a low-stress job where you don't take your work home with you).

Either explicitly or implicitly, the goal you set is a proxy for an expected-value equation, balancing the benefits that you're trying to gain against the costs you'll bear to get them.

This is all part of the process of setting the goal. But what happens to that calculus once you've set the goal and you're pursuing it?

After we set a goal, it becomes a fixed object. This thing that is a proxy for something else becomes the object itself. The goal is the thing we're trying to achieve, instead of all the values expressed and balanced when we originally set the goal.

The goal becomes fixed even as all the inputs that led to choosing that particular goal evolve. The conditions in the world change. Our knowledge changes. The weights we attach to the benefits and costs change. Our preferences and values change.

As these things change, if we were to rerun the cost-benefit analysis, the output would surely be different. But we don't rerun it.

To achieve the things we want to achieve, we have to be responsive to the way the world is changing around us and the way that we ourselves are changing. That would mean unfixing our goals, but we don't naturally do that.

In combination, the pass-fail and fixed nature of goals causes us to just keep on toward the finish line, even when the finish line is no longer what we should be running toward.

Inflexible goals aren't a good fit for a flexible world.

Every Goal Needs At Least One Unless

Goals are powerful tools. They can make it possible to accomplish worthwhile things. But the mere fact of having a goal can cause escalation of commitment, where you end up sticking to a goal that's no longer the best way to achieve the things you want to achieve.

Of course, it's partly the fixed nature of goals that wreaks this havoc. Once we set a goal, we learn new information. The world changes. We change. We solve for certain monkeys. Creating more flexible goals is a way to address this.

An "unless" is a powerful thing. Adding a few well-thought-out unlesses to our goals will help us achieve the flexibility that we're seeking, be more responsive to the changing landscape, and reduce escalation of commitment to losing causes.

"I'm going to pursue this lead *unless* I can't get an executive in the room."

"I'm going to stay in my job *unless* I have to consistently take my work home or I find myself dreading the start of the workday and that feeling persists."

"I'm going to keep developing this product *unless* I fail to hit clear benchmarks within the next two months that I've set with my quitting coach."

"I'm going to continue to run this marathon *unless* I break a bone."

This is why having kill criteria is so important. When you set a goal, creating a list of kill criteria gives you the unlesses that you need to be more rational about when it's the right time to walk away.

Those kill criteria could be about what the world is signaling to you, like observing behavior that tells you that your boss is toxic, or interest rates are rising, or a fog is rolling in, or there's an onset of a pandemic.

Or they could be about changes in yourself, whether it's the pain you might feel that precedes your fibula snapping or, as in my case, an illness you've been struggling with becoming acute.

Or it could just be that your preferences change or that the things you value evolve. That a job in the service industry is no longer for you. Or that the sport you used to love now makes you miserable.

To make these unlesses most effective, we need to create strong precommitment contracts that set out how we're going to follow through on those kill criteria. Then, to make sure that we're picking the unlesses that are going to get us to the fastest answer about whether the thing we're doing is worth pursuing, we need to do the work of identifying monkeys and pedestals.

Doing this work with a quitting coach who can hold you accountable to those unlesses is even better.

These unlesses, of course, require advance planning. You're trying to anticipate as many scenarios that might unfold as possible. But you can't anticipate every circumstance under which you might stick and every circumstance under which you might quit.

That means you have to keep checking back in on the cost-benefit analysis that the goal is a proxy for. You should reevaluate, on a regular cadence, whether the values that you're trying to privilege are still being privileged and whether the values that you're deprivileging, the costs that you're bearing, are still worth it. Those check-ins also offer an opportunity to reevaluate old kill criteria and set new ones.

Good unlesses allow us to escape the pull of short-term goals that don't actually help us achieve the long-term goals that we're striving for.

It's so easy for us to get trapped in trying to win a single hand of poker, or in trying to make sure that we don't cash out of a game as a loser. But those local goals can impede us from acting in a way that embodies the reality that life is one long game. That means trying to maximize the expected value over our lifetime, which requires us to sometimes give up on these interim finish lines.

There are lots of unlesses you can apply in poker. I'll keep playing, unless I've lost a certain amount of money, or unless new players have joined the game who are significantly better than the ones who've left, or unless I've played past a certain number of hours, or unless I'm feeling emotional or tired or sick. Unlesses can get us out from under the forces that will keep us playing in the short run, chasing a win, and align our behavior more closely with our long-term best interests.

Sticking to something that's no longer worthwhile is going to stop you from reaping the benefits that were the original reason for setting the goal in the first place, or it's going to cause you to incur more costs than you were originally willing to bear.

Your goals should change because the world changes and you change. To keep up with all that change, you need to check back periodically on whether you're taking the fastest route to the finish line, or if you're even running to the right place.

Marking Progress along the Way

It's a pretty rigid view of the world that defines success only as crossing the finish line.

It's not just that we need to set more flexible goals. We ourselves also need to be more flexible in the way we evaluate success and failure.

The way we view goals as pass-fail is, by definition, inflexible and categorical, causing us to discount or completely ignore any progress that we've made. That means, to counteract this problem, we need to find ways to mark that progress, to celebrate the things that we've accomplished on the way to the finish line.

If you're trying to summit Everest because you get a lot of value out of that physical and mental challenge, you're not *objectively* in the losses if you make it to Camp 1, 2, 3, or 4, or 300 feet from the summit, certainly not in comparison with not having tried at all.

Of course, that's not our subjective experience. That's what we need to change.

We need to find a way to flip the script and stop measuring ourselves solely by how far we are from the finish line. We need to start giving ourselves more credit for how far we are from where we started.

If we do that, a silver medal will feel much less disappointing, because in reality it's a huge accomplishment, as measured against where any figure skater has ever started. Doing that would let you see what an accomplishment it is to earn acceptance as a private student from Itzhak Perlman or, in my case, to have completed five years of graduate-level work.

It's easier to mark and celebrate your progress toward a goal if the goal itself is not so all-or-nothing. There are some goals that you set where there is little of value that you can glean if you come up short. While there are other goals where there are lots of things of value that you can accomplish or learn along the way, no matter whether you actually cross the finish line.

Those are the types of goals we should prioritize.

This is something Astro Teller really gets. If he has a choice between a project where there is little technology or learning that will come out of the trying versus one where there is, he will prioritize the project where he gets more out of it along the way.

The hyperloop offers an example of an all-or-nothing type of goal. Building track was something that was old technology. Getting the train to accelerate and run at high speeds, likewise, was something that had already been figured out. Accomplishing those things would not demand developing anything new. The monkey, whether they could get passengers on and off safely, was the technological challenge. The problem was that they had to build all those pedestals before they could figure out whether they could tackle that monkey. And if they failed to do so, they would come away with nothing new.

Contrast that with a project like Loon, whose mission was to bring internet access to remote areas using giant balloons. There were lots of different approaches for how to get the balloons to talk to the ground. One of the first things they tried was to invent new laser technology to do that. That turned out to not be the best solution, so they pivoted to a different approach, but the laser technology they developed became very valuable to X on a later project. Loon's team of laser experts became part of Taara, which is rolling out a significant increase in telecommunications bandwidth.

On a big scale, Teller is thinking hard about how you can create a culture that celebrates the wins along the way, that celebrates the 5Ks and 10Ks and half-marathons we run, even if we fall short of 26.2 miles.

This is an important lesson for leaders in general to learn because the way that we lead can exacerbate the problems that both the pass-fail and the fixed nature of goals can create. Leaders commonly fall into the trap of evaluating people solely by whether they've achieved a goal or not. When they do that, they're increasing the potential for escalation of commitment.

If leaders act like success is just whether you hit the target or goal or deadline, then the people they're leading are going to learn pretty quickly that they need to get across the finish line at all costs. They won't speak up if they think the goal isn't worth pursuing any longer. They're going to be unwilling to quit even when the situation warrants it, because leadership will evaluate that as a failure.

One of the nice features of unlesses is that they give you another way to win. A good set of kill criteria means you can win by achieving a goal *or* by successfully following those kill criteria. Quitting when the time is right is accomplishing something valuable. Following through on an unless gives you a way to live that.

The unlesses we attach to the goals we set allow us to follow through on the trope "process over outcome." The goal itself is outcome oriented, but the unlesses focus on process.

Goal-Induced Myopia

We've already seen ways in which our single-minded fixation on achieving a goal can cause us to fail to see clear and obvious evidence that we should quit, obvious to someone who's not in it, at least.

But it's not just that goals cause us to ignore changes that occur along the path that we're on or changes that are occurring in ourselves as we're heading down that path. Goals can also cause a myopia that makes it so we can't see other paths that are available to us, the other opportunities we might be able to pursue instead.

You're already familiar with the problem of opportunity cost neglect. Goal setting can exacerbate this issue. Once we settle on a finish line and a path to get us there, we become myopic, failing to explore other paths that might be available to us or other finish lines that might be better for us to head toward.

We don't see them, and that's not just a flaw in our peripheral vision.

Merely pursuing a goal can cause us to fail to notice what's right in front of us. That's certainly what happened to Stewart Butterfield when he had Slack under his nose. He couldn't fully appreciate its potential until he quit *Glitch*, closing that account and forcing him back into exploration mode. That's certainly what happened to me with poker, which I couldn't see as a possible career until I was forced to leave my graduate program.

Our lives are better if we have a larger portfolio of skills and opportunities available to us. The myopia that goals cause limits the size of that portfolio, because we don't look for or see alternatives.

In this way, ants have it better than humans, because they're a colony, a collection of individuals working together. This makes it easier for ants to explore *and* exploit at the same time. Some of the ants follow the pheromone trail, while other ants explore new food sources. Even if the ants along the pheromone trail are myopic, it doesn't matter to the colony because other ants are still looking around.

But we're just us. You're just one person. Once you've established a pheromone trail to follow, you become myopic, making it hard to see those other opportunities that your ant friends otherwise would be looking for.

One of the most famous studies showing that being fixated on a task or goal can cause you to literally not see what's right in front of you is the invisible gorilla experiment, conducted by Harvard psychologists Daniel Simons and Christopher Chabris in 1999. Participants watched a video of a group of people passing a basketball back and forth and were tasked with counting the number of passes.

Halfway through the video, a woman in a full gorilla suit walked through the scene.

After completing the task of counting the number of times the basketball was passed, the participants were asked if they noticed anything unusual. If they said no, they were asked if they saw anything or anyone other than the six players. If they said no to that, they were asked, "Did you see a gorilla walk across the screen?"

More than half of the participants (56%) answered "no" to all those questions.

The gorilla was obvious to anyone just watching the video, with no directive to count anything. Indeed, when the experimenters showed them the video a second time, the participants were consistently shocked that they missed it.

If they couldn't see the gorilla right in front of their noses, what do you think you are missing when you are pursuing a goal?

You need to be really wary of this myopia because it's counterproductive to seeing the opportunities around you. That's another reason why developing an exploratory mindset is so important. You have to be making sure that you've got a good view of the landscape, that you are taking calls from recruiters, that you're exploring other functions, and that you're generally trying out new things, so that you can start to add to and expand your portfolio.

Quitting coaches can also reduce myopia, because they can generally see the opportunities that are available to you better than you can.

Quit Thinking about Waste

When we think about the friction that makes it hard for us to quit, we can see how goal-setting piles onto the katamari. We loathe closing mental accounts in the losses. But as soon as we set a goal, we start ourselves in the losses. This adds to the ruckus caused by all those other biases that gaff the scale against quitting.

We are endowed to our goals, and they can easily become part of our identity. They become the status quo. Once we start toward a finish line, we accumulate the sunk costs of time and effort and money spent trying to get there.

What makes it so hard to quit, if we were to sum up everything that we've talked about in this book, is that when we quit, we fear two things: that we've failed, and that we've wasted our time, effort, or money.

We need to redefine what "failed" and "wasted" mean.

When we worry that quitting means we've failed, what exactly are we failing *at*? If you quit something that's no longer worth pursuing, that's not a failure. That's a success.

The way we naturally think about failure is to have stopped something short of the goal, as in failing to make it to the finish line. But if you're continuing to pursue something that's no longer worth pursuing, isn't that a failure? How do we start to redefine that and think about failure as failing to follow a good decision process?

Success means following a good decision process, not just crossing a finish line, especially if it is the wrong one to cross. That means appropriately following kill criteria, listening to our quitting coaches, and recognizing that the progress we've made along the way counts for a lot.

We also need to redefine what waste is. What does it mean to waste your time or money or effort? Our problem is that we tend to think about these things in a backward-looking way. We feel like if we walk away from something, that means we've wasted everything that we put into it.

But those are resources that are already spent. You can't get them back.

We need to start thinking about waste as a forward-looking problem, not a backward-looking one. That means realizing that spending another minute or another dollar or another bit of effort on something that is no longer worthwhile is the real waste.

Once you think about it that way, you realize how much time has actually been wasted in the service of the idea that if you quit, the time you've already spent will be for naught. Just look at the California bullet train, where they're continuing to dump money into something for fear that they will have wasted the time and taxpayer money that they've already put into it.

We need to redefine failure. We need to redefine waste. But ultimately, what we need to do is rehabilitate the very idea of quitting.

Lots of hard things are worth pursuing and grit is good for getting you to stick with it when it's right. But lots of hard things are not worth pursuing and the ability to walk away when it's right is also a skill worth developing. Hopefully this book has given you the tools to do that.

Ultimately, where you're going—where we're all going—is along whatever route will have the greatest expected value throughout our lives. *That* path is going to involve a lot of quitting.

Contrary to popular belief, winners quit a lot. That's how they win.

Chapter 11 Summary

- Goals can make it possible to achieve worthwhile things, but goals can also increase the chances that we will escalate commitment when we should quit.
- Goals are pass-fail in nature. You either reach the finish line or you don't, and progress along the way matters very little.
- Don't just measure whether you hit the goal, ask what you have achieved and learned along the way.
- Set intermediate goals and prioritize goals that allow you to recognize progress along the way or acquire something valuable even if you don't reach the goal.
- Goals, when set, are a proxy for an expected-value equation, balancing the benefits that you're trying to gain against the costs you're willing to bear.
- Inflexible goals aren't a good fit for a flexible world.
- With better advance planning (like identifying monkeys and pedestals and kill criteria) and the help of a good quitting coach, you can make goals more flexible, setting at least one "unless" and planning regular check-ins on the analysis that initially led to setting the goal.
- In general, when we quit, we fear two things: that we've failed and that we've wasted our time, effort, or money.
- Waste is a forward-looking problem, not a backward-looking one.

ACKNOWLEDGMENTS

I am so grateful for the help of so many scientists, authors, innovators, entrepreneurs, investors, and leaders who engaged with me in discussions about quitting and were incredibly generous with their insights and time: Stuart Baserman, Max Bazerman, Colin Camerer, Keith Chen, Ron Conway, David Epstein, Shane Frederick, Laurence Gonzales, Tom Griffiths, Alex Imas, Daniel Kahneman, Ken Kamler, Jennifer Kurkoski, Libby Leahy, Cade Massey, Michael Mauboussin, William McRaven, Michael Mervosh, Katy Milkman, Mark Moffett, Don Moore, Scott Page, Riley Post, Dan Raff, Eric Ries, Maurice Schweitzer, Ted Seides, Maya Shankar, Barry Staw, Hal Stern, Cass Sunstein, Joe Sweeney, Astro Teller, Phillip Tetlock, Richard Thaler, Tony Thomas, Richard Zeckhauser, and Kevin Zollman.

Thank you to the people who were willing to share their stories with me, stories that helped me develop and refine my ideas with their hard-earned insights: Stewart Butterfield, Sasha Cohen, Mike Neighbors, Sarah Olstyn Martinez, Maya Shankar, and Andrew Wilkinson. Thanks also to Barry Staw, who, in addition to his other contributions to this book, spent hours with me stitching together the narrative about his larger-than-life father, Harold.

I want to single out the collaboration of Katy Milkman, Ted Seides, and Richard Thaler. Katy and Ted read drafts of every chapter as I went along, offering insightful feedback and encouragement along the way.

Richard also read many versions of the manuscript and spent hours with me on Zoom, helping me to clarify the concepts laid out in the book, so many of which relied so heavily on his body of work. *Quit* is so much better for that thought partnership, for which I am deeply grateful.

I am also indebted to Alex Imas, Daniel Kahneman, Barb Mellers, Don Moore, Dave Nussbaum, Ogi Ogas, Brian Portnoy, Barry Staw, and Phillip Tetlock, who also read drafts of the work in progress and offered their invaluable comments.

One aspect of the generosity of my friends and colleagues (and those who became my friends during the course of writing this book) has been their willingness to connect me to others they thought would be helpful in this journey. Thank you to Josh Kopelman for introducing me to Stewart Butterfield, Ron Conway, and Andrew Wilkinson; Michael Mauboussin for introducing me to Sasha Cohen and Laurence Gonzales; Richard Thaler for introducing me to Shane Frederick and Maya Shankar; David Epstein for introducing me to Riley Post; Max Bazerman for introducing me to Stuart Baserman; Maya Shankar for introducing me to Jennifer Kurkoski, who in turn introduced me to Barry Staw and Astro Teller; Ted Seides for introducing me to Michael Mervosh; and Mark Moffett for reintroducing me to Ken Kamler.

This is my third book with the same pillars of professional support: Jim Levine, Niki Papadopoulos, and Michael Craig. Like the previous two efforts, this book wouldn't have been possible without these dear friends.

Jim Levine has nurtured this project from the very beginning. Apart from his obvious acumen in protecting and advancing my interests as my agent, he has somehow managed to be constantly encouraging and optimistic, while maintaining a hawk's eye for challenging anything he thought would make the book better as it evolved.

Niki Papadopoulos has shaped this book as editor every step of the way. Her attention to detail is amazing, and she has an incredible capacity for understanding and directing a book's flow and organization. I trust her instincts and judgments completely. Simply put, Niki gets me. I can't overstate how important that is for getting me through the wrenching process of writing a book, nor can I express how much better this book is because of her.

I am grateful to Adrian Zackheim for his enthusiastic cheerleading of this project, as well as everyone in the Portfolio and entire Penguin Random House family, including Kimberly Meilun and Amanda Lang.

I am deeply indebted to Michael Craig, who has been essential to producing this book. In addition to being a great friend, he has been incredibly generous with his talents as editor, researcher, test-audience member, contributor of ideas and examples, compiler, and organizer of this material. I am confident that this book would not exist without him.

I'm also grateful to my research assistant, Antonio Grumser, as well as for the work of Meghna Sreenivas at the start of this project.

This book benefited tremendously from the input and feedback I received from all the companies, conferences, professional groups, and executives who have hired me, giving me an opportunity to workshop my ideas through consulting, coaching, keynotes, and retreats over the years. A special thank-you to the people at mParticle, who made possible a great illustration of kill criteria in action and gave their permission to mention the company by name.

This book is better because of the experiences I've had working with the Alliance for Decision Education, a nonprofit dedicated to building the field of decision education in K–12. My thanks to executive director Joe Sweeney, his entire staff, the board, the advisory council, the ambassador council, all the guests on the Alliance's *Decision Education Podcast*, and everyone who helps support the organization.

Thank you to Jenifer Sarver, Maralyn Beck, Luz Stable, Alicia McClung, and Jim Doughan for the constant, desperately needed help they provide in keeping my professional life together.

I am so grateful to my family, my husband, my children, my dad, my brother, my sister, and their entire families. These are the people most responsible for making me the happiest I have ever been. They have supported me every plodding step of the way. I'm thankful beyond words for them.

One last, final thank-you to the late Lila Gleitman, my mentor and best friend. Right up until the week she passed, Lila would inquire about this project, excited about the topic and eager to be my thought partner. A mentor's work lives on through their students and I hope she would have been proud of the finished project. I miss her every day.

NOTES

Prologue

MUHAMMAD ALI

The major events of Muhammad Ali's professional boxing career and post-boxing life are widely reported. Along with many other sources, you can find these established facts in the following books about Ali: Jonathan Eig, *Ali: A Life* (Boston: Mariner, 2017); Dave Hannigan, *Drama in the Bahamas: Muhammad Ali's Last Fight* (New York: Sports Publishing, 2016); Thomas Hauser, *Muhammad Ali: His Life and Times* (New York: Simon and Schuster, 1991); David Remnick, *King of the World: Muhammad Ali and the Rise of an American Hero* (New York: Random House, 1998); David West, ed., *The Mammoth Book of Muhammad Ali* (New York: Running Press, 2012).

Ali's ignoble end against Trevor Berbick in the Bahamas in December 1981 is the subject of Hannigan's entire book. In addition, the following sources provide similar and some additional details about the litany of problems dominating the final showcase of the greatest showman in the history of sports: BoxRec, "Trevor Berbick vs. Muhammad Ali" (including quotes from the contemporaneous reporting on the fight), last modified March 3, 2016, boxrec.com/media/index.php/Trevor_Berbick_vs._Muhammad_Ali; Mark Heisler, "From the Archives: Ali's Last Hurrah Turns into Circus with Few Laughs," *Los Angeles Times*, August 5, 2015 (original article date, December 12, 1981), latimes.com/sports/la-sp-ali-last-hurrah-19811212-story.html. See also Eig; Hauser; Remnick; West.

Muhammad Ali's subsequent diagnosis with Parkinson's and the accumulation of all the physical punishment, especially between the Foreman fight and the end of his career, is described in depth in all the books cited above.

GRIT VS. QUIT (INSPIRATIONAL QUOTES)

The specific inspirational quotes attributed to the list of luminaries are as follows:

Babe Ruth: "You just can't beat the person who never gives up."

Vince Lombardi: "Once you learn to quit, it becomes a habit." And, of course, "Winners never quit and quitters never win."

Bear Bryant: "Never quit. It is the easiest cop-out in the world. Set a goal and don't quit until you attain it. When you attain it, set another goal, and don't quit until you reach it. Never quit."

Jack Nicklaus: "Resolve never to quit, never to give up, no matter what the situation."

Mike Ditka: "You're never a loser until you quit trying."

Walter Payton: "If you start something, you shouldn't quit; that is what we were taught. If you're going to play, you might as well play to be your best."

Joe Montana: "My mother and father, Joe and Theresa Montana, brought me along and taught me never to quit, and to strive to be the best."

Billie Jean King: "Champions keep playing until they get it right."

Conrad Hilton: "Success . . . seems to be connected with action. Successful men keep moving. They make mistakes, but they don't quit."

Ted Turner: "You can never quit. Winners never quit, and quitters never win."

Richard Branson: "Treat failure as a lesson on how not to approach achieving a goal, and then use that learning to improve your chances of success when you try again. Failure is only the end if you decide to stop."

These quotes and countless others like them can be found on the quotation-aggregation websites, such as azquotes.com, brainyquote.com, or notable-quotes.com. If you go on shopping sites like Amazon or Etsy or numerous specialty retailers, you can find most of these on T-shirts, coffee mugs, paperweights, and posters.

The original sources for these quotes have not been verified for this book, though the point is not what any of these individuals actually said or meant. It's that the message in favor of grit is ubiquitous.

The source investigating the misattribution of one of the rare pro-quitting quotes is Quote Investigator, "If at First You Don't Succeed, Try, Try Again. Then Quit. There's No Use Being a Damn Fool about It," August 11, 2013, quoteinvestigator.com/2013/08/11/try-again.

GRIT VS. QUIT (SYNONYMS)

The synonyms for these terms are from merriam-webster.com and thesaurus.com and include different forms of these words as well as synonyms for "perseverance."

WRAPPED IN EUPHEMISM (LINDSEY VONN)

Lindsey Vonn posted her retirement announcement on Instagram on February 1, 2019, instagram.com/p/BtWBLQsnKXD. Her remarkable career accom-

plishments and numerous comebacks from serious injuries are mentioned by
Bill Pennington, "Lindsey Vonn to Retire," *New York Times*, February 1, 2019;
Clare Menzel, "Lindsey Vonn's Toughest Recovery Yet May Be Healing the
Heartbreak of Retiring," *Powder*, December 2019.

WRAPPED IN EUPHEMISM (THE BUTCHER GAG)

Milton Berle's gag appeared in Milt Rosen, ed., *Milton Berle's Private Joke File:
Over 10,000 of His Best Gags, Anecdotes, and One-Liners* (New York: Three
Rivers, 1989), 118.

Chapter 1

THE OPPOSITE OF A GREAT VIRTUE IS ALSO A GREAT VIRTUE

When I began considering quitting as the subject matter for a book, I discussed
it with Phil Tetlock, a mentor and friend. One of the things he said in that
conversation, paraphrasing a great quote from the past, was "The opposite of
a great virtue is a virtue. The opposite of grit is quitting, which is also a great
virtue."

That idea was an early North Star for me in developing this book. This is actually
the substance of *two* great quotes. Thomas Mann, in a 1929 essay on Sigmund
Freud, said, "A great truth is a truth whose opposite is also a truth." According
to Hans Bohr, son of physicist and Nobel Prize winner Niels Bohr, one of his
father's favorite maxims was "Profound truths [are] recognized by the fact
that the opposite is also a profound truth." (When King Frederick IX of Den-
mark conferred the Order of the Elephant on Niels Bohr in 1947, Bohr designed a coat of arms with the motto *"Contraria sunt complementa"* ("opposites
are complementary").

THE INVISIBLE MEN AT THE TOP OF THE WORLD

Much of the information about the Everest narrative is from Jon Krakauer's *Into
Thin Air: A Personal Account of the Mount Everest Disaster* (New York: Vil-
lard, 1997). I also reviewed portions of Lou Kasischke's memoir, *After the
Wind: Tragedy on Everest, One Survivor's Story* (Harbor Springs, MI: Good
Hart, 2014), especially pp. 125–127 (on the importance of turnaround times
on Everest) and 167–179 (with his first-person account of the decision to turn
around on summit day in 1996).

There are small differences in the two versions, understandable given the chaos
of the situation and the difficulty of thinking clearly under those extreme
conditions. Kasischke is more specific in identifying Rob Hall's earlier-stated
turnaround time (1 p.m.) than Krakauer (1 p.m. or 2 p.m.). Kasischke also

puts the time of when Stuart Hutchison and John Taske told him they were turning around at "close to noon," which is a bit later than the time frame of 11 to 11:30 a.m. mentioned by Krakauer. He also mentions briefly following the other climbers continuing to the summit before making the decision to, like Hutchison and Taske, return to Camp 4.

I was also fortunate to have the opportunity to discuss decision-making high on Everest with Ken Kamler, who has been the doctor for four Everest expeditions. This included a 1995 expedition, when he turned around just 300 feet from the summit, and in 1996, when he was one day from his own summit attempt and he abandoned that to provide medical care to seriously wounded survivors. I had conversations and correspondence with Dr. Kamler for this book, as well as discussing his experiences on Everest and decision-making on "Episode 013: Everest and Extreme Decision-Making with Dr. Ken Kamler," *The Decision Education Podcast*, September 8, 2021, alliancefordecision education.org/podcasts/episode-013-everest-and-extreme-decision-making -dr-ken-kamler. See also Ken Kamler, *Doctor on Everest* (Adarsh, 2014, reprint edition).

Ken Kamler provided the source for the eightfold increase in death rates on the descent from the summit. His insight on summit fever, though expressed by others, influenced my use of decision-making examples about mountain climbers throughout the book: "Your goal becomes getting to the summit and you forget about everything else. Even to the fact that getting to the summit, you're only halfway there. They think the ultimate goal is getting to the summit, but it's not. Your goal is getting back down."

I also had conversations for this book with Laurence Gonzales, an author and speaker on decision-making in dangerous environments. Gonzales helped me with his insight on how we don't "see" the quitters: "Quitting is such an anathema to you. You don't even see it when it happens in front of you. This is an important thing. We have to learn to see quitting, because we all imitate one another. We imitate victory. You see football players pounding their fists in the air. You have to see quitters, too."

QUITTING IS A DECISION-MAKING TOOL

For descriptions and advantages of the product development strategy of "minimum viable product," see Eric Ries, *The Lean Startup*. Famous examples of companies that started with MVPs include Amazon, Foursquare, Groupon, Zappos, Airbnb, and Facebook. Laura Holton, "11 Standout Examples of Minimum Viable Products," MYVA360, myva360.com/blog/examples-of -minimum-viable-products.

I first learned of Richard Pryor's dedication to experimentation at the Comedy Store in episode 2 of the five-part Showtime documentary *The Comedy Store*,

2020, written and directed by Mike Binder. Corroborating and additional details about Pryor, his process, and the Comedy Store appear in the following books: William Knoedelseder, *I'm Dying Up Here: Heartbreak and High Times in Stand-Up Comedy's Golden Era* (New York: PublicAffairs, 2009); Kliph Nesteroff, *The Comedians: Drunks, Thieves, Scoundrels and the History of American Comedy* (New York: Grove, 2015). References to Pryor's place in the history of stand-up comedy are from Ranker, "Comedy Central's 100 Greatest Standups of All Time," updated June 24, 2021, ranker.com/list /comedy-central_s-100-greatest-standups-of-all-time-v1/celebrity-insider; and Matthew Love, "50 Best Stand-Up Comics of All Time," *Rolling Stone*, February 14, 2017, rollingstone.com/culture/culture-lists/50-best-stand-up -comics-of-all-time-126359/richard-pryor-2-105990. Quotes of praise and acknowledgment about Pryor appear on richardpryor.com, "Praise of Richard Pryor," richardpryor.com/praise.

THE SIREN SONG OF CERTAINTY

In one of my conversations for this book with Richard Thaler, he said, "The only time that you're sure you should quit is when it's no longer a decision."

THE SUPER BOWL IS A CORPORATE GRAVEYARD

Journalist Jon Erlichman (@jonerlichman) wonderfully tweeted on the day of the 2021 Super Bowl a list of some of the businesses that advertised during Tom Brady's first Super Bowl appearance nineteen years before: twitter.com /jonerlichman/status/1358528486076526592?s=21.

"KNOW WHEN TO HOLD 'EM, KNOW WHEN TO FOLD 'EM": BUT MOSTLY, FOLD 'EM

Songwriter Don Schlitz wrote the lyrics to "The Gambler" in 1976. The song was recorded most famously by Kenny Rogers and released on the album of the same name, produced by Larry Butler, in November 1978. The single version of the song was released on November 15, 1978.

Chapter 2

The biographical information about Stewart Butterfield and the details of his development of *Game Neverending*, Flickr, *Glitch*, and Slack are from the following sources: Carlos Chicas Berti, "Slack Co-founder Stewart Butterfield on Thriving through Failure," *Business Class*, Fall 2018, onlineacademiccommunity .uvic.ca/gustavson/2019/05/01/slack-co-founder-stewart-butterfield-on -thriving-through-failure; E.B. Boyd, "A Flickr Founder's Glitch: Can a Game That Wants You to Play Nice Be a Blockbuster?," *Fast Company*, September

27, 2011, fastcompany.com/1783127/flickr-founders-glitch-can-game-wants
-you-play-nice-be-blockbuster; Deborah Gage, "Slack Raises $80 Million
Fund to Support Platform Strategy," *Wall Street Journal*, December 15, 2015,
blogs.wsj.com/digits/2015/12/15/slack-raises-80-million-fund-to-support
-platform-strategy; Erin Griffith, "Slack Stock Soars, Putting Company's
Public Value at $19.5 Billion," *New York Times*, June 20, 2019, nytimes.com
/2019/06/20/technology/slack-stock-ipo-price-trading.html; Reid Hoffman,
"How to Turn Failure into Success: Lessons from Slack's Stewart Butterfield
on the *Masters of Scale* Podcast," *Medium*, April 12, 2018, reid.medium.com
/how-to-turn-failure-into-success-lessons-from-slacks-stewart-butter
field-on-the-masters-of-scale-dfad48f2bbd2; Reid Hoffman, "*Masters of Scale*
Episode Transcript: Stewart Butterfield," *Masters of Scale*, mastersofscale
.com/stewart-butterfield-the-big-pivot; Mat Honan, "The Most Fascinating
Profile You'll Ever Read about a Guy and His Boring Startup," *Wired*, August
7, 2014, wired.com/2014/08/the-most-fascinating-profile-youll-ever-read
-about-a-guy-and-his-boring-startup; Maya Kosoff, "14 Surprising Facts about
Slack CEO Stewart Butterfield," *Inc.*, September 2, 2015, inc.com/business
-insider/behind-the-rise-of-stewart-butterfield-and-slack.html; Daniel Thomas,
"The $5bn Tech Boss Who Grew Up without Electricity," BBC, June 24,
2018, bbc.com/news/business-44550312; Aaron Tilley, "Salesforce Confirms
Deal to Buy Slack for $27.7 Billion," *Wall Street Journal*, December 1, 2020,
wsj.com/articles/salesforce-confirms-deal-to-buy-slack-for-27-7-billion
-11606857925.
Specific explanations of Butterfield's process of quitting *Glitch* and starting
Slack are from conversations with Stewart Butterfield for this book. References to emails and information about marketing and customer acquisition
and retention are from copies of those materials he shared with me during and
after those conversations.

QUIT WHILE YOU STILL HAVE A CHOICE
The information about the success rate of managerial hires and the cost of an
average hiring mistake are from the introduction of Geoff Smart and Randy
Street, *Who: The A Method for Hiring* (New York: Ballantine, 2008).

QUITTING DECISIONS ARE EXPECTED-VALUE DECISIONS
The information about Sarah Olstyn Martinez is from our conversations and
correspondence when she sought me out for advice and for this book. The
source for the information about firearm violence in the North Lawndale
neighborhood of Chicago is an article by Veronica Fitzpatrick et al., "Nonfa-
tal Firearm Violence Trends on the Westside of Chicago Between 2005 and
2016," *Journal of Community Health* 44, no. 5 (2019): 866–73.

TIME TRAVELERS FROM THE PAST

The information about Admiral McRaven's use of this concept in military decisions is from conversations and correspondence with William McRaven for this book.

FLIPPING COINS

See Steven Levitt, "Heads or Tails," 2021.

JUMPING THE SHARK

Fred Fox Jr., an extremely successful TV writer and producer between the mid-1970s and the late 1990s, is credited as the writer of the *Happy Days* episode (along with Garry Marshall as series creator) "accused" of the original instance of jumping the shark. Fox wrote a spirited, good-natured defense of the episode. See Fred Fox Jr., "First Person: In Defense of 'Happy Days'' 'Jump the Shark' Episode," *Los Angeles Times*, September 3, 2010, latimes.com/archives/la-xpm-2010-sep-03-la-et-jump-the-shark-20100903-story.html. That article also includes the information on the air date, ratings, and viewership of the episode.

THE QUITTING BIND

The information and quotes in this section are from the following sources: Jim Carnes, "Dave Chappelle Lets Rude Crowd Have It, Sticks Up for Cosby Comment," *Sacramento Bee*, June 17, 2004; Christopher John Farley, "On the Beach with Dave Chappelle," *Time*, May 15, 2005, content.time.com/time/magazine/article/0,9171,1061415,00.html; Josh Wolk, "EW Investigates the Disappearance of Dave Chappelle," *Entertainment Weekly*, May 16, 2005, ew.com/article/2005/05/16/ew-investigates-disappearance-dave-chappelle; Kevin Power, "Heaven Hell Dave Chappelle," *Esquire*, April 30, 2006; Oprah, "Chappelle's Story," February 3, 2006, oprah.com/oprahshow/chappelles-story; Hilton Als, "Who's Your Daddy?," *New Yorker*, July 14, 2014, newyorker.com/magazine/2014/07/07/whos-your-daddy; CBS News, "Dave Chappelle on Fame, Leaving 'Chappelle's Show' and Netflix Special," March 20, 2017, cbsnews.com/news/dave-chappelle-netflix-comedy-fame-leaving-chappelles-show; Biography, "Dave Chappelle," January 29, 2018, biography.com/performer/dave-chappelle.

Chapter 3

The seminal study on cab drivers' dependence for daily quitting-or-sticking decisions on whether they've reached an earnings target from Camerer et al., "Labor Supply of New York City Cabdrivers," 1997.

Princeton economist Henry Farber has conducted three studies that question findings of the Camerer et. al. study. See Farber, "Is Tomorrow Another Day?," 2005; Farber, "Reference-Dependent Preferences and Labor Supply," 2008; Farber, "Why You Can't Find a Taxi in the Rain," 2015.

Farber's 2005 study found that daily income effects on cab-driver stopping were small. But he did find that drivers used the reference-dependent heuristic of daily hours spent in the cab. That made an improvement to the behavior Camerer found, but was still suboptimal in making decisions whether to quit or continue based on demand. In his 2008 study, he concluded, "While there may be a reference level of income on a given day such that there is a discrete increase in the probability of stopping when that income level is reached, the reference level varies substantially day to day for a particular driver. Additionally, most shifts end before the reference income level is reached."

His 2015 study, based on data of all cab-driver trips in New York from 2009 to 2013, more directly contradicted Camerer, concluding "there is little evidence that reference dependence is an important factor determining the labor supply of NYC taxi drivers." He also noted the positive role of experience: "The estimated labor supply elasticity grows substantially with experience, and new drivers with small labor supply elasticities are more likely to quit."

Two studies of Singapore cab drivers reported findings similar to Camerer's. See Chou, "Testing Alternative Models of Labor Supply," 2002; Agarwal et al., "Labor Supply Decisions," 2013.

Economist Kirk Doran of Notre Dame reported in a 2014 study that, consistent with Camerer's results, "many workers decrease their daily hours in response to short-term wage increases that last less than a day." Doran, "Long-Term Wage Elasticities," 2014.

PAPER GAINS AND PAPER LOSSES

The material introduced in chapter 3 about aspects of Daniel Kahneman's work has been shaped by my conversations and correspondence with Kahneman during the course of writing this book.

Richard Thaler also shaped this chapter (and others, as will be noted) through my conversations and correspondence with him during the course of writing this book.

Kahneman and Tversky first laid out prospect theory in "Prospect Theory: An Analysis of Decision under Risk," 1979. They developed a subsequent version of prospect theory in "Advances in Prospect Theory," 1992. Kahneman described prospect theory in detail in *Thinking, Fast and Slow*.

A 2020 paper by Kai Ruggeri and more than thirty coauthors summarized the massive influence of prospect theory: "It is difficult to overstate the level of importance that Prospect Theory has had on science, policy, management, financial services, government and beyond." In addition, they cite prospect theory as "the most influential theoretical framework in all of the social sciences," and "the most cited economic paper and is among the most-cited in psychological sciences." This international roster of coauthors re-created the methods and procedures of the original *Econometrica* study in nineteen countries and thirteen languages. They concluded that "the principles of Prospect Theory replicate beyond any reasonable thresholds." Ruggeri et al., "Replicating Patterns of Prospect Theory," 2020. See also the prepublication version, "Not Lost in Translation," 2019.

Because of loss aversion's importance as an aspect of prospect theory, the citations above also describe Kahneman and Tversky's foundations of loss aversion. See also Kahneman and Tversky, "Choices, Values, and Frames," 1984; Tversky and Kahneman, "Loss Aversion in Riskless Choice," 1991. Nathan Novemsky and Kahneman described a history of loss aversion, including numerous theoretical and experimental contributions by other scientists. Novemsky and Kahneman, "The Boundaries of Loss Aversion," 2005, 120. For some estimates of the size of the asymmetry of the emotional impact of losses compared to equivalent gains, see Kahneman, *Thinking, Fast and Slow*, 284; Thaler, *Misbehaving*, 34.

QUIT WHILE YOU'RE AHEAD?

One of the few aphorisms that encourage quitting is "Quit while you're ahead." The quote originated with a priest named Baltasar Gracian, who wrote it as advice in a 1647 book named *The Art of Worldly Wisdom*. (Gracian added, "All the best gamblers do.")

TAKE THE MONEY AND RUN

The study referred to in this section is Heimer et al., "Dynamic Inconsistency," 2020 and 2021. This section is also based on conversations and correspondence with Alex Imas for this book.

Imas's research and insights were especially valuable because his study specifically looked into the quitting of retail traders compared with their *planned* quitting (in the form of take-profit orders and stop-loss orders). The general tendency of investors to sell winning investments too soon and hold losing investments too long is well documented. See, as an example, the famous study by Terrance Odean, "Are Investors Reluctant to Realize Their Losses?," 1998.

HOW SMART IS THE SMART MONEY?

Henry Farber's work is cited in the "cab drivers" note in this chapter.

The study about buying and selling decisions of experienced, successful portfolio managers is Akepanidtaworn et al., "Selling Fast and Buying Slow," 2019.

Information and findings from the study are also from conversations and correspondence with Alex Imas for this book.

Interlude I

Most of the details described are from viewing the 2018 documentary *Free Solo*, directed by Jimmy Chin and Elizabeth Chai Vasarhelyi. For the credits on *Free Solo*, see IMDb, *Free Solo*, "Full Cast & Crew," imdb.com/title /tt7775622/fullcredits, especially for the lengthy lists of camera, sound, and other technical crew involved. Some details not in the film are from the following articles: Daniel Duane, "El Capitan, My El Capitan," *New York Times*, June 9, 2017, nytimes.com/2017/06/09/opinion/el-capitan-my-el-capitan .html; Peter Gwin, "How Jimmy Chin Filmed Alex Honnold's Death-Defying Free Solo," *National Geographic*, November 2018, nationalgeographic.com /culture/article/alex-honnold-jimmy-chin-free-solo-yosemite-el-capitan -explore-through-the-lens; Matt Ray, "How Free Solo Climber Alex Honnold Conquered El Capitan," Red Bull, February 8, 2019, redbull.com/us-en/alex -honnold-interview-free-solo.

Chapter 4

The main source for Harold Staw's story was his son, Barry Staw. He shared the story and the details included here during several conversations and in subsequent correspondence. Barry Staw also wrote a brief summary of his father's story in "Stumbling toward a Social Psychology of Organizations," 2016, 10.

Some details on the merger with Sage, the stock offering of the post-merger company (Sage International), the initial valuation based on the offering, and the Staw family's share ownership are from "Sage International Files for Stock Offering," *Securities and Exchange Commission News Digest*, May 1, 1962, p. 2, sec.gov/news/digest/1962/dig050162.pdf.

WAITING UNTIL IT HURTS

Rubin and Brockner, "Factors Affecting Entrapment in Waiting Situations," 1975. The introduction to that study mentions the U.S. involvement in the Vietnam War as an entrapment situation, 1054.

Rubin and Brockner initially referred to the phenomenon as "entrapment" or "escalation traps," though they later adopted the term "escalation of commitment." Their influential later work includes the following: Rubin et al., "Factors Affecting Entry into Psychological Traps," 1980; Brockner et al., "Factors Affecting Entrapment in Escalating Conflicts," 1982; Brockner and Rubin, *Entrapment in Escalating Conflicts*, 1985; Brockner et al., "Escalation of

Commitment to an Ineffective Course of Action," 1986; Brockner, "The Escalation of Commitment to a Failing Course of Action," 1992.

Chapter 5

The original plans, goals, and projections for the California bullet train are from documents of the Authority, specifically *California High-Speed Train Business Plan*, November 2008; *Report to the Legislature*, December 2009.

The delays, increases in cost, and extensions of the completion date appear in the Authority's biennial business plans: *Building California's Future*, April 2012 (Revised 2012 Business Plan); *Connecting California*, April 30, 2014; *Connecting and Transforming California*, May 1, 2016; *Transforming Travel, Expanding Economy, Connecting California*, June 1, 2018; *Recovery and Transformation*, submitted April 12, 2021 (Revised 2020 Business Plan); *Draft 2022 Business Plan*, February 2022. See also *Project Update Report to the California State Legislature: Delivering High-Speed Rail to Californians*, May 2019; "The Economic Impact of California High-Speed Rail," 2022.

Information about the belated recognition of the challenges, costs, and uncertainties in tunneling under the Pacheco Pass and Tehachapi Mountains is from the 2018 business plan, *Transforming Travel, Expanding Economy, Connecting California*, pp. ii, 17–18, 23, 28, 45–46, 47, 57, 114 (California High-Speed Rail Peer Review Group Letter); *Recovery and Transformation* (Revised 2020 Business Plan), pp. 73–74.

The description of developments on the California bullet train are also from reporting by the following sources: Jeff Daniels, "California's $77 Billion 'Bullet Train to Nowhere' Faces a Murky Future as Political Opposition Ramps Up," CNBC, March 12, 2018, cnbc.com/2018/03/12/californias-77-billion-high-speed-rail-project-is-in-trouble.html; Adam Nagourney, "A $100 Billion Train: The Future of California or a Boondoggle?," *New York Times*, July 30, 2018, nytimes.com/2018/07/30/us/california-high-speed-rail.html; Reihan Salam, "Gavin Newsom's Big Idea," *The Atlantic*, February 15, 2019, theatlantic.com/ideas/archive/2019/02/governor-newsom-addresses-californias-housing-crisis/582892; Associated Press, "California Bullet Train Cost Rises by Another $1 Billion," *U.S. News & World Report*, February 12, 2020, usnews.com/news/best-states/california/articles/2020-02-12/california-bullet-train-cost-rises-by-another-1-billion; Nico Savidge, "Got $13 Billion? Planning for High Speed Rail's Bay Area Link Continues, without Money to Make it Happen," *San Jose Mercury News*, May 3, 2020, mercurynews.com/2020/05/03/got-13-billion-planning-for-high-speed-rails-bay-area-link-continues-without-money-to-make-it-happen; Dustin Gardiner, "California's Bullet-Train Project Faces Unprecedented Woes," *San Francisco Chronicle*, July 9,

2020, sfchronicle.com/politics/article/California-s-bullet-train-project-faces
-15356051.php; Associated Press, "California Again Pushes Back High-Speed
Rail Construction Deadline," KTLA, February 5, 2021, ktla.com/news/cal
ifornia/california-again-pushes-back-high-speed-rail-construction-deadline;
Kim Sloway, "What's Behind the California Bullet Train Project's Latest
Woes?," *Construction Dive*, April 8, 2021, constructiondive.com/news/whats
-behind-the-california-bullet-train-projects-latest-woes/597850; Kathleen
Ronayne, "California Bullet Train's Latest Woe: Will It Be High Speed?,"
San Jose Mercury News, October 13, 2021, mercurynews.com/2021/10/13
/california-bullet-trains-latest-woe-will-it-be-high-speed; Ralph Vartabedian,
"Costs of California's Trouble Bullet Train Rise Again, by an Estimated $5
Billion," *Los Angeles Times*, February 8, 2022, latimes.com/california/story
/2022-02-08/california-bullet-train-costs-rise-roughly-5-billion.

THE SUNK COST EFFECT

Two of the most influential scholarly papers identifying and explaining the sunk
cost effect are Richard Thaler's "Toward a Positive Theory of Consumer
Choice," 1980; and Arkes and Blumer's "The Psychology of Sunk Cost," 1985
(including the results of ten experiments demonstrating the sunk cost effect
and the example of the Tennessee-Tombigbee Waterway).

WHEN "PUBLIC WORKS" IS AN OXYMORON

Facts and quotes about the Tennessee-Tombigbee Waterway are from Arkes and
Blumer, 1985. Facts and quotes about the Shoreham Nuclear Power Plant are
from Ross and Staw, "Organizational Escalation and Exit," 1993. See also Flyvbjerg, Holm, and Buhl, "Underestimating Costs in Public Works Projects," 2002.

KATAMARI

Little did I know that the devotion of my oldest daughter to a video game and the
hours I spent watching her play *Katamari Damacy* a decade and a half ago
would offer me such a whimsical but totally appropriate metaphor for escalation of commitment.

Information on the original version of the game is from the following sources:
L. E. Hall, *Katamari Damacy* (Boss Fight, 2018); Ivan Sulick, "Katamari
Damacy," originally posted September 16, 2004, updated December 12, 2018,
IGN, ign.com/articles/2004/09/16/katamari-damacy; Steven Kent, "Katamari
Damashii: The Snowball Effect," April 8, 2004, GameSpy, ps2.gamespy
.com/playstation-2/katamari-damashii/504503p1.html; Malindy Hetfield,
"The Joy of Katamari Damacy," December 14, 2018, Eurogamer, eurogamer
.net/articles/2018-12-14-the-joy-of-katamari-damacy.

HOW BIG DOES THE KATAMARI GROW?

See Staw, "Knee-Deep in the Big Muddy," 1976.

Staw, along with several collaborators, used this same general design with modifications to establish specific aspects of escalation of commitment and the effectiveness (or ineffectiveness) of different means of combating this escalation. See Staw and Fox, "Escalation: Determinants of Commitment," 1977; Staw and Ross, "Commitment to a Policy Decision," 1978; Fox and Staw, "The Trapped Administrator," 1979; Simonson and Staw, "Deescalation Strategies," 1992.

MENTAL ACCOUNTING

As I was struggling with an early draft of a section about mental accounting, I had a conversation with Richard Thaler, during which he reminded me of the importance of including the concept and getting it right, at one point saying, "I think everything in life is about mental accounting." Conversations and correspondence with Thaler played an enormous role in making the explanation of mental accounting, if not "right," definitely far better.

Mental accounting is, like loss aversion, a cornerstone of prospect theory. Kahneman and Tversky first described mental accounting in the paper "Choices, Values, and Frames," 1984. In the article, the authors noted the importance of Thaler's work, including his writings in progress not published until shortly after this paper appeared. (On page 346: "Our analysis of mental accounting owes a large debt to the stimulating work of Richard Thaler, who showed the relevance of this process to consumer behavior.") Thaler's first explanation of this concept and its connection with prospect theory, along with so many other groundbreaking ideas, appeared in "Toward a Positive Theory of Consumer Choice" in 1980, as part of an "individual's psychic accounting system."

In addition to Thaler's personal contribution, his most influential papers on mental accounting include "Mental Accounting and Consumer Choice," 1985; "Mental Accounting Matters," 1999. See also Thaler, *Misbehaving*, 56–84, 115–24; Thaler and Sunstein, *Nudge*, 49–52; Kahneman, *Thinking, Fast and Slow*, 342–52.

See Flepp, Meier, and Franck, "The Effect of Paper Outcomes versus Realized Outcomes on Subsequent Risk-Taking," 2021.

Raphael Flepp of the University of Zurich and colleagues studied individual-level results of more than four thousand slot machine players making an average of six casino visits during a four-month period. Because they used personalized player cards, their gains and losses were open until they left the casino, at which time a money transfer took place.

The researchers found that during a casino visit, the players significantly increased their risk-taking when they had paper losses, and the effect increased with the size of their unrealized loss, demonstrating the aversion to closing mental accounts in the losses. Once the players left the casino and those outcomes became realized losses, they did not take those risks on subsequent visits. In fact, in contrast to their behavior during visits ending in a big loss, they significantly *decreased* their level of risk-taking when they next played at the casino.

THE HARDEST COST TO BEAR

General Thomas told me this story during a conversation about sunk cost and other issues related to this book.

See also Arkes and Blumer, 126 (use of past casualties in the Vietnam War to justify continuation of the war); Teger, 1 (Vietnam); Barry Schwartz, "The Sunk-Cost Fallacy: Bush Falls Victim to a Bad New Argument for the Iraq War," *Slate*, September 9, 2005, slate.com/news-and-politics/2005/09/bush -is-a-sucker-for-the-sunk-cost-fallacy.html (quoting an August 2005 speech by then president George W. Bush justifying staying the course in Iraq by saying, "We owe [the two thousand soldiers who had already died] something. We will finish the task that they gave their lives for."); Van Putten, Zeelenberg, and Van Dijk, "Who Throws Good Money after Bad?," 2010, 33 ("one of the most important reasons to continue the way in Iraq was to prevent acknowledging that soldiers who fell in battle died in vain").

THE DIFFERENCE BETWEEN KNOWING AND DOING

The facts in this story are from a conversation with Don Moore, who also wrote an account of it in *Perfectly Confident,* 131–32, as well as Rubin's obituary by Wolfgang Saxon, "Jeffrey Z. Rubin, 54, an Expert on Negotiation," *New York Times*, June 9, 1995, nytimes.com/1995/06/09/obituaries/jeffrey-z-rubin-54 -an-expert-on-negotiation.html. General background about one hundred highest peaks in New England is from Lindsey Gordon, "A Quick Guide to the New England 100 Highest," March 27, 2019, *TheTrek*, thetrek.co/quick -guide-new-england-100-highest.

YOU CAN'T JEDI MIND TRICK BEING FRESH TO A DECISION

See Simonson and Staw, "Deescalation Strategies," 1992.

Chapter 6

The facts and descriptions about Astro Teller's leadership at X, X's mission and culture, particular projects at X, monkeys and pedestals, and kill criteria are from conversations and correspondence with Astro Teller and Libby Leahy, head of communications at X, and the following additional sources: x.com pany; Astro Teller, "Failure, Innovation, and Engineering Culture," video recorded at re: Work with Google event, May 24, 2016, youtube.com/watch?v=3SsnY2BvzeA; Astro Teller, "A Peek Inside the Moonshot Factory Operating Manual," *X* (blog), July 23, 2016, blog.x.company/a-peek-inside-the-moonshot-factory-operating-manual-f5c33c9ab4d7; Adele Peters, "Why Alphabet's Moonshot Factory Killed Off a Brilliant, Carbon-Neutral Fuel," *Fast Company*, October 13, 2016, fastcompany.com/3064457/why-alphabets-moonshot-factory-killed-off-a-brilliant-carbon-neutral-fuel; Astro Teller, "Tackle the Monkey First," *X* (blog), December 7, 2016, blog.x.company/tackle-the-monkey-first-90fd6223e04d; Kathy Hannun, "Three Things I Learned from Turning Seawater into Fuel," *X* (blog), December 7, 2016, blog.x.company/three-things-i-learned-from-turning-seawater-into-fuel-66aeec36cfaa; Derek Thompson, "Google X and the Science of Radical Creativity," *The Atlantic*, November 2017, theatlantic.com/magazine/archive/2017/11/x-google-moonshot-factory/540648; Alex Davies, "Inside X, the Moonshot Factory Racing to Build the Next Google, *Wired*, July 11, 2018, wired.com/story/alphabet-google-x-innovation-loon-wing-graduation; *"The Gimbal V2.0,"* July 2018, storage.googleapis.com/x-prod.appspot.com/files/the_x_gimbal_v2.10_web.pdf ("a guide to X's moonshot factory culture"); Astro Teller, "Tips for Unleashing Radical Creativity," X (blog), February 12, 2020, blog.x.company/tips-for-unleashing-radical-creativity-f4ba55602e17; Astro Teller, "Loon's Final Flight," X (blog), January 21, 2021, blog.x.company/loons-final-flight-e9d699123a96.

Background facts about Teller and X are from the following sources: "Astro Teller, Captain of Moonshots," *X*, x.company/team/astroteller; "Biography," Astro Teller, astroteller.net/about/bio; several of the articles collected on astroteller.net, "Articles," astroteller.net/press/articles; Thompson, "Google X and the Science of Radical Creativity"; Alphabet's 2020 annual report and SEC Form 10-K, as of December 31, 2020.

The direct quotes from Teller and the description of X's consideration of a hyperloop project are from conversations and correspondence with Astro Teller.

KILL CRITERIA
See Simonson and Staw, "Deescalation Strategies," 1992.

FUNNEL VISION
The example is from my work with mParticle.

STATES AND DATES
The example from the raid on Osama bin Laden is from conversations and

correspondence with Admiral McRaven. The example of setting a date for a tenure-track position is from conversations and correspondence with Kevin Zollman.

Interlude II

The basis for much of the information about Sasha Cohen's story is from conversations and correspondence with her for this book. Additional details for this interlude came from the following sources: Sasha Cohen, "An Olympian's Guide to Retiring at 25," *New York Times*, February 24, 2018, nytimes.com /2018/02/24/opinion/sunday/sasha-cohen-olympics-pyeongchang.html; the 2020 documentary *The Weight of Gold* (Podium Pictures), directed by Brett Rapkin, written by Aaron Cohen and Rapkin, in which Cohen appeared; Jessica Lachenal, "Figure Skater Sasha Cohen Has a Surprising New Career Off the Ice," *Bustle*, July 29, 2020, bustle.com/entertainment/what-is-sasha -cohen-doing-now; Megan Sauer, "Sasha Cohen: Embracing Uncertainty," U.S. Figure Skating Fan Zone, March 30, 2021, usfigureskatingfanzone.com /news/2021/3/30/figure-skating-sasha-cohen-embracing-uncertainty.aspx. Some details of Cohen's competitive record were from Cohen's Wikipedia page, en.wikipedia.org/wiki/Sasha_Cohen.

Chapter 7

Information about Andrew Wilkinson's background and successes with MetaLab, Tiny Capital, and other investments are from "Warren Buffett for Startups, Andrew Wilkinson," *The Hustle*, July 27, 2020, thehustle.co/warren-buffett -for-startups-andrew-wilkinson; Allen Lee, "10 Things You Didn't Know about Andrew Wilkinson," *Money Inc.*, December 26, 2020, moneyinc.com /andrew-wilkinson.

Wilkinson's experience with Flow came to my attention through a long Twitter thread he posted on March 30, 2021, twitter.com/awilkinson/status /1376985854229504007. The details of his Flow story are from that thread as well as conversations and correspondence with Andrew Wilkinson.

That Dustin Moskovitz had a different interpretation of what happened at his meeting with Wilkinson is obvious from Moskovitz's replies in the Twitter thread above, as well as in another thread started by Wilkinson on December 27, 2019, twitter.com/awilkinson/status/1210696247587139584, in which Wilkinson weighed in on a Twitter debate on bootstrapping versus venture capital. I described Wilkinson's view of the meeting because of the likelihood that his perception affected his future decisions. Therefore, it wasn't necessary to determine the degree to which Wilkinson's description or interpretation was correct (or reasonable) or not.

THE ENDOWMENT EFFECT

Richard Thaler named the endowment effect in his 1980 paper "Toward a Positive Theory of Consumer Choice." That's also where he told the wine-collecting story. The update is from Kahneman, Knetsch, and Thaler, "The Endowment Effect, Loss Aversion, and Status Quo Bias," 1991. Kahneman identified their wine-loving friend in *Thinking, Fast and Slow* as the late Richard Rosett, longtime economics professor and former dean of the University of Chicago Booth School of Business. Thaler did the same in *Misbehaving*, also noting that when he sent Rosett a copy of an article in which he told the story and referred to Rosett as "Mr. R," Rosett's two-word reply was, "Ah fame!" *Misbehaving*, 17.

The papers by Jack Knetsch referred to in this section, in addition to the 1991 paper with Kahneman and Thaler cited above, are Knetsch, "The Endowment Effect and Evidence of Nonreversible Indifference Curves," 1989; Kahneman, Knetsch, and Thaler, "Experimental Tests of the Endowment Effect," 1990.

The reference to the review of the endowment-effect literature is from Morewedge and Giblin, "Explanations of the Endowment Effect," 2015.

The reference to the IKEA effect study was from Norton, Mochon, and Ariely, "The IKEA Effect," 2012.

The following papers examined the application of the endowment effect to psychological ownership, which includes possession of our ideas, beliefs, and choices, as well as connections we make with organizations with which we affiliate: Dommer and Swaminathan, "Explaining the Endowment Effect through Ownership," 2013; Morewedge et al., "Bad Riddance or Good Rubbish?," 2009; Pierce, Kostova, and Dirks, "Toward a Theory of Psychological Ownership in Organizations," 2001; Pierce, Kostova, and Dirks, "The State of Psychological Ownership," 2003; Reb and Connolly, "Possession, Feelings of Ownership and the Endowment Effect," 2002; Shu and Peck, "Psychological Ownership and Affective Reaction," 2011.

See also Peck and Shu, *Psychological Ownership and Consumer Behavior*, 2018 (an entire book of scholarly papers on topics related to psychological ownership).

The explanations in this section also reflect conversations and correspondence with Richard Thaler and Daniel Kahneman for this book.

PRO SPORTS TEAMS AND THEIR ESCALATING COMMITMENT TO HIGH DRAFT PICKS

The original studies demonstrating the effect of draft order, independent of skill or productivity level, are Staw and Hoang, "Why Draft Order Affects Playing Time," 1995; Camerer and Weber, "Econometrics and Behavioral Economics of Escalation of Commitment," 1999.

In the post-*Moneyball* era, there is naturally the question of whether the emphasis on decision-making driven by analytics has corrected for irrationalities based on sunk costs, the endowment effect, or escalation bias. Quinn Keefer, in 2017, found that in the NFL, "despite being no more productive, the first round selections receive a compensation premium, which leads to them starting significantly more games." See Keefer, "Sunk-Cost Fallacy in the National Football League," 2017, 282.

This is consistent with additional work by Keefer finding a relationship (again, independent of skill or productivity) between playing time and the salaries (which for newly drafted players are increasingly standardized in the NFL, NBA, and MLB based on draft order). See Keefer, "Decision-Maker Beliefs and the Sunk-Cost Fallacy," 2018; Keefer, "Sunk Costs in the NBA," 2021. See also Hinton and Sun, "The Sunk-Cost Fallacy and the National Basketball Association," 2020, 1019 (finding a "small but significant sunk-cost effect"). Salary and draft order are not interchangeable measures of endowment or sunk cost but are both relevant to these issues and increasingly related for pro athletes in team sports at the beginning of their careers.

Daniel Leeds, Michael Leeds, and Akira Motomura presented the contrary finding, that there is no sunk cost effect from NBA draft order, in "Are Sunk Costs Irrelevant?," 2015.

THE STATUS QUO IS HARD TO QUIT

See Samuelson and Zeckhauser, "Status Quo Bias in Decision Making," 1988. The 1991 paper by Kahneman, Knetsch, and Thaler, in addition to its importance on the endowment effect, is also regarded as one of the foundational explanations for status quo bias.

Marketing professors David Gal and Derek Rucker, who have disputed the validity of loss aversion as a generalized principle, consider much of the behavior attributed to loss aversion as the result of status quo bias. Gal and Rucker, "The Loss of Loss Aversion," 2018; see also Gal, "A Psychological Law of Inertia," 2006.

The overlap and differences between status quo bias and omission-commission bias are beyond the scope of this book. For discussion of this issue, as well as explanation of omission-commission bias, see Ritov and Baron, "Status-Quo and Omission Biases," 1992; Baron and Ritov, "Reference Points and Omission Bias," 1994; Ritov and Baron, "Outcome Knowledge, Regret, and Omission Bias," 1995; Schweitzer, "Disentangling Status Quo and Omission Effects," 1994.

The Keynes quote is from John Maynard Keynes, *The General Theory of Employment, Interest, and Money*, 1936, 79–80 (International Relations and

Security Network edition, files.ethz.ch/isn/125515/1366_KeynesTheoryof
Employment.pdf).

THE PRICE OF STICKING

For a video of the MIT Sloan Sports Analytics Conference event featuring Rich-
ard Thaler, see "The Sports Learning Curve: Why Teams Are Slow to Learn and
Adapt," 2020, sloansportsconference.com/event/the-sports-learning-curve
-why-teams-are-slow-to-learn-and-adapt. The video includes the slide deck
"Learning by Sports Teams" by Chris Avery, Kevin Meers, and Richard Thaler.
See also Mauboussin and Callahan, "Turn and Face the Strange," 2021.

Chapter 8

Business stories chronicling Sears's decline, divestitures, and fall (which also con-
tain historical information): Robert Lindsey, "Sears, Roebuck: Nation's Banker?,"
New York Times, April 17, 1977, nytimes.com/1977/04/17/archives/sears
-roebuck-nations-banker-sears-roebuck-nations-banker.html; Stanley Ziemba,
"Sears Slips to No. 3 in the Retail Kingdom, Behind Wal-Mart, K," *Chicago
Tribune*, February 21, 1991, chicagotribune.com/news/ct-xpm-1991-02-21
-9101170011-story.html; "Sears Approves Spinoff of Dean Witter, Discover
& Co.," UPI, June, 18, 1993, upi.com/Archives/1993/06/18/Sears-approves
-spinoff-of-Dean-Witter-Discover-Co/4516740376000; Barnaby Feder, "Sears,
Returning to Its Roots, Is Giving Up Allstate," *New York Times*, November
11, 1994, nytimes.com/1994/11/11/us/sears-returning-to-its-roots-is-giving
-up-allstate.html; Genevieve Buck, "Allstate, Sears Set to Split Up," *Chicago
Tribune*, March 31, 1995, chicagotribune.com/news/ct-xpm-1995-03-31
-9503310328-story.html; Peter Truell, "Morgan Stanley and Dean Witter
Agree to Merge," *New York Times*, February 6, 1997, nytimes.com/1997/02/06
/business/morgan-stanley-and-dean-witter-agree-to-merge.html; Lorene Yue,
"Citigroup Buys Sears Credit Division," *Chicago Tribune*, July 16, 2003,
chicagotribune.com/news/ct-xpm-2003-07-16-0307160208-story.html.
Additional timelines and histories of Sears: "Sears, Roebuck & Co.," Encyclopedia
of Chicago, encyclopedia.chicagohistory.org/pages/2840.html; Vicki Howard, "The Rise and Fall of Sears," *Smithsonian*, July 25, 2017, smithsonian
mag.com/history/rise-and-fall-sears-180964181; Tiffany Hsu, "Sears Went
from Gilded-Age Boom to Digital-Age Bankruptcy," *New York Times*, October
15, 2018, nytimes.com/2018/10/15/business/sears-bankrupt-history-timeline
.html; Chris Isodore, "Sears' Extraordinary History: A Timeline," CNN,
October 2018, cnn.com/interactive/2018/10/business/sears-timeline/index
.html; "History of Sears, Roebuck and Co.," Reference for Business, n.d., ca.

1996, referenceforbusiness.com/history2/88/Sears-Roebuck-and-Co.html; Kori Rumore, "Rise, Fall and Restructuring of a Chicago Icon: More Than 130 Years of Sears," *Chicago Tribune*, April 24, 2019, chicagotribune.com /news/ct-sears-company-history-timeline-htmlstory.html; searsarchives.com; Mike Snider, "A Look Back at Some of Sears Ventures, Beyond Retail Stores, Through the Years," *USA Today*, October 15, 2018, usatoday.com/story /money/nation-now/2018/10/15/sears-had-far-reaching-legacy-beyond-retail -into-brands-and-financials/1645882002.

For a timeline of Allstate, see "Allstate History & Timeline," Allstate, allstate .com/about/history-timeline.aspx.

Studies and scholarly papers (which also include historical information): Shoshanna Delventhal, "Who Killed Sears? Fifty Years on the Road to Ruin," Investopedia, September 26, 2020, investopedia.com/news/downfall-of-sears; Gillan, Kensinger, and John Martin, "Value Creation and Corporate Diversi-fication," 2000; Raff and Temin, "Sears, Roebuck in the Twentieth Century," 1999; Lawrence J. Ring and John S. Strong, "Sears and Kmart, a Sad, Sad Story," July 2017, babson.edu/academics/executive-education/babson-insight /strategy-and-innovation/sears-and-kmart-a-sad-sad-story/# (referring to the Sears-Kmart merger as "a double suicide"); Varadrajan, Jayachandran, and White, "Strategic Interdependence in Organizations," 2001.

Some of the information about Sears's IPO is from "Landmark IPO Helps an American Retailing Icon Achieve the Next Level of Growth," Goldman Sachs, goldmansachs.com/our-firm/history/moments/1906-sears-roebuck-ipo.html.

Conversations and correspondence with Barry Staw were instrumental in bring-ing the Sears story to my attention as a potential topic related to escalation of commitment. I also had a conversation with Daniel Raff.

THE CULT OF IDENTITY

See Festinger, Riecken, and Schachter, *When Prophecy Fails*.

At the end of this section, in the summary about the broad impact identity has on our quitting decisions, I benefited from insights in conversations for this book with behavioral scientist Maya Shankar (whose story appears in chapter 10). She reminded me that we set children on the path of connecting their identity to an adult job: "When kids are growing up, they're often asked what they want to be when they grow up, which means they're attaching their iden-tity to a sole profession. That increases the friction that they will have from departing from that identity."

COGNITIVE DISSONANCE

The development, significance, and applications of dissonance theory go far be-yond the scope of this book. The study of cognitive dissonance, if marked from *When Prophecy Fails* and Leon Festinger's massively influential *A Theory of Cognitive Dissonance*, is now in its eighth decade. For a recent introduction, history, and overview of cognitive dissonance theory, see Harmon-Jones and Mills, "An Introduction to Cognitive Dissonance Theory," 2019.

Elliot Aronson, a student of Festinger, has researched and written about cognitive dissonance since 1960. After more than thirty years of work, he was in the position of writing about the theory's "comeback." Aronson, "The Return of the Repressed," 1992. (The quote from Aronson in this section is on pp. 304–305 of this paper.) Nearly thirty years after *that* paper, he wrote (with Carol Tavris) about the application of cognitive dissonance to the pandemic. "The Role of Cognitive Dissonance in the Pandemic," 2020. Aronson and Tavris also describe Festinger's work, cognitive dissonance in general, and some of the history and breadth of dissonance research in their book, *Mistakes Were Made*.

See also Beasley and Joslyn, "Cognitive Dissonance and Post-Decision Attitude Change," 2001; Fried and Aronson, "Hypocrisy, Misattribution, and Dissonance Reduction," 1995; Harmon-Jones, *Cognitive Dissonance*.

THE MIRROR AND THE WINDOW

The papers referred to on the size of the effects of internal and external identity in escalation of commitment are Staw, "Knee-Deep in the Big Muddy," 1976; Fox and Staw, "The Trapped Administrator," 1979.

Several of Staw's most influential papers on escalation of commitment explain the relation to dissonance theory as well as internal and external aspects of identity. Staw and Fox, "Escalation: The Determinants of Commitment," 1977; Staw and Ross, "Commitment to a Policy Decision," 1978; Staw, "The Escalation of Commitment to a Course of Action," 1981; Staw, McKechnie, and Puffer, "The Justification of Organizational Performance," 1983; Chatman, Staw, and Bell, "The Managed Thought," 1986; Ross and Staw, "Understanding Behavior in Escalation Situations," 1989; Ross and Staw, "Managing Escalation Processes in Organizations," 1991; Simonson and Staw, "Deescalation Strategies," 1992.

OUT ON A LIMB

See Beshears and Milkman, "Do Sell-Side Stock Analysts Exhibit Escalation of Commitment?," 2011.

The quote from Andrew Wilkinson was from a conversation with him for this book.

MISTAKEN IDENTITY

The quotes are from conversations with Sarah Olstyn Martinez for this book.

A RAY OF HOPE

If you want an example of a company that seems at first glance like it would be susceptible to being trapped by its identity, it would be Philips. The Dutch company has been instantly identifiable for more than a century for making light bulbs. The founders of the company, in 1891, were brothers Gerard and Anton Philips. For its first *eighty* years, it had just four CEOs: the Philips brothers, Anton's son-in-law, and Anton's son. Of course, the Philips brothers, going back to 1914 (if not earlier), showed that having a family member in charge or the family name on the company or on its products did not constrain it from expanding or changing the composition of the business.

Sources for the Philips story are the following: corporate websites and Wikipedia.org pages for Philips, Philips USA, the Philips Museum, and Signify (the corporate name adopted in 2018 by what was formerly known as Philips Lighting, spun off in 2016); Philips, "Philips Celebrates 100 Years of Research," news release, January 9, 2014, dev.usa.philips.com/a-w/about/news/archive/standard/news/press/2014/20140109-Philips-celebrates-100-years-of-research.html; "Philips to Spin of Lighting Branch in 'Historic' IPO," *IndustryWeek*, May 3, 2016, industryweek.com/finance/article/21972654/philips-to-spin-off-lighting-branch-in-historic-ipo; Philips *2020 Annual Report*, philips.com/c-dam/corporate/about-philips/investors/shareholder-info/agm-2021/Philips%20Annual%20Report%202020.pdf; Signify, *2020 Annual Report*, signify.com/static/2020/signify-annual-report-2020.pdf.

Chapter 9

Ron Conway's approach described in the narrative is from conversations and correspondence with Ron Conway for this book.

Information about Ron Conway's background, successful investments, aspects of his approach, and/or the esteem in which he is held among founders, venture capitalists, and throughout Silicon Valley is from the following sources: "The Ronco Principle," Paul Graham, January 2015, paul-graham.com/ronco; Max Chafkin, "Legendary Angel Investor Ron Conway Isn't Looking at Your Idea, He's Looking at You," *Fast Company*, March 5, 2015, fastcompany.com/3043196/ron-conway-and-y-combinator-a-love-story; Aric Jenkins, "Silicon Valley Investing Legend Ron Conway on the Lessons Learned from Napster," *Fortune*, December 2, 2020, fortune.com/2020/12/02/ron-conway-sv-angel-napster-google-facebook (in which Conway described frequency of failure in his start-up investments: "About 60% of all the companies we invest in go out of business; we don't make a nickel. Another 30% of them, maybe we will get our money back. And it's that slight balance, 10% to 20%, that you make more than you put in, and it's enough to pay for all the ones that went out of business."); "Ron Conway: Founder and Co-Managing Partner," SVAngel, svangel.com/team.

(OVER) OPTIMISM

The number of copies sold of the books on the power of optimism is from the numbers stated on the Amazon pages for *The Power of Positive Thinking*, *Think and Grow Rich*, and *The Secret*.

Most of the information in this section is from conversations and correspondence with Don Moore for this book; Moore, *Perfectly Confident*; Tenney, Logg, and Moore, "(Too) Optimistic about Optimism," 2015.

The famous survey of three thousand entrepreneurs referred to is from Cooper, Woo, and Dunkelberg, "Entrepreneurs' Perceived Chances for Success," 1988.

DIVIDE AND CONQUER

See Staw, Barsade, and Koput, "Escalation at the Credit Window," 1997.

In addition to the references already mentioned in notes for this chapter related to conversations with Ron Conway and Don Moore, many of the quotes and explanations about quitting coaches are from conversations and correspondence for this book with Daniel Kahneman, Richard Thaler, Andrew Wilkinson, Admiral William McRaven, and Astro Teller.

Interlude III

Conversations and correspondence for this book with the following sources (and review of some of their writing on the subject): Mark Moffett, as well as his book *Adventures among Ants: A Global Safari with a Cast of Trillions* (Berkeley: University of California Press, 2010); and Michael Mauboussin, as well as his book *More Than You Know*, 187–197.

Of course, the body of work of Dr. Moffett's mentor, the late Edward O. Wilson, influenced this material, specifically Bert Hölldobler and E. O. Wilson, *The Superorganism: The Beauty, Elegance, and Strangeness of Insect Societies* (New York: W. W. Norton, 2009); Edward O. Wilson, *Tales from the Ant World* (New York: W. W. Norton, 2020).

Articles and studies of foraging by ant colonies and ant algorithms: J. L. Deneubourg, S. Aron, S. Goss, and J. M. Pasteels, "Error, Communication and Learning in Ant Societies," *European Journal of Operational Research* 30, no. 2 (June 1987): 168–172; J. L. Deneubourg, J. M. Pasteels, and J. C. Verhaeghe, "Probabilistic Behaviour in Ants: A Strategy of Errors?," *Journal of Theoretical Biology* 105, no. 2 (1983): 259–271; Marco Dorigo, Gianni A. DiCaro, and Luca Maria Gambardella, "Ant Algorithms for Discrete Optimization,"

Artificial Life 5, no. 2 (April 1999): 137–172; Drew Levin, Joshua Hecker, Melanie Moses, and Stephanie Forrest, "Volatility and Spatial Distribution of Resources Determine Ant Foraging Strategies," *Proceedings of the European Conference on Artificial Life*, 2015, 256–263; E. David Morgan, "Trail Pheromones of Ants," *Physiological Entomology* 34, no, 1 (March 2009): 1–17; Masashi Shiraishi, Rito Takeuchi, Hiroyuki Nakagawa, Shin I. Nishimura, Akinori Awazu, and Hiraku Nishimori, "Diverse Stochasticity Leads a Colony of Ants to Optimal Foraging," *Journal of Theoretical Biology* 465 (March 2019): 7–16.

See also Deborah Gordon, "Collective Wisdom of Ants," *Scientific American*, February 2016, 44–47; Deborah Gordon, "Colonial Studies," *Boston Review*, September–October 2010, 59–62.

Chapter 10

The information for the Maya Shankar narrative is from the following sources: conversations and correspondence with Maya Shankar for this book; E. J. Crawford, "Getting to Know You: Maya Shankar," Yale Alumni, July 22, 2021, alumni.yale.edu/news/getting-know-you-maya-shankar-07; "Maya Shankar: Behavioral Science: From the White House to Google," The Decision Lab, thedecisionlab.com/thinkers/psychology/maya-shankar; Robert Lipsyte and Lois Morris, "How Do You Get to Camp? Practice, of Course: Teenagers Who Play Music, Not Tennis," *New York Times*, June 27, 2002, nytimes.com/2002/06/27/arts/how-do-you-get-to-camp-practice-of-course-teenagers-who-play-music-not-tennis.html; mayashankar.com; "The Power of Nudges: Maya Shankar on Changing People's Minds," *Knowledge at Wharton*, June 1, 2021, knowledge.wharton.upenn.edu/article/power-nudges-maya-shankar-changing-peoples-minds; "Maya Shankar, Aspiring Concert Violinist Turned Cognitive Scientist at the White House, UN and Google," *Rediscover STEAM*, March 21, 2021, medium.com/rediscover-steam/maya-shankar-aspiring-concert-violinist-turned-cognitive-scientist-at-the-white-house-un-google-e22d072ef72e; Sarah Stillman, "Can Behavioral Science Help in Flint?," *New Yorker*, January 23, 2017, newyorker.com/magazine/2017/01/23/can-behavioral-science-help-in-flint; Shankar Vedantam and Maggie Penman, "Loss and Renewal: Moving Forward after a Door Closes," NPR, December 31, 2018, npr.org/2018/12/28/680679054/loss-and-renewal-moving-forward-after-a-door-closes.

NOTES FROM THE LONDON UNDERGROUND

See Larcom, Rauch, and Willems, "The Benefits of Forced Experimentation," 2017.

JUST ONE DAY

The information for the Mike Neighbors narrative is from the following sources: conversations and correspondence with Mike Neighbors for this book; "Mike Neighbors," Arkansas Razorbacks, arkansasrazorbacks.com/coache/mike -neighbors; Doug Samuels, "A Major College Coach Defends His Decision to Practice ONCE Per Week," FootballScoop, March 26, 2019, footballscoop.com /news/major-college-coach-defends-decision-practice-per-week; "Operating Bylaws, Article 17—Playing and Practices Seasons," *2021–22 NCAA Division I Manual*, 235–332, web3.ncaa.org/lsdbi/reports/getReport/90008. Information about the roster and results for the 2013–2014 Washington Huskies women's basketball team is from Wikipedia, en.wikipedia.org/wiki/2013 %E2%80%9314_Washington_Huskies_women%27s_basketball_team.

THE GREAT RESIGNATION

The term appears to come from Texas A&M professor Anthony Klotz, quoted by Arianne Cohen in "How to Quit Your Job in the Great Post-Pandemic Resignation Boom," *Bloomberg Businessweek*, May 10, 2021, bloomberg.com /news/articles/2021-05-10/quit-your-job-how-to-resign-after-covid -pandemic. ("The great resignation is coming," says Anthony Klotz, an associate professor of management at Texas A&M University who's studied the exits of hundreds of workers.")

Data for this section is from monthly news releases (and accompanying tables and statistics) of the U.S. Department of Labor's Bureau of Labor Statistics, titled "Job Openings and Labor Turnover" (known as JOLT) and dated for the month of the data, typically the period two months before the release date. This includes the following releases: "JOLT—April 2021" (released June 8, 2021), bls.gov/news.release/archives/jolts_06082021.htm; "JOLT—June 2021" (released August 9, 2021), bls.gov/news.release/archives/jolts_08092021.htm; "JOLT—July 2021" (released September 8, 2021); "JOLT—August 2021" (released October 12, 2021), bls.gov/news.release/archives/jolts_10122021 .htm; "JOLT—September 2021" (released November 12, 2021), bls.gov/news .release/archives/jolts_11122021.htm; "JOLT—October 2021" (released December 8, 2021), bls.gov/news.release/archives/jolts_12082021.htm.

Some of the background information and aspects of the public discussion about the "meaning" of the Great Resignation are from the following articles: Paul Krugman, "The Revolt of the American Worker," *New York Times*, October 14, 2021, nytimes.com/2021/10/14/opinion/workers-quitting-wages.html; Eli Rosenberg, Abha Bhattarai, and Andrew Van Dam, "A Record Number of Workers Are Quitting Their Jobs, Empowered by New Leverage," *Washington Post*, October 12, 2021, washingtonpost.com/business/2021/10/12/jolts -workers-quitting-august-pandemic; Scott Schieman, "Surprise: Workers

Actually Like Their Jobs. Here Are the Real Reasons They're Quitting in Droves," *Fast Company*, December 17, 2021, fastcompany.com/90706474 /surprise-workers-actually-like-their-jobs-here-are-the-real-reasons-theyre -quitting-in-droves; Derek Thompson, "What Quitters Understand about the Job Market," *The Atlantic*, June 21, 2021, theatlantic.com/ideas/archive /2021/06/quitting-your-job-economic-optimism/619242; Derek Thompson, "Where Did 7 Million Workers Go?," *The Atlantic*, October 23, 2021, theat lantic.com/ideas/archive/2021/10/how-do-you-make-7-million-workers -disappear/620475; Derek Thompson, "Three Myths of the Great Resigna-tion," *The Atlantic*, December 8, 2021, theatlantic.com/ideas/archive/2021 /12/great-resignation-myths-quitting-jobs/620927; Abby Vesoulis, "Why Literally Millions of Americans Are Quitting Their Jobs," *Time*, October 13, 2021, time.com/6106322/the-great-resignation-jobs; Matthew Yglesias, "The Myth of the 'Great Resignation,'" *Slow Boring*, January 13, 2022, slowboring .com/p/the-myth-of-the-great-resignation.

Chapter 11

As far as I know, there is no central collection or registry of people persisting after injuries in distant races. I focused on the London Marathon and other dis-tance races in Great Britain because, in the brief time I searched for such sto-ries, I quickly noticed that there were two instances in approximately the same place during the 2019 London Marathon. Neither of the stories referred to the other, though in both (as in most of these marathon-injury stories) the medical professionals on site or at local hospitals express utter disbelief that such a thing is possible. I then found another example in Edinburgh four weeks later (along with another I didn't describe, at a half-marathon in Plym-outh in the week before Edinburgh). Then I found a 2014 London Marathon story with the same injury, and occurring in the same spot, as one of the 2019 injuries, along with another pair of London Marathon stories from 2012 and 2021.

I found several such examples in distance races in the United States and Japan during my limited search, but this obviously wasn't an attempt to comprehen-sively document such stories, nor was I singling out the London Marathon.

The news stories reporting the stories of marathoners in this section are as follows: "Stratford Dad Finishes London Marathon despite Broken Leg," *Cov-entry Telegraph*, May 1, 2012, coventrytelegraph.net/news/coventry-news /stratford-dad-finishes-london-marathon-3024241; "London Marathon Run-ner Finishes despite Broken Bone," BBC, April 14, 2014, bbc.com/news/uk -england-hampshire-27028222; "Thirty-Eight Guinness World Records Ti-tles Achieved at the 2019 Virgin Money London Marathon," MarathonGuide,

April 29, 2019, marathonguide.com/pressreleases/index.cfm?file=London Marathon_190429; Gianluca Mezzofiore, "A Firefighter Ran 18 Miles on a Broken Foot in the London Marathon," CNN, April 30, 2019, cnn.com /2019/04/30/europe/firefighter-london-marathon-broken-foot-trnd/index .html; Georgia Diebelius, "Woman Ran 18 Miles of the London Marathon with a Broken Ankle," May 1, 2019, *Metro*, metro.co.uk/2019/05/01/woman -ran-18-miles-london-marathon-broken-ankle-9375118; Fiona Pringle, "Edinburgh Marathon Runner Completes Race with Broken Leg," *Edinburgh Evening News*, May 28, 2019, edinburghnews.scotsman.com/news/people /edinburgh-marathon-runner-completes-race-broken-leg-546182; Ben Hobson, "Runner Breaks Leg at Edinburgh Marathon but Still Finishes the Race," *Runner's World*, May 29, 2019, runnersworld.com/uk/news/a27621746/edin burgh-marathon-broken-leg; "Woman Runs London Marathon with Broken Leg," BBC, October 8, 2021, bbc.com/news/uk-england-shropshire-58840890.

The scientific literature on goals encompasses far more than I could summarize here. The most influential work encouraging setting specific, difficult goals is from Professors Edwin A. Locke and Gary P. Latham. See *A Theory of Goal Setting and Task Performance*; *New Developments in Goal Setting and Task Performance*; "Goal Setting: A Half Century Retrospective," 2019.

The problems that goals can create in interfering with smart quitting behavior (their pass-fail nature, their inflexibility when things change, and the myopia they can cause) as well as strategies that address those problems, as developed in this chapter, include conversations and correspondence for this book with the following people: Maurice Schweitzer, Katy Milkman, Barry Staw, and Richard Thaler.

The references to published work by Schweitzer and colleagues are from Schweitzer, Ordóñez, and Douma, "The Dark Side of Goal Setting," 2002; Ordóñez et al., "Goals Gone Wild," 2009; Ordóñez et al., "On Good Scholarship, Goal Setting, and Scholars Gone Wild," 2009. See also Dai et al., "Quitting When the Going Gets Tough," 2018.

Those sources, along with others consulted for this chapter, generally discuss multiple problems with goals as well as solutions. See Beshears et al., "Creating Exercise Habits," 2021; Heath, Larrick, and Wu, "Goals as Reference Points," 1999; Lucas et al., "When the Going Gets Tough," 2015; Milkman, *How to Change*; Oettingen, *Rethinking Positive Thinking*; Staw and Boettger, "Task Revision," 1990.

The famous "invisible gorilla" study is Simons and Chabris, "Gorillas in Our Midst," 1999. See also Simons and Chabris, *The Invisible Gorilla*. In the original study, they reported similar results with other participants where the video of basketball passes, instead of featuring a woman in a gorilla suit, had a tall woman carrying an open umbrella walking through the scene. These videos were each seventy-five seconds long, with the unexpected events lasting five seconds, at forty-four to forty-eight seconds into the video.

They tried exaggerating the effect of the gorilla walking through by making an additional, shorter video (sixty-two seconds) where the gorilla was present almost twice as long (nine seconds). They also had the gorilla stop in the middle of the players, look into the camera, and thump its chest. They gave twelve participants the same task of counting the basketball passes and even then, only half noticed the gorilla.

BIBLIOGRAPHY

BOOKS

Brockner, Joel, and Jeffrey Z. Rubin. *Entrapment in Escalating Conflicts: A Social Psychological Analysis.* New York: Springer-Verlag, 1985.

Christian, Brian, and Tom Griffiths. *Algorithms to Live By: The Computer Science of Human Decisions.* New York: Henry Holt, 2016.

Dalio, Ray. *Principles: Life and Work.* New York: Simon and Schuster, 2017.

Duckworth, Angela. *Grit: The Power of Passion and Perseverance.* New York: Scribner, 2016.

Duke, Annie. *How to Decide: Simple Tools for Making Better Choices.* New York: Penguin Random House, 2020.

Duke, Annie. *Thinking in Bets: Making Smarter Decisions When You Don't Have All the Facts.* New York: Penguin Random House, 2018.

Ellenberg, Jordan. *How Not to Be Wrong: The Power of Mathematical Thinking.* New York: Penguin Press, 2014.

Epstein, David. *Range: Why Generalists Triumph in a Specialized World.* New York: Riverhead, 2019.

Festinger, Leon. *A Theory of Cognitive Dissonance.* Stanford, CA: Stanford University Press, 1957.

Festinger, Leon, Henry W. Riecken, and Stanley Schachter. *When Prophecy Fails.* Mansfield Center, CT: Martino, 2009.

Gonzales, Laurence. *The Chemistry of Fire.* Fayetteville: University of Arkansas Press, 2020.

Gonzales, Laurence. *Deep Survival: Who Lives, Who Dies, and Why: True Stories of Miraculous Endurance and Sudden Death.* New York: W. W. Norton, 2017.

Gonzales, Laurence. *Everyday Survival: Why Smart People Do Stupid Things.* New York: W. W. Norton, 2008.

Grant, Adam. *Think Again: The Power of Knowing What You Don't Know.* New York: Penguin Random House, 2021.

Harmon-Jones, Eddie, ed. *Cognitive Dissonance: Reexamining a Pivotal Theory in Psychology*. 2nd ed. Washington, D.C.: American Psychological Association, 2019, n.d.

Kahneman, Daniel. *Thinking, Fast and Slow*. New York: Farrar, Straus and Giroux, 2011.

Kahneman, Daniel, Olivier Sibony, and Cass R. Sunstein. *Noise: A Flaw in Human Judgment*. New York: Little, Brown Spark, 2021.

Kahneman, Daniel, Paul Slovic, and Amos Tversky, eds. *Judgment under Uncertainty: Heuristics and Biases*. Cambridge, UK: Cambridge University Press, 1982.

Komisar, Randy, and Jantoon Reigersman. *Straight Talk for Startups: 100 Insider Rules for Beating the Odds—from Mastering the Fundamentals to Selecting Investors, Fundraising, Managing Boards, and Achieving Liquidity*. New York: HarperCollins, 2018.

Levitt, Steven D., and Stephen J. Dubner. *Freakonomics: A Rogue Economist Explores the Hidden Side of Everything*. New York: William Morrow, 2006.

Levitt, Steven D., and Stephen J. Dubner. *Superfreakonomics: Global Cooling, Patriotic Prostitutes, and Why Suicide Bombers Should Buy Life Insurance*. New York: HarperCollins, 2009.

Locke, Edwin A., and Gary P. Latham, eds. *New Developments in Goal Setting and Task Performance*. New York: Routledge, 2013.

Locke, Edwin A., and Gary P. Latham. *A Theory of Goal Setting and Task Performance*. Englewood Cliffs, NJ: Prentice Hall, 1990.

Mauboussin, Michael J. *More Than You Know: Finding Financial Wisdom in Unconventional Places*. New York: Columbia University Press, 2013.

Mauboussin, Michael J. *The Success Equation: Untangling Skill and Luck in Business, Sports, and Investing*. Boston: Harvard Business School Press, 2012.

Milkman, Katy. *How to Change: The Science of Getting from Where You Are to Where You Want to Be*. New York: Portfolio/Penguin, 2021.

Moore, Don A. *Perfectly Confident: How to Calibrate Your Decisions Wisely*. New York: Harper Business, 2020.

Oettingen, Gabriele. *Rethinking Positive Thinking: Inside the New Science of Motivation*. New York: Current, 2014.

Page, Scott E. *The Model Thinker: What You Need to Know to Make Data Work for You*. New York: Basic Books, 2018.

Peck, Joann, and Suzanne B. Shu, eds. *Psychological Ownership and Consumer Behavior*. New York: Springer, 2018.

Ries, Eric. *The Lean Startup: How Today's Entrepreneurs Use Continuous Innovation to Create Radically Successful Businesses*. New York: Crown Business, 2011.

Simons, Daniel, and Christopher Chabris. *The Invisible Gorilla: How Our Intuitions Deceive Us*. New York: Crown, 2010.

Tavris, Carol, and Elliot Aronson. *Mistakes Were Made (but Not by Me): Why We Justify Foolish Beliefs, Bad Decisions, and Hurtful Acts.* Boston: Mariner, 2020 (updated edition).

Teger, Allan I. *Too Much Invested to Quit.* New York: Pergamon, 1980.

Tetlock, Phillip. E., and Dan Gardner. *Superforecasting: The Art and Science of Prediction.* New York: Crown, 2015.

Thaler, Richard H. *Misbehaving: The Making of Behavioral Economics.* New York: W. W. Norton, 2015.

Thaler, Richard H., and Cass R. Sunstein. *Nudge: Improving Decisions about Health, Wealth, and Happiness.* New Haven, CT: Yale University Press, 2008.

Thaler, Richard H., and Cass R. Sunstein. *Nudge: The Final Edition.* New York: Penguin Books, 2021.

Van Bavel, Jay J., and Dominic J. Packer. *The Power of Us: Harnessing Our Shared Identities to Improve Performance, Increase Cooperation, and Promote Social Harmony.* New York: Little, Brown Spark, 2021.

PAPERS

Agarwal, Sumit, Mio Diao, Jessica Pan, and Tien Foo Sing. "Labor Supply Decisions of Singaporean Cab Drivers." *SSRN Electronic Journal* (2013): 1053 .doi.org/10.2139/ssrn.2338476.

Akepanidtaworn, Klakow, Rick Di Mascio, Alex Imas, and Lawrence Schmidt. "Selling Fast and Buying Slow: Heuristics and Trading Performance of Institutional Investors." *SSRN Electronic Journal* (2019). doi.org/10.2139/ssrn .3301277.

Anderson, Christopher J. "The Psychology of Doing Nothing: Forms of Decision Avoidance Result from Reason and Emotion." *Psychological Bulletin* 129, no. 1 (2003): 139–67. doi.org/10.1037/0033-2909.129.1.139.

Ariely, Dan, Daniel Kahneman, and George Loewenstein. "Joint Comment on 'When Does Duration Matter in Judgment and Decision Making?'" *Journal of Experimental Psychology: General* 129, no. 4 (2000): 524–29. doi.org /10.1037/0096-3445.129.4.524.

Ariely, Dan, and George Loewenstein. "When Does Duration Matter in Judgment and Decision Making?" *Journal of Experimental Psychology: General* 129, no. 4 (2000): 508–23. doi.org/10.1037/0096-3445.129.4.508.

Arkes, Hal R., and Catherine Blumer. "The Psychology of Sunk Cost." *Organizational Behavior and Human Decision Processes* 35, no. 1 (February 1985): 124–40. doi.org/10.1016/0749-5978(85)90049-4.

Aronson, Elliot. "The Return of the Repressed: Dissonance Theory Makes a Comeback." *Psychological Inquiry* 3, no. 4 (October 1992): 303–11. doi.org /10.1207/s15327965pli0304_1.

Aronson, Elliot, and Carol Tavris. "The Role of Cognitive Dissonance in the Pandemic." *The Atlantic*, July 12, 2020. theatlantic.com/ideas/archive/2020/07/role-cognitive-dissonance-pandemic/614074.

Baron, Jonathan, and Ilana Ritov. "Reference Points and Omission Bias." *Organizational Behavior and Human Decision Processes* 59, no. 3 (September 1994): 475–98. doi.org/10.1006/obhd.1994.1070.

Basili, Marcello, and Carlo Zappia. "Ambiguity and Uncertainty in Ellsberg and Shackle." *Cambridge Journal of Economics* 34, no. 3 (May 2010): 449–74. doi.org/10.1093/cje/bep008.

Beasley, Ryan K., and Mark R. Joslyn. "Cognitive Dissonance and Post-Decision Attitude Change in Six Presidential Elections." *Political Psychology* 22, no. 3 (September 2001): 521–40. doi.org/10.1111/0162-895x.00252.

Beshears, John, Hae Nim Lee, Katherine L. Milkman, Robert Mislavsky, and Jessica Wisdom. "Creating Exercise Habits Using Incentives: The Trade-off between Flexibility and Routinization." *Management Science* 67, no. 7 (July 2021): 4139–71. doi.org/10.1287/mnsc.2020.3706.

Beshears, John, and Katherine L. Milkman. "Do Sell-Side Stock Analysts Exhibit Escalation of Commitment?" *Journal of Economic Behavior & Organization* 77, no. 3 (March 2011): 304–17. doi.org/10.1016/j.jebo.2010.11.003.

Bitterly, T. Bradford, Robert Mislavsky, Hengchen Dai, and Katherine L. Milkman. "Want-Should Conflict: A Synthesis of Past Research." In *The Psychology of Desire*, edited by W. Hofmann and L. F. Nordgren, 244–64. New York: Guilford, 2015.

Brockner, Joel. "The Escalation of Commitment to a Failing Course of Action: Toward Theoretical Progress." *Academy of Management Review* 17, no. 1 (January 1992): 39–61. doi.org/10.2307/258647.

Brockner, Joel, Robert Houser, Gregg Birnbaum, Kathy Lloyd, Janet Deitcher, Sinaia Nathanson, and Jeffrey Z. Rubin. "Escalation of Commitment to an Ineffective Course of Action: The Effect of Feedback Having Negative Implications for Self-Identity." *Administrative Science Quarterly* 31, no. 1 (March 1986): 109–26. doi.org/10.2307/2392768.

Brockner, Joel, Jeffrey Z. Rubin, Judy Fine, Thomas P. Hamilton, Barbara Thomas, and Beth Turetsky. "Factors Affecting Entrapment in Escalating Conflicts: The Importance of Timing." *Journal of Research in Personality* 16, no. 2 (June 1982): 247–66. doi.org/10.1016/0092-6566(82)90080-0.

Camerer, Colin F. "Prospect Theory in the Wild: Evidence from the Field." In *Advances in Behavioral Economics*, edited by Colin F. Camerer, George Loewenstein, and Matthew Rabin, 148–61. Princeton, NJ: Princeton University Press, 2004.

Camerer, Colin, Linda Babcock, George Loewenstein, and Richard Thaler. "Labor Supply of New York City Cabdrivers: One Day at a Time." *Quarterly*

Journal of Economics 112, no. 2 (May 1997): 407–41. doi.org/10.1162/00335 5397555244.

Camerer, Colin, and Dan Lovallo. "Overconfidence and Excess Entry: An Experimental Approach." *American Economic Review* 89, no. 1 (March 1999): 306–18. doi.org/10.1257/aer.89.1.306.

Camerer, Colin, and Roberto Weber. "The Econometrics and Behavioral Economics of Escalation of Commitment in NBA Draft Choices." *Journal of Economic Behavior and Organization* 39, no. 1 (May 1999): 59–82.

Camilleri, Adrian R., Marie-Anne Cam, and Robert Hoffmann. "Nudges and Signposts: The Effect of Smart Defaults and Pictographic Risk Information on Retirement Saving Investment Choices." *Journal of Behavioral Decision Making* 32, no. 4 (October 2019): 431–49. doi.org/10.1002/bdm.2122.

Chatman, Jennifer, Barry Staw, and Nancy Bell. "The Managed Thought: The Role of Self-Justification and Impression Management in Organizational Setting." In *The Thinking Organization: Dynamics of Organizational Social Cognition*, edited by Henry P. Sims Jr. and Dennis A Gioia, 191–214. San Francisco: Jossey-Bass, 1986.

Chen, M. Keith, and Michael Sheldon. "Dynamic Pricing in a Labor Market: Surge Pricing and the Supply of Uber Driver-Partners" (working paper). 2015. anderson.ucla.edu/faculty_pages/keith.chen/papers/SurgeAndFlexibleWork _WorkingPaper.pdf.

Chou, Yuan K. "Testing Alternative Models of Labor Supply: Evidence from Taxi Drivers in Singapore." *Singapore Economic Review* 47, no. 1 (2002): 17–47.

Cooper, Arnold C., Carolyn Y. Woo, and William C. Dunkelberg. "Entrepreneurs' Perceived Chances for Success." *Journal of Business Venturing* 3, no. 2 (Spring 1988): 97–108. doi.org/10.1016/0883-9026(88)90020-1.

Dai, Hengchen, Berkeley J. Dietvorst, Bradford Tuckfield, Katherine L. Milkman, and Maurice E. Schweitzer. "Quitting When the Going Gets Tough: A Downside of High Performance Expectations." *Academy of Management Journal* 61, no. 5 (2018): 1667–91. doi.org/10.5465/amj.2014.1045.

Dommer, Sara Loughran, and Vanitha Swaminathan. "Explaining the Endowment Effect through Ownership: The Role of Identity, Gender, and Self-Threat." *Journal of Consumer Research* 39, no. 5 (February 2013): 1034–50. doi.org/10.1086/666737.

Doran, Kirk. "Are Long-Term Wage Elasticities of Labor Supply More Negative than Short-Term Ones?" *Economic Letters* 122, no. 2 (February 2014): 208–10. doi.org/10.1016/j.econlet.2013.11.023.

Duckworth, Angela L., Christopher Peterson, Michael D. Matthews, and Dennis R. Kelly. "Grit: Perseverance and Passion for Long-Term Goals." *Journal of Personality and Social Psychology* 92, no. 6 (June 2007): 1087–1101. doi .org/10.1037/0022-3514.92.6.1087.

Ellsberg, Daniel. "Risk, Ambiguity, and the Savage Axioms." *Quarterly Journal of Economics* 75, no. 4 (November 1961): 643–69. doi.org/10.2307/1884324.

Farber, Henry S. "Is Tomorrow Another Day? The Labor Supply of New York City Cabdrivers." *Journal of Political Economy* 113, no. 1 (February 2005): 46–82. doi.org/10.1086/426040.

Farber, Henry S. "Reference-Dependent Preferences and Labor Supply: The Case of New York City Taxi Drivers." *American Economic Review* 98, no. 3 (June 2008): 1069–82. jstor.org/stable/29730106.

Farber, Henry S. "Why You Can't Find a Taxi in the Rain and Other Labor Supply Lessons from Cab Drivers." *Quarterly Journal of Economics* 130, no. 4 (November 2015): 1975–2026. doi.org/10.1093/qje/qjv026.

Flepp, Raphael, Philippe Meier, and Egon Franck. "The Effect of Paper Outcomes versus Realized Outcomes on Subsequent Risk-Taking: Field Evidence from Casino Gambling." *Organizational Behavior and Human Decision Processes* 165 (July 2021): 45–55. doi.org/10.1016/j.obhdp.2021.04.003.

Flyvbjerg, Bent, Mette K. Skamris Holm, and Søren L. Buhl. "Underestimating Costs in Public Works Projects: Error or Lie?" *Journal of the American Planning Association* 68, no. 3 (2002): 279–95. doi.org/10.1080/01944360208976273.

Fox, Frederick V., and Barry M. Staw. "The Trapped Administrator: Effects of Job Insecurity and Policy Resistance upon Commitment to a Course of Action." *Administrative Science Quarterly* 24, no. 3 (September 1979): 449–71. doi.org/10.2307/2989922.

Fried, Carrie B., and Elliot Aronson. "Hypocrisy, Misattribution, and Dissonance Reduction." *Personality and Social Psychology Bulletin* 21, no. 9 (September 1995): 925–33. doi.org/10.1177/0146167295219007.

Gal, David. "A Psychological Law of Inertia and the Illusion of Loss Aversion." *Judgment and Decision Making* 1, no. 1 (2006): 23–32.

Gal, David, and Derek D. Rucker. "The Loss of Loss Aversion: Will It Loom Larger Than Its Gain?" *Journal of Consumer Psychology* 28, no. 3 (July 2018): 497–516. doi.org/10.1002/jcpy.1047.

Gillan, Stuart L., John W. Kensinger, and John D. Martin. "Value Creation and Corporate Diversification: The Case of Sears, Roebuck & Co." *Journal of Financial Economics* 55, no.1 (January 2000): 10337. doi.org/10.1016/S0304-405X(99)00046-X.

Güllich, Arne, Brooke N. Macnamara, and David Z. Hambrick. "What Makes a Champion? Early Multidisciplinary Practice, Not Early Specialization, Predicts World-Class Performance." *Perspectives on Psychological Science* 17, no. 1 (January 2022): 6–29. doi.org/10.1177/1745691620974772.

Halevy, Yoram. "Ellsberg Revisited: An Experimental Study." *SSRN Electronic Journal* (July 2005): 1–48. doi.org/10.2139/ssrn.770964.

Harmon-Jones, Eddie, and Judson Mills. "An Introduction to Cognitive Dissonance Theory and an Overview of Current Perspectives on the Theory." In
Cognitive Dissonance: Reexamining a Pivotal Theory in Psychology, 2nd ed.,
edited by Eddie Harmon-Jones, 3–24. Washington, D.C.: American Psychological Association, n.d., 2019.

Heath, Chip, Richard P. Larrick, and George Wu. "Goals as Reference Points."
Cognitive Psychology 38, no. 1 (February 1999): 79–109. doi.org/10.1006
/cogp.1998.0708.

Heimer, Rawley, Zwetelina Iliewa, Alex Imas, and Martin Weber. "Dynamic
Inconsistency in Risky Choice: Evidence from the Lab and Field." *SSRN
Electronic Journal* (2020). doi.org/10.2139/ssrn.3600583.

Heimer, Rawley, Zwetelina Iliewa, Alex Imas, and Martin Weber. "Dynamic Inconsistency in Risky Choice: Evidence from the Lab and Field." Discussion
Paper No. 271, Project C 01, University of Bonn, Collaborative Research Center, March 2021. wiwi.uni-bonn.de/bgsepapers/boncrc/CRCTR224_2021
_274.pdf.

Hinton, Alexander, and Yiguo Sun. "The Sunk-Cost Fallacy in the National
Basketball Association: Evidence Using Player Salary and Playing Time."
Empirical Economics 59, no. 2 (August 2020): 1019–36. doi.org/10.1007
/s00181-019-01641-4.

Kahneman, Daniel. "Cognitive Limitations and Public Decision Making." In
*Science and Absolute Values: Proceedings of the Third International Conference
on the Unity of the Sciences*, 1261–81. London:" International Cultural Foundation, 1974.

Kahneman, Daniel, and Jack L. Knetsch. "Contingent Valuation and the Value
of Public Goods: Reply." *Journal of Environmental Economics and Management*
22, no. 1 (January 1992): 90–94. doi.org/10.1016/0095-0696(92)90021-N.

Kahneman, Daniel, and Jack L. Knetsch. "Valuing Public Goods: The Purchase
of Moral Satisfaction." *Journal of Environmental Economics and Management*
22, no. 1 (January 1992): 57–70. doi.org/10.1016/0095-0696(92)90019-s.

Kahneman, Daniel, Jack L. Knetsch, and Richard H. Thaler. "Anomalies:
The Endowment Effect, Loss Aversion, and Status Quo Bias." *Journal of
Economic Perspectives* 5, no. 1 (Winter 1991): 193–206. doi.org/10.1257
/jep.5.1.193.

Kahneman, Daniel, Jack L. Knetsch, and Richard H. Thaler. "Experimental
Tests of the Endowment Effect and the Coase Theorem." *Journal of Political
Economy* 98, no. 6 (December 1990): 1325–48. jstor.org/stable/2937761.

Kahneman, Daniel, Jack L. Knetsch, and Richard H. Thaler. "Fairness and the
Assumptions of Economics." *Journal of Business* 59, no. 4 (October 1986):
285–300. jstor.org/stable/2352761.

Kahneman, Daniel, Jack L. Knetsch, and Richard Thaler. "Fairness as a Constraint on Profit Seeking: Entitlements in the Market." *American Economic Review* 76, no. 4 (September 1986): 728–41. jstor.org/stable/1806070.

Kahneman, Daniel, and Dan Lovallo. "Timid Choices and Bold Forecasts: A Cognitive Perspective on Risk Taking." *Management Science* 39, no. 1 (January 1993): 17–31. doi.org/10.1287/mnsc.39.1.17.

Kahneman, Daniel, and Dale T. Miller. "Norm Theory: Comparing Reality to Its Alternatives." *Psychological Review* 93, no. 2 (1986): 136–53. doi.org/10.1037//0033-295x.93.2.136.

Kahneman, Daniel, and Richard Thaler. "Economic Analysis and the Psychology of Utility: Applications to Compensation Policy." *American Economic Review* 81, no. 2 (1991): 341–46. jstor.org/stable/2006882.

Kahneman, Daniel, and Amos Tversky. "Choices, Values, and Frames." *American Psychologist* 39, no. 4 (1984): 341–50. doi.org/10.1037/0003-066X.39.4.341.

Kahneman, Daniel, and Amos Tversky. "Intuitive Prediction: Biases and Corrective Procedures." *Management Science* 12 (1979): 313–27.

Kahneman, Daniel, and Amos Tversky. "On the Psychology of Prediction." *Psychological Review* 80, no. 4 (1973): 237–5l.

Kahneman, Daniel, and Amos Tversky. "On the Reality of Cognitive Illusions." *Psychological Review* 103, no. 3 (1996): 582–91. doi.org/10.1037/0033-295X.103.3.582.

Kahneman, Daniel, and Amos Tversky. "On the Study of Statistical Intuitions." *Cognition* 11, no. 2 (March 1982): 123–41. doi.org/10.1016/0010-0277(82)90022-1.

Kahneman, Daniel, and Amos Tversky. "Prospect Theory: An Analysis of Decision under Risk." *Econometrica* 47, no. 2 (March 1979): 263–91. doi.org/10.2307/1914185.

Kahneman, Daniel, and Amos Tversky. "The Psychology of Preferences." *Scientific American* 246 (January 1982): 160–73.

Kahneman, Daniel, and Amos Tversky. "Subjective Probability: A Judgment of Representativeness." *Cognitive Psychology* 3 (1972): 430–54.

Kahneman, Daniel, and Amos Tversky. "Variants of Uncertainty." *Cognition* 11 (April 1982): 43–157.

Keefer, Quinn A. W. "Decision-Maker Beliefs and the Sunk-Cost Fallacy: Major League Baseball's Final-Offer Salary Arbitration and Utilization." *Journal of Economic Psychology* 75 (December 2019): 1–16. doi.org/10.1016/j.joep.2018.06.002.

Keefer, Quinn A. W. "The Sunk-Cost Fallacy in the National Football League: Salary Cap Value and Playing Time." *Journal of Sports Economics* 18, no. 3 (2017): 282–97. doi.org/10.1177/1527002515574515.

Keefer, Quinn. "Sunk Costs in the NBA: The Salary Cap and Free Agents." *Em-*

pirical Economics 61, no. 3 (2021): 3445–78. doi.org/10.1007/s00181-020 -01996-z.

Knetsch, Jack L. "The Endowment Effect and Evidence of Nonreversible Indifference Curves." *American Economic Review* 79, no. 5 (December 1989): 1277–84. jstor.org/stable/1831454.

Knetsch, Jack L. "Environmental Policy Implications of Disparities between Willingness to Pay and Compensation Demanded Measures of Values." *Journal of Environmental Economics and Management* 18, no. 3 (May 1990): 227–37. doi.org/10.1016/0095-0696(90)90003-H.

Koellinger, Philipp, Maria Minniti, and Christian Schade. "I Think I Can, I Think I Can: Overconfidence and Entrepreneurial Behavior." *Journal of Economic Psychology* 28, no. 4 (August 2007): 502–27. doi.org/10.1016/j.joep .2006.11.002.

Koning, Rembrand, Sharique Hasan, and Aaron Chatterji. "Experimentation and Startup Performance: Evidence from A/B Testing." Working Paper 26278, National Bureau of Economic Research, September 2019. doi.org/10.3386 /w26278.

Larcom, Shaun, Ferdinand Rauch, and Tim Willems. "The Benefits of Forced Experimentation: Striking Evidence from the London Underground Network." *Quarterly Journal of Economics* 132, no. 4 (November 2017): 2019–55. doi.org/10.1093/qje/qjx020.

Leeds, Daniel M., Michael A. Leeds, and Akira Motomura. "Are Sunk Costs Irrelevant? Evidence from Playing Time in the National Basketball Association." *Economic Inquiry* 53, no. 2 (April 2015): 1305–16. doi.org/10.1111 /ecin.12190.

Lerner, Jennifer S., and Philip E. Tetlock. "Accounting for the Effects of Accountability." *Psychological Bulletin* 125, no. 2 (1999): 255–75. doi.org/10.1037 /0033-2909.125.2.255.

Levitt, Steven D. "Heads or Tails: The Impact of a Coin Toss on Major Life Decisions and Subsequent Happiness." *Review of Economic Studies* 88, no. 1 (January 2021): 378–405. doi.org/10.1093/restud/rdaa016.

Locke, Edwin A., and Gary P. Latham. "The Development of Goal Setting Theory: A Half Century Retrospective." *Motivation Science* 5, no. 2 (2019): 93–105. doi.org/10.1037/mot0000127.

Lovallo, Dan, and Daniel Kahneman. "Living with Uncertainty: Attractiveness and Resolution Timing." *Journal of Behavioral Decision Making* 13, no. 2 (April 2000): 179–90.

Lucas, Gale M., Jonathan Gratch, Lin Cheng, and Stacy Marsella. "When the Going Gets Tough: Grit Predicts Costly Perseverance." *Journal of Research in Personality* 59 (December 2015): 15–22. doi.org/10.1016/j.jrp.2015.08.004.

Massey, Cade, and Richard H. Thaler. "The Loser's Curse: Decision Making and Market Efficiency in the National Football League Draft." *Management Science* 59, no. 7 (2013): 1479–95.

Mauboussin, Michael, and Dan Callahan. "Turn and Face the Strange: Overcoming Barriers to Change in Sports and Investing." Morgan Stanley, Counterpoint Global Insights, September 8, 2021. morganstanley.com/im/publication/insights/articles/article_turnandfacethestrange_us.pdf.

Milkman, Katherine L., Todd Rogers, and Max H. Bazerman. "Harnessing Our Inner Angels and Demons: What We Have Learned about Want/Should Conflicts and How That Knowledge Can Help Us Reduce Short-Sighted Decision Making." *Perspectives on Psychological Science* 3, no. 4 (July 2008): 324–38. doi.org/10.1111/j.1745-6924.2008.00083.x.

Milkman, Katherine L., Todd Rogers, and Max H. Bazerman. "I'll Have the Ice Cream Soon and the Vegetables Later: A Study of Online Grocery Purchases and Order Lead Time." *Marketing Letters* 21 (2010): 17–35. doi.org/10.1007/s11002-009-9087-0.

Moore, Don A., and Daylian M. Cain. "Overconfidence and Underconfidence: When and Why People Underestimate (and Overestimate) the Competition." *Organizational Behavior and Human Decision Processes* 103, no. 2 (July 2007): 197–213. doi.org/10.1016/j.obhdp.2006.09.002.

Moore, Don A., John M. Oesch, and Charlene Zietsma. "What Competition? Myopic Self-Focus in Market-Entry Decisions." *Organization Science* 18, no. 3 (May-June 2007): 440–54. doi.org/10.1287/orsc.1060.0243.

Morewedge, Carey K., and Colleen E. Giblin. "Explanations of the Endowment Effect: An Integrative Review." *Trends in Cognitive Sciences* 19, no. 6 (June 2015): 339–48. doi.org/10.1016/j.tics.2015.04.004.

Morewedge, Carey K., Lisa L. Shu, Daniel T. Gilbert, and Timothy D. Wilson. "Bad Riddance or Good Rubbish? Ownership and Not Loss Aversion Causes the Endowment Effect." *Journal of Experimental Social Psychology* 45, no. 4 (July 2009): 947–51. doi.org/10.1016/j.jesp.2009.05.014.

Northcraft, Gregory B., and Margaret A. Neale. "Opportunity Costs and the Framing of Resource Allocation Decisions." *Organizational Behavior and Human Decision Processes* 37, no. 3 (June 1986): 348–56. doi.org/10.1016/0749-5978(86)90034-8.

Norton, Michael I., Daniel Mochon, and Dan Ariely. "The IKEA Effect: When Labor Leads to Love." *Journal of Consumer Psychology* 22, no. 3 (July 2012): 453–60. doi.org/10.1016/j.jcps.2011.08.002.

Novemsky, Nathan, and Daniel Kahneman. "The Boundaries of Loss Aversion." *Journal of Marketing Research* 42, no. 2 (May 2005): 119–28. doi.org/10.1509/jmkr.42.2.119.62292.

O'Connor, Kathleen M., Carsten K. W. De Dreu, Holly Schroth, Bruce Barry,

Terri R. Lituchy, and Max H. Bazerman. "What We Want to Do versus What We Think We Should Do." *Journal of Behavioral Decision Making* 15, no. 5 (December 2002): 403–18. doi.org/10.1002/bdm.426.

Odean, Terrance. "Are Investors Reluctant to Realize Their Losses?" *Journal of Finance* 53, no. 5 (October 1998): 1775–98. doi.org/10.1111/0022-1082 .00072.

Ordóñez, Lisa D., Maurice E. Schweitzer, Adam D. Galinsky, and Max H. Bazerman. "Goals Gone Wild: The Systematic Side Effects of Overprescribing Goal Setting." *Academy of Management Perspectives* 23, no. 1 (February 2009): 6–16. doi.org/10.5465/amp.2009.37007999.

Ordóñez, Lisa D., Maurice E. Schweitzer, Adam D. Galinsky, and Max H. Bazerman. "On Good Scholarship, Goal Setting, and Scholars Gone Wild." *Academy of Management Perspectives* 23, no. 3 (April 2009). doi.org/10.2139/ssrn .1382000.

Patil, Shefali V., Vieider, Ferdinand, and Philip E. Tetlock, "Process versus Outcome Accountability." In *The Oxford Handbook of Public Accountability*, edited by Mark Bovens, Robert E. Goodin, and Thomas Schillemans, 69–89. New York: Oxford University Press, 2014. doi.org/10.1093/oxfordhb/97801 99641253.013.0002.

Pierce, Jon L., Tatiana Kostova, and Kurt T. Dirks. "The State of Psychological Ownership: Integrating and Extending a Century of Research." *Review of General Psychology* 7, no. 1 (March 2003): 107–84. doi.org/10.1037/1089 -2680.7.1.84.

Pierce, Jon L., Tatiana Kostova, and Kurt T. Dirks. "Toward a Theory of Psychological Ownership in Organizations." *Academy of Management Review* 26, no. 2 (April 2001): 298–310. doi.org/10.2307/259124.

Polman, Evan. "Self–Other Decision Making and Loss Aversion." *Organizational Behavior and Human Decision Processes* 119, no. 2 (November 2012): 141–50. doi.org/10.1016/j.obhdp.2012.06.005.

Preller, Rebecca, Holger Patzelt, and Nicola Breugst. "Entrepreneurial Visions in Founding Teams: Conceptualization, Emergency, and Effects on Opportunity Development." *Journal of Business Venturing* 35, no. 2 (March 2020): 105914. doi.org/10.1016/j.jbusvent.2018.11.004.

Rabin, Matthew, and Max Bazerman. "Fretting about Modest Risks Is a Mistake." *California Management Review* 61, no. 3 (May 2019): 34–48. doi.org /10.1177/0008125619845876.

Raff, Daniel M. G., and Peter Temin. "Sears, Roebuck in the Twentieth Century: Competition, Complementarities, and the Problem of Wasting Assets." In *Learning by Doing in Markets, Firms, and Countries*, edited by Naomi R. Lamoreaux, Raff, and Temin, 219–52. Chicago: University of Chicago Press, 1999.

Reb, Jochen, and Terry Connolly. "Possession, Feelings of Ownership and the Endowment Effect." *Judgment and Decision Making* 2, no. 2 (April 2007): 107–14. journal.sjdm.org/vol2.2.htm.

Ritov, Ilana, and Jonathan Baron. "Outcome Knowledge, Regret, and Omission Bias." *Organizational Behavior and Human Decision Processes* 64, no. 2. (1995): 119–27.

Ritov, Ilana, and Jonathan Baron. "Reluctance to Vaccinate: Omission Bias and Ambiguity." *Journal of Behavioral Decision Making* 3, no. 4 (October/December 1990): 263–77. doi.org/10.1002/bdm.3960030404.

Ritov, Ilana, and Jonathan Baron. "Status-Quo and Omission Biases." *Journal of Risk and Uncertainty* 5 (1992): 49–61. doi.org/10.1007/BF00208786.

Robertson-Kraft, Claire, and Angela Lee Duckworth. "True Grit: Trait-Level Perseverance and Passion for Long-Term Goals Predicts Effectiveness and Retention among Novice Teachers." *Teachers College Record* 116, no. 3 (March 2014): 1–27. doi.org/10.1177/016146811411600306.

Ross, Jerry, and Barry M. Staw. "Managing Escalation Processes in Organizations." *Journal of Managerial Issues* 3, no. 1 (Spring 1991): 15–30. jstor.org/stable/40603896.

Ross, Jerry, and Barry M. Staw. "Organizational Escalation and Exit: Lessons from the Shoreham Nuclear Power Plant." *Academy of Management Journal* 36, no. 4 (August 1993): 701–32. doi.org/10.2307/256756.

Rubin, Jeffrey Z., and Joel Brockner. "Factors Affecting Entrapment in Waiting Situations: The Rosencrantz and Guildenstern Effect." *Journal of Personality and Social Psychology* 31, no. 6 (January 1975): 1054–63. doi.org/10.1037/h0076937.

Rubin, Jeffrey Z., Joel Brockner, Susan Small-Weil, and Sinaia Nathanson. "Factors Affecting Entry into Psychological Traps." *Journal of Conflict Resolution* 24, no. 3 (September 1980): 405–26. doi.org/10.1177/002200278002400302.

Ruggeri, Kai, et al. "Not Lost in Translation: Successfully Replicating Prospect Theory in 19 Countries." Pre-publication version, August 21, 2019. osf.io/2nyd6.

Ruggeri, Kai, et al. "Replicating Patterns of Prospect Theory for Decision under Risk." *Nature Human Behavior* 4 (2020): 622–33. doi.org/10.1038/s41562-020-0886-x.

Samuelson, William, and Richard J. Zeckhauser. "Status Quo Bias in Decision Making." *Journal of Risk and Uncertainty* 1, no. 1 (February 1988): 7–59. doi.org/10.1007/BF00055564.

Schwartz, Barry. "The Sunk-Cost Fallacy: Bush Falls Victim to a Bad New Argument for the Iraq War." *Slate*, September 9, 2005. slate.com/news-and-politics/2005/09/bush-is-a-sucker-for-the-sunk-cost-fallacy.html.

Schweitzer, Maurice. "Disentangling Status Quo and Omission Effects: An Experimental Analysis." *Organizational Behavior and Human Decision Processes* 58, no. 3 (June 1994): 457–76. doi.org/10.1006/obhd.1994.1046.

Schweitzer, Maurice E., Lisa Ordóñez, and Bambi Douma. "The Dark Side of Goal Setting: The Role of Goals in Motivating Unethical Decision Making." *Academy of Management Proceedings* 2002, no. 1 (2002): B1–6. doi.org/10.5465/apbpp.2002.7517522.

Shu, Suzanne B., and Joann Peck. "Psychological Ownership and Affective Reaction: Emotional Attachment Process Variables and the Endowment Effect." *Journal of Consumer Psychology* 21, no. 4 (October 2011): 439–52. doi.org/10.1016/j.jcps.2011.01.002.

Simons, Daniel J., and Christopher F. Chabris. "Gorillas in Our Midst: Sustained Inattentional Blindness for Dynamic Events." *Perception* 28, no. 9 (September 1999): 1059–74. doi.org/10.1068/p281059.

Simonson, Itamar, and Barry Staw. "Deescalation Strategies: A Comparison of Techniques for Reducing Commitment to Losing Courses of Action." *Journal of Applied Psychology* 77, no. 4 (1992): 419–26. doi.org/10.1037/0021-9010.77.4.419.

Sivanathan, Niro, Daniel C. Molden, Adam D. Galinsky, and Gillian Ku. "The Promise and Peril of Self-Affirmation in De-Escalation of Commitment." *Organizational Behavior and Human Decision Processes* 107, no. 1 (September 2008): 1–14. doi.org/10.1016/j.obhdp.2007.12.004.

Sleesman, Dustin J., Donald E. Conlon, Gerry McNamara, and Jonathan E. Miles. "Cleaning Up the Big Muddy: A Meta-Analytic Review of the Determinants of Escalation of Commitment." *Academy of Management Journal* 55, no. 3 (2012): 541–62. doi.org/10.5465/amj.2010.0696.

Spranca, Mark, Elisa Minsk, and Jonathan Baron. "Omission and Commission in Judgment and Choice." *Journal of Experimental Social Psychology* 27, no. 1 (January 1991): 76–105. doi.org/10.1016/0022-1031(91)90011-t.

Staw, Barry M. "Attribution of the 'Causes' of Performance: A General Alternative Interpretation of Cross-Sectional Research on Organizations." *Organizational Behavior and Human Performance* 13, no. 3 (June 1975): 414–32. doi.org/10.1016/0030-5073(75)90060-4.

Staw, Barry M. "The Escalation of Commitment to a Course of Action." *Academy of Management Review* 6, no. 4 (October 1981): 577–87. doi.org/10.2307/257636.

Staw, Barry M. "The Experimenting Organization." *Organizational Dynamics* 6, no. 1 (Summer 1977): 3–18. doi.org/10.1016/0090-2616(77)90032-8.

Staw, Barry M. "Knee-Deep in the Big Muddy: A Study of Escalating Commitment to a Chosen Course of Action." *Organizational Behavior and Human Performance* 16, no. 1 (June 1976): 27–44. doi.org/10.1016/0030-5073(76)90005-2.

Staw, Barry M. "Stumbling Toward a Social Psychology of Organizations: An Autobiographical Look at the Direction of Organizational Research." *Annual*

Review of Organizational Psychology and Organizational Behavior 3 (March 2016): 1–19. doi.org/10.1146/annurev-orgpsych-041015-062524.

Staw, Barry M., Sigal G. Barsade, and Kenneth W. Koput. "Escalation at the Credit Window: A Longitudinal Study of Bank Executives' Recognition and Write-Off of Problem Loans." *Journal of Applied Psychology* 82, no. 1 (1997): 130–42. doi.org/10.1037/0021-9010.82.1.130.

Staw, Barry M., and Richard D. Boettger. "Task Revision: A Neglected Form of Work Performance." *Academy of Management Journal* 33, no. 3 (September 1990): 534–59.

Staw, Barry M., and Frederick V. Fox. "Escalation: The Determinants of Commitment to a Chosen Course of Action." *Human Relations* 30, no. 5 (May 1977): 431–50. doi.org/10.1177/001872677703000503.

Staw, Barry M., and Ha Hoang. "Sunk Costs in the NBA: Why Draft Order Affects Playing Time and Survival in Professional Basketball." *Administrative Science Quarterly* 40, no. 3 (September 1995): 474–494. doi.org/10.2307/2393794.

Staw, Barry M., Pamela I. McKechnie, and Sheila M. Puffer. "The Justification of Organizational Performance." *Administrative Science Quarterly* 28, no. 4 (December 1983): 582–600. doi.org/10.2307/2393010.

Staw, Barry M., and Jerry Ross. "Behavior in Escalation Situations: Antecedents, Prototypes, and Solutions." *Research in Organizational Behavior* 9 (January 1987): 39–78.

Staw, Barry M., and Jerry Ross. "Commitment to a Policy Decision: A Multi-Theoretical Perspective." *Administrative Science Quarterly* 23, no. 1 (March 1978): 40–64. doi.org/10.2307/2392433.

Staw, Barry M. and Jerry Ross. "Understanding Behavior in Escalation Situations." *Science* 246, no. 4927 (October 1989): 216–20. doi.org/10.1126/science.246.4927.216.

Steinkühler, Dominik, Matthias D. Mahlendorf, and Malte Brettel. "How Self-Justification Indirectly Drives Escalation of Commitment." *Schmalenbach Business Review* 66, no. 2 (2014): 191–222. doi.org/10.1007/bf03396905.

Tenney, Elizabeth R., Jennifer M. Logg, and Don A. Moore. "(Too) Optimistic about Optimism: The Belief That Optimism Improves Performance." *Journal of Personality and Social Psychology* 108, no. 3 (March 2015): 377–99. doi.org/ 10.1037/pspa0000018.

Tetlock, Philip E. "Close-Call Counterfactuals and Belief-System Defenses: I Was Not Almost Wrong but I Was Almost Right." *Journal of Personality and Social Psychology* 75, no. 3 (1998): 639–52. doi.org/10.1037/0022-3514.75.3.639.

Thaler, Richard. "Mental Accounting and Consumer Choice." *Marketing Science* 4, no. 3 (August 1985): 199–214. doi.org/10.1287/mksc.4.3.199.

Thaler, Richard H. "Mental Accounting Matters." *Journal of Behavioral Decision*

Making 12, no. 3 (September 1999): 183–206. doi.org/10.1002/(sici)1099 -0771(199909)12:3<183::aid-bdm318>3.0.co;2-f.

Thaler, Richard H. (featured). "The Sports Learning Curve: Why Teams Are Slow to Learn and Adapt." Video of discussion at MIT Sloan Sports Analytics Conference, March 2020. sloansportsconference.com/event/the-sports -learning-curve-why-teams-are-slow-to-learn-and-adapt.

Thaler, Richard H. "Toward a Positive Theory of Consumer Choice." *Journal of Economic Behavior & Organization* 1, no. 1 (March 1980): 39–60. doi.org /10.1016/0167-2681(80)90051-7.

Thaler, Richard H., and Eric J. Johnson. "Gambling with the House Money and Trying to Break Even: The Effects of Prior Outcomes on Risky Choice." *Management Science* 36, no. 6 (June 1990): 643–60. doi.org/10.1287/mnsc.36.6.643.

Thibodeau, Ruth, and Elliot Aronson. "Taking a Closer Look: Reasserting the Role of the Self-Concept in Dissonance Theory." *Personality & Social Psychology Bulletin* 18, no. 5 (October 1992): 591–602. doi.org/10.1177/0146167 292185010.

Tversky, Amos, and Daniel Kahneman. "Advances in Prospect Theory: Cumulative Representation of Uncertainty." *Journal of Risk and Uncertainty* 5 , no. 4 (1992): 297–323. jstor.org/stable/41755005.

Tversky, Amos, and Daniel Kahneman. "Availability: A Heuristic for Judging Frequency and Probability." *Cognitive Psychology* 5, no. 2 (September 1973) 207–32. doi.org/10.1016/0010-0285(73)90033-9.

Tversky, Amos, and Daniel Kahneman. "Belief in the Law of Small Numbers." *Psychological Bulletin* 76, no. 2 (August 1971): 105.

Tversky, Amos, and Daniel Kahneman. "Causal Schemas in Judgments under Uncertainty." In *Progress in Social Psychology*, edited by Martin Fishbein, 49– 72. London: Psychology Press, 1980.

Tversky, Amos, and Daniel Kahneman. "Causal Thinking in Judgment under Uncertainty." In *Basic Problems in Methodology and Linguistics*, edited by Robert E. Butts and Jaakko Hintikka, 167–90. Dordrecht, Netherlands: Springer, 1977.

Tversky, Amos, and Daniel Kahneman. "Evidential Impact of Base Rates." In *Judgment under Uncertainty: Heuristics and Biases*, edited by Daniel Kahneman, Paul Slovic, and Amos Tversky, 153–60. Cambridge, UK: Cambridge University Press, 1982.

Tversky, Amos, and Daniel Kahneman. "Extensional vs. Intuitive Reasoning: The Conjunction Fallacy in Probability Judgment." *Psychological Review* 90 (October 1983): 293–315.

Tversky, Amos, and Daniel Kahneman. "The Framing of Decisions and the Psychology of Choice." *Science* 211, no. 4481 (January 1981): 453–58. doi.org /10.1126/science.7455683.

Tversky, Amos, and Daniel Kahneman. "Judgment under Uncertainty: Heuristics and Biases." *Science* 185, no. 4157 (September 1974): 1124–31. doi.org /10.1016/0010-0285(73)90033-9.

Tversky, Amos, and Daniel Kahneman. "Loss Aversion in Riskless Choice: A Reference Dependent Model." *Quarterly Journal of Economics* 106, no. 4 (November 1991): 1039–61. doi.org/10.2307/2937956.

Tversky, Amos, and Daniel Kahneman. "Rational Choice and the Framing of Decisions." *Journal of Business* 59, no. 4 (October 1986): 251–78. jstor.org /stable/2352759.

Tversky, Amos, Paul Slovic, and Daniel Kahneman. "The Causes of Preference Reversal." *The American Economic Review* 80, no. 1 (March 1990): 204–17. jstor.org/stable/2006743.

Van Putten, Marijke, Marcel Zeelenberg, and Eric van Dijk. "Who Throws Good Money after Bad? Action vs. State Orientation Moderates the Sunk Cost Fallacy." *Judgment and Decision Making* 5, no. 1 (February 2010): 33–36. journal.sjdm.org/10/91028/jdm91028.pdf.

Varadrajan, P. Rajan, Satish Jayachandran, and J. Chris White. "Strategic Interdependence in Organizations: Deconglomeration and Marketing Strategy." *Journal of Marketing* 65, no. 1 (January 2001): 15–28. doi.org/10.1509/jmkg .65.1.15.18129.

Von Culin, Katherine R., Eli Tsukayama, and Angela L. Duckworth. "Unpacking Grit: Motivational Correlates of Perseverance and Passion for Long-Term Goals." *The Journal of Positive Psychology* 9, no. 4 (March 2014): 306–12. doi .org/10.1080/17439760.2014.898320.

Weber, Martin, and Colin F. Camerer. "The Disposition Effect in Securities Trading: An Experimental Analysis." *Journal of Economic Behavior & Organization* 33, no. 2 (1998): 167–84. doi.org/10.1016/S0167-2681(97)00089-9.

Wrosch, Carsten, Gregory E. Miller, Michael F. Scheier, and Stephanie Brun de Pontet. "Giving Up on Unattainable Goals: Benefits for Health?" *Personality and Social Psychology Bulletin* 33, no. 2 (February 2007): 251–65. doi.org /10.1177/0146167206294905.

Wrosch, Carsten, Michael F. Scheier, Charles S. Carver, and Richard Schulz. "The Importance of Goal Disengagement in Adaptive Self-Regulation: When Giving Up is Beneficial." *Self and Identity* 2, no. 1 (2003): 1–20. doi.org/10.1080 /15298860309021.

Wrosch, Carsten, Michael F. Scheier, Gregory E. Miller, Richard Schulz, and Charles S. Carver. "Adaptive Self-Regulation of Unattainable Goals: Goal Disengagement, Goal Reengagement, and Subjective Well-Being." *Personality and Social Psychology Bulletin* 29, no. 12 (December 2003): 1494–1508. doi.org/10.1177/0146167203256921.

INDEX

Italicized page numbers indicate material in tables or illustrations.

permission and, giving and getting, 194–96

Teller, Eric, as, 195–96

quitting while you're ahead, 55–59

rational actor theory, cab drivers and, 49

Rauch, Ferdinand, 217

realism, optimism and, 188

Realogy Holdings, 163

recruiter calls, 215–16

relationships, 14, 15, 97, 125, 189–90

retail trading, 57–62, *60, 61,* 90–91, 97

Riecken, Henry, 164

rock climbing, 67–70

Rogers, Kenny, 18, 257*n*

Rosett, Richard, 269*n*

Ross, Jerry, 94

Rubin, Jeffrey, 82–83, 103–4

Rucker, Derek, 270*n*

Ruggeri, Kai, 260*n*

"Rumble in the Jungle," xv–xvi

Sage Stores, 76–78, 262*n*

sales, 117–22

Samuelson, William, 150

Santos, Laurie, 208

Saturday Night Live, 46

Schachter, Stanley, 164

Schlitz, Don, 257*n*

Schweitzer, Maurice, 231

Sears

bankruptcy of, 160, 162

diversification and, 223

holdings and divestitures of, 161–63

identity and, 163, 167, 176–78

mail-order growth and success of, 158–59

Morgan Stanley buying, 162–63

Philips compared to, 176–78

retail problems of, 159–60

Seeger, Pete, 80

Seekers, 164–68, 170

Seinfeld, 45–46

self-image concerns, 170–73

"Seven Summits," 7

shadow books, 64

Shankar, Maya

academic accomplishments of, 207–8

backup plans and, 214

as behavioral science adviser, 209

on children and identity, 273*n*

forced quitting and, 206

musical achievements of, 205–6

Shavers, Earnie, 30

Shoreham Nuclear Power Plant, 94

shot selection, in NBA, 154–55

Silicon Valley, 12

Simons, Daniel, 244

Simonson, Itamar, 105–6, 116–17

skiing, xxi–xxii

Slack, 28–29, 136

"A Slight Change of Plans" podcast, 209

slot machines, 266*n*

Smart, Geoff, 31

Spinks, Leon, xvi

S.S. Kresge, 76

Stallone, Sylvester, xvi–xvii

stand-up comedy, 12–14, 257*n*

start-ups, 34–35, 135, 179–85. *See also specific companies*

states and dates, 122–25

status quo bias, 150–56

Staw, Barry, 262*n*

advance planning and, 116–17

bank loan approval and, 192–93

escalation of commitment and, 80, 81, 100, 105–6

NBA draft and, 146–49

prior commitment and, 98–100

ABOUT THE AUTHOR

ANNIE DUKE is the bestselling author of *Thinking in Bets* and *How to Decide*. She is also a corporate speaker and consultant in the decision-making space. As a former professional poker player, Annie won more than $4 million in tournament poker before retiring from the game in 2012. She is the cofounder of The Alliance for Decision Education, a non-profit whose mission is to improve lives by empowering students through decision skills education.

A Frightening Discovery

Randal opened the door and stepped into his room—only to come to a sudden halt on the other side of the threshold.

Magic! But this magic was strange, like nothing he had known before. Randal looked around the room, which was lit by an eerie, blue-white glow.

"Wizard . . ."

The faint whisper came from his bed, over in the corner. Randal looked, and saw a man lying there, his features drawn and ashen in the cold blue light. Randal forced himself to go over to the cot and grasp the man by the shoulder.

The young wizard pulled his hand back quickly. *He's dying,* he realized. *He's dying of magic.*

CIRCLE OF MAGIC

CITY BY THE SEA

by Debra Doyle and James D. Macdonald

Illustrated by Judith Mitchell

Troll Associates

Library of Congress Cataloging-in-Publication Data

Doyle, Debra, (date)
  The city by the sea / by Debra Doyle and James Macdonald;
  illustrated by Judy Mitchell.
      p.   cm.—(Circle of magic; #3)
  Summary: A legacy from a dying stranger sends fifteen-year-old
journeyman wizard Randal on a dangerous journey to find the rightful
place of an artifact of power, which tempts him to succumb to its
tainted magic.
  ISBN 0-8167-1830-X (lib. bdg.)   ISBN 0-8167-1831-8 (pbk.)
  [1. Fantasy.]   I. Macdonald, James, 1954-   II. Mitchell,
Judy, 1951-   ill.   III. Title.   IV. Series: Doyle, Debra, 1952-
Circle of magic; #3.
PZ7.D7735Ci   1990
[Fic]—dc20   89-5213

A TROLL BOOK, published by Troll Associates,
Mahwah, NJ 07430

To the Siren of Seal Beach, who sang to us while we were stranded on a foreign shore—and read our manuscripts, too.

I.

Old Friends Meeting

RANDAL OF DOUN, a sturdy black-haired youth of about fifteen, pulled up the hood of his dark robe and hurried through the narrow streets of the Woodworkers' District. Here in Cingestoun the afternoons were cool, even though the season was not yet autumn. The River Donchess flowed through the middle of town, and the wind brought damp air off the water.

He paused at the corner and looked quickly up the next street. A man he'd spoken with earlier had told him that Alured Carpenter had a helper named Nicolas. That could only mean one thing: Randal's friend Nick, from the Schola Sorceriae—the School of Wizardry in Tarnsberg—was still working here.

In the old days, when Randal had despaired of completing his own apprenticeship, Nick's help and advice had sometimes been the only things that kept him going. But in the middle of Randal's second year, Nick had startled everybody by leaving both the Schola and the practice of wizardry. Nick had traveled north, to Cingestoun, to work in a carpenter's shop.

This street, Carpenters' Lane, was the place. Randal

1

looked into the open front of each shop as he came to it. Then, at last, Randal spotted his friend—a young man with a curly brown beard, leather-aproned, with a hammer in his hand and a trickle of sweat rolling down his forehead.

"Nick!" Randal shouted.

The young man looked up. "Who—Randy!" The journeyman carpenter put down his hammer and hurried to the front of the shop. "Come in, come in. I never expected to see you again after I left Tarnsberg, but I should have known someday you'd come walking in the door!"

Nick clasped Randal around the shoulders, nearly squeezing the life out of him with a friendly bear hug. "Let me take a look at you." Nick stepped back, and gave Randal an appraising glance. "And wearing a journeyman's robes, too. So you made it. I knew that no one would ever beat my record as the apprentice wizard who went the longest without becoming a journeyman."

He steered Randal inside the shop and over to a bench. "Sit down and tell me the news. Cingestoun may be a big town, but not much word from the outside world comes through the gates."

Randal sat, accepted the cool drink that Nick offered, and began to tell what he'd seen and heard on the road. "Times are hard," he said. "Crops are failing from one side of Brecelande to the other, and robbers are everywhere."

"Then nothing much has changed since I last left the city," Nick said. "Now, tell me the news from Tarnsberg.

Whatever happened to Lys? Is she still playing the lute and singing at the Grinning Gryphon Inn?"

"You can see for yourself," Randal replied. "We've been traveling together, and she's here in Cingestoun, singing at the Green Bough."

Nick's face lit up. "She is? That's wonderful! I have to watch the shop tonight for Alured, but tomorrow, I promise you, I'll stop by and see her again."

Randal smiled. Lys and Nick were his two best friends from his days in Tarnsberg. In fact, aside from his cousin Walter, who'd shared Randal's boyhood at Castle Doun, they were the best friends he had in the world.

"And how is everyone at the Schola?" Nick asked. "Mistress Pullen and all the rest?"

"Well enough," Randal replied. "Pieter's a master now."

"That's good news," said Nick. The former apprentice looked wistful for a moment. "Sometimes I wonder what might have happened if I'd stayed . . . but never mind the might-have-beens. Tell me what's become of Master Laerg—Head of the Regents and running the whole Schola by now, I shouldn't wonder."

Randal looked down, suddenly unable to speak. He flexed his right hand, where a raised scar ran across the palm.

"No," Randal said quietly. "No, Master Laerg doesn't run the Schola."

He looked up, directly into Nick's eyes. "You might as well hear it all," he said. "Master Laerg is dead, and I killed him. With a sword."

"You what?" Nick asked in disbelief. Of all the laws

3

and traditions binding wizards, the rule against using steel for attack or defense was the oldest and most revered.

Randal looked down at his lap. "I didn't have a choice," he said. "Laerg was summoning up demons . . . he wanted to destroy the Schola, and then rule all of Brecelande with the demons' help. He'd promised them a sacrifice and I was it."

"But to use a sword . . ."

Randal clenched his fist. The scar ached with the movement, as it always did—a reminder of the choice he'd made, when he'd cut himself to the bone grasping the blade of Laerg's ceremonial sword.

"I paid for it," Randal said quietly. "The Regents made me give my sworn word not to use magic until I'd gone on a quest for forgiveness to Master Balpesh off in the eastern mountains. But Balpesh let me use magic again, and taught me a few things, as well. And since then I've been living as a journeyman in truth, traveling up and down the land and seeking more magic than the Schola could teach me."

He looked about the carpenter's shop. "But what about you?" he asked Nick. "Do you use any magic at all, now that you've left the Schola?"

Nick shook his head. "I asked the Regents to put a binding spell on me," he said. "There's nothing worse than a half-taught wizard. Better to be an honest carpenter and save myself the temptation."

The street out front was dark now, and shadows filled the corners of the shop. "I have to get back," Randal said. "I was in the university library all day, and Lys will be wondering where I am."

Nick stood up and saw Randal to the door. "Better be careful, Randy. Cingestoun gets rough after dark."

Randal paused on the threshold, his wizard's robes swirling around him, and looked back at his friend.

"Don't worry, Nick. I'll be all right."

Nick shook his head. "This isn't Tarnsberg, remember? A black gown isn't going to keep you out of trouble—not when you've got people here who don't know a journeyman wizard from a stable hand."

"I've been a stable hand, too, and I'm not exactly helpless," Randal pointed out. "I sat through Master Issen's lectures on magical self-defense, just like everybody else."

"Of course you did," said Nick. "But as far as some people can see, you're still a half-grown boy, and a shock spell won't do you a bit of good after somebody's hit you over the head from behind with a club."

Randal laughed. "For what—five copper pennies and a book of spells?"

"For the boots on your feet," Nick told him. "Like you said, times have been bad, and this year isn't any better. People are looking out for themselves."

"I know," said Randal, his laughter dying. "I told you about some of the things that are happening up around Tattinham—the robbers and bandits—but I didn't think I'd be seeing it here on the King's Road, right in the middle of Brecelande."

"It's everywhere," said Nick. "So don't get so involved

in working out spells in your head that you forget to keep an eye out for trouble."

"I won't," Randal promised his friend. "I'll see you tomorrow, then."

"Until tomorrow."

The door of the carpenter's shop swung shut, leaving Randal alone in the dark. He took a firmer grasp on the tall walking staff he carried and turned down the street.

The waning moon shone down on Randal as he made his way through Cingestoun's narrow alleys to the inn where he was staying. In spite of his words to Nicolas, he wasn't particularly worried. Randal still had the strength and quick reflexes developed by his boyhood training as a squire in his uncle's castle of Doun. Although he would never use a sword again, as a journeyman wizard he had other defenses at his command.

His mind still dwelling on days past, he turned down Hornpipers' Street and entered the Green Bough, the inn where he was staying. He paused in the common room, where a clear alto voice came to him over the murmur of the crowd of patrons:

"I wish the wind would never cease,
Nor waters in the flood,
'Til all my sons come home to me
In earthly flesh and blood."

He waved to the performer, a slender, black-haired girl dressed in boy's clothing. She sat on a makeshift stage at the other end of the room and played a lute as she sang. She nodded to him, and kept on playing without losing a beat.

Randal took a seat at the back of the room and listened. Lys was a lute-player, singer, and acrobat, a native of Occitania in the far south. She made her own way as best she could with her voice and lute.

Her song done, she came across the room and took a seat by Randal. "How did your day go?" she asked.

"Fine," he said. "The university here didn't mind a journeyman wizard poking around in their library. I didn't find anything magical in there, but you never know with old books. But guess what—I found Nick! He's doing just fine at a carpenter's shop. He said he'd come by here tomorrow."

Lys smiled. "That's marvelous! If he hadn't loaned me that lute of his when I was starving, I wouldn't be able to earn my living now. I still have to sing one more time tonight—will you stay?"

"No, it's been a long day already. I think I'll go up and turn in early."

"I'll see you in the morning then," she said.

"In the morning," Randal replied, standing up. Leaving the lute-player behind, he headed across the crowded common room toward the stairs.

The innkeeper met him at the foot of the staircase. "A word with you, wizard."

Randal halted, one foot on the bottom step. "If it's about those rats I charmed out of your pantry, I told you a long-term warding spell costs more than just my room and board."

"No," said the innkeeper. "Day by day is fine. They're

7

still gone. But if you could do the same for the fleas and the bedbugs . . ."

"Ten coppers," Randal said automatically.

"Six," the innkeeper replied.

"Eight," said Randal. "Half in advance."

"Done," said the innkeeper. "I'll pay you in the morning."

Randal smiled to himself as he mounted the steep steps to the upstairs hall. *Eight copper pennies, and five more in my pocket—not bad.* Compared to the riches he'd left behind when he chose to study wizardry instead of becoming a knight, thirteen pennies didn't look like much—but here in Cingestoun, one penny was more than enough to buy a meal at the Green Bough, and sleeping space on the floor besides.

His own small use of magic had done him even better, purchasing the luxury of a room upstairs. As he paused with one hand on the latch, he murmured the words of the doorkeeping spell. An alarm sounded in his mind. Someone had entered his room since the morning, and that someone was still there.

Nick's words of caution came to him. Was there a thief waiting inside? *Well, he'll be the one getting the surprise,* Randal thought as he prepared a shock spell. Then he opened the door and stepped into the room—only to come to a sudden halt on the other side of the threshold.

Magic! Unfamiliar magic. The scar on his right palm began to throb. But this magic was strange, like nothing he had known before. Randal called up a small ball of cold-flame, and looked around the room by its eerie, blue-white glow.

He heard a creaking noise from the bed in the corner. Heart pounding, he spun toward the sound.

"Wizard. . . ."

The faint whisper came from his bed. Randal looked and saw a man lying there, his features drawn and ashen in the cold blue light. Randal forced himself to go over to the cot and grasp the man by the shoulder.

One touch, and the young wizard pulled his hand back. The man lying on the bed wore the ragged traces of what once had been a journeyman's robe like Randal's own, now grown soiled and tattered with age. But it wasn't the torn robe that had caused Randal to draw away; it was the sickening, hollow feeling he experienced when his fingers closed on the man's shoulder—as if the man was both empty and filled with a sense of power and energy greater than Randal had ever before encountered.

He's dying, Randal thought. *Dying of magic.*

Randal prepared the most powerful healing spell he knew, one that he'd learned earlier in the summer from master wizard Balpesh. He fought back a shudder of revulsion at the thought of touching that dead-but-living flesh a second time, and laid his hand on the man's cold, sweating forehead. In a low voice, he murmured the spell of restoration, and felt his own magical energies flowing out into the dying man, helping his weakened lungs to take in air and his laboring heart to beat.

"*Spira.*" He whispered the spell words again in the Old Tongue, the language that all wizards used to cast their spells and record their magical observations. "*Spira vive-que.*"

9

But Randal knew in his heart that the magic wasn't strong enough. Whatever was killing the stranger kept on drawing strength—the more Randal gave to the spell, the more it took from the man he was trying to heal. At last, the young wizard pulled away, defeated.

The attempt had given the man some strength, at least. He raised himself up from the thin mattress and said again, "Wizard. They told me you were a wizard, down below. You have to help me."

"I am trying to help you," said Randal as calmly as he could. *What good is knowing how to stop bleeding and lower a fever, against something like this?* he wondered. *How do you cure a man under a death spell? Balpesh would know.*

But Balpesh was a master wizard who'd spent years learning the healer's art, and Randal was only a journeyman. Already, the effects of Randal's spell were starting to fade. With the last of his strength, the stranger brought something out from under the pillow where it had lain hidden: a leather bag closed with a drawstring cord.

"Take this," he said. "Help me."

Randal hesitated. Something about the sack—the way it seemed to press down the man's hand with an unnatural weight, or the way shadows collected in its folds—hinted at the presence of powerful magic. *What manner of thing is this?* he wondered. Magical objects were not accepted carelessly, but he felt drawn toward it just the same.

"Please," said the stranger. "You are a wizard . . . you will know what to do. . . ." His breath came in ragged

10

gasps, and he had to pause before going on. "Dagon wants this . . . he waits at the Rooster and Roundels."

Still, Randal paused. The object in the bag seemed to call to him and repulse him at the same time. Before he could act, the stranger collapsed back onto the pillow and the leather bag fell from his lifeless hand.

Randal stood for a moment in shock. He had seen death before, but never like this, in a man he'd been trying to help. And never death caused by magic.

Worse yet, Randal thought numbly, *the man made a request, calling on me as a wizard. And as a wizard, I can't refuse.*

He picked up the sack. It was lighter than he had expected it would be from the way the stranger had handled it. A cold feeling walked up his spine.

There's powerful magic here indeed, he thought. *But not of any kind that I've ever known before.*

The wisest course of action, Randal knew, would be to hand over the bag unopened to Dagon, whoever he might be—but curiosity, as they said at the Schola, was always a wizard's greatest vice. *And after all, that's why the Schola sends apprentices out to be journeymen—to learn more about magic.*

Carefully, Randal opened the bag and peeled it away from the object it contained: a little statue about a foot tall, carved from ivory long since gone golden with age, representing an old woman leaning on a staff.

He held up the carving and looked at it from all angles. It was more than well made—the old woman almost seemed real. Each wrinkle of her face was lovingly rendered. The hand that grasped the staff was knobby and thin. A few strands of hair escaped from under her hood.

11

Looking at it, Randal got the odd sensation that the figure was alive.

He shuddered slightly. The feeling of magic was overwhelming. Fortunately, the statue wasn't his problem. It was Dagon's. All that remained was to find this Dagon and get rid of the unsettling piece of artwork.

II.
Midnight Dealings

RANDAL SLIPPED THE little statue back into its protective sack. He paused for a moment to examine the leather—soft and fine, like the best pigskin, but even more delicate. Pulling the drawstrings tight, he tied the sack to his belt and then looked down at the dead man lying in his bed. He didn't like the idea of just leaving him there, but the man had died trying to hand over the bag and what it contained.

"Whatever your name was," he promised the dead man, "I'll try to get back soon and take care of you—but I'll carry out your errand first. Wherever you've gone, fare well."

Randal extinguished the cold-flame, stepped out into the hall, and cast a locking spell on the bedroom door. As he finished, he heard a familiar light tread coming up the stairs and turned to see Lys, with her lute in its leather case slung over her shoulder.

She looked at him curiously. "You're going back out at this hour? I thought you were going to turn in early."

"I was," said Randal. "But something . . . came up, and I have to take care of it."

14

She looked at him sharply. "Trouble?"

"Bad trouble," said Randal. "There's a dead man in my bed, and magic killed him."

Even in the dim light, he could see her eyes widen and her lips move in an exclamation in her native southlands tongue. Then she dropped back into the language of Brecelande again and asked, *"You* didn't—?"

"No," said Randal. "I never have, and I don't even know if I could. I don't know what happened to him. But before he died, he gave me an errand to run."

"And that's where you're headed now?"

Randal nodded. "To a place called the Rooster and Roundels. Do you know how to find it?"

"You're not going there alone?" Lys asked sharply.

"Yes, I am," said Randal. The statue in its leather bag made a heavy weight at his belt. "I've been given something I don't understand," he said, "and I don't want my friends getting in trouble on my account."

"The Rooster and Roundels is over near the river docks," said Lys. "You can't go there alone. You'll need someone to watch your back."

"I can take care of myself," said Randal.

"Right," said Lys. She didn't sound convinced.

Randal sighed. "Since you're probably going to follow me whether I ask you to or not, you might as well come along."

A damp fog had risen outside, making Randal glad of the thick cloth of his wizard's robe as he and Lys made their way to the dockside district. The River Donchess, flowing out of the dense Wilderness of Lannad to the west, ran through the center of Cingestoun, and the

15

boatmen gathered in cheap inns along the waterfront. The street facing the river was lined with rough, dangerous places, of which the Rooster and Roundels looked to be one of the worst: foul smelling, and dimly lit by a scattering of smoky rushlights.

"This is the sort of place I wouldn't sing in without an armed guard," Lys muttered as she and Randal stepped through the door and into the hazy common room. She stuck close to his shoulder, and kept one hand on the hilt of the small knife she wore at her belt.

Randal nodded agreement. "If I hadn't made a promise to a dead man," he said, "I wouldn't be here."

He'd already marked how the boatmen and gamblers drinking at the rough-hewn tables had eyed them as they entered, and then had looked away again. *Nick worries too much,* he thought. *They still recognize a wizard's robes.* The knowledge gave him a little more confidence. A couple of boys—for so Lys appeared at a casual glance—might be ripe victims for robbery, kidnapping, or worse, but a wizard was something else.

Just the same, Randal scanned the room warily as he and Lys made their way through the close-packed tables to where the landlord stood filling tankards from an open keg. *Two doors . . . windows on three walls . . . lots of ways in and out . . . and as scummy a bunch of wharf rats as I've ever seen.*

"I'm looking for Dagon," Randal said to the landlord. "Is he here tonight?"

"Maybe," said the landlord. He eyed Randal narrowly. "What's it to you, wizard?"

"Private business," said Randal. He reached into the

16

deep inside pocket of his journeyman's robe, past the small leatherbound spell book that he kept there, and pulled out one of the five copper pennies. The young wizard held out the coin. In the orange glow from the rushlights, the long scar across his palm made a raised white line against the surrounding flesh.

"Can you point Dagon out for me?" he asked.

The landlord took the coin. "Over there," he said, nodding toward a table where a dark, thickset man sat with his back to the wall. "That's him."

Randal frowned briefly as he took in the dark man's studded jacket of hardened leather—the armor of a mercenary foot soldier. *A fighting man? For something like this, I was expecting a wizard. That man in my room had to know more than a little of the Art, or he'd never have gotten past the spells on my door. But this fellow . . .*

Dagon watched without expression as Randal and Lys crossed to his table and took seats across from him. Randal began without buildup. "Are you Dagon?"

The dark man took a deliberate pull from his mug before answering. "I don't think I know you."

"If you *are* Dagon," Randal continued, "then I met a man today who said he had something for you."

A gleam of interest showed in the man's eyes. "And if I *was* Dagon, then what would that thing be?"

"A statue."

Dagon let out his breath in what could have been either satisfaction or relief. "Bryce got it, then. What does he want for it? Tell him that I already paid him, and he won't get a copper more."

17

That's the truth, thought Randal, *whether you meant it to be or not.*

"It isn't like that," he said. "He asked me to give it to you. . . ."

Dagon sat up straighter, and leaned forward. "You have it here? Hand it over."

Seeing the avid gleam in Dagon's eyes, Randal suddenly felt reluctant to pass the ivory carving across. *That statue holds powerful magic of a kind I've never experienced— what could a man like this want with such a thing? He isn't going to think past the money it'll bring him when he sells it.*

Still, giving the statue to Dagon had been the dying man's own request. *Since you couldn't save him,* Randal told himself, *you ought to at least do that.*

He took the bag from his belt and opened it. Reaching in, he pulled out the figurine. "Is this what you were expecting?"

Randal set the carving upright in the center of the table. The flickering light made it seem as if the old woman was in motion, even though she was only dead ivory. Once again, Randal felt the prickling sensation that told of powerful magic.

"Yes," Dagon said. "That's mine." The mercenary reached out a hand to take the carving.

Before his fingers could close around it, the two doors of the Rooster and Roundels smashed open. A dozen armored men in yellow surcoats came crashing in, their swords out and ready. Randal heard the racket of a table falling over, and the metallic whisper of a broadsword coming out of its sheath. Then the six windows of the

18

tavern's bottom story crashed in, and more men-at-arms came clambering through, swords drawn.

"Fess's men!" exclaimed Dagon, leaping to his feet and drawing his sword as he rose. "Time to get out of here."

The table rocked and tilted dangerously when he bumped into it, and the ivory figurine started sliding toward the floor. Lys grabbed the statue as the table went over, and thrust the carved figure out toward Randal. His fingers closed around the cold ivory.

"Give it to him and let's run," she said hurriedly. "It's not our quarrel." Then her eyes widened and she cried out, "Quick, Randy—duck!"

He ducked, and a sword-blade whizzed over his head as one of the yellowcoated men took a swing at him. The young wizard flashed a bright light in the man's face, and boomed some thunder in his ear—easy spells, but enough to stun the man and buy some thinking time.

"We're with you," Randal said to Dagon. "Let's go."

The three went out the nearest window. The street outside held more men, wearing the same yellow surcoats as those in the tavern. Some of them carried torches, and all of them were armed. Randal called up another flash of light into the midst of the troop, this time making it bright enough to dazzle the yellowcoats into temporary blindness.

"This way!" yelled Dagon. "Hurry!"

The mercenary led the way down a winding alley. Randal and Lys followed, running lightly, their leather soles making only a faint slapping sound against the fog-slicked cobblestones.

A few minutes later, the three paused in the shadow of some empty casks stacked at the foot of one of the city wharves.

"That wasn't bad, what you did back there," said Dagon. "A wizard, are you?"

"You saw for yourself," Randal told him. *No point in letting him know I'm only a journeyman. A wizard doesn't lie . . . but what a man thinks is his own business.* "And I don't like what's going on. Who's Fess, and why is he after you?"

Dagon chuckled grimly. "You must be new around here if you don't know who Lord Fess is. And he's not just after me anymore—not since everybody in the Rooster and Roundels saw you handing over that piece of ivory. Speaking of which . . ."

Randal shook his head. "Not until you tell me what it is and why you want it. For something that small, it's caused too much trouble already."

"I don't know what it is," Dagon admitted. "All I know is that Varnart wants it, and he's paying good money for it. That's enough for me."

"Not for us," said Lys, at the same time as Randal asked, "Who's Varnart?"

"I thought all you wizards knew each other," said Dagon. "The statue is really his—or so he told me. He only wanted it back."

"Sure he did," said Lys. "Tell us another."

Randal ignored her. "If the statue is Varnart's, then who is Fess?"

Dagon gave a world-weary sigh. "Cingestoun's a free town, but Lord Fess holds just about everything outside the city walls. And sometimes things turn up in his trea-

20

sure room that don't have any business being there, if you take my drift."

Lys put her hands on her hips and looked straight at the mercenary. "You stole it, didn't you?"

"Not me," said Dagon. "That was Bryce's job. I'm just returning the carving to its rightful owner."

Randal's lips tightened, and he folded his arms on his chest. "So you took the safe part for yourself."

"You call being chased halfway across Cingestoun by Fess's yellowcoats 'safe'?" said Dagon indignantly.

Randal nodded. "Bryce is already dead."

"I see," said Dagon. "Too bad. He was a friend of mine." He gave the young wizard a measuring glance. "Your doing?"

There was a note in the mercenary's voice that Randal didn't like at all. *I don't want to fight this man,* he thought. *I'd have to use something a lot more permanent than bright lights and loud noises.*

"I found him in my room," Randal said aloud. Carefully, in the back of his mind, he began readying a shock spell in case he needed it. "I don't know how he got there, but he was already dying. He gave me the statue, and said it was for you."

"If that's what happened," Lys cut in, "then I say let's hand the thing over and say good night."

"It's not that simple," said Randal. "Not with magic involved." In fact, he felt less and less sure that he ought to give the statue to Dagon. The mercenary clearly had no idea how to deal with a magical artifact. True, Randal had promised . . . but only to find Dagon, nothing more.

Maybe I ought to give the statue to Varnart myself, he

21

thought. *Wizard to wizard. If we're dealing with an artifact of power, that would be the safest thing to do.*

"Let's talk about this someplace warm and dry," Randal said finally. "I think we've shaken Fess's men, so it's probably safe to go back to the Green Bough."

Dagon scowled at him for a moment longer, and then shrugged. "Sounds good to me."

But when they reached the Green Bough, Randal stopped short with an exclamation of dismay, and gestured the others back into the shadows of the alley. Two men-at-arms in yellow surcoats were coming out of the inn. They took places on either side of the doorstep, as if standing guard.

"I don't like the looks of this," said Lys. "I'm sure nobody back at that other place knew me or Randal by sight, so how could they have gotten here before we did?"

"Bryce," said Dagon. "Someone must have followed him into town." The mercenary shook his head. "Careless of him."

"He was probably dying already," said Randal. "And as soon as somebody breaks down the locking spell on my door, Fess's men are going to find his body."

"Then we'd better leave town," said Lys at once. "You'll never convince Lord Fess that you didn't do it."

"Smart girl," said Dagon—Lys's disguise apparently hadn't survived the conversation. "I have to meet a fellow outside town tomorrow anyway. But getting out of Cingestoun's likely to be harder than it sounds. Fess's men will be watching all the gates by now, and those fellows who hit the Rooster and Roundels got a good look at all of us."

Lys bit her lip. "So what do we do now, Randy? Climb over the walls?"

"I've heard worse ideas," said Dagon. "But we'd still have to reckon with the city guards."

Lys wasn't paying any attention to the mercenary. "Well?" she asked, still looking at Randal.

"Let me think. . . ." The young wizard frowned. *I've never been all that good with disguises and illusions*, he thought. *I couldn't cover all three of us, or even just Lys and me, for more than a little while. Not if we're all moving. And fighting our way out's no good either—not when we're one mercenary, a lute-player, and a journeyman wizard up against Lord Fess's personal troops. We'll have to smuggle ourselves through the gates somehow. . . .*

"I've got it," he said. "Come on."

Dagon didn't move. "Where are you going?"

"I have a friend in town," said Randal. "With any kind of luck, Fess's men don't know about him, and with a bit more luck, he'll be willing to help us."

The young wizard led the way back along the route he had followed at the start of the evening, from the Green Bough to Carpenters' Lane. Now the sky overhead was beginning to go from black to gray, and the stars were gone. Soon a smell of resin and sawdust filled the dawn air.

"Nick's shop is close by here," said Randal to Lys. A moment later he stopped before a barred and shuttered shop-front.

23

Dagon frowned. "How do we get in without waking up the whole street?" the mercenary asked.

"Like this," Randal said, laying his hand on the shop door. He muttered a quiet spell of opening, and the bolt shifted. He pushed at the door, and it swung open. "Let's get inside before somebody spots us."

Once all three of them were inside the shop, Randal called up a sphere of cold-flame. The cold light played over the workbench and the tools, the carpenters' aprons hanging from pegs along the walls, the motes of sawdust, and a curled woodshaving that had escaped the evening cleanup. Dagon looked about the shop with a fighter's usual contempt for a tradesman, but Lys's dark blue eyes were interested, and a little sad.

"This is a long way from the Schola," she murmured.

"It's honest work," said Randal, in the same low tones. "And safer than life on the road. You two stay down here, and I'll go wake up Nick."

He started for the stairs that led to the upper levels of the shop, but stopped at a muffled exclamation from Dagon.

"Someone's coming!" said the mercenary.

Randal turned, and saw that Dagon already had his sword half-drawn. "Put that away," said Randal. "I told you this man's a friend."

Dagon looked unconvinced. "Yours maybe—not mine." The mercenary met Randal's gaze for a long minute before slamming the sword back into its scabbard.

By the time he had done so, Nick was already coming down the stairs into the blue glow of the cold-flame, a heavy wooden club at the ready in his right hand.

24

III.

A Friend in Need

"WHAT," SAID RANDAL, half laughing, "a club and not a dagger?"

"Old habits die hard," said Nick, tucking the club into his belt with a look of relief. "I suppose I stayed too long at Tarnsberg. I still don't feel right about using steel." He saw Lys and broke into a delighted smile. "Lys! I've been looking forward to seeing you ever since Randy told me you were in town. But what brings you to the shop at this hour?"

"We have to get past the town gates without being spotted," Randal answered. "Can you help us?"

"Are you in trouble?"

"Not if we aren't seen," Lys replied.

"Then there's nothing easier," said Nick. "Mind telling me who's chasing you, just so I'll know who to avoid?"

"Fess's men," said Randal. "We have something they want, and they're acting serious about getting it."

Nick frowned. "Those yellowcoats are a nasty bunch. I'll still help you, but I'd like to know what you're trying to keep away from them."

"This," said Randal. He unwrapped the ivory statue from the bag that protected it, and set it down on the carpenter's workbench. As before, the old woman seemed to have moved since the last time he'd seen her, even though he couldn't pinpoint a particular change. "I think it's an artifact of power."

Nick reached out to touch the smooth ivory of the carving. He ran a forefinger along the curve of the figure's wrinkled cheek, and then drew his hand back with an odd expression. "It's . . . certainly something very strange," he said. "I don't recall ever reading or hearing about anything like it."

"Me, neither," said Randal. "So what do you think?"

Nick stroked his curly brown beard, all the while frowning at the ivory figurine. "I haven't done magic since I quit the Schola," he said finally, "and that thing still makes my skin prickle. I'd say get rid of it as soon as you can—but not to Lord Fess."

"Don't worry," said Dagon. "I've already got a buyer."

Nick glanced over at the mercenary, and then back to Randal. When he spoke again, it was in the Old Tongue. *"Who is that person?"*

"One of my other problems," said Randal, in the same language. *"His name is Dagon, and I don't trust him. He says the artifact is supposed to go to someone called Varnart."*

"I see," said Nick. He switched back to the language of Brecelande. "Come help me harness up the lumber wagon. The guards at the North Gate are used to passing me through early in the morning when I go to the

26

Oseney woodlots for timber. You can hide in the back of the wagon, and I'll drive you out of town."

A few minutes later, Alured Carpenter's lumber wagon rolled out of the stable in the back of the shop. On the wagon-driver's seat, Nick whistled a cheerful tune as the wagon rumbled down the alley into the broader stretch of Carpenters' Lane. In the box of the wagon, Randal, Lys, and Dagon huddled under a canvas cloth.

Good thing Nick was in town and willing to help, Randal thought, as he breathed the close, resin-scented air. *Otherwise I'd be stuck with trying to make the three of us look like rag collectors or something.*

"Your friend could get a pretty sum from Fess for turning us in," Dagon muttered low-voiced at Randal's elbow.

"Don't worry," said Lys. Even in the darkness, Randal could tell that she was angry. "Nick wouldn't even think of doing a thing like that."

"You'd better hope he doesn't try," said Dagon. "If I so much as get suspicious—"

"You'll keep your mouth shut and hold still," Randal said sharply. "I told you before, Nick is my friend."

The whistling from the driver's seat stopped. "Better be quiet back there," came Nick's voice. "We're coming up on the North Gate."

Randal half knelt and peered through a chink in the wooden slats that formed the front and sides of the lumber wagon. Through the narrow gap, he could see Nick's head and shoulders silhouetted against the orange torchlight coming from the North Gate guardhouse. Armed men moved about in the road ahead.

27

Yellow surcoats, observed Randal, as the lumber wagon trundled closer to the guardhouse. *Dagon was right. Fess's men are watching the gates already.* He turned and whispered to the others, "Don't move. I may have to try an illusion to get us past."

Nick drove the lumber wagon up to the guardhouse, and then brought the four-horse team to a halt. Randal watched from beneath the canvas as the regular night guard came up, holding a lantern. A pair of yellowcoated men came with the gatekeeper, one on either side.

Randal pursed his lips in a silent whistle, and shook his head. *Lord Fess isn't taking any chances.*

"Where do you think you're going?" one of the yellowcoats demanded.

"Out to Oseney," Nick called back. "Ebert, tell these fellows who I am."

The night guard held up the lantern so that the yellow light shone directly on Nick's face. Randal, crouched in the wagon-box and squinting through the little space between the canvas and the wood, saw that his friend's lips were tight and his jaw was set under the dense brown beard.

The guard gave Nick no more than a cursory glance before lowering his lantern with a nod. "I know you," he said. He turned to the yellowcoat on his right. "It's just Alured Carpenter's journeyman. He comes by here three, four times every month."

Fess's man frowned. He took a step forward and looked up at Nick. "You, journeyman—what brings you through the gates this early in the morning?"

Randal tensed. He heard the catch in Lys's breathing,

28

and the faint sliding sound of her dagger coming out of its sheath. From Dagon, he heard nothing at all—and that, he somehow knew, was an even more dangerous sign. *It's not enough that I have to worry about the gate guards,* thought Randal. *If Dagon gets it into his head that Nick's sold us out . . .*

But Nick only ran a hand across his face as if he were still half-asleep, and blinked down at the guard. "I need wood, the same as always, and it's a long way out to Oseney."

The regular guard scratched his head. "Didn't you come through looking for wood just three days past?"

Nick swallowed a yawn, and then shrugged. "Business is good lately. I go fetch wood when Alured tells me to."

The second of Fess's men nodded at the four-horse team. "Why so many horses to pull the wagon?"

Nick yawned again. "Load's heavy sometimes."

"Then you won't mind if I look in the back."

The words were a statement, not a question, and the yellowcoat had already headed around toward the rear of the wagon before Nick could reply. Randal clenched his hands on the rim of the wagon-box, and pressed his forehead against the wood.

Illusion, he thought, listening to the heavy footsteps growing closer. *We need an illusion.*

He closed his eyes and spoke the words that created a false appearance. As he finished, the guard's footsteps reached the back of the wagon. He couldn't hear Lys's breathing at all now, and the silence from Dagon seemed even heavier than before. If the mercenary decided to make good on his earlier threat, there was no way Randal could stop him—not without dropping the fragile illusion spell first.

Randal heard the stiff rustle of the canvas being lifted, and felt cold sweat break out on his forehead with the effort of keeping up the illusion.

Bare boards and shadows . . . let Fess's man see only bare boards and shadows.

The canvas rustled again as the guard let it drop. The footsteps went back around to the front of the wagon, and Randal heard the voices of the three guards in muttered conference.

"She's empty, all right. You vouch for this man, Ebert?"

"Known him this past year or more, and a more honest sort you won't find between here and Widsegard."

"Right, then. Off you go, carpenter . . . and if you happen to see a pair of boys and a man-at-arms anywhere between here and Oseney, make certain you tell us about it double quick."

Randal heard Nick give another smothered yawn as the gates creaked open. "I'll keep an eye out," promised the apprentice wizard turned carpenter, and then called to the horses: "Gee up!"

The lumber wagon lurched forward, and rolled out through the North Gate into the graying light of dawn. With a sigh of relief, Randal let the illusion go. He was shivering as he sank back down to a seated position on the wagon-bed, and his teeth were chattering.

He felt the light touch of Lys's hand on his arm. "Are you all right, Randy?"

The young wizard nodded, although he knew she

30

couldn't see him in the darkness under the canvas. "I'm fine—just tired, that's all. Illusions are hard work."

Especially when you've never been very good at them in the first place, he added to himself, but he knew better than to say it out loud. Only Dagon's grudging respect for his magical skills had kept the mercenary cooperative so far. *If he ever figures out how little I really know, he'll kill me the next time I turn my back.*

"Rest while you can," came Nick's voice from the front of the wagon. "I'm taking the three of you well clear of town before I stop the wagon and let you get off."

"Do what Nick says," Lys told Randal. "I'll keep alert in case of trouble."

Randal started to protest, and found himself yawning instead. Almost in spite of himself, he leaned back against the side of the wagon and fell asleep.

He woke to the feel of the wagon coming to a halt. A moment later, pale light struck his closed eyelids, and he opened his eyes to see Nick pulling back the canvas cover from the wagon-box. Randal looked around and saw nothing, for the moment, that appeared threatening or even interesting—only the nondescript brown and green of the grasslands that surrounded Cingestoun. The sky overhead was gray and watery, and a light mist dampened everything as soon as the canvas was raised.

"We're almost to Oseney," said Nick. The journeyman carpenter was smiling cheerfully, in spite of the beads of moisture silvering his brown hair and beard. "That was a good job you did back there at the gate. I was afraid we were done for."

Lys pushed herself away from the side of the wagon

31

and stretched. Her lute, which she'd carried with her during all the night's adventures, lay on the floor of the wagon near her feet. "So was I," she said to Nick. "Thanks, Randy."

Randal shrugged. "The dark night, the torchlight, the fact that they didn't really expect to find us . . . it wasn't really much work, as illusions go."

Next to Randal, Dagon sat up and yawned. The mercenary had fallen asleep himself on the road out of Cingestoun; wood chips and scraps of bark from the floor of the wagon clung to his hair and clothing. "It was enough," he said as he brushed himself off. "Now that we're past the gates, you can hand over Bryce's package like you agreed."

Randal shook his head. "Oh, no. I never agreed to that." He closed his hand around the statue inside its leather bag. "We were going to talk things over at the Green Bough."

Dagon turned to face Randal directly. "You're quibbling, wizard. That statue doesn't belong to you. It's Varnart's, and I'm going to see that it goes to him." He looked at Randal for a moment. "I thank you for your help so far, and now I'll thank you to hand over that carving."

"I know it's not mine," said Randal. "I don't want it, and I'll be happy to get rid of it. But I'm going to give it to Varnart myself."

Lys gave him a doubtful glance. "Are you sure you want to get yourself mixed up in something like this?"

"No," Randal said. "But there's something about that statue . . . take a good look at it."

32

He opened the leather bag, and pulled out the ivory figurine. The light of day brought out even more clearly the fineness of the unknown artist's work: He could see the very wrinkles on the knuckles of the old woman's hand where it gripped the staff, and her eyes, under their deep brows, seemed ready to blink and gaze about.

Lys regarded the figurine for a long moment. "If that thing were mine," she said finally, "I'd drop it in a well. I don't like the looks of it."

Surprisingly, Dagon nodded. "I don't either, but Varnart's the one who's paying for it. And don't think you'll be getting a reward for giving him that piece," he added suspiciously. "His agreement was with me, and me alone."

"You can have Varnart's money," said Randal. "I don't want that either. But I'm almost certain this statue is an artifact of power. If that's so, then you need a wizard to handle it."

"I had Bryce," said Dagon. "But you tell me he's dead."

Nick was frowning. "If Randy says your friend's dead," he told the mercenary, "then he's dead. And if that thing really is an artifact of power, then the sooner it gets safely to Varnart and out of our hands, the better."

"For a carpenter, you sure talk a lot about magic," Dagon said. He looked at Nick curiously. "What's an artifact of power?"

Randal slid the ivory carving back into its protective bag. "All objects contain magic," he explained. For a moment, considering the mercenary's question, he was back at the Schola in Tarnsberg, sitting safe in a warm,

33

dry room and listening to Master Crannach lecturing on magical theory.

He put the memory behind him and continued. "Most of the time, though, objects don't contain very *much* magic. But once in a while, an object turns up that has so much magic it can act by itself. If it's properly controlled, it can be the key to great things."

Lys looked nervously at the now-closed leather bag. "What happens if it isn't controlled?"

Randal and Nick exchanged glances.

"Then you've got trouble," said Nick. "A thing like that doesn't have much use for people."

Dagon scratched the stubble on his jaw and scowled. "Sounds like a demon to me."

"It's worse. Demons aren't of this world," said Randal, quoting what he had heard during those classes in Tarnsberg that now seemed so long ago. "You can send them back where they came from. But artifacts *are* of this world. They're in this world, and contain part of the world in themselves. You can't destroy one without destroying part of our own world, and the world fights that."

"And you think Varnart's figurine is one of those artifacts," said Dagon thoughtfully.

Randal nodded. "I'm almost certain of it."

"Then it can't hurt to have a wizard along until I turn it over," said the mercenary at last. "The meeting place isn't too far from here. We can make it on foot if we have to."

"No need," said Nick. "You three wait here, and I'll take the lumber wagon to Oseney and bring the horses back. They know me at the woodlot; Alured's wagon will be safe there while we're on the road."

"Wait a minute," said Randal. " 'We'?"

"I'm coming with you," said the one-time apprentice wizard. He grinned through his beard at Randal. "This one looks like too much fun to miss."

"It's your neck," grunted Dagon as he climbed out of the wagon. The mercenary looked back at Randal and Lys. "Come on. The less time we spend hanging around by the side of the road, the better."

Lys vaulted over the side of the wagon with an acrobat's easy grace. Randal followed more slowly, and stood for a moment leaning against his walking staff. Nick called to the horses, and the wagon creaked off down the road.

IV.
Power

"LET'S GO," said Dagon. "That wooded patch over there looks good enough for laying up a while."

Soon Randal, Lys, and Dagon were sitting on their cloaks in the middle of a stand of trees. This close to the great Wilderness of Lannad, the ancient forest that extended across southern Brecelande, the trees were thick and old. The light mist of early morning had thickened into a steady drizzle. The drops of water collected on the twigs and branches overhead, and plopped heavily down onto the dead leaves below.

"So far, so good," said Dagon. "I'm close to the place where I'm supposed to meet Varnart, and in plenty of time. Just as long as Fess's yellowcoats aren't coming along behind. . . ." He looked at Randal. "You're a wizard—can you tell if anybody is chasing us?"

Randal stifled a groan. *Please,* he thought, *not when I'm already hurting all over.* His joints and muscles ached from the bumpy ride in the lumber wagon, and his head felt fuzzy from lack of sleep. But with Dagon watching, he didn't dare refuse.

"Give me something I can look into," he told the mer-

36

cenary. "A dish of clear water's best, or a crystal, but we haven't got either of those. Ordinary polished metal will work in a pinch."

"Crystal, did you say?" Dagon pulled his dagger from its sheath on his belt, and held out the weapon hilt first. It was a fighter's weapon, long bladed and double edged, with a metal cross guard—forged for use, not for beauty. The massive blue gemstone set into the pommel looked out of place against the plain metal.

"Yes," said Randal. "That will work."

The mercenary regarded the sapphire with a fond expression. "I've had good luck with it myself," he said. "I've pawned it a dozen times if I've pawned it once, and I've always been able to buy it back."

Randal took the dagger. His scarred hand closed awkwardly on the grip, reminding him again that he had forsworn the use of such weapons when he first set out to study the wizard's art. He'd broken that vow only once, to stop his teacher, Master Laerg, from destroying the entire School of Wizardry—and he'd almost lost his own magic as a result.

This is different, he told himself. *You're using the stone, not the steel.*

He planted the dagger point first in the earth—ignoring Dagon's squawk of protest—and focused his attention on the sapphire. Time passed. He could sense Dagon and Lys moving about restlessly, somewhere outside his narrowed range of vision. He forced away the awareness of them, willing himself to sink deeper and deeper into the sapphire's azure depths.

A light flickered within the gem. It steadied, and

showed a nest in a tree—a bird's nest, but empty and broken, with a small bird perched forlornly on a nearby twig. Beneath the tree, a yellow-eyed cat circled. The bird took fright and flew off. The cat grew yellow feathers and became a bird of prey, a golden falcon that mounted skyward and followed as the bird flew on.

As Randal bent down to see the images better, a harsh oath broke his concentration, and a hand swept down and pulled the dagger free of the earth.

"Your friend's back," said Dagon. "Haven't you seen anything yet?"

Randal's head ached. He pressed his palms against his forehead. *Yellow eyes . . . yellow feathers . . . yellow, like the surcoats.*

"Fess's men," he muttered. "Following behind us."

"Close?" That was Nick's voice.

"Not yet, I think." Randal used his walking staff to pull himself to his feet. He turned to Dagon. "Let's get on to your meeting. The sooner we can hand over that carving to Varnart, the safer we'll all be."

The mercenary wiped the dirt off his dagger and slammed it back into its sheath. "Right. Everybody mount up. We're making for a ruined watchtower about a league past the turn-off for Oseney. The meeting with Varnart is supposed to take place halfway between noon and sunset. Let's go."

They rode for a couple of hours, and reached the watchtower at about midafternoon, just as the rain was ending and the clouds were breaking up. Once the tower had stood to keep the High King's peace, but now its

38

moss-grown walls were open to the sky, and the fallen roof lay in rubble on the floor.

Randal glanced about at the piles of stones half covered with dead leaves and dirt. "You're sure this is the place?"

"Of course I'm sure," said Dagon. He turned to Lys and Nick. "You two stay outside and hold the horses. This'll just be the wizard and me."

Nick ignored the mercenary. "Do you want me along, Randy?"

The journeyman wizard shook his head. "Don't worry—I can handle it. As soon as Varnart shows up, I'll give him the carving and that'll be that."

Dagon and Randal walked through an empty doorway into the shell of the watchtower. Lys and Nick stayed outside, out of sight behind the curving wall.

Inside the tower, Randal and Dagon waited while the afternoon shadows grew slowly longer. Randal sat on a block of stone and watched the sunlight move across the wall. Dagon paced about restlessly, moving from door to window to broken wall, one hand always on the hilt of his sword.

Then a lean man—tall, dressed in elegant gray clothing, clean-shaven that very morning—stepped without warning through a gap in the crumbling stone. Randal came to his feet at once, but the stranger seemed not to notice him. Instead, he looked at Dagon and smiled.

"It's always a pleasure," the man said, "to deal with someone who keeps his word. Did you have any trouble getting the object?"

Dagon halted his pacing, and faced the new arrival.

"Just who are you, anyway?" he asked. His feet were planted wide, and his right hand gripped his sword hilt. "Too many people I don't know are mixed up in this already."

"I come from the one who hired you," said the newcomer. "I have orders to pay you, but I warn you, sir, I have also been instructed that I must not return without the carving." He gave a slight nod to one side, and two other men stepped out of hiding from behind the stones. These men were also dressed in gray, and carried swords and daggers.

Dagon looked from one of the armed men to the other, without moving a hairsbreadth from where he stood. "If you've got the gold, I've got the statue. But first, tell me the name of the man who hired you."

While the two mercenaries spoke, Randal was at work casting a spell of magical resonance: a simple spell, but one that would, if done correctly, tell him whether another wizard was nearby. As he'd half expected, the only magical echo for miles around came from the carving itself. The stranger who stood before them was no wizard . . . as if the sword at his hip had not already proved that to be true.

The tall man laughed a bit, but his smile did not reach his eyes. They were cold gray in the afternoon sunlight. "I am hired by Master Varnart, to fetch back a statue of a woman, so big . . ." the man held up his hands a little less than a foot apart. "So, as one hireling to another, take your payment and be gone."

Dagon turned to Randal. "Give it to him."

Randal hesitated. This man was a stranger, and no

wizard. But he came from Varnart, whose claim to the statue was as good as anybody's. Randal held out the leather bag.

The tall man pulled the bag into his hands. He opened it, pulled out the statue, examined it briefly, and put it back into the sack. He nodded again, and stepped back.

A whisper of sound in the grass outside made Randal turn his head. Lys and Nick came around the broken wall into the tower, walking at swordpoint before three more of the gray-clad men.

The stranger smiled. "Good," he said. "Now kill them."

"Double-crosser!" Dagon yelled, drawing his sword and sidestepping at the same time, so that a sudden lunge by one of the men in gray passed cleanly by him.

In the same brief instant between the tall man's order and his men's response, Lys somersaulted forward like the acrobat she was. She curled into a tight ball as she rolled away through the debris. The sword thrust aimed at her shoulderblades passed over her as she spun.

Randal stepped back as well, and cast a shock spell at the leader of the band. But the hastily prepared magical blow did nothing, its power fading even before it reached its target. Too late, Randal saw the bronze medallion on the stranger's chest.

It's an amulet, Randal realized. *He's protected against magic.*

Randal tried another shock spell, this time at one of the two men who were attacking Dagon. The man he aimed at staggered and missed his stroke. Dagon took

41

advantage of the distraction to cripple the man with a leg blow before turning back to his one remaining foe.

Randal glanced around again. Lys was nowhere to be seen, but Nick had taken a wound, and now the former apprentice was retreating step by step in front of two men who paced toward him, trying to get him into killing range. Soon his back would be to the wall.

Then Randal lost track of the others as he, too, was attacked by a sword-wielding fighter with murder in mind. *I don't want to use lightning,* he thought, blocking the first blow with his walking staff. *It might kill him, and this isn't really my quarrel.*

Instead, he cast a heat spell on the hilt of the man's sword. Flesh sizzled, and the man dropped his weapon. *I can't use steel,* Randal thought, *but I'm not helpless.*

He swung his walking staff against the man's skull, and the attacker went down. In the momentary breathing-space, he looked around and saw that Nick's assailants had backed the journeyman carpenter up against the wall on the other side of the rubble. The two men were about to strike when a heavy chunk of rock crashed down onto the head of one. Lys followed it down, leaping from the top of the wall to land on the other man's shoulders. Swordsman and player went down together in a tangle of arms and legs.

The leader of the gray men still had not drawn his sword. *Maybe that's not a sword at all,* Randal thought in alarm. *Just a hilt attached to a sheath, to fool us. Could this man be a wizard himself—his true nature hidden by whatever's protecting him?*

Then Randal saw that the tall stranger was moving—

42

grasping the amulet on his chest, pulling it off and casting it away from him.

He is *a wizard,* thought Randal, with sudden conviction. *The same amulet that hid him, stopped him from using magic. And now he's going to kill us all if I can't stop him.*

He tried to call up a lightning bolt—but nothing happened. He staggered, exhausted, and barely recovered his balance in time to see the tall wizard's hand move in the opening gestures of a shock spell. Sluggishly, Randal countered with a shielding of his own—and again the spell was weak. Most of the stranger's power came through anyway, and sent Randal stumbling backward.

The stranger raised his hand to cast the shock spell again. This time, Randal knew, the blow would be a fatal one.

Then, suddenly, he became aware of another source of power: magical energy stronger and more plentiful than any he had ever felt before. With the last of his failing strength, he dipped into the new source, and cast the lightning spell again.

The power tore its way through Randal like a searing flame. For an agonizing moment, the spell threatened to go out of control and turn on him. With a wrench of effort, he mastered it. In the next second a harsh voice he barely recognized as his own cried out in the Old Tongue, *"Ruat fulmen!"* and the lightning struck.

The other wizard fell. In the sudden quiet, Randal strode over to where he lay and pulled the bag from his lifeless fingers. Then the rush of power left Randal as suddenly as it had come, and the journeyman wizard collapsed onto the ground, sitting with his head bowed.

I told Lys just last night that I didn't know if I could kill a man with magic, he thought unhappily. *And now I have.* He pressed his forehead against his knees and sat there, shivering uncontrollably even though the late-afternoon air was warm.

Before long he heard footsteps, and lifted his head to see Lys, Nick, and Dagon coming toward him. Lys was breathing hard, and both men were bleeding. All three sat down near Randal among the dirt and rubble, and for a little while there was silence.

Finally Dagon spoke. "We won," he said.

"So what do we do now?" asked Nick.

"Just savor the fact that you're alive," said Dagon. "The simple pleasures of life are the best."

The mercenary stood up and walked over to the man who had taken the statue. He turned over the body with the toe of his boot, and then bent to scoop up the amulet from where it lay on the dirt. "I hope you got good value for your money," he said to the dead man. "As for me, I'll take this pretty toy for my trouble."

Randal shook his head. There was a sour taste in his mouth, and his limbs were trembling from the backlash of the lightning bolt. "Why would Varnart's man want to kill us?" he asked.

"Dead men don't talk," answered Dagon. "It seems that Master Varnart doesn't want me spreading his dirty little secret." The mercenary laughed briefly. "I wonder what sort of reception that fellow would have gotten when he brought the statue home."

"It doesn't matter," said Randal. "Fess's men are still looking for the carving. And we still have it."

45

His voice sounded hoarse and cracked even now that he'd rested a little. Lys gave him a sudden concerned glance.

"Are you hurt, Randy?"

"No. They didn't touch me."

Nick frowned at him. "I took a sword cut, and I feel better than you look right now. What happened?"

Randal paused for a moment. "I tapped into a source of power," he said finally, "and it was polluted." His mouth tasted of bile. He swallowed, and went on, "When a man is dying of thirst, he'll drink from a puddle in the middle of the street, even though the memory of it will turn his stomach for the rest of his life. I just did something like that."

"I hope you're able to ride," said Dagon harshly. "If Fess's men are hunting for that statue, then we need to be somewhere else."

Randal straightened. "I can ride," he said. "But what about you and Nick?"

The mercenary gave a shrug that ended in a grimace. "Neither one of us is going to die before nightfall."

"We'll travel faster if you aren't losing blood the whole time," said Randal. "Give me another moment to rest, and I'll try healing you both."

The spells that stopped bleeding and closed wounds were simple enough that every village healwife knew them—so simple that more than one Schola-trained wizard regarded them with scorn. Nevertheless, Randal found that tending Dagon's and Nick's injuries left him drained and exhausted. He could barely haul himself onto the back of one of the draft horses that had pulled Alured Carpenter's lumber wagon.

"All right," said Dagon to Nick when all four had mounted. "Let's go to Oseney and get you started back to Cingestoun with the wagon."

"Sounds good to me," said the carpenter. "With luck, I'll come out of this with nothing more than a few hard words from Alured for taking off without his leave."

"You've already given us help beyond the claims of friendship," Randal said. "I wish I could have stayed in town a little while longer."

They traveled the rest of the way to the road in silence. When they reached the road, Randal saw that the dirt bore traces of the passing of many horses since they'd turned off the track and headed for the tower. He wasn't the only one to notice; Dagon frowned at the sight, and the mercenary's frown grew deeper the closer the four of them got to Oseney.

At length, he turned the frown on Randal. "When you did your scrying, wizard, why didn't you see what just happened?"

"You asked for news of pursuit behind us," said Randal. "So that's what I was looking for. Scrying is like that—you get answers to the questions you ask, and not to the ones that you should have asked instead."

"What exactly *did* you see?" asked Nick.

"A yellow cat," said Randal. "And a bird being chased by a golden falcon."

"Fess's men," Nick said, with a nod. "Yellow surcoats."

"So I thought," Randal told him. "But you remember

47

how it is—everything has two meanings. At least. It's possible the cat waiting below the nest might have been the ambush—"

"Wait a minute," said Nick. "This cat. Did it come before the falcon or afterward?"

"Before," said Randal. In spite of his exhaustion, he found himself enjoying the discussion. He'd been in dozens like it, back at the Schola, as apprentices and masters pried apart their dreams and visions for the meaning of each detail.

He sat up straighter on the back of Alured's carthorse, and went on, "There's more. The bird's nest was broken . . . my room, that Bryce broke into, or Fess's treasury, that Bryce broke into, or Bryce himself, empty of life. Maybe all three at once. And another thing—"

"Birds," said Dagon, in tones of disgust. "Cats. Nests. We're caught between the most powerful wizard and the most powerful warlord for miles around, and you sit there telling animal stories."

"Be careful," Lys cut in sharply. "Someone's coming up the road."

V.

The Watches of the Night

"IT'S ALL RIGHT," said Nick. "I know that man." He raised his voice and called out, "Ho, now, Swayn Steven's son—any gossip from Oseney?"

The other man—a farmer about Nick's age, carrying a covered basket over one arm—called back, "More than a little, Nick Wariner. I heard you mentioned in the marketplace today."

Dagon glowered. Randal half expected him to attack the unsuspecting Swayn, and the young wizard began readying a shield spell just in case it became necessary to protect the farmer.

But Nick ignored both of them, and asked Swayn cheerfully, "Oh? And how did that happen?"

The farmer lowered his voice. "The market was full of men-at-arms in yellow surcoats, asking about anybody who'd come to Oseney from the big town since yesterday—and that's you and no one else. They want to talk to you when you come back from looking at the timber lots. But more than that, they're asking about three strangers."

Swayn pointed with his chin at Randal and the others.

"They're offering silver coin for any word of two boys and a man who look exactly like the ones riding your horses."

"Is that so?" asked Nick.

Swayn nodded. "Not that I've seen anybody like that around here," he added with a wink.

"Thanks for the news," said Nick, smiling in return. "And good day to you."

The farmer touched his cap and said, "Good day to you too, my friend," to Nick, and walked on past the four riders. Dagon slewed around in his saddle to watch the farmer's departing back, and then turned around again to glare at Nick and Randal.

"Cats and birds," he muttered. "What next?"

"I think we'd better forget about the wagon," said Randal.

"These horses still belong to Alured," Nick protested. "I have to get them back to him."

"Today isn't the day to do it," said Lys. "We have to get away. The Wilderness isn't far, but we'll reach it quicker if we keep the horses and ride. From there we can go on foot, and you can go back with the horses. You won't be in any worse trouble, and maybe Fess's men won't be looking for you tomorrow."

"I suppose so," Nick said reluctantly.

"Then enough talking," Dagon snapped. "Let's go."

They rode until darkness overtook them, and then kept on riding well into the night. Randal kept his seat on the broad back of the carthorse by sheer willpower—aided by the fact that for the first twelve years of his life he had been destined for knighthood, and trained to stay on his horse no matter how hurt he was or how hard the going became.

Finally, he heard Nick say to Dagon, low-voiced, "We have to rest. If we keep this up, we'll kill the horses and then where will we be?"

"Same place we'll be if Fess's men catch us," replied the mercenary. "Still, stopping's probably worth the risk."

"Randal," Lys asked, "can you hide our camp like you hid us in the wagon?"

Randal shook his head to clear away the fuzziness of exhaustion. "I think so. But not unless we really have to—I'd have to stay awake the whole time the illusion is going."

And even then it'll only work if Fess's men don't trample us by mistake, he added silently. *And if none of them are looking for magic, and if they haven't guessed exactly how we got out of town this morning. . . .*

"That'll be hard on you," said Nick. "You're as tired as any of us, maybe more."

"I know," said Randal. "But there's no choice. The important thing is giving the horses a chance to rest— you said so yourself."

"And what about you?" asked Lys. Randal couldn't see her face in the dark, but she sounded almost angry. "When do we give *you* a chance to rest?"

"I'll be all right," said Randal. "I can sleep while we're riding if I have to." He gave a tired laugh. "Just pick me up when I fall off."

Lys muttered something in her native Occitanian. A

51

few minutes later, Dagon called a halt. "I hope you're as good as your word, wizard," he told Randal.

They settled down for the night. Dagon had found a clearing among some saplings a furlong from where the deeper woods of the Wilderness began. Randal scratched a circle around their camp, drawing a line in the dirt with a pointed stick, but he left the spells themselves uncast. *Time for that,* he thought, *if we come to needing it.*

Then he stretched out on the ground, wrapped himself up in his wizard's robe for warmth, and fell into an exhausted sleep. He woke in the middle of the night to feel Nick shaking him by the shoulder.

"Someone's coming," the carpenter whispered. "You can see them down the slope, using torches to search the ground."

Randal shoved a hand through his hair. "Don't they sleep? Don't their *horses* sleep?"

"Guess not."

"I'll take it from here, then."

Randal cleared his mind, using the techniques he'd learned at the Schola, and spoke the spell of visible illusion. The circle he'd scratched in the dirt earlier flickered for a moment with blue fire, then darkened. Randal sat down on a log near the center, and prepared to watch through the night.

"That's it," he said to the others. "You can go back to sleep now."

Dagon looked at him doubtfully. "Is the illusion up?"

Randal shrugged. "Either it is, or it isn't."

"You mean you can't tell?"

"Not until somebody sees through it."

Dagon didn't seem happy about that, and rolled back up in his cloak with his bare sword close at hand. Within the hour, a troop of yellowcoats appeared, but they passed by the camp without glancing at it. Dagon turned over, and began to snore.

Randal relaxed a little. *At least the spell is working,* he thought. After a few minutes, Nick came over and sat beside him. The two looked into the fire in silence for a few minutes. Then Randal glanced over at Nick. "I've gotten you into a lot of trouble, I'm afraid. Do you have someplace you can go until the search dies down?"

"I'll stick with you," replied the apprentice wizard turned carpenter. "If I'd kept on working at the Art, I'd have been out on the road as a journeyman by now . . . and I've wondered, sometimes, how I would have managed."

"You'd have done fine," said Randal. "Better than I have, certainly." The midnight air was cold; he pulled his black robe tighter around his shoulders and moved a little closer to the fire. "I never did understand why you left the Schola in the first place. Magic always came so easily to you—a lot easier than it did to me."

"I'm not sure myself why I left," said Nick. For once, his bearded features were serious. "But I couldn't think of any reason why I should stay, either. When it got to where I couldn't recall why I'd left home for the Schola to start with, I knew it was time to quit."

"Home. . . ." For a moment, Randal was quiet, fighting the sadness that still came over him sometimes when he thought about Castle Doun. *It's been more than three*

53

years since I left, and who knows if I'll ever see it again. It'll all be changed. . . .

He glanced over at Nick, and saw an expression on the former apprentice's face that mirrored his own feelings. Like most of the students at the Schola, Nick had never spoken much about whatever he might have left behind to study wizardry. *But everybody leaves something,* Randal thought. *And most of us don't go back.*

"Are you from Cingestoun, then?" he asked.

Nick shook his head. "Not me . . . I'm from Widsegard, down on the southern border. I left home bragging that I was going to come back as a wizard or never come back at all."

"So you never went back."

"I couldn't," said Nick. "How could I face the Wizards' Guild in Widsegard, after the way the Guild sent me off to the Schola with such glowing recommendations?"

"Don't let it worry you," Randal said. "Remember what Master Tarn always used to say—'Only one candidate in ten who comes to Tarnsberg is allowed to become an apprentice. And of those, only one in ten goes on to become a journeyman.'"

"I know," Nick replied. "And every night, when I go to bed, I try to convince myself that the reason I didn't become a journeyman was because I wasn't cut out for magic. I keep telling myself that that's the reason—but by the time I'm done, I'm always sure I left because I was afraid to go on. It's no fun waking up every morning thinking I'm a coward."

Nicolas poked at the fire with a stick, knocking the red

coals apart and sending a brief burst of heat outward. "So if you don't mind, now that I've seen the start of this adventure, I'll stay with you and see the end of it as well."

Then he brightened a bit. "Besides, between here and Tarnsberg is the whole Wilderness of Lannad. If you plan to travel off the road, the wild beasts alone will make you glad of another hand."

"If you're sure . . ." Randal began hesitantly.

"I've been thinking about this for a long time," Nick said. "And after seeing you again, I'm not certain that I didn't make a mistake when I left off studying the Art. I haven't forgotten everything I learned at the Schola; when we get back to Tarnsberg, maybe I can take up where I left off."

"You'd make a fine wizard," Randal told him. "I'm sure the Regents would let you back in if you asked."

They sat by the fire for a while more. "Go to sleep," Randal said finally. "At least one of us should get some rest."

The night was clear and chilly, with a wind blowing through the trees. Randal sat alone, listening to the sighing leaves while he kept up the illusion that hid the camp. By midnight, the stars shone down from a sky empty of clouds, and the moon lit the clearing with light strong enough to cast a few pale and wavering shadows. Dagon, Lys, and Nick stirred restlessly in their sleep, as if troubled by disturbing dreams. Out near the tree line, a movement caught Randal's eye.

A man was approaching, coming alone and on foot out of the Wilderness of Lannad.

He was just a pale figure at first. But then the figure

grew closer, and Randal felt a chill even colder than the night wind strike through him like a knife.

I know him, Randal thought. The raised scar on his right hand throbbed, and he pressed his palms together to stop their trembling. He remembered the day he had gotten that scar—*the circle, and the demons coming to drink my blood, and only Laerg's ceremonial sword standing between me and death.*

The man came nearer. He crossed the line of the circle inscribed in the dirt, but the circle did not break. "May I sit beside you?" the man asked. "I've walked far this night, farther than I like to think."

Randal could only nod in dumb agreement, too frightened to say no.

The voice was the same. The eyes were the same. This golden-haired man in wizard's robes—Randal knew him. This was his teacher, the wizard Laerg, who with the help of demons had tried to kill all the magicians in the realm. This was Laerg, sitting on a stone, his arms clasped around his knees for warmth, his face haggard and gaunt, a stubble of beard on his previously clean-shaven jaw—Master Laerg, whom Randal had seen buried in Tarnsberg many months past.

Randal found his voice. "Would you care for something to eat, stranger?"

"No, although I thank you," the man replied. Randal noticed that he could see the trees on the other side of the clearing, mistily, through the man's body. "But surely an apprentice ought to know his old master?"

"I'm not your apprentice anymore," Randal said carefully. "I'm a journeyman. And you're dead."

56

I remember the sword in my hand, he thought, *and my own blood dripping down onto the floor of your study, and then the blade striking home.*

"A journeyman already? How gratifying." Laerg looked directly at Randal for the first time. "And yes, I know you killed me. Let me thank you for that: You stopped me from making a great mistake. And I forgive you, too—the pain was momentary, and I've learned so much since then."

"But . . . why are you here now?"

Laerg smiled. "Let us say that I feel some lingering concern for a promising apprentice."

"Some lingering concern" . . . you made me a wizard, I'll give you that much. But you had your own reasons.

"I'm not sure I trust you," he murmured aloud.

The ghost nodded, as if acknowledging a point made in one of the Schola's many debates. "I'll admit that our last meeting was scarcely the kind of thing to inspire confidence."

"Planning to sacrifice me to demons, you mean? Hardly. Take power in the kingdom, destroy the Schola—little things like that?" Randal's voice had risen as he spoke, and now it came close to breaking. "Master Laerg, why did you do it?"

"I am a man, as other men"—the ghost looked down at his semi-transparent self and gave a faint laugh—"or I was, anyway. I had all the usual weaknesses, but I didn't know it. Through them I let myself be used by forces that I didn't understand." The ghost met Randal's eyes. "There's a lesson there for you, if you want to dig it out."

"Thanks for the thought." The sword-cut across Ran-

58

dal's hand was aching badly now. He clenched his fist over the pain. "I've got a reminder that I can make mistakes. I carry it with me all the time, thanks to you. If you really are you. For all I know, you could be a demon in Laerg's form."

The ghost raised the shadow of a golden eyebrow. "Inside your own circle? No, Randal . . . believe me or not as you will, but I have only your good at heart."

"If you wish me well," said Randal slowly, "then tell me, what do you know about the object I carry?"

"The statue?" asked Laerg. "One thing I can tell you: Master Varnart never owned it."

"He told Dagon that he did."

The ghost shook his head, and looked at Randal with what might almost have been fondness. "Randal, Randal—you were always so charmingly innocent. There are a hundred ways to convey an untruth without ever lying."

Laerg's voice took on an echo of the tone that Randal remembered from a hundred lectures back in Tarnsberg. "Suppose that Master Varnart called this Dagon to him," the ghost went on, "and said, 'Lord Fess has stolen property in his castle.' A true statement, as it happens. And then: 'In his treasury is a certain ivory carving.' Again true. Then, finally, 'Lord Fess has no right to it. Bring it to me, and you will be richly rewarded.' All these things are true, and who can blame Varnart if Dagon hears something more than what was said?"

The ghost paused. "I never played those games myself. A man must have his pride—and I had somewhat more than most."

Randal blushed in the dark, knowing that he himself had spoken just such half-truths to Dagon more than once. Still, he said nothing of that to Laerg, but only asked, "What else do you know about this statue?"

"That Varnart wants it, that it is magical—but those things you already know." The ghostly wizard rose to his feet, and looked down at his former apprentice. "One thing more, Randal—that carving is a thing of evil. I speak as someone who knows more than a little about evil, and I tell you, that statue is dangerous. Death follows it, and luck deserts it."

The sky was graying to the east. The birds were waking in the trees. Randal was surprised by how fast the time had gone. "Can't you tell me more than that?" he asked.

"Daybreak draws near," said the ghost, "and I have a long journey ahead of me." Laerg was looking more transparent by the moment. His voice was faint, nothing more than a whisper in the wind. "Only one thing more. Be careful, for your friends' sakes. Being near you can be deadly."

Randal drew a deep breath, hoping to question the ghost further—but before he could speak, Laerg had departed, as had the mist, torn on the light breeze of morning.

VI.
Running

ONE BY ONE, the others awoke.

Lys was the first, coming awake with a violent start and reaching out immediately for her lute in its leather case, as if she feared to find it gone. She relaxed when she saw Randal.

"Looks like we're still alive after all," she said with relief. "But if that's what sleeping inside a magic circle is like, don't ask me to do it again. I had nightmares the whole time."

Dagon yawned and stretched. "So did I. I dreamed I got an honest job."

The mercenary picked up his sword from where it had lain beside him all night long, sheathed it, and buckled the swordbelt around his hips. Then he looked around the campsite with a satisfied expression, and chuckled. "But there're no enemies in sight, which is worth a few bad dreams as far as I'm concerned. I have to hand it to you, wizard—when you promise, you deliver."

Randal swallowed an exhausted yawn of his own. "I'm glad you approve," he said dryly. "And I'd trade my night for yours if I had the chance."

Nick was the last to wake, rousing slowly and rubbing his eyes to clear away the last traces of sleep. He blinked at Randal, and said, "You look like death warmed over—how long did you have to keep the circle up?"

"It's still here. Can't you feel it?" said Randal, and added, in the Old Tongue, *"I had a dead man visit me during the night."*

Nick looked at him more closely. *"In the circle?"*

"Yes. A master wizard, the one I told you about."

"I won't ask more," said Nick. Then he switched back to the common speech of Brecelande. "But it's not surprising that I had strange dreams."

"I think we all did," said Lys. Her dark blue eyes clouded over with memories. "I dreamed of the day I found my family all murdered by bandits, and me left alone to starve."

"Not a good dream to wake up on," agreed Nick soberly. "My own dreams weren't bad, just odd. I dreamed that your statue had come alive, Randy—I was in Alured's shop back in Cingestoun, and that same old woman came walking in the door as large as life."

"What did she want?" asked Randal sharply. He seemed to hear again Master Laerg's final warning. *The carving is a thing of evil. . . . Be careful, for your friends' sakes.*

Nick shook his head. "I don't know. I said to her, 'You look like you've come a long way,' and she said, 'From Widsegard on the Southern Sea.' Then I thought she was going to ask me for something, but I woke before she could say anything more."

"Widsegard," repeated Randal. Other than Nicolas, he didn't know anyone who came from there. Once it had been part of Brecelande, but after the High King's death the city merchants had shut the gates and raised their own banner. "I wonder . . . was the statue made there in the first place?"

"Possibly," said Nick. "I thought the carving looked like southern work."

"What does it matter?" Dagon demanded. "It's here now."

Randal thought for a moment, and turned to the mercenary. "Tell me," he said, "are you still determined to hand over the statue to Varnart?"

"Master Varnart and I had a bargain," said Dagon. "And he went back on it. Nobody gets the chance to cross me twice."

"And we've seen how dearly Fess's henchmen love us," said Lys. She looked at the young wizard. "What are you thinking, Randy? What should we do with that thing?"

Dagon grunted. "Drop it in a well, like you said yesterday, if I can't find a buyer for it in a hurry."

"No," said Randal. "I have a better idea. We can take it to Tarnsberg. The School of Wizardry is there, and maybe the masters can tell us what kind of thing we have."

And besides, he added to himself, *evil things don't stay down. If we threw that carving into a well, it would only crawl out again and do harm somewhere else.*

Dagon was frowning. "More wizards? I don't like it. But I can't stay here, whatever I do. If I'm going to run, I might as well head for Tarnsberg and try to sell the statue there."

63

He cast a penetrating glance at Randal. "I suppose you'll want to keep on carrying the thing yourself?"

Randal nodded. "That's right." The young wizard was uncomfortably aware that he was working with partial truths again, but something about dealing with Dagon seemed to call them forth. *If this thing is really an artifact of power, then it's too dangerous to abandon—and too dangerous to sell.*

Once again Laerg's warning echoed in his mind—*be careful, for your friends' sakes*—and he turned to Lys and Nick. "Cingestoun isn't healthy for either of you right now, but once you're not with me and Dagon, you should be able to make it to Castle Doun. Lord Alyen is my uncle, and a good man. Ask him for refuge. You'll be safe there."

Lys and Nicolas exchanged glances. Nick spoke first. "I'll stick with you," he said.

"I don't think you should do that," said Randal uneasily. "The statue is dangerous, and I don't want you and Lys to get hurt."

"What kind of friend would I be," Nick asked, "if I ran out on you when the trouble started? Like I said last night, I'm coming with you."

"I see," said Randal. He still didn't feel right about Nick's insistence on coming along, but the former apprentice's jaw was set in a stubborn line. Randal turned to the lute player. "How about you, Lys?"

"Tarnsberg was as much my home as anywhere," she said. "I'll be glad to see it again. And you need somebody with common sense to keep you out of trouble."

Randal sighed. "Tarnsberg for all of us, then. Let's get out of here before Fess's men come back."

The four of them remounted Alured's carthorses and rode out. But Randal's words turned out to be prophetic. No sooner had they crossed the perimeter of the magic circle than a band of horsemen in yellow surcoats burst out of the trees and charged toward them.

"Ambush!" Dagon shouted. "Move out!"

The mercenary had his sword ready, and was riding hard for a gap in the ring of horsemen, heading for the trees that marked the edge of the wilderness. He didn't wait to see if anyone was following him.

Fess's men, thought Randal. *They must have surrounded the spot where our tracks vanished, and then waited until morning to see what happened.*

He looked around for the others. Dagon had already disappeared into the trees, and Nick had almost reached shelter as well. But Lys hadn't yet won free of the clearing— and a pair of Fess's riders was closing in on her.

Randal gestured to call forth the flashing lights and booming thunder that could panic both men and horses. But Fess had trained his troopers well—they faltered, but didn't stop.

Their brief confusion, however, allowed Lys to slip away into the trees. Randal turned to fend for himself. He threw a shock spell at a nearby rider, and the man tumbled from his horse. Randal kicked his own horse into a gallop, and headed for the woods. The forest closed around him, but he could hear the sound of hoofbeats in pursuit.

I have to slow them down, Randal thought. *The only reason we just got away is because we rested our horses last night, and they didn't.*

A spell of tangling and confusion would do the trick—but he had never cast such a spell before on his own, and the long watch over the magic circle had already left him drained. Once again, he became aware of the statue's power.

Use me, it seemed to say. *Use me, and become mightier than you have ever dreamed.*

"I don't want your power," he muttered aloud, "but if I don't use you, Fess's men will catch us all."

He brought the carthorse to a halt, and began the spell. This time he was ready for the unpleasant surge of energy, and directed it all into a maze of confusing tracks and deceptive images that Fess's men would find if they followed him into the woods.

"Fiat!" he cried, and the spell was ended. Then the backlash of the power took him, and he collapsed onto his horse's neck, clutching the coarse mane in his hands.

Although the spell had weakened him, Randal found that drawing on the statue's power hadn't disgusted him as much as it had the last time. *I have to be careful,* he thought, *and not use it unless I have to. I might get to liking it.*

After a moment, he straightened, and rode on. It wasn't long before he saw Lys and Nick waiting among the trees ahead. He shook his head to clear away the fog that casting the spell had left behind, and asked, "Where's Dagon?"

"Don't know," said Nick. "But I'd guess he saved his own skin—he certainly rode out fast enough."

66

"So did you all," said Dagon, riding up from behind them. "And you've been so noisy since then that I'm amazed we're not all crow's meat by now. Maybe I'd have more luck if I took that statue myself, and left you to your own devices."

"I don't think so," said Randal wearily. "The spell of confusion I put on our trail will last until noon or so. That gives us a good head start if Fess's men want to follow us through the Wilderness."

They pushed on hard the rest of the day, always fearful that Fess's men would overtake them again. Night was falling before they paused.

"I figure we have half a day's lead on them," said Nick.

"Maybe," said Dagon. "And maybe not. In the meantime, we're in a horse race to Tarnsberg." He looked over at Randal. "Will the city take you in?"

"The Schola has to," said Randal. He swallowed what would have been a jaw-cracking yawn. The carthorse's jolting gait had given him no chance to rest all day, and he felt tired in his very bones. "And Tarnsberg is a free city. Its Council won't hand us over to a baron's riders, no matter how powerful Lord Fess may be around Cingestoun."

"Good," said Dagon. "Then let's concentrate on not losing our way."

Darkness fell suddenly in the woods, and they camped that night without a fire. When the first gray light came trickling through the thick foliage above, they rose and rode on.

Each day seemed the same, after that. They searched rivers for fords. They went around the heavier brush, or through it if need be. For several days they passed through craggy land, took shelter in caves, and never saw other living men.

"Do you suppose they're still following us?" Lys asked one evening as they sat beside a small stream that fell bubbling over the broken rocks.

"We can't afford to think they aren't," said Dagon. The mercenary was using his dagger to whittle a trap from a bit of broken wood. Every evening since they had entered the Wilderness, they had set out such snares, so that each morning brought them meat for the coming day.

Randal listened to the conversation without taking part. Once again, the day's riding had left him weak and shaken. His skin was hot and dry, and his head felt like it belonged to someone else. He sat leaning against a tree at the edge of the campsite, with his forehead resting on his upraised knees.

I'm glad I don't have to do magic, he thought. *I don't think I have the strength to work a single spell.*

After a while, Nick came over and sat beside him.

"Are you feeling well?" Nick asked.

"No," Randal answered, without lifting his head.

"I didn't think so," said the former apprentice. "If you want to know what I think, *I* think that statue is draining you somehow. You've looked pale and tired ever since you started carrying it around with you."

"Maybe," said Randal. The thought was a disturbing one. *Did the statue kill Bryce?* he wondered. *Did it take all his magic and then leave him empty? Is that what it's doing to me?* He shivered, feeling suddenly fearful. "We have to get to Tarnsberg as fast as we can," he said aloud.

Lys joined them in time to overhear the last few words of their conversation. "Just when are we going to reach Tarnsberg, anyway?" she asked. "We've been wandering in these gloomy woods for a long time, with no sign of breaking out on the far side."

Randal looked up at the sound of Dagon's deep-voiced chuckle from the other side of the little camp. "I've got bad news for all of you," said the mercenary. "We aren't going to Tarnsberg."

Nick turned to glare at Dagon. "What do you mean?"

"We've been heading through the forest from north to south," said Dagon, "not east to west." The mercenary looked at the others. "Haven't you seen the slant of the sunlight? Haven't you noticed how each detour forces us southward?"

Lys had her hand on her dagger. "You didn't mention any of this before."

"If you weren't complaining, I wasn't going to stop you." The mercenary chuckled again. "That piece of ivory will bring a far better price from the merchant princes of the south." He went back to his work, still laughing to himself.

Nick, Lys, and Randal glanced at each other. "If we've been heading southward," said Lys, after a long pause, "then we're probably coming up to Widsegard."

"Then my dream about the old woman—" began Nick.

"—may not have been just a dream," Randal finished for him. "Few dreams are, after all."

"But what does it all mean?" asked Lys. "The dreams, and the confusion?"

"I don't know," said Randal. "That's why I want to find a master wizard. This statue has too many puzzles wrapped around it for my liking."

"Why don't you put some kind of protection spell on it?" suggested Nick. "If it really is an artifact of power from somewhere around Widsegard, it could have been influencing our footsteps all this time."

Randal nodded slowly. "That's a good idea. If anybody's been tracing us by magic, the spell will make us harder to follow as well."

But a protection spell is something I should have thought of a long time before this, he reflected to himself. *Maybe the statue really has been working on me, like Nick said.*

Later that evening, after a scanty supper of rabbit grilled on sticks over a small campfire, Randal went off a little way into the forest. Kneeling on the mossy ground, he called up a pale cold-flame, and then took the statue out of its leather bag. He looked at the carved figure by the witchfire's flickering light, and once again felt certain that the figure had shifted its position. Perhaps the old woman's hand was a bit lower on her staff, or her mouth was a bit more open—he couldn't tell.

He put the statue down on the ground, and traced a circle around it with a twig he'd broken from a nearby tree. He frowned for a moment in concentration, and then wrote in the proper mystic signs at the four directions.

As he did so, the fog in his mind cleared for a moment, and he realized something. *Dagon was right: We've been traveling southward all along. The statue—or something—has been blurring our sense of direction.*

Quickly, while his mind was still clear, Randal began his conjuration. The spell was hard to work, even harder than he'd thought it would be. His head felt stuffed with rags, so that he could hardly remember the words, and he could feel the power in the statue wriggling and twisting as it tried to keep a way open to the outside world.

But at last the circle gave a flash of blue, and the spell was complete. He turned his attention to the bag, speaking the words that would turn it into a magical bag of holding to contain the power of the artifact. This spell slipped into place much more easily, and he realized that this wasn't the first time such a spell had been placed on the bag.

Who broke the spell before, and what became of him? Randal wondered. *Was it Bryce?*

But there wasn't any time to think about that now—he had to finish his work while the spell on the statue itself was still fresh. Moving rapidly, he picked up the statue and placed it in the bag. Then he pulled the leather drawstrings tight and tied the bag shut, sealing the knot with the words of binding.

For a moment he doubted that the spell had taken—the words were in his spell book, copied down during a long-ago lecture, but he had never before tried them in the real world. Now, though, it seemed to him that the bag pulsed with the energy it contained.

"Did you put the spell on it?" Nick asked when Randal walked back into the camp, carrying the bag in his hand.

Nicolas and Lys were alone there, while Dagon was out placing his snares for tomorrow's meat.

"I did," said Randal, "as much as I could, anyway. I don't believe I'd have had any luck at all if the bag hadn't already been marked with magic. But the statue's power is contained now, as long as no one opens the bag."

The next day, they came to the first signs of human habitation they had found in weeks, and by evening they broke out of the Wilderness entirely. And just as Dagon had predicted, they emerged on the southern border of Brecelande—a region so far removed from the center of the kingdom that most people no longer considered themselves to be from Brecelande at all, but gave their loyalty to the nearest town or city, after the manner of the people of the far south.

"Not a healthy place to be," Nick commented. "The people here may not be loyal to Lord Fess, but they certainly aren't friendly to us. The threat of a blow or the promise of silver will get us handed over to anyone who asks."

"On the other hand," Randal said, "the people here aren't likely to be in Varnart's pay—and when we find Widsegard we'll find a Wizards' Guild as well. It's not the same as going back to the Schola, but at least it'll have some master wizards who can give us help."

They camped for the night at the edge of the forest, and in the morning continued on, hoping to keep ahead of the pursuit they weren't certain still existed. Late in the afternoon of the second day they came to the crest of a hill overlooking the ocean. At the edge of the blue water, golden towers sparkled in the low sunlight, and Randal looked down in wonder at the largest city that he had ever seen.

VII.

Widsegard

WIDSEGARD WAS LARGER than Tarnsberg, larger
than Tattinham in the eastern mountains, larger even
than Cingestoun. The city walls were high and long, and
colorful banners floated from the towers and gate-
houses. Buildings inside the city took on the color of bur-
nished gold in the light of the setting sun, and the roads
coming and going were crowded with travelers on foot
and on horseback, and with the wagons of merchants.
Armed guards stood on the parapets, and the dying sunlight flashed from their polished spearpoints.

"Well," said Nick at last. "There it is. Do we go in?"

"I don't think we have much choice," said Randal.
"I'm afraid we were meant to come here from the first.
And that worries me."

"Then onward," said Dagon, with a laugh.

When they rode through the gates of Widsegard, the
opening in the city wall above them was ten times the
height of a man, with battlements above and towers on
each side. The road was so wide that even though they
were riding four abreast, none of them rode next to the

wall. More travelers, on horseback and on foot, filled the road on either side.

The guards at the gate didn't bother to stop them. Randal looked at the guardsmen curiously, realizing that these were fighting men of a far different stripe than the city guard back at Cingestoun. These were sturdy men, armored in mail and carrying long swords or huge double-bladed axes. They had an air of easy confidence about them, as if to say, "We are the law here, traveler, and no one challenges the law."

The four companions rode on into the city itself. Once they were past the walls, Randal asked Nick about the guardsmen at the gate.

"The city merchants pay them," Nick explained. "And with all the gold Widsegard earns from the southern trade, the city can afford to hire the best fighting men available."

They went on, riding between buildings of stuccoed brick and whitewashed stone. Shops with striped awnings spilled out their wares into booths and baskets that covered half the street. The scent of spices filled the air, the sweetness of cinnamon blending with the bite of pepper and the muskiness of sandalwood.

"One thing about a place like this," Lys said. "We're lost in the crowd."

"I wouldn't bet on that," said Dagon. "There are people in any town who earn their living trading answers for gold. Questions like, 'Did four northerners arrive the day before yesterday, and if so, where are they now?' are their daily bread."

As night fell around them, Lys saw an inn on the right. "I'm tired," she said. "Can't we rest?"

"This is as good a place as any," Randal replied. He swung down from his horse and went in. He found the innkeeper, a stocky, dour-faced man, and drew him aside.

"I'm interested in trading work for a room," said Randal. "Do you have any little problems you need taken care of—fleas in the bedding, weevils in the flour?"

The innkeeper scowled. "I run a clean inn without any wizard's tricks. You'll have to pay in coin like anyone else."

Randal didn't argue, although a room for the four of them cost him all the pennies remaining from his time in Cingestoun. "Money well spent," was Lys's comment, when Randal came out to tell them the news. "This isn't the sort of town where you can sleep out on the street."

Somewhere nearby, somebody was frying something in hot oil—Randal could hear the oil crackling, and caught the odor of cooking meat coming to him through the other city smells of garbage, spices, and sweat. He realized that he felt truly hungry for the first time since he'd taken the statue from Bryce, back at the Green Bough.

"Is there any way we can get some food?" he asked.

"I've got a coin or two," Dagon offered. "I'll stable the horses and be back soon."

The other three went up to the room in the inn. Despite the innkeeper's words to Randal, it was small, dark, and dirty. "I think you got robbed of those coppers," Nick said as they looked over the sleeping space.

76

"It's only for one night, and I can make it better," Randal answered as he set about the preparations to send the assorted vermin elsewhere, and clear a bit of the reek from the air. Lys and Nick watched him as he worked.

For Randal, the use of such simple, honest magic felt good. He had been doing nothing but hurting and hiding for much too long. "Even if this is your old home city," he said to Nick as he finished the spells, "let's do what we came to do, and then move on."

"And just what *did* you come here to do?" asked Dagon, entering the room with a loaf of bread and a basket of meat in his hands. "I came here to get some money for that cursed ivory statue you've been cuddling like a baby ever since we left Cingestoun."

"I'm looking for a master wizard," said Randal. "Or a library of the Art, or a Wizards' Guild of some kind . . . because 'cursed' is a good word for that statue, and it's more than I can handle alone. Tomorrow I'll go looking for the place, and by evening I should have an answer."

"I hope you do," said Dagon. "I'm a man of patience, but not very great patience. I have my own business to transact."

They soon turned in, but Randal was unable to sleep. The others were restless as well, and once Lys cried out from the midst of some nightmare. Nick lay on his pallet as if he were turned to stone, and sweat glistened on his forehead.

In the morning, they arose. The day was clear, but the air was heavy and oppressive with the late-summer heat.

"We'll have a storm before tomorrow, if I'm not mis-

77

taken," said Nick, glancing out the window at the sky. "We'd better take care of our business before it breaks. It's been a long time since I lived here, and I was just a boy when I left—but I think I can find the Wizards' Guildhall without getting lost."

Randal swallowed the last of a bit of bread left over from the evening before. "Then let's go."

"I'm coming, too," Lys said. "I wouldn't mind seeing a bit of Widsegard with somebody who knows where things are."

"Well, I'll stay here," said Dagon. "I'm not the one who's hunting for wizards." The mercenary gave the other three a hard look. "Just remember, if you don't come back, the horses are mine."

As soon as Randal was outside with Lys and Nick, he turned to his friends and said, "Let's get on with it. The sooner I can find a master wizard, the better—I'll hand over the statue, and it can be somebody else's problem from then on."

"I don't know," Nick said. "Our friend Dagon seems to think the statue is his to dispose of."

"Only because he stole it for Varnart," said Randal. "Or hired Bryce to steal it for Varnart, since Bryce was at least gutter-trained in wizardry and Dagon hasn't drawn a magical breath in his entire life. But the statue wasn't Varnart's any more than it was Fess's, and it isn't Dagon's."

"It's not yours, either, if it comes to that," Nick pointed out. "But I suppose someone has to see that it's taken care of." The former apprentice shook his head. "Somehow, I don't think that Alured will be seeing me

78

or his horses again. I'll have to find a way to make it up to him."

The three walked through the streets, searching for the Wizards' Guild. But the city had changed since Nick's childhood, and few of the landmarks from his memories matched reality any longer. As the morning wore on, the three travelers were reduced to asking passersby where the Guildhall might be.

"Randy," Nick said, after one such conversation, "have you noticed anything strange about how people have been looking at us in the street?"

Now that Nick had mentioned it, Randal realized that there was indeed something odd going on. In other parts of Brecelande, the loose black wizard's robe he wore over his ordinary clothing gained him respect and even a measure of protection—Dagon, Randal felt certain, would have cut his throat in a heartbeat without it. But here, the expressions he saw as he walked past were different. Some people looked curious, some alarmed, and a few even made hand signs against the evil eye and other sinister enchantments.

Something very strange is going on in this city, he thought. *Something to do with magic.*

The sun was a pale, hot disk high overhead before they found the Guild: a white-plastered building on one side of an open square. The windows on both floors were covered by painted wooden shutters, and the heavy door was closed.

"That's the Wizards' Guildhall, all right," Nick said. "But it looks different. Something's wrong."

Something was indeed wrong. The whole place had

an air of decay about it—the whitewashed walls had faded, and the paint on the shutters was peeling away. When Randal went closer, he saw that the door had been nailed shut with iron spikes. The spikes were rusty, and spiders had spun their webs around the doorjamb.

He walked back to his two companions, and the three of them retired to the other side of the square. They stood in the shadow of another stone building and looked across at the deserted Guildhall.

"Now what?" Nick asked.

"Guardsmen coming up the street," Lys said quietly, before Randal could answer. "Both directions."

Then, in carrying tones, she shrieked, "How *dare* you suggest such a thing! I'm a good girl!" and with her left hand slapped Randal so hard across the cheek that his head rang. At the same time, he felt the dagger in her right hand cutting the leather cord that tied the statue's protective bag to his belt. Before he could protest, Lys was gone, blending into the gathering crowd as a dozen guardsmen converged on the plaza.

Randal hardly had time to wonder what was going on before he found himself surrounded by guardsmen, their swords all drawn and pointed at him and Nick.

"Not a word, wizard," said the captain of the guards. "Don't try to get away. You're coming along with us."

Randal looked at Nick, and shrugged.

I could run, thought Randal. *But I wouldn't get very far— the captain's wearing an amulet just like the one Varnart's man wore at the tower. My spells wouldn't work on him. I wish I knew what Lys was up to. . . .*

He decided to put as good a face on things as possible,

80

and made a respectful bow to the captain of the guards. "My friend and I are at your service, sir."

The captain wasn't impressed. "Very pretty," he said. He nodded at one of his troop. "Search them, Freki." To Randal, he said, "Try anything on my man, wizard, and you're both dead where you stand."

The guard called Freki searched both Nick and Randal—taking their eating knives and Randal's spell book. Randal knew better than to protest as he saw the fruit of three long years of study handed over to the captain. Just the same, he winced inwardly as the captain leafed through the painstakingly inscribed pages and snorted, "Looks like wizard stuff to me. Maybe someone at the guardhouse will be able to read it."

The guard handed the book to Freki with a curt, "Keep this for evidence," and then turned back to Nick and Randal. "You two come along."

The guards marched the two northerners through the streets of Widsegard to a huge, bleak stone building with more of the city guards standing watch at the gate and lounging around the courtyard within. The captain and Freki escorted Randal and Nick across the courtyard and up a flight of stone steps to a small room where another guardsman—this one older, with gray in his hair and beard—sat behind a wooden desk. The guard at the desk looked Randal and Nick up and down.

"What do we have? Public brawling?" the older man asked.

"No, sir," said the captain. "Show him the evidence, Freki."

Freki laid Randal's spell book on the desk. The older guard picked it up.

" 'Randal of Doun,' " he read aloud. He looked at the young wizard. "That you?"

Randal nodded. "Yes."

"We've had more than enough trouble with your kind. Possession of magical books or implements gets you a flogging through the city gates."

Randal didn't say anything. The older guard nodded to the captain. The captain turned to Freki and said, "Lock 'em up."

Freki nodded in turn and marched the two northerners out of the small room and down into the depths of the prison. They came to an underground cell, dark and foul-smelling and cold in spite of the warm air in the world outside. An iron grille barred the entrance to the cell. Freki unlocked the door and pulled it open. "In there," he said.

Randal and Nick obeyed, and the door clanged shut. Freki locked it, and strode away down the dim corridor.

"Well," said Nick, after a long pause. "What do you think our chances are of breaking out of here before morning?"

Randal moved over to the damp wall of the cell and sank tiredly down onto the dirty straw that covered the stone floor. "We can't," he said. "I can feel spells of binding on this place that go back for centuries."

He leaned his head back against the wall and closed his eyes. The sense of increased well-being that he'd felt since putting the statue and its bag into a protective binding had begun to ebb away, bringing back the dragging exhaustion that had beset him on the road from Cingestoun.

The spell wasn't broken completely when Lys cut the draw-string, he thought blearily, *but it must have been weakened. That's why I feel this way—the statue's feeding on my lifeforce. At this rate, I may not live long enough to see what kind of justice Widsegard has for wizards. I hope Lys can find somebody who can deal with that artifact. It's dangerous, and it's starting to work its way loose.*

He heard Nick saying something close by, but he was suddenly too weary to answer. With his cheek resting against the cold stone, he fell asleep.

Randal woke with a start, and stared around. Nothing had altered, it seemed—nothing had happened to account for his waking. He stood up and stretched. The weariness he'd felt before was gone, and he turned back toward the wall to give Nick a hand up onto his feet.

Two skeletons lay on the floor of the cell. The disconnected bones of the closer one were covered by a loose black robe. A wizard's robe.

Randal bit back a cry of fear. Carefully, he raised his own arm, still clad in the wide black sleeve of his Schola robe, and touched his own flesh. *Solid,* he thought. *Warm. I'm alive, and this is a dream. But where is Nick?*

"Nick?" he whispered. "Are you here, too?" But no answer came to him, and the two skeletons grinned in silent mockery.

Randal felt a slight breeze pass through the dungeon corridor, bending the flames of the smoky torches set in brackets outside the cells. *Someone must have opened a door somewhere,* he thought. *If they have doors in dreams.*

Then he heard a sound. The light tap-tap-tap of someone walking, walking with a cane, or a staff. Under his robe, Randal felt sweat trickle down his back.

Panic seized him. Whoever was coming, he knew, was coming for him. And there was nowhere to hide down here, nowhere to run to. He grabbed the bars of the door and shook them, but the door didn't budge. A shadow was growing visible in the passageway leading to the cell, a shadow walking slowly.

Then the figure came into view—an old woman, garbed in a long white cloak, with strands of gray hair floating from under the hood. In her hand she clasped the staff on which she leaned.

She walked up to the door of the cell, her staff tapping with each step she took. When Randal looked at her face, he could tell that she was blind: White film covered both her eyes. Randal recognized the old woman—she was the statue he had carried over mountain and moor from Cingestoun, grown to human size and brought to horrible life.

The woman faced in his direction and spoke. "Set me free," she said.

"How can I?" Randal asked. "I'm the one in prison, not you."

Then, abruptly, Randal saw that he was wrong. He was looking in through the door of a cell, not out as he had thought, and the woman was standing in the cubicle. Randal felt something cold in his hand. It was a ring of keys.

"Don't worry, granny, I'll help you," he heard himself saying. Even as he spoke, he was trying keys in the lock.

He found one that fit and turned it. With a howl of rusting metal, the bolt withdrew. Randal pulled the door open. "You can come out now."

The old woman took a step forward. "Take me with you. I have to find my way home."

"Come on, take my arm," Randal said. "We'll get out together."

Slowly they walked up the passageway, turned, and took the stairway up. At last they came to the small room that topped the dungeons. The light of the setting sun slanted in through the window, illuminating motes of dust with gold, and smearing red light on the walls. The room had guardsmen in it, and they moved, and they talked, but no sound came from their mouths. Still, Randal knew that he hadn't gone deaf—he could hear the buzzing of a single fly, and, farther off, the breaking of the waves on the cliffs under the city's walls.

His spell book still lay on the wooden desk. Unnoticed by the guards, he picked it up and put it into the deep pocket of his wizard's robe. Then he went on, the old woman pacing slowly by his side, her hand holding onto his upper arm with a grip so hard that it was painful. The staff went tapping before her, a steady, relentless sound.

People thronged the streets of the city, but still no one saw Randal and the old woman, though the path opened before them, as if by chance. They walked through the gaps, and the crowd closed behind them again.

Randal and the old woman continued on. At last, they faced a set of wide steps leading to the walls of the sea side of the city. *Who's guiding whom?* Randal asked himself. *Where is she taking me?*

They came to the top of the wall, the setting sun a burning orb of blood red, balanced on the horizon.

The old woman turned to Randal. "If you truly wish to follow me," she said, "you will throw yourself into the sea."

She thinks I'm one of her worshippers! Randal thought. The daze that held him broke, and he wrenched his arm out of her grasp. "No!"

"Thousands before you were honored to perform lesser acts," the woman said softly.

She raised her hand, and Randal felt a fascination with the edge of the parapet. It would be nice to stand up there. And the sea, where it rushed over the rocks a hundred feet below, looked cool and refreshing. He felt hot and sticky, and his body itched after sleeping on the prison's filthy straw. A swim would be so nice. . . .

"No!" he shouted again, and tore his gaze away from the tempting water.

He turned back to the old woman leaning on her staff, and he cast the spell of clear seeing, to look beyond illusion and see the truth.

The woman looked the same as before. No . . . wait . . . now she was younger than he had thought, not much older than he was himself, and the long cloak was a bridal gown. She beckoned to Randal and smiled.

"No," Randal said, "I'm not going to go where you lead. Your way is death."

She reached out a hand, and clenched it. Randal felt a pain in his chest, as if his heart was being pulled out of his body. Desperately, he cast a shield spell, and the pain faded. Then he tried a shock spell, to knock her away from him, but the enchantment went wild and turned into a green mist between them that made it difficult to see beyond the little patch of stone wall where they stood.

The girl came close and closer still. "Come with me," the girl said. She reached out and touched Randal's shoulder. He flinched away.

Then he awoke.

"Come with me," Lys said, kneeling over him, shaking his shoulder. "Come with me. We've got to get out of here."

VIII.

Bargains

"COME ON," said Dagon, from the open doorway of the cell. "Nobody stays bribed forever."

Randal rose to his feet. The dungeon had chilled him through and left him aching in every joint. Moving hurt. *I feel old,* he thought. *If I'd stayed home in Doun I'd still be only a squire in my uncle's castle. Instead, I'm escaping from a southlands prison, and I feel like I'm a thousand years old.*

Lys hustled him and Nick out through the door. Randal glanced at her belt as he passed. "Where's the statue?"

"Shh!" Lys said. "It's safe. Let's get out of here."

They hurried through a maze of twisted passageways, all leading down. Randal could hear Dagon counting the turnings to himself. At last, they emerged through a narrow slit of a door opening onto a dark, narrow street. Far above, Randal could see a faint sprinkling of stars.

"All right," said Nick. "Let's go someplace where the city guard won't come by in the next minute, and sort this out."

A few minutes later, the four companions were sitting around a squalid room in one of Widsegard's dirty waterfront inns. Dagon had slid the bolt home behind them as they entered, and now he leaned by the wall to one side of the door.

Randal looked about, and shook his head without speaking.

"Well," said Lys, "Nick asked for a place where the guard stayed out, and this part of town looks like it."

"I'm not surprised," said Randal finally. "How are we paying for it?" He gestured at the smoke-stained walls. "It's not much, but I've spent all my money already."

He reached into the pocket of his robe, intending to turn it inside out to demonstrate his penniless state. His fingers brushed against the coolness of leather. It was his spell book. The one the guards had taken from him.

"What's wrong, Randy?" asked Lys. "You look funny."

"You spend a night in jail and see how you look afterward," he answered. The book had been taken from him, and not returned by the guards—and despite his dream, he hadn't been out of the cell until Lys arrived. But someone, somehow, wanted him to have the book.

The statue, he thought. *That has to be it. It wants me to keep on acting as a wizard. It wants me to use my powers.*

"Got fleas from the dungeon, I suspect," said Dagon, with a knowing expression. "It happens every time."

"You still haven't mentioned where you came by the money for this room," Nick said. "Let alone for a bribe."

"Pawned my lucky sapphire again to save you, out of a spirit of fellowship." Dagon grinned at Nick. "We wound up selling the horses, too. Sorry." Nick glowered at Dagon, but the mercenary didn't seem particularly upset.

Randal had listened to the talk with only half an ear. Now he turned to Lys. "By any chance did you manage to learn what's happened in Widsegard to make wizards so unwelcome?"

"I heard stories," she said. "For starters, about three or four years ago, the city merchants threw all the wizards out of town."

"And they just left," said Dagon. "So much for the power of wizardry."

"No," said Randal. "They'd leave if the city told them to go. Staying where we aren't welcome isn't worth destroying a city for."

Lys nodded, her face grim. "The head of the Wizards' Guild told the city merchants something like that when he got the order."

Nick scratched his curly brown beard. "A bunch of merchants wouldn't do a thing like that without a reason," he said. "I learned that much, working in Cingestoun. What had the wizards been doing to start the trouble?"

Wizards wouldn't . . . Randal's thought began, and then he stopped. *By now, you know for yourself that a wizard is just as capable of villainy as anybody else.*

Lys and Dagon exchanged glances. "That's where people start getting real quiet," said the mercenary. "Nobody wants to name names . . . but I get the impression that Widsegard had a full-scale war going between two rival groups of magicians for control of the Wizards' Guild."

"The City Council left them alone at first," Lys explained, "mostly because the merchants weren't sure which side to back. All the Schola-trained wizards were on one side—but the other wizards belonged to a tradition that grew up in Widsegard years before the Schola was ever founded."

"So the Council stood by and let them fight it out for a while," finished Dagon, "but when ordinary people started getting killed, the Council threw out the whole Guild instead of picking one side over the other. And wizardry's been illegal in Widsegard ever since."

Randal felt a sudden cold stillness in the center of his bones. "But what if one side never really left?" he whispered. "If they could get their hands on an artifact of power—one from this city, even, and summon it home by magic from whatever strongroom happened to hold it—then they could control the whole city and not just the Guild."

He shivered. "We have to get back north to Tarnsberg," he said. "The longer that statue stays in Widsegard, the worse everything becomes."

"Don't worry," said Lys. "We're sneaking out by the Ragpickers' Gate as soon as I go fetch that leather bag from where I hid it."

"Is it somewhere safe?" Randal asked.

"Safer than carrying it around would be."

"And she wouldn't tell me where it was," Dagon put in, "unless I agreed to help get you out of jail." From the sound of the mercenary's voice, he might have been either irritated or somewhat amused.

For a little while, there was silence. The heat of the

day had not yet faded from the tiny room. Randal stood and walked to the window for a breath of air to clear the lingering dungeon smell from his nostrils.

The room overlooked the harbor, and the low-hanging moon blazed a silver path across the bay. Above the port district, the cliffs rose sheer, crowned at their summit by the walls of the main city above. Long breakwaters stretched out from the cliffs into the deep, and ships lined the edges of the harbor. On the end of one of the breakwaters was a lighthouse, a tower with a beacon fire that painted the harbor with a red glow.

The sky overhead was cloudless, but a low haze was rapidly gathering on the horizon. The ocean looked like a millpond, smooth but for the ripples showing on its glassy surface.

If there is a storm brewing, Randal thought, *we'd better get out of the city before it breaks.*

He looked down at the open square below, lit by moon and fire. Riding through the square, looking carefully to right and left, was a troop of horsemen in yellow livery: Lord Fess's men-at-arms, still searching for the four companions.

Randal beckoned to the others. "Trouble," he said, pointing to the riders below.

"I don't like the looks of this," Dagon said. "Don't they *ever* give up?"

"I'd say we got out of prison just in time," Nick said. "If they're looking for a wizard in this town, that's the first place they'll check." He looked over at Dagon. "We still have something to settle about those horses, but I have to thank you for saving our lives."

"Your lives aren't saved yet," Dagon pointed out.

"No," Lys said, "but this might just be our good luck. They'll spend weeks searching the city, and all the time we'll be on the road to Tarnsberg."

"We may have more trouble getting there than you think," said Randal slowly. "That statue brought us here. Powerful spells must have been cast to bring it home, and now that it's here it wants to stay. I don't know how much longer I can handle it—it has a feel of death to it, and a strength in it that needs a master wizard to control."

"Randy!" Nick exploded. "If I hear you wish one more time for a master wizard to come help you out, I'm going to hit you with a brick. You're the only wizard around here, and if magic is the problem and magic is the solution, then you're the only one who can handle it. Now, what are you going to do?"

Randal dropped his head into his hands. *Nick's right,* he thought. *That statue became my responsibility the moment I took it from Bryce. So now it's my job to decide what we do next.* He paused a moment longer to order his thoughts, and then lifted his head again.

"First," he said, "I think we should get the statue from wherever Lys hid it. If dropping it down a well was a bad idea before, leaving it lying about in Widsegard is a worse idea now. So we'll have to take it with us when we go."

"If it will let us," Lys said. She gave a shaky laugh. "See—you've frightened me with your talk."

"You mean if *I'll* let you go," Dagon said. "I still want to sell that statue and buy back my lucky dagger."

94

The candle flickered in the room, sending the shadows dancing. Lys rose to her feet. "I'll go get the statue," she said. "Now's as good a time as any. We can be gone by daybreak."

"I'll go with you," said Randal. "This time you're the one needing someone to watch your back."

Lys didn't argue the point. She and Randal left the waterfront inn together, and Lys led the way through the dark streets. The roads here in the port district all led uphill to the main city, and the steep climb left Randal panting. When they reached the point where the narrow road pierced the city wall, Lys stopped and turned to Randal.

"I have to do some climbing now," she said. "You'd better stay down here—you look done in."

Randal was too tired to protest. He nodded in agreement, and Lys disappeared into the shadows. He settled himself against the wall to wait.

Time passed, and Randal began to worry. *Lys has been gone a long time,* he thought. *Maybe too long.* His anxiety grew as the minutes passed and the lute-player failed to reappear. *I don't think she is coming back,* he thought with a rush of panic. *Something's happened to her. And there's nobody to help her but me.*

He thought about doing a scrying to find her, then shook his head. That idea was no good. There was nothing nearby for him to look in, and he had an increasing sensation that something was spreading strange magic through the night, like rings in a pool of water disturbed by a thrown rock, distorting all that it touched.

I've got to get Nick, he thought frantically, *and then we can both go find Lys.* He turned back downhill toward the waterfront, a plan already forming in his head. *We'll give Dagon what he wants—or give him something that looks like it for a little while, anyway—and then be rid of him. If he sold the horses, he's made a profit on the deal, and we don't owe him anything.*

Randal cast his eyes about for suitable objects on which to cast a spell of physical change, to produce an illusory replica of the missing statue. *When is an illusion a lie,* he wondered, *and when is it not?* At the Schola, those had been topics for scholarly debate among the student wizards—now the practical aspects were looming before him. *If I lie, I am no wizard, and my magic will never be trustworthy again.*

Randal was nearing the waterfront inn. And there he found what he needed: a torn and dirty burlap sack, and a piece of rotten fruit, discarded from one of the merchant's stalls. He placed the fruit—a peach, from the fuzzy skin and sickly-sweet odor—into the sack, and cast the spell of visual illusion. The bundle shifted and changed, taking the form and shape of the statue in its leather bag.

The effort of the spell left Randal even weaker than before. He was aware of the other, real statue somewhere in the city, a source of power calling out to him to be used. *The protection I've put on it is completely gone.* But this time he resisted the temptation to tap into that deep well of mystic energy. *Whatever I do, it must be my own effort now.*

Randal reached the inn and climbed the stairs to the dirty room. The local customs apparently included minding one's own business—no curious heads had turned as he passed through the crowded downstairs common room.

Upstairs, he knocked at the door and walked in. Before he could speak, Dagon gestured him into silence. "This man has a message," the mercenary said.

This man? Randal looked around the room. Nick was standing against the far wall, arms crossed on his broad chest and anger burning on his face. A small, gray man in greasy clothing stood beside the door.

"Good," the man said. "I see you have something with you. If it's what I think it is, you'll see the girl again. Open the bag and let me see."

I hope the illusion is good enough, Randal thought. *The bad light will be a help.*

The young wizard reached into the sack of illusory leather, and pulled out what appeared to be an ivory statue of an old woman. To Randal's eye it was only a crude copy, with none of the sinister life of the original. But maybe it would pass.

It did. "Ah, yes," the man said. "You don't know how long we've waited for her to come home. Bring it to the Crystalmen's Plaza at moonset, and we will trade the girl for that statue. Agreed?"

How long should I pause, to seem real? Long enough, but not too long.

"Agreed," Randal said at last.

"At moonset, then." The gray man gave a half-bow, slipped out the door, and vanished.

"What happened out there?" Nick asked after a moment of heavy silence. "How did they get Lys?"

Randal collapsed into the room's only chair. "She

97

climbed up somewhere to get the statue," he said in dull tones. "Someone must have captured her."

"Someone indeed," said Dagon. "It's the wizards. Fess's men would be more direct—a charge up the stairs is their style. And this was a local man, not one of Varnart's litter. Looks like you were right: Someone here wants that piece of dead bone. And it looks like wizards still aren't too finicky to hire people like me to do their dirty work."

"You can't give the statue to people like that," Nick protested. "Think of the evil that will come of it."

"I won't be giving it to them," Randal replied. "I can't. This is only an illusion. I have no idea where the real statue is, except that it's still somewhere in the city."

He pushed himself to his feet, and wearily made his way to the window. The moon was already descending into the clouds that hid the horizon. "We have to be on our way," he said. "Moonset is only a few minutes from now. Where is this Crystalmen's Plaza?"

"It's where all the glassmakers have their shops," Nick replied. "I think I know where it is."

"Then lead on."

Behind him, Randal could hear Dagon muttering. "More double-crosses. I don't like it."

Nick was able to find the plaza without too much trouble. Randal knew they were in the right place when he saw the shops of glassblowers and window and mirror makers gathered around a central square with a fountain. He took up a position near the fountain, with Nick and Dagon close behind him.

"Remember," Randal said, "whatever we do, the main thing is to get Lys back."

With the moon gone, the night had gone blacker, and heavy clouds had begun building up over the ocean. In the darkness, Randal saw Nick nod his head—a movement of shadow against shadow. "Here they come," said the carpenter.

The man from the inn room came up to them. "You have it?"

Randal held up the bag. "What you saw is still here."

The man gestured. Two other men came forward through the dark, holding a girl between them.

"Let the girl start walking toward us," Randal said. "When she gets halfway across, I'll toss you the bag."

The shadowy girl started to walk across the square. When she had come about halfway, Randal tossed the bag to the men who had released her. At the same time he called out, "Lys, run!"

The girl broke into a dash. As soon as she reached the waiting three, she collapsed against Randal. "Oh, Randy, am I glad to see you!"

"No time to talk," Nick said. "Let's go."

They ran. The four of them were a couple of streets and an alley away before they slowed.

"You sure fooled them with that fake," Dagon said to Randal. "Now let's get the real one."

"Lys?" Randal said.

"Yes, let's go do it. And then get out of this city."

Randal had his doubts about how possible that might be. The city guards would be looking for him, Fess's men had come to town and were looking for him, and now

99

these others would be looking for him as well. Randal knew they wouldn't stay fooled long. No change spell lasts forever, and sooner or later the mock statue would return to being a rotten peach.

Lys led them to another part of town. Randal recognized the section of the city wall where he had lost her before, only this time they were approaching it from the other side. He watched as she climbed up a wooden drainpipe, and retrieved something from where it had been jammed under a balcony. A bag.

"Is that it, this time?" Dagon asked.

"Yes," said Lys.

And Randal echoed, "Yes," as he took the bag. He could feel the magic of the statue reaching out to him through its protective shroud.

Suddenly, a sharp whistle sounded from the darkness. Lys cried out in alarm. Randal looked up and froze. Both ends of the alley were crowded with robed and hooded figures, all of them holding wicked, curving knives.

IX.
City Fight

THE LEADER OF the newcomers threw a leather purse down onto the pavement at Dagon's feet. Randal heard the clink of coins as it landed. As the mercenary bent to scoop it up, the other man called out, "See, we keep our bargains—here is the rest of your gold. Now hand over the *real* statue, as you promised."

These must be the outlaw wizards, Randal thought. *The ones who were calling the statue home.* He heard Lys gasp. "Dagon!" she exclaimed, making the mercenary's name sound like a curse. "Why did you do it?"

The mercenary turned to face her. "I kept telling you the statue was mine to sell," he said. "And I needed the money to buy back my dagger. Give the man the statue, like he said."

Randal felt his stomach churn. *All of our lives count for less with him than his blasted knife.* He looked in vain for some expression of remorse, or even of satisfaction, in Dagon's face—anything that would help him understand what had just happened. But the mercenary had already turned away.

The leader of the hooded strangers held out his hand

101

to Randal. "Give me the statue, wizard, and we will let you leave unharmed."

"Randy," Lys muttered, "maybe you ought to . . ."

She never completed the sentence. Lightning flashed, and thunder rang out—not magical thunder, but real thunder from the sky above. Another bolt of lightning followed closely, zigzagging down from above to strike one of the highest towers of Widsegard. Cold rain poured down. The storm that had been brewing all day had broken at last.

Over the sound of rain, Randal heard hoofbeats, loud and growing louder. Then there was an outcry from the mass of hooded men at one end of the alley, and a moment later a troop of horsemen, their swords drawn and ready, rounded the corner and burst in upon the hooded men at a gallop.

"Yellow surcoats!" Lys exclaimed. "Lord Fess's riders are attacking from the rear!"

They must have been following the statue all this time, thought Randal. With Nick and Lys, he flattened himself against one wall of the alley as horsemen in yellow surcoats fought hooded footmen in the pouring rain—a vicious, close-quarters combat pent up between the stone buildings that fronted the alley.

The three young people huddled, forgotten, against the wall. Sounds of fighting filled the night air—the clash of swords against curving knives, the harsh shouts of men in combat, the cries of the wounded. Where Dagon had gone to, or on which side he now fought, Randal couldn't tell. Then, above the noise of battle, a horn sounded.

"The city guard is coming out!" Nick shouted. "We can't let them catch us!"

A riderless horse bolted past, a coil of rope swinging wildly from the horn of the empty saddle. Nick made a grab for the horse's bridle and brought the frightened animal under control. "If we get a couple more of these," he said, "we can ride out of here."

"No," Randal said. "We'd never make it out through all the fighting. Give the rope to me, and let the horse go."

He took the loop of rope in his hands and uncoiled it. Then he dropped it onto the pavement at his feet and leaned back against the stone wall. He closed his eyes and searched deep within himself, seeking the strength to do what came next.

"Randy, are you all right?" Nick asked.

"I'm going to try something," he said, without opening his eyes. "Let Lys go first. She's the lightest."

Randal spoke the words and made the gestures of a levitation spell—one that he had last used in happier days, when he and the wizard Balpesh together had restored a ruined bridge. He reached far down into himself for the power to make the light rope uncoil and rise, snakelike, through the dark alongside the wall. It went up fast, until it hung fully extended, its top lost in the stormy night.

"Lys," he said. "Go."

Lys grasped the hanging rope and pulled herself up, hand over hand. Acrobat that she was, she took no more than a moment to make the climb. A moment longer, and she called down, "I've got it! Nick, you're next."

103

Nick turned to Randal. "You look too tired to climb. When I get up, you tie the end around your waist, and Lys and I will pull you up."

Randal nodded, and gestured to Nick to be on his way. The former apprentice grabbed the rope, set one boot against the wall, and half pulled himself up the rope, half walked up the wall. He was lost in the shadows above. Then his voice called down. "Randy! Tie on and let's go!"

Randal leaned against the wall a moment longer, then wrapped the end of the line around his waist and tied it in front of him. Reaching up, he tugged twice on the rope.

He went up the side of the wall in a quick series of yanks. Once he swung, smashing into the stone, but he didn't lose consciousness or his grip on the rope. Soon he came to the edge of a roof, and eager hands grasped him and helped him over.

Randal lay for a moment on the slick clay roof tiles, breathing hard. The storm that had broken minutes earlier was raging now. Wild lightning ripped the sky apart, making the city as bright as day for a few seconds, and then casting everything into darkness again. The rain plastered Randal's hair against his skull. The chilly droplets trickled down his neck and under his clothing, but he wasn't cold.

Instead, he burned with fever. *Nick was right, the same thing that got Bryce is getting to me,* he thought, but he was too tired to feel any emotion about the prospect. He wanted nothing more than to lie on the rooftop and let the storm wash over him—no more moving, no more problems.

Lys tapped him on the shoulder. "I've found an outside stairway leading down to the next street over," she said. "Let's get moving before somebody figures out where we've gone."

Wearily, Randal rolled over on to his side and pulled himself to his feet. He swayed, and Nick caught him. Then, with Randal leaning on Nick's arm for support, they followed Lys down the outside stair. In the alley they paused, gasping for breath, while the rain still poured down.

"How many of them do you think there were?" Lys asked.

"I don't know," Randal replied. "How many followers does a master wizard have, if he can promise them a share in the power that a magical artifact can bring? Widsegard was wrong to throw out its wizards, I think—only the good ones left."

They came to the mouth of the alley. Nick stepped out into the street, and jumped back as a bolt of magical lightning sizzled past in front of him. "That was close," he said "They're out there waiting for us."

Randal gestured to Lys and Nick to move farther back. "Let me see what I can do," he said, and reached within himself to the dark place where his deepest reserves were stored. *I didn't know I had enough magic in me to do everything I've done tonight,* he thought. *Something is stretching in me . . . power responding to need, maybe. I'm not certain if it's going to save me, or kill me—and right now I don't care.*

Gathering his energies together, Randal prepared a

shield spell for protection, and an illusion of fog to blur their images. He threw the illusion in the area around the alley's entry, then put the shield spell on himself and his friends.

"Now let's go," he said. "Make for that alley over there."

They ran. A lightning bolt flashed out of the darkness toward them, but it bounced off of the shield spell Randal had cast. As he ran, Randal threw a lightning bolt of his own in reply, but without a clear target the stroke went wild, splintering stone and gouging walls but doing no other damage. The three fugitives reached the other side of the street, then ducked down yet another alley.

"There's at least two of them still after us," said Lys.

"Randy," said Nick, "you'll have to do something stronger. They're trying to kill us."

"They're just trying to get us to drop the statue," Randal said in a ragged voice. He was exhausted, like a man who had run twenty miles to bring bad news. "They won't do anything to endanger it. Whatever they do to others, they won't hurt us."

"Maybe you should just put it down on the pavement and walk away," suggested Lys. "Let them handle it."

"No," said Randal. "I can't do that. They'd only try to use the statue for themselves, and it's too powerful for that—the evil in it has to be contained somehow, to keep it from doing any more harm."

You know better than that, said a voice in his mind. The old woman in his dream had spoken in just the same quiet, silken tones. *The magic is there for you, too. Let me help you. Open yourself to me, and I will give you great power. I can save your life.*

"No!" Randal cried aloud. His two friends looked startled.

"What is it?" Lys asked, staring at Randal.

He shook his head. "Nothing. But let's get out of town as soon as we can."

"I'm with you on that," said Nick. "This hasn't exactly been the triumphant homecoming I planned on back when I was a boy." He pointed to where the opening of a side street made a darker blotch of shadow against the night. "If I remember right, that alley leads to a shortcut to the main gate."

"Have you thought about how we're going to convince the city guard to let us go?" Lys muttered.

"We'll worry about that when we get there," Nick answered as they turned the corner. Then the carpenter cursed under his breath as the three companions found themselves facing a blank wall. "Guess I remembered wrong," Nick said. "Looks like we'll have to retrace our steps a bit."

They began walking back toward the mouth of the alley. A red glow had begun to illuminate the underside of the clouds, and a smell of smoke came through the rain-swept air. *One of the lightning bolts must have started a fire,* thought Randal. From far away came the note of a bronze bell, sounding rapidly again and again.

He shook his head. "Fire, Lord Fess's men, the city guard—how many of those others in the black robes can still be left after all that?"

"Just three of us," came a voice from the mouth of the

alley. Three hooded and robed figures stepped into the gap between the walls, blocking off all escape.

"We are the only ones to escape from the yellow riders and the city guard," said the one who had spoken, "but I am the master, and two of my acolytes are with me. And you—you are the only other wizard in this entire town. There is no need for us to fight each other. Give me the statue and you will go free. I guarantee it."

A harsh shout from behind the speaker interrupted him. "Like you guaranteed your payment to me, wizard—with gold that turned to rocks?"

"Dagon!" Nick shouted. The mercenary, still wearing his studded leather armor, his sword ready, had stepped out into the street behind the three hooded figures. Lightning flashed, and the blue light glittered from his blade.

"You betrayed me!" Dagon said to the hooded man.

"Why not?" The hooded man gave him a little bow. "You betrayed your own companions. See if they will take you back now, if you wish to share their fate."

"Don't mock me, wizard!" Dagon swung his sword against the tallest man.

The master wizard blocked with a gesture, and Dagon's sword rebounded from empty air, spitting sparks. But the mercenary didn't pause. He whirled and threw a blow against the acolyte to his left. At the same time, he glanced down the alley to where Randal and his friends stood.

"Run, you fools!" he shouted.

The three ran past where Dagon held the magicians at bay, and on down the street. The wind howled, and

108

the rain came at them in horizontal sheets. When Randal could go no farther without pausing to rest, they stopped again and huddled for shelter behind a horse trough in front of a closed building. Lights showed in the cracks of the closed shutters above.

Another body appeared out of the downpour, and thudded to a seat beside them against the trough.

"Dagon!" Lys exclaimed.

The mercenary was bleeding freely from a deep cut that ran from his left eyesocket down to his jaw. He didn't seem to notice the wound. "Who did you expect?" he asked Lys. "The High King?"

"Certainly not you," said Lys. "Not after the way you sold us out."

Dagon shrugged. "I was just taking care of myself. Who wouldn't?"

"*I* wouldn't," said Lys. "You get out of here."

"Be quiet, girl. I'm on your side. No one double-crosses me and lives."

Randal looked at him. "Suppose we said that, too?"

"Can you fight them?" demanded the mercenary. "They would have had you a hundred times by now, if it weren't for me slowing them down."

"If you aren't on their side, why haven't they blasted you with lightning yet?" Randal asked.

Dagon reached into a pocket and pulled out the amulet he'd taken from Varnart's henchman. "So far this little toy has kept me safe."

"Those charms don't last forever," Nick said. "One of these times, the magic will get through, and then we'll have one headache less. Now get out of here. We don't want your help."

"You'll be sorry," said Dagon.

Nick stood, picked the mercenary up by the front of his leather jacket, and dropped him into the horse trough. "I'm sorry already," said the former apprentice. "Now get out of my sight before I become sorrier still." He turned back to Randal and Lys. "Come on. Let's go."

The three walked off, leaving Dagon spluttering in the water trough.

"What's that booming sound?" asked Lys, after they had gone a little farther.

"The sea on the cliffs," Nick answered. "We must have gotten turned around while we were running—we're heading back toward the port again."

Randal said nothing. He'd heard that hollow pounding noise before—during his dream in the prison cell. *The old woman led me up onto the sea-wall to die,* he thought. *Is she leading me there now?*

A lightning stroke hit close overhead, and thunder rang with an ear-aching boom. The glare of the lightning showed him three hooded shadows at the end of the street—the master wizard and his two acolytes, waiting motionless for Randal and his companions to come up to them.

They're following the statue, Randal thought. *They can tell where it is. This is it—we can't hide anymore.*

"Nick," he said. "Lys. Get away while you can—they'll go for me first, to get the statue."

"We'll stick together," said Nick. The former apprentice wizard halted and put a hand on Randal's shoulder.

"Three against one are bad odds. You need another wizard on your side—if you release the binding spell the Schola put on me, I can fight them alongside you."

Randal looked down the street at the three who waited. They still hadn't moved—they just stood there, motionless. *Wherever I go, they'll find me.* "I'm only a journeyman," he protested to Nick. "How can I break a spell the Regents cast?"

A lightning bolt lit the street. Rain was streaming down Nick's face. "Make me your apprentice—give me your permission—I don't know. But I know you can do it somehow."

Randal bit his lip hard, tasting blood. He'd worked more magic tonight than he ever had before, and his own magical reserves were already almost empty. He knew that three against two made better odds—they might even have a chance that way.

"Yes," he said. "Use your magic and help me."

It was as if the simple words were a powerful spell. Randal felt the same mental snap that he did when he finished a complicated conjuration. *The binding spell must have been set to end if a wizard gave Nick permission to work magic,* thought Randal.

At the same moment, Nicolas straightened, as if a weight had fallen from his shoulders. "That's done it," he said with a laugh. "Thanks, Randy—it looks like I've come back home as a wizard after all."

The one-time carpenter turned and faced the three who waited at the end of the street. "No use waiting for them to start it," he said. He lifted his hand and began chanting.

111

Randal recognized the shock spell that Nick was speaking. He felt the magic build up and falter—Nick's skills had lain too long unused. Time and practice would bring them back to what they had once been, but Nick didn't have time. Just as Master Laerg had once done for him, Randal spoke the words of strengthening and steadying.

Nick threw the spell successfully, and one of the two hooded figures went down. At the same time, another figure broke away from the shadows between two buildings behind the hooded men and ran forward. The two cloaked and hooded ones cast a bolt of red fire. The other man, the one attacking from behind, cried in Dagon's voice, "By the moon and the stars, wizards—face me!"

Dagon swung his sword as he shouted, and one of the two hooded figures crumpled to the street. But the red fire had already found its target, and Nick fell, blasted backward, his body outlined in crimson light. Randal threw a fireball at the one remaining wizard, and then he and Lys sprinted for the spot where Nick lay.

They dragged him around the corner, with Lys taking one arm and Randal the other. *He's too hot and limp,* Randal thought, unwilling to look down for fear of what he might be forced to see.

As soon as they were out of sight of their enemies, they lowered Nick to the ground. Randal flung himself to his knees beside Nick's unmoving body, feeling desperately for any trace of a heartbeat in his friend's chest, and finding none. He called out the words of one healing spell

112

after another, drawing still deeper on his own depleted strength. Nothing worked.

At last Lys crouched beside him. "Randal," she called out over the sound of the driving rain. "You have to stop. He's dead, Randy—you can't do anything for him now."

X.

The City and the Sea

RANDAL KNELT, looking down at his friend's body, and felt colder and lonelier than he had ever felt in his life.

"Master Laerg was right," he whispered. "Being near me can be deadly."

You caused this, said the voice of the old woman from his dream, seeming to call out to him from the statue he carried. *You can still change it if you truly want to. Only take the power that I offer, and you can strike down the ones who killed your friend, or smash this whole city into rubble. . . .*

"Lies!" Randal cried out, his voice breaking. "All lies!"

You could even bring him back.

Randal pressed his clenched fist against his mouth. This time, he knew that the statue spoke the truth. The temptation to open himself to that limitless, tainted power pulled at him almost uncontrollably. For a long time the young wizard knelt on the wet cobblestones, fighting back the words that would undo all that had happened since he'd lifted the binding spell.

I want my friend back, he thought. *I don't want to have*

114

killed him. I could use the statue, and Nick would get up from the street right now. But he wouldn't be the same man that I knew before. There are some things that should never be done, no matter what the reason, and calling the dead back to life is one of them.

Still he did not move away from where Nick lay silent on the cobblestones. At last Lys pulled Randal to his feet. Tears ran freely down her cheeks, and her voice had lost all its music as she said again, "There's nothing you can do for him, Randy—we have to run."

He hesitated until finally Lys dragged him away—and still he looked backward, stumbling as he ran, until Nick's body was lost from sight behind them.

After that, Randal lost track of time and place, following where Lys led without caring where they went. The storm raged all around them, and cold water ran in the streets. Then the booming noise of the sea rose up again out of the darkness, louder and nearer than before. Lys halted and laid a hand on his arm.

"Randal," she said, "stick by me. We'll head for the sea-wall and try to find the port gate from there."

He ran on a little longer, following the lute-player's slender figure in and out of the shadows. The street turned into a series of stone steps, worn with use and slick with the driving rain. Randal mounted the steps, and found himself on the city wall overlooking the ocean—a place he had only been before in a dream. He turned to Lys, but the lute-player was nowhere in sight.

"Lys? Lys!" he cried, but his voice hardly carried above the sound of the wind. He was alone on the rain-swept height.

Then he heard the sound of laughter. "Give me the

115

statue now. Or you will meet the same fate as your friends."

The tall, black-hooded master wizard stood before Randal, blocking his path back down to the city. Behind the journeyman, the sea beat against the shattered rocks below. He had nowhere to retreat.

Randal looked around him. Lys was gone. The city walls were empty. The cold rain soaked his garments to his body, and deep, bone-numbing fatigue crushed down on him. The statue in the bag seemed the only real thing in the universe. And Randal's enemy stood before him, too strong and cruel for him to fight.

Randal stripped the leather bag away. The old woman looked at him, her face turned up in the darkness toward his.

"Is this what you want?" Randal called to the man who faced him. He held up the statue. "It is death and all the hateful things in the world."

"I know," the master wizard replied. "But it is power. Give it to me." He took a step forward.

Randal turned. The sea boomed below him. White spray flew up from the rocks, and the violent wind sent it whipping above the edge of the wall. Even the guards had hidden from the storm—no one was there to see anything that would happen.

You dreamed this. You know what to do, whispered a little voice at the back of his mind.

The master wizard of Widsegard walked slowly up the steps onto the sea-wall. His long, hooded robe swirled about him as he ascended. Randal cradled the statue in his arms and watched as the man approached.

Then Randal was aware of another man at his own shoulder—one tall and fair-haired, with embroidered robes semi-transparent in the fitful illumination of the lightning.

"Master Laerg!" Randal cried out. "Have you come to watch me die, then?"

"No, Randal," Laerg answered, "I've come to help you."

Randal shook his head. "I don't trust you."

"I suppose I deserve that," said the ghost. "But I tell you, I am more your friend than he is." Laerg pointed with a misty finger at the black-robed wizard.

Randal followed the ghost's gesture and looked at the sorcerer. He was frozen in mid-step. The sea had halted, and the rain no longer fell, but the air was full of drops hanging suspended between the clouds and the ground. The sound of the storm had quieted; Laerg and Randal stood inside an enormous circle of silence.

"What's happening?" Randal asked, curious. An eerie calmness filled him, as though all emotion had been washed out of him by the driving wind and rain.

"You are outside time, now," Laerg replied. "I am outside of time more often than in it, since that morning in Tarnsberg. Now you are close to joining me. Can't you feel it?"

Randal thought of how nice it would be to lie down and go to sleep, to not wake up, to rest. So many times tonight, only Nick or Lys pulling him along had kept him from sinking into that warm darkness.

"Yes," he said. "I feel it. Does that make you happy?"

"It would be very easy for you to join me," the ghost

117

replied. "But I must ask you not to. There is something else that you need to do."

"What is it?"

Laerg shook his head, a smile on his semi-transparent features. "I'm sorry, but I can't tell you. I'm not sure myself, only that you have a task yet to perform in the world."

"But what am I to do *now?*" Randal cried.

"That's obvious," said the ghost. "Destroy that statue."

"But it's an artifact of power," protested Randal. "Its magical energy is huge. Once it is destroyed, all that energy will be lost forever. I can't do that."

"Yes, you can," said Laerg with a hint of his old arrogant impatience. "The statue is playing you false. Just as it draws you and gives you power, it is drawing and empowering your enemy. See, even now, he is draining the magical power that you hold, taking from you so that he himself may grow stronger. Where do you think this master wizard has gotten all the energy he has used this night?

"Just break the statue and let it be gone. Don't worry about the loss of magic, there is magic enough in the world."

Laerg vanished.

Once more the sea boomed, the wind howled, and the raindrops stung Randal's cheeks.

The master wizard of Widsegard reached the top of the stairs and stepped out onto the sea-wall. He stretched out his hand, and Randal started to turn and run. Then he saw that another, smaller person walked beside the master wizard. *Lys!*

"Lys!" Randal cried aloud. "Lys! Get away! Run!"

The wizard chuckled. "No, she is one of mine. You should be happy that she is willing to die in your place."

Lys took a step closer to the edge of the wall. Spray from the breaking waves down below shot up into the air above her head. Randal remembered his dream, how the statue had called on him to jump into that very sea.

"No!" Randal shouted again. Another few steps, and Lys would be poised at the edge of the sea. He leaped forward and stood blocking her path. The cold spray cascaded over him, and he could feel the wind blowing up from the abyss at his back.

"Have it as you will," said the master wizard, and called a flaming sword to his hand. Randal could feel his energy sinking lower as the blade appeared. The weapon burned with a clear red light and shot painful beams into Randal's eyes. The master wizard lifted his blade to strike.

"Your strength is fading," said the master wizard to Randal, "even as mine grows." He swept downward with the sword.

Randal pushed Lys out of the way with all his strength, and then blocked the blow with the only defense he had—the ivory statue in his left hand. The sword of flame struck, and rebounded off the piece of carved ivory. But the shock of the impact drove Randal down onto his knees.

Burning pain filled his hand like a swarm of wasps stinging him all at once. He knew that a second blow

119

would make him drop the statue, and the third would kill him.

Above him, the master wizard laughed. "You will die, the statue will be mine, and the city will know the true meaning of magic," he said. "Die then, you and the girl together."

The master wizard stepped forward, flaming sword upraised.

Randal tried to summon a magical weapon of his own—and failed. The dark place within him where he had found power before, from which he had drawn the reserves he hadn't known he possessed, was empty.

And the sweet whisper in his mind came and said, *Now you have no choice. You are mine, and you must come to me.*

"No," said Randal aloud. "I will not. No." Still the whisper of power went on in his mind: *Come to me, use me, you have no choice.* Resolutely, he closed his ears to the tempting voice. "There is magic enough in the world," he said. He put the piece of brittle ivory against his knee and broke it in two.

The broken statue twisted and writhed in his hands like a living thing. The master wizard's flaming sword burst into a huge flare as the power of the statue escaped into the world, turning the blade's wielder into a human torch. The wizard staggered forward, tottered off the edge of the city wall, and fell, flaming, all the way into the sea so far below.

Randal staggered to his feet. Around him, streaks of blue and purple lightning flashed down from the grey, cloud-filled sky, and return strokes rose back from earth and sea to strike the clouds again. The noise of thunder came like the sound of mountains splitting in two. The wind howled. And in the driving rain, Randal saw ghosts.

Master Laerg stood at his side. The wild wind whipped through his old teacher's golden hair. "You have done well. The only correct choice."

Nick came up to him and embraced him. "I'm so proud of you, Randy. You saved the day for everyone."

Randal hugged him back, weeping unashamedly. "Oh, Nick, I'm so glad to see you. I thought you were dead."

"I am." The solid flesh of Nick's arm became air as the dead man spoke. "But Lys is alive. You have to help her."

"She's here," said Randal. "I have her safe."

"No, Randy," said Nick. "Lys isn't here."

Randal looked over at the girl he had pulled from the wall, and recoiled in horror. This was the old woman, the statue full size and brought to life, and now she stirred and stood upright.

"Come with me," she said.

Randal turned and ran down the steps toward the street. He could hear the old woman's slow footsteps following behind him as he ran. He ran through the streets of Widsegard, and always the footsteps and the tap-tap-tap of her staff sounded close behind him. No matter how fast he ran, every time he stopped for breath her dragging footsteps had drawn a little nearer.

When he tripped on a wet stone and fell to his knees, he knew he could run no farther. He knelt, sobbing, while the noise of the footsteps and the staff filled his ears.

"Come with me," a girl's voice said. The voice of his dream. He looked up. It was Lys.

He put out a hand to touch her. "Where did you come from? Are you alive?"

"Are you?" she asked. "Does it matter? Come with me."

Randal got to his feet and stumbled after her. Another hand took him by the other arm, and helped him forward—this hand belonged to a muscular arm in studded leather. It was Dagon, battered and bleeding from his wounds, but still upright.

"Move out," the mercenary said.

A tremor ran through the paving stones under their feet. Lightning played over the towers and battlements of the city. The booming of the waves increased, even though Randal and his companions were running away from the sea. A wall collapsed in front of them, and they fled down another way. All around them, the ground heaved and shivered.

They reached the Great Gate—and found it blocked by an entire troop of city guards.

"We're all dead," said Lys. "They'll never let us past."

"Well, it wasn't a long life, but I had fun," Dagon said with a chuckle. He loosened his sword in the scabbard.

"Onward, then," Randall said. He had to hold onto Dagon and Lys so that he could stand at all.

Then the Great Gate collapsed, and the walls with it, while the wind roared around them and cold water ran ankle-deep in the streets. A mob of men and women surged through the main plaza of Widsegard, driven out of the crumbling buildings by the earthquake. The three

123

companions were pushed and shoved and almost separated by the crowd, but still they moved forward.

A low moaning noise arose from the mass of people in the plaza—the sound of fear even greater than anything the storm and earthquake could bring. Randal looked up. The crushing black of the night was illuminated by the internal glow of the gigantic figure of an old woman, striding down from the hills of the Wilderness of Lannad, coming toward the gates of the City.

"I have to go face her," said Randal. He was too tired to feel anything except a kind of resignation, as though his long journey was at its unavoidable end. "There's no other wizard in the city now but me."

"You'll get killed," Dagon pointed out reasonably.

"I think I'm dead already," Randal said, feeling weary to his bones. "But it doesn't matter. Somebody has to stop her, or the entire city will perish."

"Then I'll go with you," said Lys.

"So will I," said Dagon. The mercenary laughed. "You might say I started this. I want to see the end."

"No," said Randal. He pulled away from them. "One friend died for me already tonight. No more."

Randal pushed his way through the wailing crowd, past men in yellow surcoats who never turned to stop him, past guardsmen who had eyes only for the death that came striding down upon Widsegard. Step by step, while the earth rocked and the wind shrieked around him, he mounted the rubble of the city walls. There he stood, facing the old woman one more time as she came toward the city in slow steps that spanned a league or more at every stride.

It can't be real. It doesn't really exist.

The thing came closer.

If I'm killed by unreal things, am I really dead?

"Yes, you are," said Nick from beside him. His friend's features were faint and transparent against a sky full of blue-black clouds.

"Not that there's anything wrong with being dead," said Laerg's ghost from his other side. "Eventually you will be, like it or not."

"But not now!" Randal cried. He gathered what remained of his powers to him, and nothing answered. He was as empty of magic as a broken bowl. *There's nothing left of me. I've used it all, and there's nothing left to stop death from taking the entire city.*

He looked back over his shoulder at the city behind him. Everything appeared far away, and very pale. The mass of people crowding the ruined streets had blurred and faded until he couldn't make out the individual figures at all. Only the ghosts seemed real—the ghosts, and the old woman.

Why am I seeing the dead more clearly than the living tonight? he wondered, and turned back to the semi-transparent figures beside him. "Master Laerg—Nick—what do you want me to do?"

"Save the city," Nick told him. "Put an end to the evil magic before everything is destroyed."

"I can't," said Randal. He wept at his own helplessness and felt the hot tears sting his cheeks. "My strength is gone. There's nothing left."

"You have us," Master Laerg replied. "We helped to

make you what you are, and we are a part of you forever. Let us help you now."

Randal looked from one ghostly form to the other— the teacher he had killed, the friend who had died trying to save him. "Stand beside me, then," he said. "Give me the strength to defeat this magic. Say the spell with me."

He began the words of the spell of dismissal. *"Vanesce,"* he called out in the Old Tongue. *"Fuge . . ."*

As he cast the spell he drew on the power of the ghostly wizards who stood beside him, using their magical energy as if it were his own. Laerg had the deep reserves of a master of the Art, and an almost dizzying strength. Nick was only an apprentice but his lesser power was clear and bright, untouched by the shadows that clouded Laerg.

Randal chanted on, letting the magical energy flow through him into the words of the spell. On his right and his left the two other wizards chanted along with him. He gestured, and saw the two beside him echo the movement. *Now for the end,* he thought, and pulled in all the power that he could find. Neither Laerg nor Nick would have anything left now, nor would they be able to reappear in the world—Randal was draining them to the last of their reserves—but they gave their strength to him freely.

"Redi ad umbras, figura mortis!" Randal shouted, and directed the whole force of the spell at the monstrous apparition looming above him.

The old woman faltered, then slowed. Finally, her footsteps halted at the very outskirts of the city. Her image thinned out against the stormy sky, and then drifted away like fragments of a cloud, with no more sound to mark her going than the keening of the wind. The ghosts vanished and their magic drained out of Randal, leaving him even emptier than before.

It's finally over, thought Randal. *I can rest now.* He sank to the stone under his feet, and into a sleep deeper than he had ever known.

How long he slept, Randal never knew. At first, he didn't even dream. Then there were nightmares, and voices talking someplace near, and after that, undisturbed rest again. When he finally awoke, he was lying on his back and looking up at green branches, with warm sunlight dappling down through the leaves overhead.

Randal turned his head—there was a pillow under it, and a pallet under him—and he realized that he had not collapsed here, but had been brought here and cared for in this sunny place that smelled of life and morning. He stretched, testing his strength, and sat up.

He saw that he was in an olive grove, on a patch of high ground not far from Widsegard. The hillside sloped away toward the sea, and the towers and rooftops of the great city clustered around the water in the distance.

A few feet away, Lys sat with her back against a tree, singing in a quiet voice. She didn't have her lute, but sang without accompaniment:

> "Blow up the fire, my maidens,
> Bring water from the well,
> For all my house shall feast this night
> Now that my sons are well."

Randal looked within himself once more. He had magical energy again, more and purer than he had ever known. He whispered the words that called up the spell of sound, to accompany Lys since she had no instrument of her own. She heard the music and turned to face him. "Welcome back," she said.

"I was afraid you were lost," Randal said. "I think I dreamed it. You were lost, and Nick was dead, and the whole city was destroyed . . . I can't tell where the truth stopped and the dream began."

Lys gave a shaky laugh. "The city's as whole as it ever was, or so I hear—a bit of damage down by the port, and a couple of buildings lost to a lightning-fire, but nothing you wouldn't expect from a bad storm."

Randal gave a sigh of relief. *I never wanted to tear down an entire city, not even to destroy something as evil as that statue.* He paused a moment. "And . . . Nick?"

Lys bent her head. "No, that part wasn't a dream. He's really gone."

Randal closed his eyes to stop the tears that threatened to spill down over his cheeks. When he had his voice back under control, he asked, "What happened to you at the end?"

She shook her head. "All I remember is following you through the streets, and then you were gone. I figured out later that I'd been following an illusion."

"An illusion must have been leading me as well," said Randal. "I thought that you were with me, and never noticed that we'd been separated."

"What was that statue, anyway," asked Lys, "that it could cause so much trouble and destruction?"

"An artifact of power," said Randal. "Very old and very strong. Whoever made it, long ago, never meant it for anything good . . . and over the years it grew stronger and more wicked, full of the magical energy it took from the wizards it killed. In the end," he finished with a shudder, "the statue became almost like Death itself. I don't think anybody could have controlled it."

"Why did it bring us here?"

"The statue was made in Widsegard," Randal said. "The city was its home, and the place of its greatest strength. If its power had gone unchecked, it might have gone on drawing energy into itself until all the world was drained dry."

Lys's blue eyes were almost black with remembered fear. "Was that what those wizards in the city wanted to see happen—the death of everything?"

Randal shook his head wearily. "I don't think so. They wanted the power a magical artifact can give, so they tried to call the statue to them . . . and the statue was only too glad to answer. It worked on Varnart until he hired Dagon and Bryce to steal it from Lord Fess's treasury. But Varnart would have kept the statue in Brecelande, so it killed Bryce and came to me. And I— almost—brought it the rest of the way."

He bowed his head for a moment, thinking of that last struggle on the walls of the city. How much had been real, and how much only nightmare, he would probably never know. *It doesn't matter anyway,* he realized. *Wizards fight their battles in a realm where dreams and reality are one. If I'd held back from facing the old woman, I would have awak-*

129

ened to find all of Widsegard leveled by storm and fire, and the statue lying unbroken in the rubble.

He sat in silence for a minute or two, while the salt breeze off the sea stirred the leaves in the olive grove. After a while, Randal heard the sound of footsteps coming up the hill, and turned.

A man was climbing into the grove. "Dagon!" Randal said. "Of all the people I didn't want to see . . ."

"Don't judge him too harshly," Lys said. "After the storm was over, he helped me get you out of Widsegard and up here where we could hide out from the guard and Fess's men."

"They were still looking for you then," Dagon explained, coming up beside Randal and sitting down cross-legged on the ground. "That bunch of wizards, though—they're gone for good, as far as anyone can tell. But that's old news, and I came up here with fresh, for a change."

Randal looked at the mercenary suspiciously. "You bought back your lucky dagger?"

Dagon shook his head. "I never thought you'd hold a man's mistakes against him, wizard. No, I've joined the city guard. There's been quite a shakeup lately in town, and they were recruiting. I thought you'd enjoy the joke of it—my nightmare's come true, and I've taken an honest job."

Randal regarded the older man for a moment longer, then smiled faintly in spite of himself. "More or less honest," he said, and Dagon laughed.

"Dagon's been taking good care of us," Lys told Randal, "ever since he and I found you on the sea-wall with that statue broken in your hands."

"So I did break it," said Randal. "That much was real, then. What did you do with the pieces?"

"Took the girl's advice," said Dagon, "and threw them into the ocean."

"Thank you," said Randal to the mercenary. "I think I came closer to death—in several ways—because of that statue than I want to be again. And I don't think I could have made it back without your help."

Dagon actually looked somewhat shamefaced, as if gratitude were something new to his experience. "You were shouting all kinds of nonsense," he said. "And you've been out for days. This is the first time I've seen you awake since then." He paused. "Are the two of you going to be moving along soon?"

Lys tilted her head curiously. "Should we be thinking about it?"

"Well," said Dagon, "wizardry's still outlawed in the city, and the city guard has a warrant for your friend there. Sooner or later, somebody's going to notice that you're up here and think about sending out a troop, just to make an arrest and keep things tidy."

"How long do you think we have?" Randal asked.

"Long enough to get you back on your feet," said Dagon. "But probably not much more than that. And I'd start figuring out which way you want to head, just in case you have to start off in a hurry."

"We can't go back to the north," Randal said. "Master Varnart and Lord Fess are up there, and neither one is likely to feel kindly toward me after what I did to that statue."

"We could go south," Lys said. "That's where I come from, and we'll be beyond any borders that Brecelande ever claimed."

"South," said Randal. He recalled the spices and fruits that had come into Widsegard from the southern trade. The thought called up images of warmth and light, new places without old memories to darken them, new learning, even new magic.

"Yes," he said. "We'll go south."

Randal's adventures continue in *The Prince's Players* by Debra Doyle and James D. Macdonald. Here is an exciting scene from Book Four in the CIRCLE OF MAGIC series:

Silence filled the workroom. Petrucio turned to Randal. "Today you've been shown things that most folk in Peda never suspect," said the master wizard. "Now I need your assistance. Will you give it?"

Randal thought for a moment. "If I can," he said finally. "In every honorable way."

Petrucio smiled — Randal thought for a second that he looked relieved. "Very good," said the wizard. "By now, you've probably guessed that I do more than keep Prince Vespian amused."

"I'd wondered what you were doing while I was working on magical disguises for Vincente and the rest of the actors," admitted Randal. "But what does that have to do with my room being searched? I just came to Peda this summer, and I haven't got the faintest idea as to what's going on around here."

"What you know or don't know remains a mystery to most people," said Petrucio. "And you are, after all, a wizard. They were probably just trying to find out as much as they could about you from your possessions."

Randal gave a brief laugh. "They wouldn't have found out much—except for my spell book, I don't have anything here that didn't come from the palace to start with. And the spell book stays in my pocket."

"Wise of you," said Petrucio, "since—as you may also have guessed—there are those in Peda who don't share most people's love for His Grace. Because Prince Vespian employs me to inform him of their plots, and because you are known to be my assistant, you will have come under their suspicion, as well."

Randal considered the happenings and conversations of the last few hours. "You think that somebody is conspiring to overthrow the Prince."

"I know they are," said Petrucio. The master wizard sighed. "It's a problem of long standing, I'm afraid. The Prince is a kindhearted man — sentimental, one might call him. He coddles his greatest enemy, gives him a villa outside the city walls, provides him with money and all that he might require. And how does this fellow repay that kindness? With constant plotting and treachery. But Prince Vespian is sentimental, as I said. He refuses to have Bartolomeo put to death."

"Bartolomeo?" asked Randal. "Who's he?"

"Vespian's brother," said Petrucio. "His identical twin. Some fifteen minutes younger, and as wicked as the Prince is good."